CAMBRIDGE LIBRARY COLLECTION

Books of enduring scholarly value

Religion

For centuries, scripture and theology were the focus of prodigious amounts of scholarship and publishing, dominated in the English-speaking world by the work of Protestant Christians. Enlightenment philosophy and science, anthropology, ethnology and the colonial experience all brought new perspectives, lively debates and heated controversies to the study of religion and its role in the world, many of which continue to this day. This series explores the editing and interpretation of religious texts, the history of religious ideas and institutions, and not least the encounter between religion and science.

A Commentary on the Book of Daniel

This translation of an Arabic commentary by Jephet ibn Ali (*fl.* late tenth century) was first published in 1889. Based on ten manuscripts, the text was carefully edited and rendered into English by David Samuel Margoliouth (1858–1940), Laudian Professor of Arabic at Oxford. Jephet was a leading Karaite scholar who wrote a number of biblical commentaries in his native Arabic. This was one of his mature works and perhaps the best example of his critical and exegetical powers. On the basis of the historical allusions in the commentary, Margoliouth estimated that it was composed between 990 and 1010. The work includes the Arabic text, with critical apparatus and a useful glossary of key words. Fiercely polemical against Islam, Christianity and Rabbinic Judaism, the commentary has greatly contributed to our understanding of tenth-century religious controversies. It remains an important work of Karaite literature.

T0381808

Cambridge University Press has long been a pioneer in the reissuing of out-of-print titles from its own backlist, producing digital reprints of books that are still sought after by scholars and students but could not be reprinted economically using traditional technology. The Cambridge Library Collection extends this activity to a wider range of books which are still of importance to researchers and professionals, either for the source material they contain, or as landmarks in the history of their academic discipline.

Drawing from the world-renowned collections in the Cambridge University Library and other partner libraries, and guided by the advice of experts in each subject area, Cambridge University Press is using state-of-the-art scanning machines in its own Printing House to capture the content of each book selected for inclusion. The files are processed to give a consistently clear, crisp image, and the books finished to the high quality standard for which the Press is recognised around the world. The latest print-on-demand technology ensures that the books will remain available indefinitely, and that orders for single or multiple copies can quickly be supplied.

The Cambridge Library Collection brings back to life books of enduring scholarly value (including out-of-copyright works originally issued by other publishers) across a wide range of disciplines in the humanities and social sciences and in science and technology.

A Commentary
on the
Book of Daniel

by Jephet ibn Ali the Karaite

EDITED AND TRANSLATED BY
D.S. MARGOLIOUTH

CAMBRIDGE
UNIVERSITY PRESS

University Printing House, Cambridge, CB2 8BS, United Kingdom

Published in the United States of America by Cambridge University Press, New York

Cambridge University Press is part of the University of Cambridge.
It furthers the University's mission by disseminating knowledge in the pursuit of
education, learning and research at the highest international levels of excellence.

www.cambridge.org
Information on this title: www.cambridge.org/9781108062442

© in this compilation Cambridge University Press 2013

This edition first published 1889
This digitally printed version 2013

ISBN 978-1-108-06244-2 Paperback

𝕬𝖓𝖊𝖈𝖉𝖔𝖙𝖆 𝕺𝖝𝖔𝖓𝖎𝖊𝖓𝖘𝖎𝖆

A COMMENTARY

ON THE

BOOK OF DANIEL

BY

JEPHET IBN ALI THE KARAITE

EDITED AND TRANSLATED

BY

D. S. MARGOLIOUTH, M.A.

LAUDIAN PROFESSOR OF ARABIC IN THE UNIVERSITY OF OXFORD

𝕺𝖝𝖋𝖔𝖗𝖉

AT THE CLARENDON PRESS

1889

𝔏𝔬𝔫𝔡𝔬𝔫

HENRY FROWDE

OXFORD UNIVERSITY PRESS WAREHOUSE

AMEN CORNER, E.C.

CONTENTS.

———•—————

PREFACE.

THE life of Abu 'Ali Jephet[1] has been narrated by the authorities cited by M. BARGÈS in the Preface to his edition of the Commentary on the Canticles[2], at greatest length by J. FÜRST in his *Geschichte des Karäerthums*[3], whose account is to be supplemented from the notice of Jephet in A. NEUBAUER'S *Aus der Petersburger Bibliothek*[4]. The Commentary on Daniel was one of the latest of his writings[5]; and that it cannot have been written before 990 A. D. has been shewn by PINSKER[6] from the statement in the Appendix[7] that 'the date 2300 after the Exodus is passed years ago;' now 2448 A. M. (the date of the Exodus) + 2300 gives 4748 A. M. = 988 A. D., to which at least two years must be added to justify the expression in the text. On the other hand, the Commentator speaks of the Mohammadan religion as 'about 400 years old[8],' a statement which gives us perhaps as terminus ad quem the year 1010 A. D.

---

[1] His names and titles are given in full on the Arabic-Hebrew title-page.

[2] Paris, 1884, pp. i, ii.   [3] Vol. ii. 124–130.   [4] Pp. 15–18.

[5] The phrase on p. רמח. 2 does not necessarily imply, as FÜRST thinks, that he had already commented on all the books of the תנ״ך.

[6] נספחים, ל״ק, p. 88.

[7] P. קמ. 3. FÜRST's suggestion that we should read منذ اثنتان سنين is not likely to find acceptance.

[8] P. קמז. 4. The prophecy that the end is to come in the year 400 A. H. is not Jephet's, but a false inference of the scribe from this passage.—R. Saadia Gaon's date was 350 A. H. (Bodleian MS. Opp. Add. fol. 64, p. 75^b).

The other historical allusions do not contradict this result. Jephet knows of the taking of Antioch, Tarsus, and 'Ainzarbah by the Greeks[1]; these events happened in 359, 354, and 351 respectively. The pillaging of the Ka'bah by the Carmathians under Abu Tāhir in 317 (929) is made much of[2], although the Black Stone was restored in 338, and the Temple itself repaired, of which Jephet, who has some strange opinions about the nature of the Ka'bah, does not seem to have heard; however, their prohibition of the Pilgrimage, in which he finds the fulfilment of the 'taking away of the continual,' lasted as late as 403 (1012)[3]; and although their power was on the decline after Abu Tāhir's death, they continued long to make themselves felt in Syria and Egypt. In 360 they take Damascus, Ramleh, and Jaffa[4]; in 375 (985) they capture Cufa[5]; the prophecy therefore that 'they will certainly take Baghdad[6]' was quite likely to be realised, and indeed had already been partly realised in 330[7]. We cannot therefore wonder at the important place assigned them by Jephet in the history of the Arabian empire. Further, the reference to 'the non-Abbasid lord of Islām, established at Baghdad[8],' points to a date after 334 (945), when the title of Sultan was conferred on the Buyid conqueror[9].

---

[1] P. ‏קלג‎. 16.

[2] P. ‏קלו‎. Just as the Carmathians are called here by Jephet ‏קשרים‎, so in 2 Kings ‏התקשר‎ is rendered by ‏نقرمط‎.—For the derivation of ‏قرمطى‎ see DE GOEJE, *Mémoire sur les Carmathes*, p. iii of Appendix.

[3] DE GOEJE, l. c. p. 85; *Chron. Mecc.* ed. WÜSTENFELD, ii. 249.

[4] Ibnu 'l Athīr viii. 485.

[5] Ibnu 'l Athīr ix. 29. In this year, however, ‏زال ناموسهم‎.

[6] P. ‏קלד‎. 21.

[7] Abu 'l Mahāsin ii. 297; DE GOEJE, p. 50. In 375 they have a 'representative' (‏نائب‎) in Baghdad (Ibnu 'l Athīr, l. c. p. 30).

[8] P. ‏קלד‎ *ut supra*.

[9] WEIL, *Geschichte der Khalifen*, ii. 696.—The statement that 'they were originally unbelievers' will agree with the account of their origin given *ibid.* ii. 652; but their identification with the 'king of the north' is stranger and given hesitatingly.

The matter of the Commentary—with the exception of the violent polemics against the Christians[1], Rabbanites, and Muslims[2]—is probably for the most part traditional, derived from the 'Doctors of the Captivity[3],' some of whose names are specified in the Appendix. The Commentary of R. Saadia Gaon (El-Fayyūmī), the object of Jephet's most bitter polemics, has been discovered by Dr. NEUBAUER, in a fragmentary MS. of the Bodleian[4]. This MS. is unfortunately deficient in those parts of the book where Jephet's attacks are most violent[5]; in general the agree-

---

[1] See especially the notes on xi. 14 (p. ١١٩. 14–16). Some further information on the Christian religion is to be found in the note on Obadiah 1 : וקאל פיה זרֹן

לדֹך לאנה אٿقﻊ בדيا עלى רב אלעאلﻤين ואدﻋى באלٹאلוٹ וجﻌل للﻪ ولدا כﻤا يقولو אבא ובٔרא ורﻭّﺡ קדﺷﺎ جﻞ אلﺨﺎلق ﻋﻦ צفات אلﻤﺨلوﻗين ٹם אنﻪ אدﻋﻰ برﺳﺎلة וכﺘﺎب (!) וادﻋﻰ אן ﺷريﻌة אللﻪ בﻄلت ואن כﺘﺎبﻪ ﻫﻭ אلٹﺎבת וﻋليﻪ אلﻤﺤﺻﻭﻝ وﻫذا فﻰ غﺎية ﻤﺎ يﻜون ﻤﻦ אلقﺤﺔ וﻋﻨد ﻤﺎ אﻋﺘﻘد فﻰ ﻴﺷﻮ אن ﻫﻭ ولدﻪ ﻋلﻰ ﻤﺎ يزﻋﻤﻭن וכﺎنﻭא בﻨﻰ ישראל قد صלבﻭﻩ فﻰ زﻤﺎن בﻴﺕ ﺷﻨﻰ אﻋﺘﻘדﻭא אن ישראל כلﻫﻢ ﻤﺳﺘﺤﻘين للﻌﺒﺎדﺓ וللﻫﻼك آלﺥ.

[2] The number of 'Spottnamen' employed is quite considerable : פסול for رﺳﻭﻝ, קלֹן for قﺭﺍن, מכות for ﻤﻜّة; איש הרוח is a frequent designation of the Prophet. The MSS. vary between ישו and ישוע.

[3] Some of these, perhaps, he imperfectly understood. The Commentator who derived מההצפה (p. ١٩. 13) from the Chaldee may have spoken of the latter as the language of the Pharisees=Rabbanites; Jephet's אלفﺎرﺳية would naturally mean *Persian*. His compiler in the ספר העשר renders לשון רבנים.

[4] Opp. Add. fol. 64. NEUBAUER's Catalogue, no. 2486.

[5] Yet see note on x. 3 (MS. p. 134ᵇ): וקולﻪ לחם חמדות לא אכלתי ובשר ויין : يﻜﺷف لﻨﺎ אن يﺳראﺋيﻞ فﻰ אلﺠﺎلﻭٹ ليﺱ يﺤﺭﻢ ﻋليﻫﻢ אכﻞ אللﺤﻢ ולא ﺷﺭב אلﺨﻤﺭ ولا אلﻤﻼ׼ للﺤﻼﻝ ﻤﻦ אجﻞ ﺨﺭﺍב אلقﺩﺱ (ولﻭ כﺎنﺕ אلﺘﻭﺭﺍﻫ אﺤﺭﻤﺕ ذל׼) ﻋليﻫﻢ לﻜﺎن דﺍنيﺎﻝ ونﻇﺭﺍﺅﻩ אوّﻝ ﻤﻦ يﻤﺘٹلﻫﺎ فلﻤﺎ وجﺩנﺎﻩ فﺭﺩ ٢١ يﻭﻤﺎ لﻢ يﺎכﻞ فيﻫﺎ ﻤﻦ ﻫذﻩ אلאﺷيﺎﺀ ﻋلﻤﻨﺎ אنﻪ כﺎن يﺎכلﻫﺎ قבﻞ ٢١ يﻭﻤﺎً. Jephet's observation that the Temple was then standing is answered by anticipation.—'The marvellous inventions' (p. ١٥٢. 2) of El-Fayyūmī concerning the 'end' are probably the calculations

ment[1] of the Gaon's[2] opinions with those of the Karaite are more striking than their divergence.

The opinion of Jephet's powers as a commentator held by M. BARGÈS (who has done more than any one to make them accessible) is perhaps too high. His knowledge of both Hebrew[3] and Chaldee[4] is inaccurate, although he speaks contemptuously of those 'who do not know our language.' The grammatical observations, which have won praise from NEUBAUER[5] and others, fail almost entirely in this book[6]. His acquaintance with contemporary events[7], by the light of which he occasionally interprets prophecy, is as hazy as his knowledge of earlier history

---

on p. 75 sqq. of the Bodleian Commentary; in which it is shewn that there are four possible explanations of the 'time, times and a half,' which all alike produce the result 350 A. H. for the time of the end.

[1] E. g. on the division of the four kingdoms see especially the note on ii. 33 (MS. p. 15^b): فقال اولا ان تكون براسها مدة طويلة بازاء ما قال שקוהי די פרזל. مفردا ثم تشاركها [לאדום] المملكة الاخرى. Some 'marvellous inventions' follow, by which the 'end' is fixed for 350 A. H.—Compare with Jephet's explanation of Daniel's exemption from bowing down to the statue the following passage (p. 26^b): ان يسل عن دانيال هل طولب ايضا بالسجود ام لا ... فنقول ان دانيال كان عند نבוכدנצר معبودا من المعبودات اذ ليس منكرا عند الكفار ان يعبدوا الهة كثيرة.

[2] Perhaps the Arabic Commentary may in a few cases be supplemented from the spurious work printed in Buxtorf's Bible under the Gaon's name; e.g. the opinion refuted on p. ٩. 8, 9 is held by this author. See MATHEWS, *Saadiah's Comm. on Ezra*, p. xvi.

[3] See especially ix. 25 בצוק העתים. So in Is. liii. 5 חברתו is rendered مشاركته, in Ps. xxii. 25 ענות by اجابة, etc.

[4] See especially ver. 12.

[5] *Aus der Petersburger Bibliothek*, p. 15.

[6] Some of these are decidedly striking; see BARGÈS' *Cant.* p. xvii; ibid. p. ٧٥; Comm. on Exodus (MS. 2467), p. 126^a: اعلم ان יכל יכלתי هو ماخوذ من مصدر ومثله יכלתי קטנתי יגרתי ولو كان ماخوذ من امر كان تحت الكاف فتحة مثل שמעת فالقصة للحقيقة مقام או.

[7] E. g. the history of the Carmathians, *v. supra*.

is shallow [1]. On the other hand, the present Commentary is not written *currente calamo*, for the theory which it expresses may be traced even in points of detail in his earlier writings. Thus the argument of p. רי. 18 is anticipated in the Commentary on Exodus [2]; that of p. ירס. 1 sqq. in the Commentary on Leviticus [3]; while the curious combination of the prophecies of Isaiah, Joel, and Daniel worked out especially in the notes on the twelfth chapter is to be found already stated in the Commentaries on the first two Prophets, and in part in that on the Canticles.

In the appended Translation brevity especially has been studied, and with the same end the Arabic version of the Hebrew text as well as the table of contents has been left untranslated. Where, however, Jephet's interpretation differs seriously from the Revised Version, account is taken of the difference either in the lemmata or in notes. These differences are of course never worth a moment's consideration; the idea of elucidating the Hebrew vocabulary from his native Arabic was not familiar to Jephet [4].

With the list of curious words occurring in this volume contained in the Glossary, the Editor has incorporated some occurring in the printed works of the same author, as well as in works of his existing in MS. in Oxford, London, and Paris. Of course this collection does not aim at completeness, but in some respects perhaps it may be found of interest. Most of these words are not explained in the Lexicons of FREYTAG and DOZY, although their existence will be found to be sufficiently certified; the source of several is Syriac or Persian, while a few are Hebrew words in an Arabic dress. That Jephet should think it proper to attack in this rustic dialect the classical writings of R. Saadia Gaon agrees with the

---

[1] So he makes Alexander come from Alexandria.—In the Comm. on Kings he mentions Kalilah wa-Dimnah.

[2] MS. 2467, p. 167[b].   [3] MS. 2472, pp. 80[b], 81[a].

[4] I have noted the following cases: Lev. xiii. 25, where פתחת is connected with فَكَّة as against the derivation from פחות; לוית, 1 Kings vii. 29, لَاَنِهَا تَلَوَّا; Prov. iii. 13, where יפיק is rendered وِفْق.

contempt which he frequently expresses for the learning of the Gentiles. Many of the words recur in the Lexicon of the Karaite David b. Abraham[1].

Matter has been drawn from the following printed books : BARGÈS' *Specimen* ('Spec.'), containing the Preface to the Commentary on the Psalms, with version and explanation of Pss. i and ii ; BARGÈS' edition of the complete version of the Psalms, and his edition of the Commentary on the Canticles; HOFFMANN'S edition of the Commentary on Ps. xxii ; AUERBACH'S of that on Prov. xxx ; NEUBAUER'S of that on Isaiah liii[2]. A MS. of the complete Commentary on Isaiah was kindly lent to the Editor by Canon DRIVER. He has further excerpted the fragmentary Commentary on the Minor Prophets in the Bodleian Library; that on the Proverbs in the Bibliothèque Nationale in Paris ; and a portion of the rich Schapira Collection in the British Museum, quoted by their number in the Oriental Catalogue[3].

My best thanks are due to the Delegates of the Press for undertaking this work, which I wish I could have accomplished in a more satisfactory manner ; to Dr. NEUBAUER, for multifarious help and kindness ; and to Mr. J. C. PEMBREY, to whose care and skill any degree of accuracy which may have been attained is to be ascribed.

---

[1] MS. Bodl. 1451.

[2] In *The Jewish Interpreters on Isaiah liii* by NEUBAUER and DRIVER.

[3] To the literature on Jephet must now be added Dr. HOERNING's accurate and valuable account of the *British Museum Karaite MSS.*, which appeared too late for the Editor to use.

LIST OF MSS. OF THE COMMENTARY ON DANIEL.

M = Or. 2557 of British Museum.

M² = Or. 2556 of British Museum.

Both these fragments are in the Arabic character, containing the Hebrew text (also in Arabic characters) with vowel-points and accents. The portions of the text which are found in these fragments are marked by the letters M and M² on the margin.

B = Opp. Add. 4°. 166 of Bodleian Library. (See NEUBAUER, Catalogue, no. 2494.)

P = 2nd Firkovich Collection, 420 of Imperial Library, St. Petersburg.

X = Firkovich Collection, 580 of Imperial Library, St. Petersburg.

All these are in the Hebrew character and (except P) complete. Where M and M² fail, the printed text follows X, unless the contrary is stated in the note.

D = 2nd Firkovich Collection, 314.

Fragments covering about half the work; some of the leaves have been misplaced by the binder.

K = 2nd Firkovich Collection, 315.

Commences with Hebrew of i. 6. Wants a whole sheet (ten leaves) from vii. 1 to vii. 25. Also defective from p. ﺍﺭﻪ. 15 to p. ﺍﺭﻯ. 8. Terminates at Comm. on xii. 11.

Q = 2nd Firkovich Collection, 313. Large fragments.

Kit. = Last part of كتان العتيدات, containing Commentary on chap. xii. (ending at p. ﺍﻩﺍ. 17).

C = Or. 2520 of British Museum, containing six short fragments.

All these are in the Hebrew character.

The MSS. in the Hebrew character (Heb.) were all copied from one archetype, as is shewn e. g. by their common omission of the translation of chap. viii. vers. 23 and 25, preserved in M; the occasion of that omission is obvious. That archetype was in the Arabic character, as is shewn by the nature of the mistakes; see p. ﻯ, n. 1. It contained moreover the Hebrew text written in Arabic characters, for from the nature of the transliteration many of the constant errors of the Karaitic punctuation can be explained: e. g. Qameṣ and Segol are both regularly represented by the Elif of lengthening, and Pathaḥ is occasionally represented by the same; now it is in the confusion of these three signs that the Hebrew texts in these MSS. err most[1]. To the same source may be attributed such orthographies as כסדים for כשדים. That archetype cannot

---

[1] BARGÈS, in his edition of the Canticles, reproduces the Karaitic pointing. See his observations, p. xv. The MS. copied by him is now no longer 'unicum,' since the introduction of the Schapira Collection into the British Museum.

have been either of the MSS. of which M and M² are fragments, but it may have been not earlier than these MSS., which date probably from the eleventh century, whereas it is not probable that any of Heb. are earlier than the fourteenth (C K ?), while some (B X ?) probably belong to the sixteenth. The text offered by D P Q X is practically the same ; while all have many errors in common, they supplement each other in single cases. B and K exhibit a rather different recension, in some cases agreeing with M against the others; both however are interpolated, B notably so, e. g. in the translation of ix. 25, where Jephet rendered העתים ובצוק הוקאת الاوقات وعجيبن, connecting בצוק with בצק, but the editor of B rightly corrected وبضيق, making the comment disagree with the text. See too the note on p. ٩٩. The scribe who copied B can have known very little Arabic (see note on p. v.), and this MS. is so defaced by omissions, occasioned ordinarily by homoeoteleuton, repetitions, and other errors that the Editor found it impossible to publish the text from it. By the kindness of the Imperial Russian Government and the English Foreign Office the six St. Petersburg MSS. were placed in the Bodleian for a period of four months ; during which the Editor had time to collate K and X twice, and the rest once with the exception of Q, which he occasionally consulted. The British Museum fragments, when identified, helped him to correct a number of difficult passages, but many remain with which he has been unable to grapple successfully. The various readings are quoted fully in the first few pages, afterwards only when the text of M, M², and X is deserted, or when they seemed to the Editor to possess some interest.

In the matter of *orthography* the MSS. exhibit no regularity (e. g. מֹצִי and מֹצֵא are sometimes to be found in the same line). The Editor has endeavoured in transliterating to introduce the ordinary orthography, but where the text existed in Arabic characters he has rarely departed from the MSS.

In the treatment of the vulgar forms[1] the editors have taken different lines : NEU-BAUER prints the vulgar forms without alteration; BARGÈS prints the correct forms in

---

[1] A peculiar form is the 3rd person plur. perf. masc. in ن, p. ١٤٠. 9, n. 2 ; compare Ex. xix. 8 فصارون, Ex. xxiii. 28 الذين بقون فى بلدانهم. LAGARDE, *Materialien zur Kritik u. sw. des Pentateuchs*, i. v, notices forms like استكنّت Ps. xxxi. 1 for استكننت. لم يزلوا (for يزالوا) MS. 2473 (Numbers), p. 16ᵇ, unless it be a mistake of the copyist, is curious. أقيل (for قيل) occurs in MS. 2475, p. 25ᵃ; comp. اشيتم for شُتم MS. 2478, p. 12ᵇ. Forms like بقيوا (for بقوا) are common : MS. 2478, p. 12ᵇ, ونسيوا, p. 18ᵇ. وقويوا. Prov. ix. 15 (לקרא) لتدعيين is strangely faulty. Prov. xiii. 18 فيطلبوه دويه للجاه (for ذوو=ذوى) is probably a copyist's error.

Letters regularly interchanged are ض and ظ ; both were pronounced as ز, which, as in فريزة, is sometimes written for them. س and ص are occasionally confused; لعب الصطرنج Prov. xiii. 11 (ص for ش) is unusual.—The ١ of forms of جاء is often omitted ; נו is commonly written for נה, גו for جاءت, גה for جاوا Comm. on Ex. xvi. 20.

the text, placing the vulgar forms in the notes[1]; AUERBACH prints the vulgar forms in the text, followed by the correct forms in brackets. The first of these seems clearly the right method, since these vulgar forms never create any difficulty, and it is no part of the editor's duty to correct the author's language. On the advice of friends, however, the present Editor has in the earlier sheets given in foot-notes what he believes to be the correct substitutes for the more glaring errors in the text[2].

This Commentary is excerpted (in Hebrew) in the ספר העשר, a specimen of which is given by PINSKER, l. c. p. 88. Jephet is frequently quoted by Ibn Ezra, but, as elsewhere, the quotations do not correspond with the Arabic originals. On the other hand, an opinion attributed to חכמי צדוקים 'Sadducean Doctors,' i. e. Karaites, on chap. xi, will be found stated in full in the accompanying text : יש לתמוה מחכמי צדוקים שפירשו זה לעתיד ואמרו כי המקדש היא מיכה (Mekka) שיחוגו עליה הישמעלים :

---

[1] Not, however, consistently ; e. g. he allows the Comm. on Canticles to commence לשלמה ان علمین. for علمان.

[2] The following signs have been employed in the text :

    ⟨ ⟩ denote insertions by the Editor.

    [ ] denote interpolations.

    ( ) denote alternative renderings.

References to the Old Testament are given on the margin ; the quotations have been abridged as much as possible.

ENGLISH TRANSLATION.

COMMENTARY ON DANIEL.

The book of Daniel. This book has been attributed to Daniel in particular because it contains an account of his history and prophecy. It comprises eleven chapters.

* * * * * * * *

If we add up the years occupied by this book, they make up a total of sixty-seven: [for seventy years were occupied by the reigns of Nebuchadnezzar, Evil-Merodach, and Belshazzar; all of which come within our narrative, except the first seven years of Nebuchadnezzar, as we shall see below;] this leaves sixty-three years, to which are to be added the one year of Darius and the three years of Cyrus; making a total of sixty-seven years.

I.

1. It is to be observed that the reign of Jehoiakim was divided into three parts: a. *four* years during which he was subject to the king of Egypt; b. *three* years during which he was subject to the king of Babylon (2 Kings xxiv. 1); [c. *three* years during which he was independent.] During these three years the king of Babylon was occupied with his Eastern expedition; after he had rested a little, he attacked him (in the tenth year of his reign), besieged him with his army, took his city, took him prisoner, and carried away many captives with part of the vessels of the house of God (see here).

In the third year: not 'in the tenth year,' for the following reason. Jehoiakim had originally been subject to the king of Egypt; then he became subject to the king of Babylon. Thus seven years passed; and since after this he rebelled against the king of Babylon, and became an independent king, who paid homage to no other, the writer can say *in the third year of the reign of Jehoiakim king of Judah,* dating from the time at which he became independent. The proof of our theory of the division of Jehoiakim's reign into three parts is the statement in 2 Chron. xxxvi. 4, that the king of Egypt took Jehoahaz, brother of Jehoiakim, and sent him to Egypt, and made Jehoiakim king in his stead. Now we know that he remained subject to the king of Egypt four years, and that the king of Babylon came to the throne in the fourth year of Jehoiakim; see Jer. xxv. 1, where it is stated that the first year of Nebuchadnezzar was the fourth of Jehoiakim. In that year the king of Babylon fought with the army of the king of Egypt, which was encamped on the banks of the Euphrates (see Jer. l. c.), when Syria fell into his hands (2 Kings xxiv. 7), and Jehoiakim became subject to the king of Babylon in the fifth year of his reign.

Came unto Jerusalem and besieged it: he was not satisfied with sending an army against him, but led the army himself. Had Jehoiakim come out to him, he

b   [II. 3.]

would not have besieged the city; only the former would not submit, and locked the gates, and stood a siege, thinking that the king of Babylon would grow tired and desist. The king, however, maintained the siege until he took the city.

2. Either he *stormed* the city, as some think, or the people may have opened the gates. The latter is the more likely, as no battle is mentioned. Jehoiakim, we are told, died outside Jerusalem. Either the king of Babylon tormented him till he died, or he was killed [in some other way]; or he may have killed himself.

And he carried them into the land of Shinar: i.e. rather more than three thousand men whom the king of Babylon carried away captive; they are mentioned in Jer. lii. 28. **He brought the vessels into the treasure-house of his god**: observe that we are not told the *number* of the vessels, nor their material (gold, silver, or brass); doubtless they were different vessels from those taken away with Jehoiakim (2 Chron. xxxvi. 10); they were not used by him, but put all together in a safe place; had he attempted to use them, God would not have permitted it, even as He did not permit Belshazzar, but shewed serious signs [of His disapproval].

3, 4. He ordered the chief of his ministers, under whose care the captive Israelites were, to choose from the whole multitude youths of this description without fixing a number; he was to look out for all who were possessed of these characteristics, and to take them, however few or many of them there might be.

Of the children of Israel: i.e. of those who were not of the royal stock, or of the children of the nobles, but *of the common people*. He did not regard the fact of such a person being of the common people, when found to possess these qualities; to shew that talented persons are not affected by the lowness of their station.

And he ordered him to take the *best looking of them;* it would not be seemly that a person with uncomely visage should stand in his court; such persons must have handsome features, and be comely and fair.

Of understanding in all wisdom: not wisdom in the Thōrā concerning 'unclean' and 'clean,' or sacrifices, as the king would not desire that. He rather desired persons of intelligence in all subjects into which intellect can enter, and studies connected therewith.

And knowing knowledge: most probably knowledge, like Solomon's, in the different departments of philosophy. The children of Israel were never destitute of its elements, but always taught them to their children. Even in the times of their idolatry and wickedness, the votaries of wisdom and knowledge never failed among them.

And understanding teaching: knowing the way to instruct others in their knowledge; not every scholar makes a good teacher.

So he chose all those in whom were all these virtues and desirable qualities. Since this was done at the time described, it was unlikely that there would be [many] lads among them possessing these qualities.

And such as had ability: i.e. force of patience to stand before the king, and to abstain from expectorating, spitting, etc.

And he ordered them to be **taught the writing and language** : that they might write it and talk it ; naturally they would not know either.

Had not Ashpenaz himself possessed many of these gifts and understood them, the king would not have given him this order.

The king's object in taking these youths, so described, was twofold : (1) to gratify his fancy for men of knowledge ; for it is the custom of high-minded kings to have scholars trained in their courts ; (2) to be able to boast before the nations that in his court are the greatest men in the world.

5. It was not the king's purpose to corrupt their religion, as he endeavoured to do in the story of the image which he set up ; he rather desired that they should have suitable diet, which would make them grow, and give them a healthy appearance. So he made their rations like his own food and drink ; the best food and the choicest drink.

He also designed that he should train them three years, that they might come before the king fair in form and appearance, and acquainted with the writing and language and all that was desired of them.

6. These four are mentioned on account of their abstaining from the king's food, and the rest of their achievements. Among them were some of the seed-royal, whom the Scripture does not mention. Had these four been of it, he would have said, ' there were among them of the seed-royal,' mentioning their rank. This disproves the view that Is. xxxix. 2 refers to these.

7. He surnamed them with Chaldean names ; possibly *names of honour*, since *Belteshazzar* is the name of Nebuchadnezzar's God (*inf.* iv. 5) ; the rest may be so too.

8. He bound himself not to eat the king's food or drink his drink, whatever the consequences might be ; staking his life, just as he staked it in his prayer, and as Hananiah, Mishael, and Azariah staked theirs when they would not bow down to the image. It is quite impossible that he would have staked it for a matter of no consequence as some irreligious persons have said, whom we have answered in our commentary on the commandment.

He would not defile himself: not, ' he would not eat ;' meaning that he would not eat a meat originally pure, but defiled by [coming in contact with] uncleanness. And he made no difference between the meat (consisting of animals slaughtered by Gentiles) and the drink. Possibly the former was not from an animal naturally forbidden, nor the wine naturally forbidden ; but only because it was prepared by Gentiles, though free from all taint of uncleanness. This was because he regarded the grape-juice as the original state [i.e. he regarded the wine as a transformation of grape-juice], and refused to touch that with which uncleanness was mingled.

The chief of the eunuchs is Ashpenaz. He said, ' My lord, give me not, I pray thee, food and drink which will not profit me.' But the other gave him an answer which took from him all hope that his request would be granted him.

9. **Favour and compassion** comprise two periods ; the first, sc. *favour*, had been

shewn in the previous time, and consisted in various acts of kindness shewn to Daniel which he does not describe at length; the second, *compassion*, took place at that particular time, consisting in his doing him no harm or violence, nor informing the king, but excusing himself as follows.

10. He tells him that he only refuses out of fear for his life, whenever the king should send for them, wishing to observe their condition; and if he saw the faces of the others and saw their faces different, when on enquiring he found out about the change in their food, the blame would fall on Ashpenaz, while they would not be reprehended.

According to your joy: because the wise are habitually joyous and merry, because knowledge wastes the body and destroys it.

חיבתם, like חוב in Ezek. xviii. 7.

11. As the chief eunuch would not grant his request, and he had bound himself to stake his life upon it, he tried the expedient of speaking to the man through whose hands this nourishment passed, in case *he* might do this for them, and try them, as we shall explain presently.

12. **Try us ten days**. A short time, of which account is scarcely taken ordinarily; in order to facilitate the matter, and render its accomplishment less arduous.

13, 14. He accepted their proposal and afterwards examined them, and found them fatter and fairer than the others who had been eating the king's food and drinking his wine. This must have been done by the Creator, who set in the grain something to supply the place of meat, and similarly in the water. Those who did not do as Daniel and his friends must either have argued that they were excused and that it was impossible for them to resist the Sultan, or they did so because they did not care about lawful and unlawful. And God sent leanness into their bodies, so that they did not fatten. This proves that God cares for His saints who are willing to suffer death for His law's sake.

At the end of ten days, when he found that they were increased in fairness and fatness, he continued this for a period of three years.

16. He profited by the provisions and took them for himself, without telling Ashpenaz, but doing it in secret.

פתבג includes bread and dainties. The word may be divided into two: פת 'bread,' and בג 'dainties,' i. e. bread and meat. **Pulse** is the substitute for it.

They took wheat for bread, and some other grain to cook, such as lentils, rice, pease, and beans, and they drank water. Of course they took grain that was not defiled; and water out of the river in clean vessels, as they wished.

17. They had already the wisdom described above; which God Almighty increased during these days with additional wisdom, in all book-learning and philosophy known by the sages and Chaldees. Daniel surpassed them by the possession of certain divine gifts, such as the interpretation of all visions. The Chaldees did not understand dreams. This was not *confined* to Daniel, since Hananiah and the rest

were distinguished, only Daniel was the most eminent. This was all the Creator's purpose (**he gave them**), compare *inf.* ii. 21 and Prov. xx. 6.

18. At the end of the three years, during which the king had ordained that they should be nourished and instructed in the 'writing and language,' the **Chief of the Eunuchs** brought them before him, and the king began to examine them in the different departments of science, and found none among the Jewish youths like them (**all of them** refers to the Jews). This was owing to what was mentioned before— God's bestowing on them clear intelligences. Next he tells us that they were ten times better than the king's sages. Either this is a [figure of speech or else a] real number, and we are to infer that the king called all his sages before him in their presence, and bade them ask one another questions, while he heard what passed between them on each particular head ; and doubtless he himself was a sage and understood the discourse, and comprehended what passed and how they surpassed all his sages ten times in breadth of knowledge : and perhaps there were among his sages men who had been studying science all their lives till they had grown old, who yet had not reached the stage of these four. All this was in order that God might exalt His servants who were sunk to the lowest depth, and because they had clung to His religion and had not indulged themselves with eating unlawful food, but had eaten grain instead. And among the philosophers there must have arisen mutterings against certain meats, 'Woe to him that eats defiled food and the preparation of the Gentiles, defiling his soul and removing it from holiness, and withdrawing it from God Almighty ; who finds ways of explaining away the commandments, and eats forbidden foods, and drinks the Gentile drinks, with creeping things and abominations among them.' And there is no difference between wine and any other drink, all of them being *mashqiym.* And no person during the Captivity can possibly eat the preparation of any one whom he knows to be unfaithful in his observances in the matter of preparation of meats, so that his food is of the unclean and impure. Such cases are referred to in Lev. xx. 25 and Ps. xxxiv. 10.

21. **Was:** i. e. was in the Sultan's kingdom till the first year of Cyrus, the time when the Israelites were set free to go to the Holy Land to build the Temple ; when he was set free from the duties of government and retired into religious life. He had by then grown old. As for his companions, he tells us nothing about them after the story of the image.

II.

1. Just as we said of the 'third year of the reign of Jehoiakim' that the phrase did not refer to his reign literally, so this again does not refer to Nebuchadnezzar's *reign,* as Daniel is the person who interpreted the dream. Plainly it must refer to something else. Some have supposed it to be the *second year of Jehoiakim's captivity,* which is unlikely, because Daniel had no office till after three years ; see i. 5, which shews that he licensed them after three years. Others have referred it to the *fall of Jerusalem,* imagining that he did not consider himself king till he had subdued Israel ;

which is not improbable. To my mind what is most probable is that it means [the second year] *after he had become king of the entire world (inf.* ii. 38). Now it is well known that he took Jerusalem before he took Tyre : and Tyre before he took Egypt. It is most probable that he took Egypt in the thirtieth year of his reign. This is shewn by Ezek. xxix. 11, 'neither shall it be inhabited forty years,' etc. (cp. 13). Now it was God's decree concerning the whole of the captives that they should remain in their present condition the whole seventy years, made up by Nebuchadnezzar, his son, and his son's son (Jer. xxv. 11) ; none of them returning to his country till after the completion of these seventy years. Now Egypt was the last of his conquests, as no other king stood before him save Pharaoh ; so that the words in the second year will refer to the thirty-second year of his reign, thirteen years after the destruction of the Temple. In that year Ezekiel saw the form of the Temple (xl. 1) ; for Nebuchadnezzar took the Holy City and burnt the Temple in the seventeenth year of his reign ; and if Nebuchadnezzar saw the dream in the thirty-second year of his reign, there must have passed since the destruction of the Temple thirteen years, and the appearance of the dream will have taken place in the fourteenth year [after its destruction].

Dreamed dreams. There was only one. Our view of this phrase is that he says **dreams** because the dream contains five subjects ; i. e. it embraces the account of four kingdoms and of the empire of Israel. The same expression is used of Joseph's dream (Gen. xxxvii. 7), before he saw the second dream, and that again is because the first dream contained three subjects.

His spirit was troubled, because he awoke and forgot the dream, and tried to remember what he had seen, but could not remember at all. Then he slept again ; **his sleep was upon him.**

Note that there is a difference between the dream of Pharaoh and that of Nebuchadnezzar, in two respects : 1. Pharaoh saw his dream at the end of the night (Gen. xli. 8), whereas Nebuchadnezzar saw his in the middle of the night (**his sleep was upon him**); 2. Pharaoh remembered his dream, whereas Nebuchadnezzar forgot his. The reason of this was that Pharaoh's *dream was realized after a short time,* whereas Nebuchadnezzar's is not yet fully realized. Consequently, as the former's dream was realized after a short interval, God Almighty did not suffer him to forget it ; but as Nebuchadnezzar's was not to be realized till after a long period, God caused him to forget it, so that when the dream was told him, that might be evidence of the correctness of its interpretation.

2. These **Chaldeans** had a certain wisdom which they professed. There was left no order professing to reveal secrets, which he did not summon, demanding that they should tell him the dream which he had forgotten.

3. He desired them to tell him the dream (see ver. 2).

4. Possibly he spoke to them first in some other language than the Aramaic, but afterwards addressed them in Aramaic, as they addressed him. Then they said : *Tell thou the dream that we may tell the interpretation thereof.* They did not say, 'We cannot tell thee the dream.'

5. He said, 'First I asked you for the dream; but, as you are not satisfied with that, I ask you now for the dream **and the interpretation thereof.** And if ye will not shew me the dream and the interpretation thereof, ye shall be **hewed in pieces,** i. e. your flesh shall be cut up, and your houses become confiscate to the Sultan.

6. 'But, if you shew me the dream and the interpretation thereof, I will give you raiment and dīnārs, and handsome presents, and high honours shall be bestowed upon you ; but only after you have told me the dream and its interpretation.'

When they heard his promise and his threat, and could find no deliverer, they repeated their speech a second time like the first, as follows.

7. 'We stand by our first answer; we undertake to *interpret* it.' Again they would not say 'We cannot tell thee the dream.' When he saw them . . ., he first demanded of them the dream without promising them or threatening them ; . . . afterwards, he demanded of them the dream and the interpretation thereof, and made them a promise. When they repeated their answer about the interpretation, instead of saying 'We are unable,' he said to them something different.

8, 9. **Ye are buying the time** : i. e. you are making the time pass, and imagine that I will refrain from asking you, and that you will leave me troubled in thought, with my spirit distressed, while you care not. This is because you see that the *dream has fled from me* and that I cannot remember it.

There is but one law for you : i. e. one judgment ; I will make no difference between you ; let no one imagine that I will spare you or any one of you. Others interpret : *Ye are all agreed on one thing,* i. e. to say, 'Tell us the dream, and we will interpret it,' and not to tell me the dream.

Lying and corrupt words : i. e. if ye do not tell me the dream, then ye will not tell me its interpretation either. Ye only say 'We will interpret the dream' to shift **till the time is changed,** i. e. till that with which ye are threatened is removed from you. Tell me the dream : and when ye have told it I shall know thereby that ye will tell the interpretation thereof.

The word הזדמנתם is from the root זמן, the letter ד being servile. He means, 'You have made this time different to that wherein you used to tell us that you understood secrets.' Nebuchadnezzar must have heard them say that they understood things of this sort ; otherwise he would not have demanded it of them, nor would he have killed them except because before this time they had **professed** this ; but now, when his demand had fallen upon them, and they saw no way to meet it, they said time after time, 'Tell the dream that we may interpret it,' instead of saying 'We are not equal to this ;' and simply maintained that he knew the dream and was demanding of them what he remembered, or that he had seen no dream at all, and was demanding of them what he had not seen. This is why he said **lying and corrupt words.** And when they heard this last word they were forced to declare they had lied when they professed that they could reveal secrets.

10. Note that none of them ventured to address the king save *the Chaldees,*

who were the nearest to the king of them all, and spoke for the rest. They said, 'O king, we will tell thee the truth. Do not think that any man can reveal this secret, we or any beside us, neither busy thy heart with any such fancy, nor ask of us an impossibility, nor imagine of us that we understand any such thing, or that we are trying to protract the time while thy spirit is tormented. So spare us in justice. Has any of the kings that preceded thee ever demanded of his sages this thing which thou demandest of us?'

11. Appended explanation. **And there is none other**: it is clear to me that they aimed at Daniel and his fellows as professing such knowledge; then they relegate [the king] to the angels. Hence, in ver. 10, **there is no man on the dry land** (with reference to the Jewish sages); here, **none but the angels know this.** 'So be just to us and demand not of us an impossibility.'

12. When he saw that they dealt plainly with him and gave him no hope, he was wroth, and ordered the slaughter of all of them that were present in Babylon, and that others who were dispersed outside Babylon should be brought before him, after the slaughter of these, that he might hear what they had to say. The words, **and they sought Daniel and his comrades,** point to the fact that they had not been present with them during the colloquy which passed between the Chaldees and the king; and this was because they had never professed that they understood mysteries as these had professed; only the wise men of Babylon must have said, 'We and others are partners in taking the king's supplies; why should we be killed and not they? Let them be killed too.' And when the news reached Daniel, he hastened and came before the king's executioner so that he learned the matter from him, and went before the king and asked of him a respite, and promised him what he had asked of the wise men.

14, 15. אדין comes from אז like ומן אדין (Ezra v. 16); עטה comes from עצה.

מהחצפה (it is said) is from the language of the Pharisees, in which the insolent is called חציפא. He tells us that Daniel referred the counsel and the guidance to Arioch, after he had asked him to explain the matter clearly; and he took his advice and his bidding about the question, whether he should enter unto the king and ask him for a respite, or should not enter unto him for fear of the Sultan's wrath and lest he might not give him time, but order him to be slain. And Arioch, knowing that the king would give him time and would not deal hastily with him, counselled him to enter unto him. Perhaps he asked permission for him, so that he might enter in and ask him for the respite, and the king answered him favourably. The executioner had been executing the wise men of Babel one after another; and perhaps had begun with the most honourable.

16. **An interpretation**: plainly not without the dream; for the person who did not know the dream could not possibly interpret it. He could only interpret when he knew both dream and interpretation. Daniel must have promised the king what he had demanded of the wise men, both dream and interpretation; and he did so because it was plain to him, and he was convinced and assured that Almighty God had made

him forget the dream in order that He might prove the wise men of Babylon liars in their professions, and reveal the matter to Daniel, that he might magnify his people who serve the True God, Who alone sheweth dreams and revealeth secrets.

17. I. e. he told them the cause of the massacre and what he had promised the king.

18. I. e. the four stood crying to God and begging mercy of Him, in that He would reveal this secret, that they might not be killed with the rest ; for they knew that they would not be left while the others were killed, especially after Daniel's promise to the king.

19. As there was no use in the revelation of the mystery to all four of them, one of them sufficing, He revealed it to Daniel, who was the principal of them, especially as the king had not demanded that all the wise men of Babylon should shew him the dream, but if one told him, he would excuse the rest ; do you not see that Daniel said to the executioner, 'Destroy not the wise men of Babylon'? Next he tells us that when Almighty God had revealed it unto him, he blessed God for that. Evidently He shewed Daniel the dream which the king had seen, i. e. the figure of the image, and the cutting of the stone out of the mountain, and the breaking of the image and the wind carrying away its dust, and how the stone became a mighty mountain.

20 sqq. Observe that he tells us that they asked of Almighty God that He would reveal the mystery to them, that they might not be slain like the rest of the wise men of Babylon ; and he tells us that Daniel thanked Almighty God for having revealed the mystery to him, but does not record any thanksgiving by him for their deliverance from death ; because the Glory of God was to his mind more important than the deliverance of their souls ; and further, if the mystery were revealed, they were beyond doubt delivered. Then he thanked Almighty God according to what the subject of the dream suggested ; **for wisdom and might are His**: as He had furnished him with wisdom which no one else had mastered (cp. v. 23 a). Now he ascribed *wisdom* to Him in one of two senses : either he meant, 'He is the wise and mighty ;' or he meant, 'He giveth wisdom and might to whom He will' (compare for *wisdom* Prov. ii. 6, and for *power* Deut. viii. 18, Is. xl. 29). **He changeth the seasons and times**: *seasons :* i. e. seasons of the year, 'cold, heat, summer, and winter ;' *times :* i. e. night and day. No one can do this save the Creator. **He removeth kings and setteth up kings,** inasmuch as He is possessor of the whole world, He setteth up whom He will and removeth whom He will. **Removeth** is put before **setteth up,** because kings had been in the world from the beginning, ever since the reign of Nimrod, after the flood (cp. Eccl. i. 2). **He giveth wisdom unto the wise** : with the same meaning as above; **wisdom** being intellect and discrimination, whereby mankind surpass the brutes and each other. We also learn that the wise men and sages of the world are so not of themselves, but only because God has given them their wisdom and their knowledge. **He revealeth the deep** : alluding to the unseen world which he compares to an object lying in the deep, so that it cannot be reached ; or to something hidden and concealed, so that it is unknown, with the same idea as Is. xli. 10; or

possibly he means, 'He revealeth what is in man's heart, which none understand save the Creator of the heart and reins, which are concealed from every one, but known to Him' (Jer. xvii. 10). **He knoweth what is in the darkness:** which is also hidden from mankind, inasmuch as the organ of sight cannot see in the dark : whereas the Creator of darkness and light knows what is in the one as He knows what is in the other (Ps. cxxxix. 12); the purpose being that He, knowing hidden things, knew what the king had seen, and had revealed it to Daniel. After mentioning these five classes, all corresponding with the matter and circumstances of the dream (*wisdom and strength* with the amount of both which He had bestowed on Daniel, *changing of seasons* with the vicissitudes undergone by Israel and other nations, shewn by the removing of a kingdom and the establishment of a kingdom contained in the dream; and so with the *revealing of secrets*, etc.), he said **O thou God of my fathers** : referring to the fathers and forefathers whom God had chosen and exalted, Who had dealt so with Daniel because he was of their offspring. He praised God for the wisdom and might which He had vouchsafed him, which had brought him to his high station before Nebuchadnezzar saw the dream; now it was a period of twenty-two years from the time that he had obtained this rank in the king's palace to the present. **And hast now made known unto me what we desired of Thee** : referring to the revelation of the king's secret (cp. *b*). He first described how God had dealt with him from the time of his standing before the king till the present crisis ; then he described how He had dealt with him in the present business ; and in this matter he associates his companions with himself, in contrast to the previous time, in the words, **what we desired of Thee** : i. e. I and my companions ; similarly **Thou hast made known unto us.** He associates his companions with himself, to shew that, although the revelation was made to him and not to them, nevertheless it belonged to all of them, since all of them were sought for execution, and all had prayed and humbled themselves (ver. 18). After praising Almighty God for this, he went to Arioch without delay, because he had already pledged his word, and a fixed time had been appointed him by the king. Possibly he had asked of him a day and no more ; and while they four stood praying, it came to pass that he fell asleep and saw the dream, and woke rejoicing, and told his companions, and they too blessed the Almighty Creator. Possibly he rose in the night, at once, and went to the king to delight him with the news, and to calm the people's horror and anguish ; as doubtless the country was dismayed at the massacre of the wise men, and at the thought that the land would be left without wise men ; which is one of the worse misfortunes that can befall a country.

24. He went to Arioch at once, for two reasons : (1) that he might stay the massacre ; (2) that he might introduce him before the king.

25. The words, **I have found a man,** when the king must have known of Daniel certainly, are plainly a refutation of the words of the wise men : the speaker points out that by the children of the captivity, who were of inferior rank and low esteem among the wise men, behold, this secret shall be made known.

26. He had already promised the king that he would tell him the interpretation at

the time appointed. But the king had no confidence in this. Therefore he said, '*Canst thou* do this?' i. e. 'tell me the dream and the interpretation thereof; let us see what thou wilt say.' He employs in this place the name which the chief eunuch surnamed him, because it was an honourable one.

27 sqq. By the declaration that neither the wise men of Babylon nor any one else could do what the king had demanded of them, he does not mean to excuse them; his only object therein is to give the lie to all the sages of the Gentiles who professed to know mysteries. He will state after this that he too had not learned this secret of himself, but the Creator had revealed it to him. Then he told him that God Almighty revealed secrets to whom He would, because it was He who shewed men dreams; adding that God had made manifest to him (Daniel) the fancies which had entered into Nebuchadnezzar's mind concerning the future.

28. **Thy dream and the visions of thy head :** i. e. thou hast indeed demanded of us what thou hast seen: and, lo, I will shew thee what thou didst see, and thou shalt recognize that I have not added nor taken away from it.

29. He mentions, first, a matter not appertaining to the dream, nor to what the king had forgotten : 'before thou didst sleep or see the dream thou wast thinking of what should happen hereafter to thy kingdom, which has reached the summit of its exaltation; and who should receive the kingdom after thee. And since this was already in thy mind, and thou didst desire to know it, the Revealer of secrets shewed thee what should come to pass hereafter, that thou mightest know it, and mightest know that the kingdom is to belong to that dynasty which shall outlast all the dynasties.'

30. 'I have not learned this secret by wisdom found in me, and peculiar to me above the rest of [mankind], as scholars excel one another in different sciences.' The other side [i. e. the power by which he had learned it] he does not explain further than by saying, 'God has revealed this to me that thou mayst know what is to happen, and that on which thou wast pondering and which thou didst desire to understand.' Now the purpose of God in shewing him the dream was, first, that he might know the truth of Israel's assertion that the kingdom is to be given to them and no other nation, and that the kingdom of Nebuchadnezzar shall cease and be transferred to another and an inferior, to increase his confusion; and to shew him also that the assertion of Israel is true that God Almighty reveals to them secrets which none beside them understand; and that the secret of which his wise men stated, that none but the angels could understand it, had been shewn by Almighty God to Daniel; and that Almighty God had delivered Daniel and his fellows from death, and that they had delivered the other wise men of Babylon (ver. 24). Doubtless, while he was interpreting the dream, a crowd was present listening to his voice. And at the words *As for thee, O king, thy thoughts came into thy mind upon thy bed,* the king said, 'It was so.' That too was a mystery revealed to him by God.

31. He attributes to the image four qualities:

(1) *Greatness :* i. e. length, breadth, and height; referring to the length of their duration, and the greatness of their power.

(2) *Order* [1] *:* referring to the good order of their empire(s), and the organization of their kingdom(s).

(3) *Comeliness:* because each one of them had armies.

(4) *Fearfulness and awfulness:* because each dynasty was fearful and terrible, especially to Israel.

32–35. He tells the king his dream as he had seen it; and the king bore witness to his accuracy. Then he said, 'And now we will interpret it to thee :' for none of his wise men could interpret it any more than they could interpret his second dream.

37–43. He notices in the interpretation one of the features of the image which he had not noticed in the dream ; in the dream he says **his feet part of iron and part of clay,** but in the interpretation, **the feet and toes,** for a reason which we shall explain.

A kingdom powerful and strong : powerful, referring to the number of his armies; **strong,** to his vigour; **hard,** referring to the amount of his wealth and supplies, and the obedience of mankind.

And wheresoever men dwell : meaning that all mankind were beneath his sway, so much so that even the beasts and birds were beneath his sovereignty, meaning that he could do with them what he pleased when he assailed them. Some say there is an allusion to his being with them during the seven years in which he 'abode with them.' This is unlikely, as the words are a description of his present condition, and do not refer to anything in the future. Compare Jer. xxvii. 6, referring to the terror which he inspired in the heart of all beasts and birds. Another fancied it referred to the inhabitants of wildernesses and remote islands. Daniel continues : 'And because thou hast reached this station, and art the first and most splendid of the four kingdoms, thou art the fine golden head.' This is the interpretation of the head ; 'and he that shall arise after thee is *inferior to thee ;*' ארע is derived from ארעא 'earth,' and is used metaphorically ; meaning, even as the ground is below man's feet. Of this second kingdom he says **another** because its religion and laws were different from those of the Chaldees : he does not explain this, just as he does not dwell on the description of the third kingdom, contenting himself with saying that it is inferior to the silver. **That shall rule over the whole earth :** to distinguish between the second and the third kingdoms; the second kingdom owned three quarters of the world, but the third four quarters ; we shall give the reader all these explanations in full in the commentary on Daniel's dream. Then he described the fourth kingdom, which he compares to iron, not meaning that it was inferior to the brass, but on account of its hardness (**strong as iron**), and because this kingdom should pulverize armies as iron pulverizes gold, silver, and brass. **It breaketh in pieces and subdueth all :** i.e. it crushed the kingdoms of its time, as we shall explain on ver. 35. This is the kingdom of Rome, before the kingdom of Arabia arose.

---

[1] The words רכן רב are rendered in the translation ' composite.'

He makes the head the first kingdom, and the breast and arms the second kingdom, and the belly and thighs the third kingdom : and he makes the upper parts of the legs the fourth kingdom before the kingdom of Arabia.   Now he does not say of the fourth kingdom 'another,' as he said of the second and third, because the Greeks are the founders of the kingdom of Rome, as we shall shew in chap. viii.   **And whereas thou sawest the feet and toes** : feet refers to the instep of the foot ; then he mentions the **toes**, and tells us that the feet and toes of this image were like the feet and toes of a man, two feet and ten toes ; probably, however, the statue resembled a human being also in its erect posture, its back, hips, legs, as well as feet and toes. He unites the **feet and toes** in the sentence because they were all of the same material, iron and clay (cp. ver. 33).   The *iron* represents the Romans, and the *clay* the Arabs ; and this is because the Romans reigned a hundred years before the Arabs ; then the Arabs began to reign, but the kingdom of the Romans remained, as is witnessed in our own day.   He compares the kingdom of the Arabs to *clay*, because they have neither power nor force like those of the Romans.   **A divided kingdom** : i. e. from the time of the reign of the Arabs, inasmuch as the kingdom was first to the Romans only, then the Arabs reigned with them.   **And part of iron** : to shew that this iron which is mixed with the clay is not other than the former iron, but the same. The interpretation is that the kingdom of the Romans shall remain simultaneously with the kingdom of the Arabs, and that the Arabs shall be partners with them therein ; hence, **and part of clay shall be therein.   Mixed with miry clay** : not a mixture in which the ingredients mingle, as gold mixes with silver ; as this is not possible between such substances as iron and clay ; but a mixture like that of wheat and barley, or similar substances ; part, therefore, of the instep of the foot is iron and part clay.   This is possible because of the length of the instep.   The same is the case with the toes.   In the description of the toes, **part of iron and part of clay**, probably this iron does not belong to the Romans, but is to be interpreted of the Arabs only. In the interpretation of this he says **so the kingdom shall be partly strong and partly broken.**   Either he means that its beginnings were powerful (as we shall explain in the proper place in this book), and its end feeble ; in which case the toes where they joined the instep must have been iron, and the ends clay.   Or he may be referring to the kingdom of certain of the children of 'the Master' (Muḥammad), who were powerful, and others who were to follow them and be weak like clay.

   And whereas thou sawest the iron mixed with miry clay does not refer to the mixture of the toes, since he does not use the word *mixture* of them, but says only **part of them were iron and part clay**.   This can only refer to the mixture of the feet, of which he had said **forasmuch as thou sawest**, etc.   This is the mixture of the Romans and the Arabs ; he tells us that just as they are associated in empire (**a divided kingdom**), so they shall be mixed in the matter of marrying and begetting children, neither party disapproving of this, as Israel does ; for this reason, too, he said **they shall mingle themselves with the seed of men.**   For the Moslem does not refuse to take a wife of the Christian religion, nor the Christian to take a wife of the religion of Islām.

But they shall not cleave to one another : since they disagree with one another on the fundamental doctrines, the one confessing One God, and believing that 'Īsā (Jesus), the son of Maryam (Mary), was a mortal; whereas the others believe that He is the Creator of the heavens and earth, as is well known concerning the Christian religion. Similarly do they differ about the Qiblah and many other subjects too long to explain. This is why he says **they shall not cleave one to another** ; which is explained in the words **even as iron**, etc., i. e. as iron does not mingle with clay.

So far for the description of the statue. Now for the interpretation of it. It means four kingdoms which are to arise in the world. The *first* is the kingdom which laid waste Jerusalem and took the people captive from their homes. *After* it came the kingdom of the Persians, which ordered the House to be built, and permitted the people to go thither, and gave the money and charges and offerings out of its treasures. The *third* is the kingdom of the Greeks, which neither took the people captive nor laid waste their dwellings : however, harm was done the nation by them, as the Jews have handed down in their books and records, though the books of the Prophets do not expressly state it. As for the *fourth* empire, it has carried Israel into captivity, as the first did, and gone further than it in enmity and injury; and as for the Arabs, they have not indeed acted like the others in exiling them and destroying them, but they have injured the nation in the way of contempt and scorn and humiliation, etc., of which we shall mention some specimens in the commentary on the dream of Daniel and his prophecy. He represents all these empires as attached to each other, because there was not a follower of the truth among them, though their systems differed : and he makes them all one piece.

After giving the interpretation of the image he gives that of the stone which was cut from the mountain and brake the image.

44, 45. He compared the four kingdoms to a wrought image, but the kingdom of Israel to a stone cut out of a mountain, because their kingdom is eternal : either it means the *nation*, or the *Messiah*, who is of them, or of the seed of David. He said in the dream that it *brake the feet of the image*, i. e. that they shall crush Edom (i. e. Rome) and Ishmael. Then he says **then were broken in pieces together**, inasmuch as the religion of each kingdom and some, too, of the people shall remain till the Messiah's kingdom. He tells us that it shall break and destroy the remnants of the three previous kingdoms, them and their religions; **it shall break in pieces and consume all these kingdoms.** He points out the difference between these four kingdoms and that of the Messiah. Of every one of these four kingdoms the dominion ceases, and is given to another : but this kingdom shall not pass away, nor be given to another. And he did not say of the image that God Almighty had set it up, as he says of the kingdom of the Messiah **the God of heaven shall set up a kingdom,** because they are weak and few in number, and it is God who will raise them from the dust, and bring down the others from the height, since it was He who brought them down from the height (Lam. ii. 12) and raised the empire of the others (ibid. ii. 14); and He will do the same in the time to come, raising the estate of Israel and afflicting the empires (cp. Ps. cxiii. 5). And God Almighty shewed this dream to Nebuchadnezzar, because he was the first of the kings and the greatest of them; to shew to him and every king who should arise, the superiority of Israel, and what should come to pass in the latter days, and that every dynasty should be destroyed when her empire began, and that none should think itself a lasting dynasty; and that it will be well for them not to afflict Israel, because they are suffering discipline, that is all; and if they do otherwise, God will be wroth with them and punish them. And thereby too He teaches His people to be patient, knowing the transitoriness of these empires and the durability of their own, and that all nations shall bow before them. And therein is their great consolation.

And the dream is certain and the interpretation thereof sure: i.e. this dream came not from fancy, or occupation of spirit, as men sometimes see in dreams what they have been doing or pondering, and when they see it, there is no interpretation to be realized in the future; no, this is a dream which God purposed to shew him.

And the interpretation thereof sure: i.e. this interpretation of mine is accurate, and there is no explanation other than what we have given.

46. Believing that there was in Daniel a portion of the divine power, like what the Christians hold of the Messiah, he put him in the place of God, and fell on his face before him and bowed down to him, and commanded that sacrifices should be brought to him, as they are brought to a god; he does not say that he *brought* them to him: most probably Daniel prohibited him from doing so.

47. **Of a truth**: he acknowledges that God is the God of gods, and that it was thereby that Daniel could know this mystery. Then he called him **Rabbi** [1], i.e. made of himself his pupil and his slave. Then he bestowed on him many splendid gifts, as he had promised the Chaldees, ver. 6; adding a distinction which he had not expressly mentioned to them, viz. making him sultan of the province of Babylon and chief of all the wise men of Babylon.

49. When he had attained high station it was impossible for him that his fellows should be left with none. As for himself, he was established in the king's gate,—not as porter, but rather to inspect men's business in the same way as Joseph did: so that the king had the title and Daniel gave the commands and prohibitions. The writer tells us of the rank of his associates by way of introduction to the sequel.

III.

The matter narrated belongs to the history of Nebuchadnezzar, but Hananiah, Mishael, and Azaria enter into it. It is told us on account of the great edification to be got from it.

---

[1] Translation of ver. 48: ' Then the king called Daniel my lord, and my master,' etc.

The first thing necessary to explain is, What moved Nebuchadnezzar to make this image? Our answer is, that when he became master of the world he made it, and the herald proclaimed that whosoever should not come forward and bow down should be cast into the fiery furnace. By doing this they would shew their allegiance to him; before they were under his sovereignty he could not have done it. He had already another deity whom he served (ver. 14). His will was accomplished as soon as it was seen that all mankind—except the Jews mentioned in the Scripture—bowed down to it. He records its *height* and its *size;* the latter containing its length and breadth. He set it up in the plain of Dūra because it could contain a great crowd of men standing. He made its *height sixty cubits*, that they might see it from a distance and bow down to it from every quarter. He did not set it up before collecting the people: rather, he made it first, then sent and brought the people from all the cities of the world, and when they were come to Babylon set it up and ordered them to bow down to it. He brought the nobles, not the common people, which would have been impossible; the world would have been desolated and the place could not have contained them either. Those who came must have left substitutes to keep their places till they returned. He tells us that when they were summoned *they came* and did not disobey; which fact, by itself, shewed their allegiance to him. And when they were gathered in Babylon, he made a banquet in honour of the image; and the people gathered and bowed down, and after that went to eat and drink; they did not eat before they had bowed. Probably he had slaughtered victims and made them ready for them. Then, after they had gathered together, he set up musicians with their instruments, and when they were standing in front of the image, he bade the heralds go about among the people and say: 'Ye tribes of men, take heed, and fail not to bow down to the image; whensoever ye hear the sound of the musical instruments, let every one fall on his face bowing to the image, and whosoever shall not bow down, that moment shall he be cast into the fiery furnace.' This shews that he must have built a great furnace in order that if any man disobeyed he might be thrown into the fire. Most probably he had sent some persons before him to go about among the people who had come from the countries, to see whether any one disobeyed or not. Then the writer informs us that all who were present bowed down after they had heard the sound of the musical instruments, except the three mentioned above. We are left with one of two alternatives. Either he desired the people to abandon their religions and serve a god other than their own; or he desired their allegiance only. As it is not probable that he desired them to give up their gods, since the religions remained intact, each nation serving its god, we must suppose that he desired of them allegiance and nothing more. What we must remember about all the Jews who were in Babylon is that the king did not require this of the common people, but only of the dignitaries and nobles: not of the others. Had not Hananiah, Mishael, and Azaria been dignitaries—as was mentioned before—he would not have made them appear in the throng, nor have required them to bow down. As for the case of Daniel, he was not required to bow down to the image because his station was too high, as he occupied the place of a god with the king (ii. 46). Those who accused them were minions of the king, whom he had ordered to take note of the people.

12. **They serve not thy god** : i. e. the god whom he served before he set up the image.

We learn that when he was told that they *bowed not down to the image,* **he was filled with wrath and his colour changed.** Either this was because *   *   * or because opposition had come from *them;* [and he feared] that, when this was known to others, his authority would be weakened ; and had it not been for that, he would not have thought it a grave matter. The latter is more probable to my mind. He did not know what to do, and perhaps did not finish the dedication of the image.

He ordered them to be brought before him and began to upbraid them ; perhaps, he thought, they would make an excuse of some kind, so that their joy need not be troubled [i. e. so that they need not be punished].

15. **Now are ye ready?** i. e. 'did ye just now hear the proclamation, or has the herald not yet come forward with it ?' Perhaps he said this in order that they might make some excuse, that the people might know that they did not slight him ; though the time for bowing had already passed ; for he only desired the people to bow down at the time when they heard the sound of the musical instruments. But the answer they returned was not an excuse ; on the contrary, they spoke plainly to him, so that it became necessary, in his view, for him to do what he did.

16. **We do not need** : i. e. 'it is not necessary for us to make any excuse, as perhaps thou wouldst suggest ; and as for thy saying "**What god is he,**" thou art to know that our God is able to deliver us from the fiery furnace wherewith thou threatenest us in many ways, and if thou command us to be slain by some other means, He is able to deliver us from that too.'

18. **And if not** : this does not mean 'if He is not able,' which would be in contradiction to their assertion, ver. 17. It means, 'if He should not deliver us ; for He will not leave us in thy hand out of inability. Nor do we serve Him in order that He may deliver us from punishment in this world, but only that we may be delivered from punishment in the next world, and receive our eternal reward ; so thou mayest know that what was told thee of us is true ; we have not served thy god, nor thy image, nor shall we serve them in time to come either.' And this they said in the presence of the crowds that had bowed down to the image.

From this verse we learn that it is unlawful to bow down to an image, even though a man does not believe in its sanctity. The foundation of this is in the law (Ex. xx. 5). We also learn that there is another world of rewards. For, if there were no other world after this, in what did they trust, that they did not bow down to the image? And for what did they hope, that they gave their bodies to be burnt ? Or why did Daniel let himself be thrown into the lions' den ? The words **if not** shew that in their opinion it was possible that God might let His servants be tormented and slain by the hand of unbelievers, to reward them for it in the next world. They knew all this, and yet did not commit the crime.

d

[II. 3.]

He ordered them to throw in **seven times as much wood** as was ordinarily thrown in, to terrify them, that they might **repent** and humble themselves; but they did not care for his words or think about them. Then we are told that he commanded them to be bound **in their clothes**; and the king's order was obeyed.

פטישיהון, **their vests.**

כרבלתהון, **their belts.**

לבושיהון, either **their turbans**, or **their bonnets**, as they were dressed like governors.

They were *thrown* with engines, because the furnace was high, and raised above the level of the ground, and they were thrown over the top of it. They were not introduced by the door of the furnace, because the king wished to make the scene as terrible as possible, and in order that the crowds of bystanders might look on at a distance, on some high ground. Possibly he flung in each one separately, one after the other; he threw in, let us suppose, Hananiah first, that the two might take fright; but they did not care; so he threw in the second, and the last did not care.

22. The writer now tells us how those who threw them in were slain by the heat of the sparks of fire. This was because the fuel flew up when they fell in; a fierce flame came out of it; and when the heat caught them, they perished. Nebuchadnezzar was standing on the high place when they flung them out of the engine, looking on the furnace; there can have been no smoke ascending, which would have hidden the furnace from view; and he beheld them, and lo, they were going to and fro in the flame. And he was terrified and amazed thereby (ver. 24), and spoke to his courtiers as recorded. Either these were present with him, but did not see what he saw, through God hiding it from them (as happened to Daniel when he saw the angel whom no one else saw, as we shall explain *infra*), so that they saw neither the angel nor the three. Or it may be that his courtiers saw the three, but did not see the angel.

24. **Were not three men?** He tells them that he sees something they do not. Perhaps he asked first for information from them, to know whether they saw it or not; and then he said ' Did not we throw in three men and no more?' And they said ' Aye.' Then he said, ' Lo, I see four persons, only the fourth is like the angels.' The other three were, of course, Shadrach, etc. Then, when he saw them going to and fro in the furnace, not going out of the furnace, he said in himself, ' These men will not go out, however long they stay; it is as if they were in a garden, taking their pleasure.' So he approached the door of the furnace to ask them to go out from the furnace, since there was no way out save by the door; apparently they wished to shew that the person who should take them out must be himself, and that they would not go out save by his command. So he approached the furnace and said to them, ' Come out, come;' the angel must have been with them till they left the furnace, because so long as he was with them no mischief from the fire could come to them. When they went out, they were not naked, but covered with their clothes; in

their tunics only, out of all their clothes, since only these are mentioned. And the Creator and Worker of miracles caused these tunics to remain, to cover them, and that all might see the marvel that some of their clothes should be burnt, while others remained unburnt. We are told above that the fire did not attack any part of their *bodies*, so that even in the nails of the feet and the hands, in which no great harm would be done, they were not injured by it. **Their hair was not singed** : as hair naturally is by a little fire, when it comes near it. **Nor had the smell of fire passed on them** : it could not be smelt in their bodies or in their tunics ; this is not astonishing, as a work of the Almighty Creator ; He put a screen between the fire and them, by one of those mercies of which He is capable, but not between the fire and their garments ; blessed be He, Worker of miracles impossible to His creatures (cp. Ps. cxxxvi. 4). This overthrows the doctrine of those who would do away with miracles, and reject this narrative. Now God Almighty displayed this mighty miracle in the time of Nebuchadnezzar, as He displayed His miracles in Egypt, annulling thereby the systems of the Magicians till they confessed and said, ' This is the finger of God ' (Ex. vii. 15). And so, when Nebuchadnezzar and the rest of his princes had witnessed this, they believed in the work of the Creator, and thereafter he blessed the Creator, saying : **Blessed is their God, etc.** An hour before his language to them had been : **And who is the God who shall save you from my hand ?**

Who sent His angel : he had witnessed the angel going with them ; God Almighty had sent the angel to make him certain that this was His work, and none other's.

And saved His servants : observing that they were saved through relying on Him, not caring for his threats, and **changing the king's word**.

But gave up their bodies : i. e. they gave over their bodies to the fire, and all that they might serve no other god.

And a decree is set forth by me : he ordered that a stop should be put to the societies of religious speculation, wherein the doctrines of the Unitarians were reprobated. **That whoever speaketh error against their God shall be hewn**, i. e. his body cut in pieces, and his property be confiscate to the sultan.

For there is no other god : he decides that among all the gods there is none able to deliver his servants from afflictions and punishments like Him.

After this he tells us what the king did with them afterwards. **He promoted**, i. e. he increased their rank and dignity.

People may ask about the previous assertion of Nebuchadnezzar at the time in which Daniel interpreted his dream to him, ' Of a truth your God, etc.,' and they may say, ' Does not this language shew that he believed in God Almighty and His miracles ? How then can he have dealt so with them or said, " And who is the God who shall save you from my hand ?" ' The answer is that it was not more extraordinary than that our ancestors should have witnessed God's wonders and His talking with them on Mount Sinai, and after a few days should have served the calf, explaining away in some manner what they had witnessed. How much more natural that such should be the conduct of Nebuchadnezzar the idolator! At the time, probably, he believed; afterwards he apostatised by the aid of some of these false explanations. Doubtless God punished him for his apostasy, and for admitting doubts into his mind.

(Fourth Chapter.)

31. These are the letters written by king Nebuchadnezzar to all the people of the world, after the completion of the seven years which passed over him when he was among the wild beasts. When his reason had returned to him and he was once more king, he wrote the letters, in which he narrates the story; beginning with **Signs and wonders** and ending with **and those that walk in pride.**

32. **Signs and wonders** : alluding to what had happened to him during the seven years, which we shall recount in its place. **It was pleasing before me** : meaning that he felt bound to tell them to the world, and not to refrain from publishing and proclaiming them, and thanking God for them.

33. **His signs** : i. e. both the wonderful works recorded above, and those which God is constantly performing. Shewing that he believed in them, and did not reject them as the philosophers do.

His kingdom is an everlasting kingdom : meaning (1) that it endures infinitely; (2) that He does what He thinks fit in His world, and that His dominion is over all while the times and periods change (cp. Ps. cxlv. 13).

IV.

1. He tells us that he saw the dream at the time when he was at peace, and no necessity for expeditions occurred : the world being completely at his feet, without enemies or rivals; his affairs and business being all in due order.

Green in my palace refers to his bodily health and personal appearance when his affairs were settled, as opposed to the condition in which he was during the periods when he was engaged in wars.

2. He tells us that he saw a dream which made an impression on him, and which he did not forget as he had forgotten the first dream : and when he woke, lo, he was in terror. Or, the first part may be a description of his condition during the time in which he was seeing the dream and hearing the voice of the angels, **Cut down the oak** ; and the words **and thoughts on my bed troubled me**, an account of his condition after waking, meaning that he was pondering on what he had seen, and troubled and amazed, not knowing the interpretation.

3, 4. He did not, we see, send for Daniel to appear before him, and ask him to interpret the dream, notwithstanding that Daniel was present in Babylon. He sent first to the wise men of Babylon for the following reason : when he demanded of them the first dream, they said repeatedly, 'Tell us the dream and we undertake to interpret it.' So when he saw this dream, knowing that the interpretation of it was difficult, he determined to tell it to the different orders of the wise men of Babylon, in order that, when they were found unable to interpret it, their inferiority might be clearly proved to themselves and to mankind in general ; and that he might afterwards send for Daniel, who would tell him the dream before them, and explain it step by step; so that his superiority would come out as clearly as that of Joseph, when the wise men of Egypt were unable to interpret the dream of Pharaoh, and they all acknowledged his wisdom (Gen. xli. 38).

5, 6. He had called him **Belteshazzar, the name of his god,** because of the **spirit of the holy gods** which was to be found in him; the name was a distinction.

According to the name of my god : some have supposed that in spite of all the events which had happened to him, he continued to worship idols, owing to some delusion or other, or else for political purposes ; as, if he proclaimed to the world that he adopted the religion of the Jews, their laws would be incumbent on him, and he would fall. He was therefore unwilling to withdraw himself from his god, so that he magnified the God of heaven, but did not give up his own religion. Or it may refer to that which he had been accustomed to serve before he believed in God Almighty.

Whom I know, from what had occurred in the first dream, when the secret had been revealed to him.

7 sqq. After being told the dream, and how 'none but thee of the wise men of Babylon can interpret it, but thou canst because of the divine wisdom that is in thee, so tell the interpretation thereof,' Daniel pondered and did not commence interpreting till the king spoke to him. This was not bewilderment on Daniel's part concerning the interpretation, owing to the matter being concealed from him ; he was rather pondering how to approach the king, it being improper to approach him directly with the interpretation, owing to its content, viz., misfortunes to happen to the king ; he also saw that it would not be well when the king asked him for the interpretation that he should fail to give it. He thought it therefore the safest course to ponder till the king spoke and asked him. The severe effort of thinking had made his colour change ; when the king saw him thus he said, **Let not the dream or its interpretation trouble thee,** thinking that he would require to ponder deeply over it. Daniel answered that he had not held back the interpretation because it had troubled him, but only on the king's behalf; otherwise he might have hastened to interpret it at once.

19. **The dream be to them that hate thee** : an expression of civility and courtesy, it being improper to commence otherwise. It has been thought that Daniel may have meant the *enemies* of God Almighty, and *those that hate* Him, Nebuchadnezzar being one of them. Then he proceeded to divide the dream into three parts, and to interpret each part separately.

20. 'The greatness, might and height of the tree that thou sawest, with food therein for all animals, and dwelling for them beneath it and in it,' represents the height of the kingdom and its extension to the end of the world. One thing is left unexplained, sc. v. 21: **Whose leaves were fair and the fruit thereof much** ; the first refers to the beauty of his armies and his children, and the second to the quantity of goods that he had collected from the countries. **In it was meat for all,** refers

to his stores. **The beasts of the field had shadow under it**: i.e. the nomads. The **fowls** symbolize all those who had come to him from all countries, and attached themselves to his dominion and housed themselves under his protection. **And all flesh was fed of it** most probably refers to the profit enjoyed by mankind after his dominion had been established. Then he expounds the *second part*, the voice of the angels which he had heard (ver. 14). Observe that of these two angels one was in the height, the one that said **Hew down the tree,** who is called a watcher, and was higher in rank than **the holy one,** who asked the 'watcher' to let the roots of the tree remain in their place (ver. 15). **The sentence is by the decree of the watchers,** refers to **Hew down the tree,** etc.; **the demand is by the word of the holy one,** to the demand that the **stump of his roots** should be left. The names are used first in the singular (ver. 13), afterwards in the plural (ver. 17); this shews that they were a multitude; and that a number of *watchers* commanded, and a number of *holy ones* asked on behalf of the tree: God shewed him this that he might know that both matters were by command of the Almighty Creator; both Nebuchadnezzar's personal calamity, and the preservation of the kingdom for him till he returned from the wilderness.

Hew down the oak means removing him from mankind: **cut off its branches** refers to the cutting off of his armies. **Even with a band of iron and brass** refers to his being among the animals during that period, like a man bound, unable to move hither or thither, and remaining with the wild beasts. **In the tender grass of the field** means that he would live in a place which produced grass for him to feed upon, and that he would be a graminivorous not a carnivorous animal.

With the dew of heaven refers to his being day and night under heaven, having no shelter to take refuge in from the dew.

Let his heart be changed refers to the cessation of his reason, and his becoming deprived of the power of discrimination which he had.

Three things, it is to be observed, are literal: (1) **grass like an ox,** etc.; (2) **let it be wet with the dew of heaven**; (3) **let his heart be changed**; the rest are all symbolical.

And let seven times pass over him: some persons have thought these 'times' mean 'seasons,' making a total of less than two years; others, that they were 'years,' which is more probable; the period apparently was extended, and the Creator humiliated him. Then the angel states that all this had come upon him that he might know that the kingdom is God's, and that He gives it to whom He will, though he be the lowest of the people (ver. 17). This shews that his heart was swollen, and that he had clothed himself in pride: and that God had humbled him in consequence, that he might realize that God Almighty is Monarch in His world, and does therein what He will, as is explained in the following chapter. Then he proceeds to the third portion, **and whereas they commanded,** whereas thou heardest it said 'leave the stump of the roots of the tree,' the meaning thereof is that the kingdom remaineth for thee, and shall not be taken away from thee. Then after he had interpreted the dream he proceeded to give him counsel, which he had only to follow to avert the threat.

24. This points to his having tyrannized over the people (cp. Ezek. vii. 11; Jer. xxi. 35); he may have made heavy demands from them or enacted cruel laws. The words **by shewing mercy to the poor** refer to hard-heartedness on his part towards *the weak:* by whom some have thought that the *weak* Israelite nation is intended, since apparently he was more furious against them than any others. Now these are two great offences committed by unbelievers for which God punishes in this world; thus he destroyed the generation of the Flood on their account (Gen. vi. 13), and so too Sodom and Gomorrah, and so too the people of Nineveh till they repented (Jonah iii. 8).

So there shall be a lengthening of thy tranquillity: i.e. God will divert it from thee for a time, as he diverted the disaster in the time of Hezekiah. God would bring it upon him owing to his oppression and tyranny: but if he mended his ways, God would divert it from him: it will be according to the **sentence of the watchers,** if thou remainest in all thy sins.

25. This verse is not part of Daniel's address to the king, but an observation of the writer, informing us that Nebuchadnezzar did not accept Daniel's counsel, and therefore that which the dream symbolized overtook him.

26, 27. This saying only was not the cause of what happened to him, but his continuance in his guilt and transgression. God gave him a year's grace from the time that he saw the dream: but as he did not repent, and this saying was added thereunto, God delayed his punishment no longer. It happened that he had gone up to the roof of the palace and looked down over the city, and observed the beauty of its buildings, till he said **Is not this great Babylon?** which shews that he had rebuilt it after his own fancy to make it his capital; and all his stores were therein, whence the words **for the might of my power,** etc.

28, 29. The voice which he heard was from heaven; possibly no one heard it save he; or possibly others did hear it, the voice being loud that mankind in general might know this.

30. Doubtless as soon as he heard this voice which descended from the heavens reach him, his reason stopped, and he fell down from his palace-roof, and went blindly forward, and was guided by the Creator into the wilderness; he was not stopped, especially as his story was known, and Daniel had told them about it, so that they did not attend to him.

Till his hair was grown points to the length of his sojourn, which was seven years.

31, 32. At the end of the seven times his reason returned to him, and he found himself among the wild beasts in the wilderness, and perceived the state of his body, the mass of his hair and the length of his nails, and realized that there had come upon him all that had been told him. After that he raised his eyes to heaven and spoke as above.

His kingdom is an everlasting kingdom, inasmuch as the kingdom of men and their dominion ceases and terminates.

And all the inhabitants of the earth: the great and the little alike are counted as nothing; since they come to an end and die : and in this sense the verse will refer to ordinary people, and their general condition. The prophets and saints however are the pillars of the world. If Nebuchadnezzar refers to death and the termination of man's career, then it is a general sentiment ; but if it refers to rank and power, then the prophets and saints are not included.

And He doeth according to His will in the army of heaven: i. e. either the angels ; or the stars, which eclipse, blacken, and fall.

And among the inhabitants of the earth : here too he may refer to mankind,— whom God slayeth and maketh alive, enricheth and maketh poor—or it may include all the animals.

And none : including the host of heaven and the inhabitants of the earth.

Can strike upon His hand : i. e. upon God's hand ; or perhaps on his own hand, to warn Him off. The first is more probable. None among the host of heaven and the inhabitants of the earth can stay Him from His will, or express displeasure at His work, saying to Him, 'What is the work that Thou hast done? It is not fair' (cp. Eccles. viii. 4). He notices this because it corresponds with his own case ; since he had been unable to impede God's dealings with himself, or be displeased thereat, for He had been just in His work ; Daniel had warned him, but he had not taken his advice ; and so earned all that happened to him.

33. He said above (ver. 31) **mine understanding returned unto me** in order to annex to it **and I blessed the Most High ;** here he repeats it to tell us how he returned and was established in his sovereignty and his glory. Daniel had said to him **thy kingdom shall be sure unto thee,** assuring him that he would certainly return to his throne.

My counsellors and my lords sought unto me : Daniel had reckoned up the times, and when they were full, he commanded the army and the nobles to go out after him, and to disperse in different regions to seek him, till they found him seeking the inhabited world, and took him and brought him back.

And excellent greatness : he was not humiliated in their eyes when the disaster had fallen upon him, but on the contrary, they gave him increased might and majesty. This was because he dealt justly with the people, and gave up oppression, wrong, and tyranny. Fear of him was in consequence put into the hearts of men, and he increased in power and glory. The Scripture does not tell us how the world fared during these seven times without a king to govern. Some say Daniel governed the kingdom ; others that the king's son Evil sat on the throne till the return of the father.

37. Just as if he had been reading out to them this section from the beginning till this place, in copies transmitted to them, he finishes with the words ' I bless and exalt the blessed Creator for all His works.'

This is the end of the history of Nebuchadnezzar. Then he proceeds to tell us the history of Belshazzar, his grandson ; the history of his son Evil Merodach is omitted, because no act was done by him like those done by his father and his son Belshazzar.

Of Evil Merodach we only hear of the kindness that he shewed to Jehoiakin. Probably he was the best of them.

V.

1. Belshazzar reigned three years at the least; and he made this feast quite at the end of the time (ver. 3, *inf.*). The book does not explain the reason for which the feast was made. Possibly he had counted the seventy years which God had appointed them; and when he saw that the seventy years were completed, and the kingdom remained unchanged, he made the feast out of joy thereat, thinking that all that had been said had fallen to the ground: and this was why he ventured to take the vessels of the house of God which Nebuchadnezzar his father had put away, and abstained from employing; when Belshazzar saw the seventy years completed and the kingdom remaining, he said, 'These vessels are mine and there is no return:' so he began to praise his gods, in whom he now believed, wherein he was too hasty; and, indeed, this was one of the causes of his ruin. He did not invite any besides the nobles, their attendants and followers; who, he tells us, were a **thousand** souls. **And drank wine before the thousand**: they were in his hall, and he drank in their presence.

2. **While he tasted the wine**: some make this mean that his intoxication excited him to this, whereas, had he been sober he would not have done so, but would have refrained from bringing them out and drinking out of them; others, that while the wine was pleasant to him, he wished to drink out of the vessels of the house of God, these being vessels fit to drink out of, such as 'cups' and 'bowls,' etc.

Vessels of gold and silver in ver. 2; in ver. 3 the *silver* is omitted: either for brevity; there being no doubt, if the gold were brought, that the silver would be brought too; or he may have ordered them to be brought, and afterwards preferred the gold exclusively. Then they praised the god[s] of the images; and did not praise the blessed Creator, despising Him in their hearts, and thinking that they were masters of the vessels of the house of God; and just then came the term which God had fixed.

5. **The fingers of a hand**: this shews that he saw a hand appear, but did not see the arm, or the person; so, too, Ezekiel (viii. 3) saw a hand only; and likewise Daniel on a later occasion (x. 7).

On the plaister of the wall of the palace: referring to the white plaister; the writing was black, so that it shewed: and the king saw it alone of those who were in the hall, just as Nebuchadnezzar only saw Hananiah, Mishael, Azariah, and the angel.

6. When he saw this miracle, fear and tremor came upon him, and owing to the greatness of his terror the vertebrae of his spine were loosened, and his knees struck against each other.

7. He immediately summoned these to tell him the writing and its interpretation; promising the person who should read it, and shew him the interpretation, that he

e   [II. 3.]

would clothe him in royal garments, and put a gold chain about his neck, while a herald cried before him that he was lord over a third part of the kingdom. This is like what Pharaoh did to Joseph, only he entrusted his affairs to Joseph without making him a partner in the kingdom, whereas Belshazzar meant that of all the taxes that came to him Daniel should have a third part, and a third in every benefit which the king enjoyed. His grandfather Nebuchadnezzar had made no such offer to the person who should tell him his dream and its interpretation, but had merely offered presents, rewards, and dignities, inferior to the sovereignty. This was because this matter made more impression on Belshazzar than the other had made, and because of the fright, fear, and impatience that had seized him.

8. The writing was not unlike any existing writing; on the contrary, it was an existing character, whether Hebrew or some other. The answer (to the problem) is that the letters were not *arranged* in order, but inverted, the letters of מנא being arranged אנם: and similarly all the letters of the four words were transposed. Hence they did not understand them: and, when they read them, they got no intelligible word, much less its interpretation. And his heart was nigh breaking thereat, so that when Daniel, after the others had failed, read it and interpreted it, he was able to address him as he did in presence of the throng, and explain to him his sin and the wickedness of his conduct, as described at the outset of the chapter.

9. He had hoped that his wise men would understand it, and tell him its interpretation: so when they did not understand it, his horror increased and his colour changed. It is not improbable that he saw the hand while the others did not see it, and that on account of this they were astonished and confounded when he said, 'Ye peoples, lo, I see a great hand which has written this, and lo, terror confounds me!'

10. This **queen** was his grandmother, wife of Nebuchadnezzar, and was acquainted with these matters from their beginning.

By reason of the affairs of the king: this refers to the terror and fright that had seized the king, and the change of the expression of his face, and the bewilderment of his nobles, and [the fears] that had fallen on them on the king's account, whence their joy had been changed into this plight. Her heart pained her on his account, since he was her son's son, now that this trouble had fallen upon him, and she feared that he might die of the fright which had beset his heart; at any rate that he would not rest till there came the person who had power to read to him the writing and understand its interpretation.

11. She informs him that there is present in the city Daniel, who will read the writing, and interpret it to him; that he might cease from [the terror] that had fallen upon him. Then she began to recount to him some details of Daniel's wisdom, and how he was above all his father's wise men, having been the most eminent of them, that he might be convinced in his mind that Daniel would understand that, and a more difficult thing too. The most probable account of this matter is that Daniel had never come before him, and had never known him at all, having been absent from Babylon during this year (see on viii. 1); after which he returned, very probably

for this very purpose, providentially. Next she described Daniel to him that he might know him and his skill.

In verse 11 she ascribed to him four characteristics: (1) **spirit of the gods**; (2) **light**; (3) **understanding**; (4) **wisdom**. In the next verse she repeats some of them in the same words, and others with a change of expression. Probably an **excellent spirit** means the same as **spirit of the holy gods**; **knowledge** is the explanation of **wisdom like the wisdom of the gods**; **interpreting of dreams** the specification of **light**; this word נהירו may either mean 'that which is correct' according to the Hebrew, or 'light' according to the Aramaic (cp. ii. 22); meaning that he can shew up hidden things, which are as it were in dark places, so that they can be seen and understood.

An excellent spirit: referring to his inspiration, the like of which was not to be found among the wise men of Babylon.

Knowledge: the philosophical sciences, as in i. 4.

Understanding: reasoning power.

Interpreting of dreams: referring to difficult dreams, as happened to him when he explained the tree (chap. iv).

Shewing of dark sentences: this is not illustrated in the book; 'dark sentences' are, in the language of the philosophers, striking sayings constructed in language made up of hints, like Samson's riddle.

12. **Dissolving of knots**: a form of expression which is thought to be simple, but which the wise man can analyse into its parts. She added that his grandfather had set him above all his wise men because these qualities were united in him; and that he also called him by the name of his god on that account.

13. The queen had not told him that Daniel was of the Jews. Possibly he asked those present about him, and they told him so. This remark of Belshazzar was not meant contemptuously at such a time: he must have said it to him because the Jews were famous for prophecy and the divine sciences.

16. He said in the first verse (14) 'that a spirit of the gods and light and prudence;' in the second (this verse) he adds 'solutions' also, according to what the queen had stated.

17. He would not accept any of the things he mentioned for several reasons. First, because he did not want his favours, which were not proportionate, but dictated by ignorance and insolence. Secondly, because they were honours which would be annulled at once. Thirdly, that it might not be said that he had interpreted it for the sake of what he was going to get. He said, 'I will not take from thee, so, if thou wilt give, give some one else, whom thou mayest choose. I will read the writing and tell thee the interpretation thereof: that only is thy desire and thy request.'

18–22. He prefixes this introduction to shew him that he was not greater than his grandfather, who had reached in sovereignty and power and terror and majesty a height which his grandson had not reached: yet, when he grew proud, and put on the garb of tyranny, the Creator humbled him to a degree beyond which there was no further degradation; and that God raises the humble, and humbles the proud, and slays mighty kings, and does whatever else He will, none being able to oppose Him, or thwart His will.

22. **Though thou knewest all this**: shewing that Belshazzar knew all that had happened to his grandfather, so that he should have taken warning thereby. He then tells him that his seizure of the vessels of God's house was presumption towards Him and contempt of Him in his soul. Then Daniel looked towards the hall and the people therein, and saw the vessels of the house of God, and how they had been used for drinking; and told him how they had been praising their gods, and had not praised God Almighty as was His due, but had praised instead the idols which can do nothing, being mere images and semblances. Then after shewing him the inferiority of his gods, and his folly and audacity, he said to him, ' On account of this the author of this writing was sent.'

24-27. He tells him that on account of his action, as described, the angel had been sent and had written these four words. He then combined the fifteen letters into words, saying **number** twice; the first referring to the number of seventy years which God had appointed for Nebuchadnezzar, his son, and his son's son (Jer. xxvii. 7), the second to the reign of Belshazzar. He had numbered to them three kings and seventy years; when these were completed, they had nothing more left. **Tekel** he interprets **thou art weighed**; implying that one who is *wanting* cannot be taken, but only one who is full weight; i. e. whose intelligence, wisdom, piety, etc. are so; now in his father and grandfather there had been a certain number of laudable characteristics, but in him there were none, all his qualities being *wanting*. **Pharsin** he interprets **fragments**, comparing him to a thing that is broken, wherein nothing serviceable is left; referring to the destruction of all his supporters in the kingdom, and his own murder. This is why *Pharsin* is in the plural; signifying his own destruction, i. e. death, and afterwards the destruction after him of all the supporters of the Chaldean rule. Then he informed him that that rule would be transferred to the *Medes and Persians*.

29. The king's promise had necessarily to be fulfilled, and Daniel could not resist, though he knew that this sovereignty was transitory.

30. Darius knew that a word spoken by Daniel would be fulfilled, and that the kingdom was destined for the Medes and Persians. It may be that Daniel had told him that he and no other would be king, whence he was encouraged to kill Belshazzar. Or he may have been killed by some of his servants, since the Scripture does not record who the murderer was.

31. **Received the kingdom**: i. e. received it from the Chaldees; cp. *inf.* ix. 1. We are not told how he was established in the sovereignty, nor how he became seated in Babylon on the royal throne; but the writer tells us that Darius was born in the year in which Nebuchadnezzar took captive Jehoiakin king of Judah, to shew that in the very year in which he did so much in Jerusalem, and won so great a victory, God raised up one against him, who should take his kingdom

from him. For this reason we are given the number of his years at the time of his receiving the kingdom from the Chaldees. Since there was no purpose in telling us the age of any other of the kings of the Gentiles or of the Israelites [?] at the time of their coming to the throne, it is nowhere else given.

VI.

1–3. Darius was certain that the kingdom was established in his hands, and that he had not to march out to fight opponents. He appointed therefore these hundred and twenty governors, to each of whom belonged a particular province, wherein he left a viceroy, while he himself remained with the king in the capital. And he appointed three presidents, to whose word and command they were to refer ; and he appointed the hundred and twenty that they might govern the kingdom, and the king might not have to be fatigued with all the business. This is the same sort of plan as Pharaoh adopted, when he appointed Joseph to govern the kingdom, giving himself up to amusement, and retaining merely the title.

3. With עשׁית cp. Jonah i. 6 and Ps. cxlvi. 4. He set the three over the hundred and twenty, and Daniel, who was one of the three, over both the governors and the presidents, so that none of them could do anything save by his consent or command. He did this, **because an excellent spirit was in him.** He was never found incompetent, nor his orders and counsels false. So the king was, observe, **planning** to remove the others, and establish Daniel by himself ; i.e. it was not practicable for him to establish Daniel at once ; such a matter, he knew, required gentle strategy. So he went to the chief nobles of the empire, and did not remove them from their high station till his sovereignty was established. When it was established he began to plot and to plan to remove them little by little ; and when they perceived this they began to plot to remove him from the kingdom altogether.

4. The presidents and governors agreed together by reason of the envy of him which had penetrated their hearts. The king, they said, has only exalted him above us owing to the excellence of his counsel ; so we must plan some device to convince the king of some error or shortcoming on his part, that he may remove him from the sovereignty altogether. They sought, he says, for an error, but could not find one.

Error or mischief: ‘error’ means oppression of the subjects. ‘Mischief,’ wrong done in reference to the king, or wasting the revenue.

5. Despairing of finding a means of attack on the side of the king, they thought they would attain their will in respect of him in the matter of the worship of his Lord. Their object and intention therein was not to endeavour to shew that he neglected any of his religious duties, but of another sort.

7–9. **Have consulted together** : indicating that they had assembled and consulted about a measure which could establish the king in his sovereignty, so that the people would obey him ; and that it was necessary that this should be done, and if the king failed to do it, his kingdom would become insecure. They bound themselves to this, in order that Daniel might not be able to serve God, which was their real object, which object the king did not know : which was part of their treachery against him ; for had the king known, he would not have agreed to their counsel nor accepted it, nor set his signature. Then they said to him, 'Set thy signature that it may be read to the people in the streets and in the assemblies, that none of them may oppose it.' They included in their phrase that every man the followers of every religion, not confining the law to religions other than their own ;—a stroke of policy, to make it apply to Daniel. They appointed it for the space of thirty days, to make it last long ; that being with them the utmost space for which they could remain without worship of their deity. Had that not been allowed by their religion, he would not have enacted it. They also forbade people to make any request of each other, as they had forbidden them to make any of God ; but their object was only the latter. This they did that none besides themselves might know their object. Then they excepted *the king* for two reasons. First, because it was absolutely necessary ; since otherwise the nation would have perished from mutual outrages and difficulties that would arise. Secondly, they exalted the king above all gods to magnify his estate. All this was to shew him that by this statute his kingdom would be confirmed and set in order. When the king saw that they were agreed about it, it was clear to him that, unless he did that on which they were agreed, his power would be shaken. So he did it. He did not take Daniel's opinion beforehand, because they had told him that it was a part of the administration wherein Daniel had absolutely no concern.

11. Daniel may have known what was in their minds, and their purpose, i. e. that he and no other was their mark ; and he knew too what the king had done. But he did not tell the king, committing the business to the Creator of all. He mentions the windows, because they looked in at him through them, and surprised him, and behold he was praying.

Towards Jerusalem : this does not mean that the windows were opened towards Jerusalem, but rather that he stood facing Jerusalem, the Qiblah.

As he did aforetime : shewing that it was not a thing which he commenced then ; it implies that he had habitually done so, and that it is an obligatory duty which cannot be neglected. The three times probably mean evening, morning, and midday. From the words he kneeled upon his knees we learn that that is one condition of prayer (cp. Ps. xcv. 6).

12. Doubtless he had perceived that they had come to see him ; he did not, however, interrupt his prayer, but continued till the end, so that when they came down upon him he was still praying. These men were the governors and presidents.

13 (12). His answer, the thing is true, means 'it is so,' and none may transgress it ; whoever transgresses shall be cast into the den of lions. When they heard this saying of the king, and had reminded him of his decree, they proceeded.

14 (13). Of the children of the captivity : contemptuous, indicating that he was of the vilest of the people : 'yet thou hast raised him above them all, and he has

opposed thy edict, and loosed that wherewith thou hast bound the nation.' And they desired the king after this speech to order that he be thrown into the den of lions.

15. When he heard them say that the violator of the decree was Daniel, he perceived that they had laid the plot against him : so he began to make excuses for Daniel; such as that he did not count as one of the multitude to whom the prohibition applied : ' since he is the ruler of the kingdom, and the persons intended were others.' This and similar things he kept saying to them till sunset, opposing their proposition and excusing Daniel. Some have supposed that he said to them, ' Daniel cannot have known what was written ; had he heard of it, he would not have disobeyed our decree.' But when the sun set, Daniel rose and prayed, so that the king had no longer any excuse for him.

16. In other words : ' If Daniel be not cast into the lions' den, the rule of the Medes and Persians will have been broken ; now if it can be broken in Daniel's case, it can be broken in other cases; and this is a principle which will extend itself ; and ruin will be the result.' Their meaning was, that if the king altered their laws they would revolt from him, seeing that it was quite impossible that one who altered their laws should be king over them.

17. Darius' language is very different from that of Nebuchadnezzar (*sup.* iii. 15). Darius believed in God's power to deliver in some miraculous manner, whereas Nebuchadnezzar believed in no such power. Those who threw the victims in that case into the furnace were killed by the sparks of fire, because they were close by it. Those who threw Daniel into the den of lions did not suffer in the same way, the lions being far away from them. Darius said to Daniel at the moment of his being thrown in, 'Doubtless the God whom thou servest continually will save thee from the lions, since He is able to do this ; and those who have plotted against thee will not see their will accomplished upon thee.'

18. Probably the den had a door, whereby the lions were introduced ; and also a mouth, by which their food was thrown to them to eat, when there was no man thrown. And it was these people's duty when any man had merited death to throw him to the lions to eat. It was Nebuchadnezzar's way to kill by fire, and of the rest to kill by the sword.

That there might be no change of purpose : he means lest, when they saw that the lions did not harm him, they might themselves throw stones upon him and kill him; since they now dealt openly with him. And the king did this because he knew that God Almighty would deliver him ; otherwise he would not have sealed the stone which was at the top of the pit.

19. טות is the Chaldee for the Heb. צלי אשׁ. His heart was on fire, he means, concerning Daniel, so that he refused music and pleasure. And through his spirit being occupied with him, he thought much concerning him, and his sleep fled, so that he got no rest till dawn.

20 sqq. He arose at dawn, his spirit being occupied with him ; then he called

to him that he might let his voice be heard, and delight his heart with [an assurance of] his safety.

My God hath sent His angel : to be taken literally. God Almighty sent His angel to deliver him, as He sent His angel to Hananiah, Mishael, and Azariah. Although the lions were hungry, He allowed them no means of harming him.

For as much as before Him innocency : referring to his righteous conduct in matters between himself and God generally, and also to what was said above, ver. 4.

And also before thee, O king, I have done no hurt : indicating that he had done nothing whereby he had earned this treatment.

24. They let down ropes, as was done in the case of Jeremiah.

25. These men were the hundred and twenty-two who had plotted against him ; and every one who had displayed any hatred towards Daniel they included with them : also their sons and wives ; because it was the rule by the Persian law to include the women and children with the men ; or perhaps their wives and their grown-up sons had displayed some joy at Daniel's misfortune and hatred towards him, and so had earned their fate in the king's mind. Probably they threw them down in parties according to the number of the lions, each lion getting one ; and when they saw that he had devoured him, they produced another till they had devoured them all. Then Daniel returned to the administration of the kingdom by himself, as the king had originally intended (ver. 3). Doubtless the king's written statute must have held good till the end of the thirty days, except [for] Daniel and those who, like him, were worshippers of God Almighty.

26 sqq. Darius acted as Nebuchadnezzar had done, when he returned from the wilderness to his throne, in circulating letters, recounting what had happened to him. He felt bound to magnify the blessed Creator and publish His miracles ; and to command mankind to fear Him ; He being the eternal God, Whose kingdom and prevailing sovereignty never cease ; and the Saviour and Deliverer of whom He will.

Doing signs and wonders in heaven and earth : signs in the heavenly hosts, such as eclipses, etc. ; and in earth, such as took place in the history of Daniel and his companions. Darius himself had witnessed this, and knew it. Then he informed them how Daniel had been cast into the lions' den, and had not been hurt ; doubtless people already knew what had been done by the hundred and twenty men till they were thrown to the lions and removed from office and others appointed in their stead.

29. He was in power and office. (Cp. i. *ad fin.*)

So far the history of what happened to Nebuchadnezzar, Belshazzar, and Darius. The history of Cyrus and the Persian kings who succeeded him is told in the book of Ezra.

VII.

1. He was already acquainted with the facts about the *four kingdoms* contained in Nebuchadnezzar's dream, as explained by him ; after this, however, he received

fuller accounts of the same ; part of which is contained in the now following dream, parts in chaps. viii, ix, x ; in all five chapters. Now the dream which Nebuchadnezzar saw, and this dream which Daniel saw mention all four kingdoms. The *Vision*, on the contrary, does not mention the first, but only three. The fourth chapter (chap. ix) contains a summary history of the Second Temple, and also a notice of what Rome, the fourth kingdom, did to Jerusalem. The fifth chapter describes the fortunes of the kings of Greece, Rome, and Arabia, etc., as we shall explain by God's help. These four chapters, composed by the blessed Daniel, may be thus divided : the first consists of what he saw in the *dream ;* the second of what he saw in the *vision;* the third and fourth of what he saw when *awake;* indicating the high stage he had reached in prophecy. God Almighty revealed this to Daniel of all mankind, owing to his anguish at our sufferings, and the interest he felt in what was going to happen to us, and his *desire* to know how long the time would be ; for which reason he is called the *man of desires.*

Then he wrote the dream : because he desired that it should have a place in the collection of documents written by the blessed prophets.

And told the sum of the matters : meaning either that he wrote down the important points of the dream ; or else referring to the heading words in the chapter, **Daniel answered and said**, as they are written ; and meaning that the events took place just as they are recorded in this book ; that it might not be supposed that only part was written, the dream being epitomized ; since the prophets do sometimes write part [of a history] and omit part ; as in the Books of Kings.

2, 3. He saw four winds stirring the great sea, i. e. the ocean. And after it had been stirred, there rose from it these four animals. Apparently he must have fancied in the dream that he was standing on the sea-shore till the animals rose. Then he begins to describe them one by one.

4–8. We must explain why these kingdoms are compared to animals, so that sometimes they are compared to *horses* (Zech. vi. 1), which are domestic animals ; and similarly *infra* the king of Persia is compared to a *ram*, and the king of Greece to a *goat*. In my opinion he (Zechariah) compared the four kingdoms to horses, because they are used in war ; since, therefore, each of these kingdoms was at war with some other, he compared them to horses. Nebuchadnezzar he compares at one time to an eagle, at another to a lion ; to an eagle as being the strongest bird of prey, and to a lion as being the strongest beast of prey ; similarly none of the four kingdoms was more powerful or braver than he. For a similar reason he compared him (chap. ii) to gold, which is more valuable than silver. The eagle again suggests the idea of flight and elevation ; both of which apply to Nebuchadnezzar (Jer. iv. 13 and Is. v. 27). The lion too has extraordinary strength, and never turns his back (Prov. xxx. 30). In this verse he is compared to the two together. The *eagle's wings* are his mighty armies.

I was gazing : i. e. at the animal that I saw with this terrible form, till I beheld,

f   [II. 3.]

and lo, **its wings were plucked off,** so that it could not fly; typifying that his journeyings and invasions were interrupted.

It was lifted up from the earth typifies what befell him during the seven years (iv. 30).

And it was made to stand on two feet as a man, and a man's heart was given unto it : a description of his condition when his reason returned to him, and he confessed the Unity of God, and renounced tyranny and transgression, and returned to his kingdom, and was increased in dignity above what he had possessed before (iv. *ad fin.*). He describes Nebuchadnezzar only, not noticing the estate of his children, because they had no estate worth noticing, i. e. they achieved no acts of heroism or conquests ; but only retained the estate left them by Nebuchadnezzar.

Next, he describes the second animal, *as like to a bear :* referring to its stupidity ; because they were believers in dualism and idolaters.

And it was raised up on one side : some take this literally, as meaning that as soon as it rose, it was in part overthrown ; referring to its dealings with Israel, i. e. those of Darius with Daniel, of Cyrus, Darius the Persian, and Artaxerxes with Israel, and of Ahasuerus after the history of Haman.

And three ribs were in its mouth : i. e. they governed three quarters of the globe (cp. viii. 4).

And they said thus unto it, Arise, devour much flesh : the words of Haman (Esth. iii. 9). He does not say that it *ate*, because this purpose was not accomplished upon Israel, but was turned against their enemies. He describes, as we observed before, the conduct of the kings of Persia, but of none of the Chaldean kings save Nebuchadnezzar. Then he speaks of the third animal, which he compares to a *leopard ;* the leopard being smaller than the bear ; similarly in the last chapter he compares the kings of Persia to a *ram*, but those of Greece to a *goat*, which is smaller than a ram. Besides, the leopard haunts the doors of cities (Jer. v. 6) ; *the leopard* is the kings of Greece collectively.

Four wings of a fowl : these are his (Cerasphorus') four disciples : see on xi. 4.

And dominion was given to it : the well-known story of Alexander.

7. (**After this.**) Now he speaks of the *fourth animal*, which he does not compare, like the rest, to a known animal ; because it had not any single religion or doctrine, nor did Daniel recognise in it any animal form to which he could liken it ; he can only tell of the horror, terror, and fear which it inspired. This is a description of the kingdom of Rome ; cp. on ii. 40.

And it had great iron teeth : i. e. TITUS THE SINNER, and the others like him, who invaded cities and shed blood ; as a wild beast tears with its teeth and tusks. The metaphor is followed up in **it devoured** (i. e. massacred), and **brake in pieces** (i. e. oppressed).

It was diverse : referring to the variety of its customs, and the great harm it did.

And it had ten horns : i. e. ten thrones ; see below on ver. 24.

8. **I considered the horns :** owing to their size. He was gazing intently on their size.

He looked, and lo, after this, this little horn had risen up amid the ten horns ; and when the little horn had come between them, three horns were thrown down before it, and there were left seven, with this little horn among them. Then he perceived that this little horn **had eyes like a man's eyes : and a mouth which spoke proud words.** He does not tell us what the words were ; see below on ver. 25.

9, 10. These *thrones* [which were cast down] are the kings mentioned above. The **Ancient of days** is an angel whose task it shall be to judge the nations on the day of Judgment (cp. Ps. l. 3). **A throne of fire,** he tells us, was set up for him, and the **wheels** of his throne were **flaming fire ;** the bodies of the supernal angels are of fire, and their thrones are of fire likewise. Then he shewed him **a river of fire issuing out from before the angel,** wherewith he punished transgressors.

Thousand thousands ministered unto him : because he was the greatest of the angels, like the great Sultan, before whom stand a multitude of ministers. Then he tells us why he sat upon the throne with these ministers standing before him : **the judgment was set and the books were opened :** i. e. the *judgment* of the world for their denial of Him (Deut. xxxii. 37). **The books were opened :** for some of their sins were of long standing, and their works were noted (*ibid.* 32). The expression refers to the ordinary custom of noting down a fact which may be of use after some time, that one may not forget it. He is using the language of the world. Compare for the same, in reference to the deeds of the wicked, Is. lxv. 6 ; and in reference to the conduct of the godly, Mal. iii. 16 and Ps. lxix. 29. Reference is elsewhere made to God's judgment of the Gentiles for the wrong they have done Israel (Joel iii. 2). He thought it appropriate to mention the day of Judgment after the termination of the four kingdoms, to shew that at the close of their sovereignty they must expect judgment, punishment, and condemnation, and that their works are taken count of against them.

11. He returns to the history of the fourth animal : the cause of the destruction of this great creature, he tells us, was the proud language used by the horn ; and though God Almighty gave it a long respite, yet every respite must end, and the time will at last have come.

(i) **The beast was slain,** and (ii) **his body destroyed,** and (iii) **he was given to the burning of fire. Was slain** refers to the slaughter of their kings and the destruction of their armies. **And his body was destroyed** most probably refers to the abolition of their worship and religions ; so that there will not be left to them a Church or place of Direction (*Qiblah*) : or it may mean the extinction of *Esau* from this world. **And was given** refers to punishment in the next world, i. e. Gehenna, which means 'the place of condemnation.'

12. After narrating the destruction of the last animal, he records the cessation of the three kingdoms previously mentioned. This corresponds to ii. 34, 5, *ubi vide.*

Yet their lives were prolonged : i. e. their religion and remnants of them-selves exist in spite of the dominance of other persons and other systems.

Until a season and a time : i. e. till the conclusion of the fourth kingdom; by **a time** is meant the dominion of Israel. So the remnants of the dominions and their cults will only pass away at the appearance of the blessed Messiah.

13. The Messiah is likened to *a man* in contrast to the four kingdoms, which were likened to beasts. For two reasons. One is, because he is *wise* and knows his Lord. A second, because he is lord of all.

With the clouds of heaven : because God Almighty [shall] send him, and men shall witness him as they witness the clouds. Then we are told how he came to the angel who sat judging the people, and how the angel let him come before him and close to him, and then how God gave the kingdom to him.

14. Three words are used of him : **dominion, glory, kingdom** : the first means the subjection of enemies and rebels ; the second, their coming to bow down to him at every feast of Tabernacles, with splendid presents ; the third, his sitting on the royal throne, and receiving the tribute, and writing mandates and signing with his name and seal. And then he adds that his sovereignty will never end as that of the other kingdoms ended, nor his rule perish as theirs perished.

15. This describes his condition when he woke, and felt as Nebuchadnezzar and others had felt when they did not know how to interpret their dreams. A marvel that Daniel the 'interpreter of dreams' should not understand this ! So he slept again, and saw angels, and asked them concerning its interpretation. Or it may be supposed that it seemed to him in the dream as if his *spirit was troubled*, and as if he was confused by what he saw, and went to the angel who stood in front of the great angel that sat upon the throne, to ask him of the interpretation of the dream.

In the midst of the sheath : i. e. of the heart, which is like the *sheath* to a sword (cp. 1 Chron. xxi. 27).

16. **He told me** probably refers to what he said on the subject of the four kingdoms ; **the interpretation of the speeches** to the end of ver. 8 (cp. ver. 25). Or the first may refer to ver. 17, and the second to ver. 19.

17, 18. A general statement, without special explanation of the four animals ; corresponding to the method of both Joseph and Daniel in the interpretation of dreams ; which is to give a general idea, resolving the knotty and difficult point. The *four animals* are interpreted as *four kingdoms,* and the *sea* as the *earth :* the **four winds** are not explained. They must be motions from God, whereat the four empires arose.

Shall receive the kingdom explains ver. 13. Daniel had no need to ask about the first three animals, but only about the fourth.

19–22. He asked him concerning four things : (i) the signification of the fourth animal, its strength, its teeth, nails and devouring ; (ii) the nature of the ten horns ; (iii) the nature of the little horn and its eyes, and how it outgrew the ten horns ; (iv) the conduct of this horn in its wars, that he saw, with the saints, and its prevailing against them. Of none of these things had he any satisfactory understanding. In Daniel's question to the angel there are certain things additional to what was mentioned in the vision—four : (i) **nails of brass** ; (ii) **a compounded horn** ; (iii) **whose look was more stout than his fellows** ; (iv) **made war with the saints.** And there are four verses about which he did not ask (9, 10, 11, 12), because he already understood their meaning. When he had asked about these riddles, the angel answered.

23, 24. Observe that he says of the fourth **diversified** ; all four were already said to be *diverse the one from the other*, in their forms, as individually described ; and this fourth is made different from the others in respect of certain characteristics recorded in ver. 7.

Shall devour the whole earth : i. e. after devastating Jerusalem and taking the people captive, they increased their dominion above all mankind. And in the ten horns are **ten kings** : i.e. ten thrones, belonging to Rome, on each of which a governor sat.

And another shall arise after them : i. e. some years after the appearance of the ten horns. It rose up, he tells us, between the ten horns ; i. e. in the midst of their dominion ; and took out of their territory *three* thrones ; according to some, ALEXANDRIA, JERUSALEM, and ACCO.

And he shall be diverse from the former : in his own opinion ; for he ascended into heaven and seated himself on His right hand, and did other things that we cannot repeat, but which are well known to all, and which we need not explain ; of him it was said, 'they have set their mouth in heaven' (Ps. lxxiii. 9) ; and this is the explanation of **a mouth speaking great things.** Then he explains the meaning of **and made war with the saints and prevailed against them,** sc. **he shall wear out the saints of the Most High** : referring to the lowering of their rank, their humiliation and degradation in all departments in matters spiritual and temporal, beyond what preceded ; their having to wear the yellow badge, and being unable to speak when reviled, or to walk on [a Moslem's] right, or to present themselves to buy goods however dear the price they offer for them, etc. etc. Then the angel added a fact about which he had not asked : **and he shall hope to change** : notice that he says **and he shall hope** ; he does not say that he shall change these for them, only that he shall *hope* to do so, which hope shall not be accomplished, because God Almighty shall give him power to humble and oppress them in worldly matters, but shall not give him power to annul their religion.

25. **Times and the law** : i. e. the holy-days, sabbaths, and feasts ; he says **to change**, not 'to abolish,' because he will not altogether abolish them, but only hope to *change* them, obliging them to do work which is unlawful for them on the sabbaths and feast-days. **The law** may be the Qiblah, and certain forms of religious observances (compare Esth. iii. 8, where the king's 'laws' refer to the order to kneel down and make obeisance before Haman) : or the *days of Purim* and similar Israelitic institutions ; it is not fully explained. The prophecy **and he shall wear**

out the saints of the Most High is now *in course of fulfilment* upon Israel; of the other, **and he shall hope,** probably part was fulfilled at his (Muhammad's) first appearance, but the greater part will be fulfilled in the 'time of tribulation,' as, by God's help, we shall explain in the last chapter.

And they shall be given into his hand until a time, times and half a time: until may either mean *till he have completed a time, times and half a time,* that being the length of his reign, from beginning to end; or it may mean that the tribulation mentioned in ver. 25 b shall proceed from him over Israel for that period. Observe that he says a time, i. e. one time; and *times* in the plural, which need not refer exclusively to two, but to three or any larger number. Similarly in *half a time,* the word is like the Hebrew חצי, which does not signify 'a half' exactly, but a *portion* of the thing called עדן, etc.; as in Is. xliv. 16, where '*half thereof* (he burns in the fire)' [is shewn] by what follows [to mean not exactly a half]. So *inf.* xii. 7 : '*a season, seasons and a half,*' which is the same period as this, not another. We shall on that passage, God willing, explain it, recording the opinions of the learned, and stating what we ourselves esteem most probable.

26. **The judgment shall sit** refers probably to ver. 10 c, and tells us that at the end of a time, times, etc., no sovereignty shall remain with any save God's angel, who shall judge the nations for their doings; v. *supra.*

And they shall take away his dominion: i. e. of the kingdom whose treatment of Israel has been mentioned in ver. 25.

They shall take away: i. e. either *Israel* shall take away, according to the original idea given in ii. 34; or the *Carmathians,* i. e. the 'Arms' (xi. 31), shall take away, as we shall explain in the last chapter.

Unto the end : shewing that it will not, like Israel, have a return.

27. **Of the kingdoms :** even if there be other kingdoms in the world besides Rome and Arabia. All of them shall obey the *kingdom of God,* i. e. of His people, and of His Messiah. Their **kingdom, too, shall not pass away:** cp. Is. ix. 6; Ps. lxxii. 17. The prophets dilate on this in numerous places.

The saints of the Most High (plur.) in this chapter: either the *saints* are Israel, and *the Most High* the Creator (cp. אלהא עלאה, iii. 26, etc.) ; and Israel being Holy to the LORD, they can be called [by a double plural] saints of the Most High: or the *Most High* may be Israel, since God has made them supreme ; cp. Deut. xxvi. 19.

28. **Hitherto is the end :** i. e. this was the last word spoken to me. After this I began to ponder on what I had seen.

And I kept the word in my heart: i. e. the interpretation, that he might ask more about it. He wrote down the dream at once (*sup.* ver. 1), but not the interpretation. This is what happened to him in the first year of Belshazzar. Now he tells us what happened in the **third year.**

VIII.

1. The reason why he wrote the Dream in Aramaic, but the Vision in Hebrew has been supposed to be that he saw the dream when in Babylon, and the vision

in Shushan the Capital. He was not with the king; see chap. v, which shews that Daniel was absent from Babylon and at Shushan Habbirah. He does not tell us the reason of his absence; it has been suggested that when he saw the dream he left the city till the seventy years of Babylon should have been accomplished, and returned on Darius' account. He must have seen the vision at the beginning or in the middle of the year.

After that which appeared unto me at the first: i.e. after the dream. As this, however, is shewn already by § *a*, the words indicate that after this there were no more 'dreams' or 'visions' concerning the kingdoms.

2. He saw things like those he might see when asleep, but was awake, and in actual presence of certain objects which he could see, although they were not really to be seen. He says: 'I saw this vision when I was in Shushan Habbirah, and I saw myself in the vision standing on the river Ulai;' just as Ezekiel when in Babylon saw himself in Jerusalem.

אובל = *river;* cp. יובל, Jer. xvii. 5. In the last chapter he is on the river Tigris.

3–14. We must give the chapter first its literal interpretation, to be followed by the interpretation of the angel, and then combine the two together, as we did with the Dream. He saw then in the Vision, as it were, a mighty ram standing on the bank of the river, on which there rose first one horn, then another afterwards; and the second horn was greater than the first. Then he beheld, as it were, wild beasts that fell on it from three quarters,—the river being to its east,—and lo, it butted every animal that confronted it; and met none, but it did with it what it chose. Probably he saw the animals at first powerful and ferocious, and afterwards found that they had all perished; and that none stood up before him, and he remained alone, when this he-goat approached him from the western quarter with speed, not approaching the ground, moving, as it were, in mid-air. Others suppose that none of the beasts approached the ground for fear of this he-goat. And he perceived that it had a horn of a mighty *aspect* between its eyes; and that it made for the ram; and when it saw that the ram neither feared it nor moved from its place, then the he-goat came upon it speedily, when it was standing by itself on the bank of the river, and came close unto it, to see whether it would run away, or butt with its horns. And lo, the ram was left quite alone. Then we are told that the he-goat was **moved with choler against it**, which means that he grew angry when he saw how the wild beasts and other animals had fled from before him and hidden themselves, but the ram remained in its place and did not flee, and so he made for the ram and slew it. Apparently the he-goat harmed no other of the beasts, because they did not stand before him; but when he saw the ram stand, he fought with him, and butted his horns with his great horn; and there was not in the ram force enough to meet him, so he threw him on the ground and trampled on him. Then he perceived that the passers-by beheld what the he-goat had done, but did not rescue it; neither had it in itself force to rescue itself, nor could it find any one to rescue it: so he *slew* it. Then he tells us what happened to the he-goat: **he magnified himself exceedingly** and rose up: and after he had magnified himself, he perceived that the great horn was broken without any beast or man breaking it: just as he had broken the horn of the ram. Then he saw how, after it was broken, there rose up four horns in its stead: which four were not attached the one to the other, but in separate quarters; one being on the left, another on the right, another between the eye-brows over the top of the nose, and another at the top of the forehead, **to the four winds of heaven.** Then he saw how there issued one horn from the midst of one of the four, i. e. the one that proceeded from his right temple: **out of one of them came forth a horn.**

From a little one: i. e. the one of the four horns whence it issued was the least of the four, and he beheld as if this horn that had issued was magnified and increased above the height of the four horns, and he beheld it inclining in the direction now of the south, now of the west, now of the land of Israel. Then it seemed to him as though it had risen to the host of heaven, and thrown some of them down. **The host of heaven** very likely refers to the signs of the Zodiac; **and some of the stars** to some of the seven planets, *Saturn*, etc. Then it seemed to him as though it trampled the stars on the ground; and then as though the horn went unto the Captain of the host and the mightiest of it; but he does not say that the horn did anything with the Captain of the host more than that it **magnified itself.**

And the continual was taken away from him: as though the Captain of the host had a place in the earth which he frequented; and he was now excluded therefrom, and the pillar thereof cast on the ground and destroyed. And it seemed to him as though part of the host that had not been trampled down by the horn were seized, together with the place which he had used to frequent, by the horn; and he calls the horn **sin**, because he saw in the vision how the horn had withdrawn from the place and exalted itself. And it seemed to him as though it came to certain persons who spoke the truth, and threw them on the ground and thrust them through: and that it stood firm, and none came to break it. And when he had seen these things, he saw two angels standing opposite him, and heard one ask the other **How long?** This he did not ask to find out himself, but only that Daniel might hear; as we learn from his saying afterwards, **And he said unto me,** not 'unto him;' as though the angel knew that he desired to understand this, just as he had desired to understand the meaning of the dream; only he had been able to accost those angels (vii. 16), but had not courage to ask these angels. So the one asked the other of that about which Daniel needed to ask. Now he did not ask concerning the whole Vision, but selected such future events as Israel needed to know; i. e. *the end of the four kingdoms.*

Then I heard a holy one speaking: i. e. the one who asks **How long? To Palmoni who spoke: Palmoni** is the answerer: the name of the asker is not given, like the names of many of the angels.

The asker says: **How long?** i. e. how long shall this person last who shall do the things mentioned in the verse, which are *three?* (i) **giving**; (ii) **the sanctuary**; (iii) **the host.** The answer in ver. 14 shall be explained below.

15–18. He saw three angels, and heard their talk; and he heard the voice of one whom he did not see. He mentions the names of two, sc. **Palmoni** and **Gabriel,** but omits to mention those of the other two. This shews that Daniel did not hear from the first two more than the question, owing to their great awfulness. Gabriel, however, was near in form to a man, so that he could associate with him. And he tells us that Gabriel did not begin of his own accord, but only when he heard another commanding him to tell Daniel; after which he came to Daniel and told him. This indicates that the angels all knew; but it is possible that the angel whose voice he heard was more terrible than the two preceding (the *asker* and the *answerer*). When Gabriel approached him, he **swooned** from fear of them, and then **fell fainting on his face.**

Understand, O son of man: for the Vision belongeth to the time of the end: i. e. thou needest to know this, because there is told in it what will be at the end of the Captivity.

18. **And he set me upright:** i. e. encouraged me and raised me up.

19. He now proceeds to summarize the contents of the dream.

20. This is said generally, and we must further interpret, as we have done in other cases. He said in the Vision that the one horn was less than the other, i. e. the horn which came up first; which symbolizes the fact that Media was less in military power [and everything else]; their sole king being Darius the Mede, who reigned one year; whereas from Persia five kings arose, who reigned fifty-five years. And by the words **I saw the ram butting** (ver. 4) is meant that he had armies which marched to the three quarters. This took place in the time of Cyrus, as is explained in Is. xlv. 1. With 4 b compare *ibid.* 2.

21. We must again return to the contents of the dream which Gabriel did not explain. **There came from the west:** supposed to be *Alexander*, who came from *Alexandria.* **And none touched the ground:** i. e. none confronted him from the time that he left Alexandria till he came to Babylon. He explains that the **notable horn between his eyes** is Alexander, the first king; and he goes on to describe what the he-goat did; **he smote the ram and broke his two horns:** i. e. he fought the two armies, sc. the force of Persia and Media; **and he cast him down to the ground:** referring to his conquering their territory, city by city, and slaying those of them who withstood him: probably he killed Artaxerxes the Persian, and when the news got into the provinces, none of them opposed Alexander any more.

And there was none that could deliver: i. e. none fought for them any more.

22, 23. He said above (ver. 8), **and when he was strong, the great horn was broken:** i. e. when Alexander had accomplished his purpose he became tyrannical, and thereafter was **broken:** i. e. died. **Four notable** he interprets **four kingdoms:**

g   [II. 3.]

i. e. four disciples who came after him, each of whom took possession of a quarter of the globe without any war breaking out among them at the beginning of their history.

Shall stand up out of the nation : shewing that these four are all Greeks. **Not with his strength :** neither individually nor collectively shall they have the strength of the first king. *Supra,* ver. 9, he said, **and out of one of them :** this is interpreted here, **and in the latter time of their kingdom :** the full interpretation is not given till the great last chapter ; only **the one of them** is the **king of the south,** because the king of Arabia sprang up between them, as was shewn in the Dream (vii. 8). To this matter we shall come back, when we shall explain what the four kingdoms are. *Ibid.,* ver. 9, **from a little :** indicating that the king of the south, at the time, was the least of the four disciples mentioned above. **And it waxed exceeding great towards the south,** etc.: i. e. none of the four got so far in any direction of the world as this horn did. **Towards the south :** i.e. according to some, *Amṣār;* to others, *Italy;* to others, *Ḥijāz.* **Towards the east :** i. e. eastern countries and Khorasān generally. **And towards the pleasant land.**

Here he adds, **a king of fierce countenance, and understanding dark sentences :** referring to his boasting against God, and lying concerning Him. **Understanding dark sentences :** referring to his stealing from the books of the Jews, and contradicting their assertions, and professing to be a prophet and to have received communications from Gabriel.

24 b interprets 10 b. **Mighty ones :** i. e. *imperial personages,* Romans, and others with whom he fought and whose towns he took. **The people of the saints :** Israel. He does not say *all* the mighty ones and *all* the saints, because he was not monarch of the entire world.

And it cast down truth to the ground, of ver. 12, is explained **and he shall corrupt wonderfully :** meaning that he railed against the law of God and the words of his Prophets, and took out of them what he pleased, of which he made up a book called Qoran, and declared the rest invalid.

Ver. 11 b is not explained here being perspicuous ; the fact will be mentioned in the great last chapter.

Ver. 11 a. **The prince of the host** is interpreted here **the prince of princes :** this *prince of princes* may be the *king of Rome :* as he took three thrones of theirs, as was mentioned in chap. vii. Others think it refers to their viceroys in Babylon, in which case this will be the doing of the CONSPIRATOR who shall arise against them (*inf.* xi. 31) : we shall leave the explanation for the 4th chapter, and elucidate it there.

It did its pleasure and prospered, of ver. 12, is explained in ver. 24. The subject recurs in the long chapter, *v. ad.* xi. 3, where we shall explain the terms **the continual** and **the place of his sanctuary, sin,** etc.

We are told here besides that **he shall be broken without a hand :** signifying that his power shall wane little by little, till he perish and pass away.

25. Having explained the chapter briefly, we shall now return and mention certain things which will not recur.   In the first two chapters (i. e. ii and vii) he speaks of *four* kingdoms, and the *reign of the Messiah :* in this chapter he mentions neither this, nor that of the Chaldees, but only the three monarchies, which are the three beasts. To the description of the kingdom of Persia three details are added : (*a*) it is a divided kingdom, between Persia and Media : (*b*) **no beasts can stand before it** : *v. ad loc.;* (*c*) it will be slain by the he-goat, etc.   These three things are to be connected with three things mentioned in chap. vii : (*a*) **it was raised up on one side;** (*b*) **three ribs were in its mouth;** (*c*) **thus they said unto it, Arise, and eat much flesh.**   There he describes how the three quarters got into its hands, and how people said to it, *Arise*, etc.   By combining the two chapters we obtain a full account of the history of the Persian kingdom.   Now let us mark what is said of the king of Greece.   There he mentioned his *expeditions* (ver. 6 : **it had on the back of it four wings of a fowl**) and its **having four heads,** corresponding to ver. 8 b here, **there came up four notable horns** : only here we get additional light in the words (ver. 5) **and the goat had a notable horn ;** since there he did not divide the kingdom so as to make part of it [the reign of] *the first king*, and part [that of] *the four disciples.*

The words **when the transgressors are come to the full** shew that they will *transgress*, whether it be in matters of religion or in political matters : probably in the former.

He further adds to our knowledge of the **little horn** by calling him **king** (ver. 23).   Ver. 24 is an addition to vii. 25.   As there was no further explanation required of what had been said of the *day of Judgment* and the *reign of the Messiah* he leaves them out.

26. **The evening and the morning** : i. e. what thou heardest Palmoni say is to be taken literally, and is no allegory like the Ram and the Goat, which are allegorical, and have to be interpreted, not meaning a Ram etc. in reality.   No, these **evenings and mornings** are real evenings and mornings : you are not to suppose that the *evening* signifies a declining kingdom, and the *morning* a rising kingdom.

Two thousand three hundred : the sum made up by evenings and mornings aggregated : making 1150 whole days ; notice that he does not say ' 2300 evenings and 2300 mornings,' as elsewhere ' forty days and forty nights.'

But shut thou up the vision : i. e. there is no doubt about it.   Some think it means *seal* this chapter, with its present contents.   **For it shall be for many days** : i. e. this is a thing which shall come to pass after many long years.

27. Having heard in this vision that 'Truth would be cast to the ground,' etc., he was vexed and distressed.   **Days** : i. e. a year ; till the death of Belshazzar.

Then I rose up and did the king's business : i. e. the office given him in the time of Darius ; it was not his own choice.   The king forced it on him.

And I was deserted : i. e. he kept aloof from society, cp. Ezek. iii. 15.

But there was none to make it understood: i.e. God Almighty did not reveal to him any of the things in his mind till the first year of Darius. Two years must have passed between the *Dream* and the *Vision;* the former being in the first year of Belshazzar, the latter in the third year. Then passed the third year of Belshazzar. So the narrative recorded in the next chapter must have been at the end of the year.

IX.

1. Probably after he had been cast into the den of lions. Darius' father's name is mentioned, because he was a noteworthy person; though not the Ahasuerus of Mordecai and Esther; the latter being a Persian and the present one of the Medes.

Which was made king: to shew that the same person is meant as in chap. v. *ult.*

2. Owing to the length of the sentence in the first year is repeated.

Of his reign: interpretation of in the first year of Darius.

I considered in the books: i.e. the books of Jeremiah. Jeremiah mentions it in a number of places (e. g. xxv. 11, xxix. 10).

For the accomplishing of the desolations of Jerusalem: it had only been waste from the nineteenth year of king Nebuchadnezzar: and at this period had been waste fifty-two years: he can therefore only have meant seventy years *of the rule of Babylon :* the words *for the accomplishing* must therefore mean *after the seventy years of Babylon had been completed.*

3. When Daniel perceived that the reign of Babylon was already over, and that of Darius had begun, and Jeremiah's prophecy (xxix. 10) was not fulfilled, he was compelled to pray and ask God concerning that.

To seek prayer: i.e. to seek *with* prayer: by way of variation from with fasting, etc. He tells us that he prayed fasting with sackcloth on his body, wallowing in ashes and prostrating himself upon them.

4. Observe here prayer and confession in contrast with *prayer and supplications* of ver. 3. The prayer contains four subjects: (*a*) Glorification of God: ver. 4 b. (*b*) Enumeration of sins and offences : vers. 5–11 a. (*c*) Enumeration of Israel's sufferings in consequence of their sins : vers. 11 b–14. (*d*) Petition that God would return from his wrath in respect of the city and the nation : and that he would forgive their sins. The word *prayer* is made to include all *four* subjects (ver. 21), or *three* only, but differently, in ver. 2 referring to the three first, in ver. 4 excluding the confession of sin, and including the remaining three. He prefaces the prayer with a record of the work of God, as is the custom with those who ask God for anything they desire: cp. Deut. iii. 24.

In this preface three qualities are mentioned : (*a*) great : i.e. the Doer of surprising things, which none save He can do ; (*b*) dreadful: meaning that He is feared when He takes vengeance upon His enemies, so that they tremble then; (*c*) which keepeth covenant and mercy: signifying that He had fulfilled the covenant, i.e. the promises He had made to the patriarchs; and the **mercy**, i.e. the promises given on Mount Sinai, and the covenant of the plains of Moab; called **mercy** because it was an *extension* of the former. The **great and terrible** will then refer to the miracles wrought by Him in Egypt, the Wilderness, and in the Land itself, whereby He fulfilled all His promises to the patriarchs.

5. **We have sinned**: Ps. cvi. 36, etc.; with reference to the seven nations.

And have dealt perversely: with reference to *abominations*, unlawful marriages, etc.

And have done wickedly: with reference to *injuries*, such as theft, oppression, etc.

And have rebelled: with reference to the slaying, beating, and imprisoning of the prophets.

And turned aside from thy precepts: i.e. rules concerning sabbath, feast-days, etc.

And judgments: referring to iniquitous verdicts.

6. We have not received their address to us: 'Return from your evil ways!' **And to all the people of the land** (after **our fathers**): either **our fathers** are the elders and the persons of authority, and **the people of the land** the subjects; or the latter may be the Gentiles.

In ver. 5 he mentioned their neglect of God's commandments in each particular; here he observes that they would not receive his admonitions or reprehensions.

7. **O Lord, righteousness belongeth unto Thee**: i.e. Thy cause against us is clear, if Thou hast not dealt kindly with us; and ours is the shame, seeing that we have neglected Thy worship and served what has no right to service (cf. Jer. ii. 26). They were ashamed before the nations of the world, when they witnessed the foulness of their deeds (Jer. vi. 15).

To the men of Judah and to the inhabitants of Jerusalem: in this verse the whole nation is spoken of collectively: so he mentions first the kingdom of Judah (the more honourable), and then the kingdom of Israel: according to the custom of the Bible in several books, which is to name Judah before Israel: perhaps, however, it is put first here because the shame of Judah is greater than that of Israel (Ezek. xvi. 51).

That are near and that are far off: i.e. from the land (cp. Deut. xiii. 7). Or, those carried away captive a short time ago, and those carried away captive a long time ago, sc. the ten tribes.

Because of their trespass which they have trespassed against Thee: 'they have transgressed Thy covenants,' because they swore to God and made a covenant with Him, and then broke it (Jer. v. 11, xi. 10).

8. **To us belongeth confusion of face** is repeated. The first perhaps refers to the multitude, the second to the court; compare the rest of the verse. **Our fathers** will then refer to the Judges and Elders (Ezek. viii. 11). Or it may be repeated merely in order to contrast their doings with those of God.

9. **Confusion,** he says, is upon us, for two reasons: (1) owing to the magnitude of our sins and breach of the covenant; (2) because, in spite of the heinousness of our doings, God has spared us and had mercy on us, and forgiven us (cp. Ezek. xvi. 61, 62).

Mercies and forgivenesses: mercies meaning that He spared them in the time of His wrath (2 Kings xiii. 23); **and forgivenesses** at the time of their contrition (Neh. ix. 17). These were their relations with Him while they were in the Land; and as for the whole time of the Captivity, His mercies still rested upon them (Ps. cvi. 46; Lam. iii. 22).

Though we have rebelled against Him: i.e. in spite of all our offences, yet His mercy is upon us.

10. In ver. 6 he said **neither have we hearkened,** which he repeats here to finish the sentence; i.e. after saying **O Lord, to us belongeth confusion of face,** and after that **to the Lord our God belong mercies and forgivenesses,** he goes on to say **although we have rebelled against Him** (meaning, as stated, that they had broken His covenant), and annexes to this the further statement **neither have we hearkened to the voice of the Lord our God**; meaning 'the prophets came to us bidding us return to Thy law, but we did not receive their counsel, so that the sin became double; since *first*, we violated the covenant, and *secondly*, we disobeyed Thy prophets, this is the reason of the repetition.

By the hand of His servants the prophets: including all prophets sent us by God, those whose prophecies are recorded in writing, and all others; shewing that the prophets urged us to walk in the laws of God.

In His laws (plur.), as being a number of special laws; compare the phrase 'This is the law for the burnt-offering and meat-offering' of the sacrifices, etc.

11. **All Israel:** not all individual members of the nation, since there were among them prophets and saints; but *all the tribes of Israel,* since no one tribe was free from sin, such as idolatry, etc. As for the history of the Calf, we know indeed that the tribe of Levi, without exception, refused to worship the Calf (Ex. xxxii. 26, where *Who?* means Who of all the tribes of Israel does not worship the Calf, but the Lord only? *and then joined themselves unto him the whole tribe of Levi*), whence they earned their high dignity (*ibid.* 29). Otherwise there was not one of the tribes that did not worship idols, and commit deadly sins; for it was done by their chiefs [and also by the common people] (Ezek. xxii. 26; Jer. ii. 8, 26). Hence he says **all Israel have transgressed Thy laws,** meaning they have neglected their contents, and 'thrown them behind their backs' (Neh. ix. 26; meaning 'have transgressed Thy word by Thy prophets'); repeated to make it clear that it was because they neglected the law and did not receive His word by His prophets that the curse recorded in His Book fell on them. The **curse** is that of Deut. xxvii. 15; the **oath** the Chapter of the Covenant. All of it, he says, has lighted on Israel.

12. **And He hath confirmed His words:** i.e. the evils recorded as threatened by the prophets.

Against our judges that judged us: the kings and judges who were unrighteous, and ruined the nation; whence destruction alighted on all.

For under the whole heaven hath not been done, etc.: i. e. their eating the flesh of parents and children, etc.

13. All that the prophets told, he says, is written in the law of Moses, the servant of God; God hath covenanted with our forefathers on these terms; so He did them no wrong, but on the contrary spared them, though their sins would have deserved something far heavier (cp. Ezra ix. 13). In spite, however, of their being visited by the affliction, owing to the magnitude of their sins, they had not returned to God and besought Him to turn from His wrath (Ezek. xxii. 30).

And have discernment in Thy truth: i. e. consider the covenant that Thou hadst made with us, so that we might have abstained from such transgressions, thinking of the covenants and agreements whereby we were bound.

14. **Therefore hath the Lord watched over the evil**: i. e. since they did not repent, He did not forgive or excuse them.

For the Lord our God is righteous in all His works: i. e. He was just in all that He brought upon them, though He did not do in any other nation of the world the like of what He had done in Jerusalem.

And we have not obeyed His voice: i. e. the exiles. In spite of every disaster that lighted on us, and our falling into captivity, nevertheless they did not receive God's admonition, or turn from their transgressions.

15. So far for the enumeration of their sins and the recounting of the disasters and tribulations that had fallen on the nation. At the end of this he says: 'And now, O Lord, Who broughtest Thy people out of Egypt by ten plagues, and hast manifested their might and their superiority above the nations of the world, Thou hast no nation save them, and we have repaid Thee by evil.'

16. **Lord, according to all Thy mercies**: i. e. deal with us according to Thy ancient custom, whereby Thou usedst to turn from Thy wrath and have mercy upon us; the seventy years are accomplished, and the land has received her due for our neglect of sabbatical years and jubilees.

Let Thine anger and Thy fury be turned away: referring to the restoration of Israel thither, that the land might be inhabited.

Thine anger: the desolation of the Holy City; **Thy wrath**: the burning of the Temple.

Connect **for our sins** with **Jerusalem**, and **for the sins of our fathers** with **Thy people**. Both became a reproach; Jerusalem, as being burnt and lying desolate; Israel, through the disasters that had fallen on them, the Captivity, and their expulsion from their City. The City and the Nation are mentioned, because he desired of Almighty God that the City should be inhabited, and that Israel might return thither out of Captivity.

17. **The prayer of Thy servant**: referring to the three portions enumerated above, *ad* ver. 4; **and his supplications**, ver. 16 to end.

And cause Thy face to shine: of which the building of the city and its habitation will be the result.

For the Lord's sake: for Thy Name's sake, which is upon it, since Thou hast called it **My House**. In the previous verse he spoke of the City and Nation, here of the Temple. He speaks of the City and Nation together, but of the Temple separately, because the City was inhabited by Israel, but the Temple was more important than the City.

18. He returns to the City, mentioning the holy cities, which were round about Jerusalem. 'O Lord,' he says, 'hear my petition, and see what has overtaken Thy holy cities, which have become waste and burnt with fire. Repeople them with their inhabitants.'

Not for our own righteousness: indicating that others were praying besides Daniel. ' It is not by our merits or good deeds that we supplicate Thee ; for we have transgressed, and multiplied our sins. No, our confidence is in Thy great mercy ; do Thou have mercy on us and our cities.'

19. This ends the prayer. **Hear** : i. e. hear our complaint concerning our condition and what has befallen us, and **forgive** our sins. **Hearken** : i. e. listen to our supplication ; and **do** sc. something for Thy people, Thy city, and Thy temple.

For Thine own sake: i.e. because Thy Name is called upon Thy city (cp. Jer. xxv. 29) ; and Thy Name, too, is 'God of Israel.' So do for the sake of Thy Name, and magnify not our sins and transgressions.

20. **Speaking**: ver. 4. **Praying**: referring to the lamentations. **Confessing**: the seventeen phrases commencing with ver. 5 and ending with 16 a.

My sin and the sin of my people: hitherto he associated himself with the nation; here he mentions his sin separately. According to some, until Daniel grew up he had been trained in his parents' training, and only when he could think for himself had thrown it off. According to others, he says **my sin**, because no son of Adam is free from sin, which some commit intentionally and others unintentionally (hence Eccles. vii. 20). Others still suppose he says this because it was impossible for him to express displeasure at evil-doers, owing to the wicked having the upper hand.

21. **Speaking in prayer** includes the whole prayer from ver. 4 to the end.

Whom I had seen in the vision at the beginning : viii. 16, where another angel sent him to Daniel, and Daniel had become familiar with him. Gabriel is one of the special angels who stand before the Glory, having six wings wherewith they fly (Is. vi. 2).

Wearily : i. e. quickly.

Touched me about the time of the evening oblation : at eventide ; some say *before* the regular prayer, others *after* it. Most probably the latter view is right, viz. he first offered up the regular prayer, and followed it with the foregoing petition.

The evening oblation : i. e. the evening *burnt-offering ;* the word מנחה means simply 'offering ' (Gen. iv. 4 ; Ps. cxli. 2).

22. **And he instructed me and talked with me** : *v. infra.*

I am now come forth: from before the Glory; and have been sent to instruct thee in what thou needest to know, and thou shall instruct Israel.

23. **At the beginning**: 'from the moment when thou didst begin to say "O LORD" (ver. 16), the answer came, and I have come to instruct thee in what I have been commanded to instruct thee.' Observe that he does not say 'at the beginning of thy prayer;' apparently, while Daniel was recounting their sins, and what had befallen Israel, lo, He was listening: but when he began to say, 'LORD, according to all Thy righteousness,' the answer came, and Gabriel came to him. This is the treatment of those who are perfect with their Creator: 'before they cry He answers' (Is. lxii. 24). To those who are not perfect in His eyes He delays the answer ten days; as was the case with Johanan the son of Kareah (Jer. xlii. 8, where the answer was not delayed on Jeremiah's account, but only on account of the people).

For thou art a man of desires: 'since thou *desirest* to know the fate of the Temple and of the Nation.'

Consider the matter, and understand the vision: i. e. all the previous words that he had heard from the angels in the Dream and the Vision. Some of these he explains in this chapter; *v. infra*. The words may be taken either as infinitives or as imperatives without difference to the meaning.

24. He tells him what is going to happen during the **four kingdoms.** Of these *seventy weeks, seven* passed in the kingdom of the Chaldees (47 years); 57 years the Persians reigned, 180 the Greeks, 206 the Romans; these are the special periods of the seventy weeks. These include the reigns of all four beasts; only the angel does not describe at length what happened to any of them save the history of the Second Temple during the time of Rome. These seventy weeks are *weeks of sabbatical years*, making 490 years; below they are divided into periods.

Are decreed upon thy people: decreed by God, like the 400 years decreed to Abraham, or the 70 years decreed to Babylon.

Upon thy people and upon thy holy place: in so far as there befell the people during this period different sorts of fortune, some commendable and others to be deprecated; six things are mentioned in this verse, three commendable, **to finish transgression, to make an end of sins, to make reconciliation for iniquity;** and three are mentioned of a different aspect, **to bring in everlasting righteousness, and to seal up vision and prophecy, and to anoint the most holy**: of these six some are to take place at the beginning of the series, others at the end of 300 years. **To bring everlasting righteousness and to anoint the most holy** refers to the first beginning of the building of the Temple; **to seal up vision and prophecy** took place during the reign of *the Greeks;* **to finish transgression** etc. was done in the middle of the 70 years of Babylon.

Transgression refers to the 'worship of other gods' and similar 'abominations;' **sins,** to the misplacing of the sabbaths and the other feasts; **iniquity** includes the other sins committed by the people amongst themselves, i. e. offences against life and property or possessions. Others interpret differently; referring **to make reconcilia-**

tion for iniquity to offerings: meaning that while they were in Babylon to the conclusion of the Babylonian empire God obtained from them satisfaction for the debt they had incurred by their sins : referring to 2 Chron. xxxvi. 21.

Similarly, to bring in everlasting righteousness is supposed by some to refer to the High Priests, and to anoint the most holy to the sanctuaries and the priests. Others again make everlasting righteousness the offerings, and the most holy the High Priest, referring to 2 Chron. xxxiii. 13. Either way it must plainly take place at the building of the Temple. There remains to seal up vision and prophecy: this must mean the cutting off of vision and prophets from Israel. Vision refers to prophecies relating to future time, such as those of Haggai or Zechariah of the future; and the prophet (i. e. prophecy) is what is told relating to the present. According to some authorities the Holy Spirit was cut off from the time of Solomon; the *Singers* remaining, who recited the Psalms (see 2 Chron. xxix. 20). Or again he may mean by to seal up vision and prophecy that the Books of the Prophets were sealed and collected, twenty-four books, and fixed by *Massorahs,* and other institutions necessary for this purpose. He puts to seal vision and prophecy between to bring everlasting righteousness and to anoint the most holy because prophecy went on between the offering of the oblations and the anointing of the most holy.

25. From the going forth of the commandment : supposed to refer to Jer. xxix. 10, or to its *going forth* from God; to return : i. e. the captives with the sacred vessels; unto the anointed one, the Khalif: i. e. the High Priest, who is *anointed* with the 'oil of anointing,' and is *the prince* of the Lord's house. Others make the anointed the High Priest, and the prince Zerubbabel son of Shealtiel. He tells him then that from the time of the destruction of the Holy Place and the captivity of the nation to the building of the Second Temple, is *seven weeks,* i.e. forty-nine years. Now the people did not cease dwelling in the city till the twenty-third year of Nebuchadnezzar; they are called (Ezek. xxxiii. 24) 'inhabitants of waste places,' and were taken captive by Nebuzaradan (Jer. lii. 30). Now if twenty-three years be taken away from the sum total of the seventy years of Babylon, there remain forty-seven years plus one year for Darius and one year for Cyrus. This makes a total of forty-nine years; to which the *seven weeks* refer.

And threescore and two weeks it shall be built again : this is the duration of the Second Temple till the coming of TITUS THE SINNER, king of Rome; 434 years. During this period, he tells him, Jerusalem will again be inhabited.

Market-place : i. e. the fora of the judges.

Decision : i. e. the performance of legal sentences of death, etc.

The dough of the times [1]: referring, it is said, to the offering of the High Priest (Lev. vi. 13). Of the times: inasmuch as half was offered in the morning, and half in the evening.

The offering of the High Priest is mentioned separately, because so long as it was offered the altar continued in service.

26. And after the threescore and two weeks : at the close of these sixty-two

---

[1] Mistranslation for ' even in troublous times.'

weeks this Anointed, spoken of in ver. 25, shall be cut off; referring to the cessation of priests from the altar.

And shall have none : i. e. no son or successor in his place; *or*, the whole time of the Captivity they shall have no royalty.

The city and the sanctuary : Jerusalem and the Temple of the Lord.

Shall destroy : shall devastate and burn (Ps. cxxxvii. 7).

The people of the prince that shall come : the army of Rome with Titus.

And his end shall be with a flood : i. e. such as are left of Israel after the massacre shall be *swept away*, i. e. carried away captive. This is the description of what befell the sanctuary, Jerusalem, and the nation.

Until the end of war : i. e. till the end of wars, sc. *the wars of Gog*, Jerusalem and the cities of Judah shall lie waste ; as has been witnessed up to our day.

27. One week is left out of the seventy ; he describes their condition therein. The enemy, he says, made a covenant with them for seven years, that he would not carry them away captive or harm them ; when half the week had passed he betrayed them, and broke the covenant. Some suppose that what induced him to do this was that he saw that the people withdrew from the city in detachments, seeing that they must certainly otherwise be taken captive or fall before the enemy ; and they said, ' Let us withdraw of our own accord : it is better.' Some say that the Israelites slew certain Gentiles that were in the city, who were Roman nobles ; when they had done this the Romans broke faith with them, took the city, burnt the Temple, and put a stop to the offerings (**he shall cause the sacrifice and the oblation to cease**). The histories further tell us that he set up in God's house an idol, and offered up swine on God's altar.

The wing of abominations: the army of the Romans, who are called 'abominations ; ' they are the devastators of the sanctuary (**one that maketh desolate**).

Even unto the consummation and the determination : i. e. till God work a *consummation* and a *determination* by causing the nations to cease, and especially Edom. The first referring to the city [of Rome] ; the second to the kingdom.

Shall be poured out upon the wasted : i. e. the wrath of God upon this city, which shall be waste till Israel come and inhabit it. God shewed this to Daniel because he desired to know what would become of the people and the Holy Place in the time of the three kingdoms ; for he knew that the Holy Place *must* one day be inhabited, and the captives *must* return ; but they *might* have continued in the condition in which they were during the time of the Persian and of the Greek empires. God shewed him that the city must again be wasted, and the people taken captive, that he might know it, and Israel might know it. Thereat his heart was pained, and he sickened.

X.

1. In the third year of Cyrus, he tells us, an angel appeared to him, who told him all that God would reveal to him. This is *the fourth section*. The same thing

happened twice in the reign of Belshazzar, and once in the reign of Darius. This is the fourth time. Apparently till the first year of the reign of Cyrus he was engaged in the Sultan's business; see on chap. i. *ult.*; and then withdrew from it, having got leave, especially after the proclamation (Ezra i. 3). Then again he had become old, and his heart was affected by what he had been told of the future capture of the city and the return of the nation into captivity, as was explained before. Then he began to lament and fast, in order to ask God of that which was in his mind; he sought help for his petition in lamentation as before, chap. ix.

A thing was revealed: i.e. a matter which was difficult, and of which the interpretation was concealed from him, became clear after being obscure.

And the thing was true: i.e. *literally* true, not like the Dream or the Vision, see on ix. 26. Notice that this word *true* occurs four times, with the same meaning; ix. 26 is the first, the present passage the second; x. 21 and xi. 2.

Whose name was called Belteshazzar: not ' *whose name was* B.' Some think the name still remained upon him, and that he did not discard it. Others infer that he was called by that name till the fall of the Chaldean empire, and that the appellation ceased with that; which is probable.

And a great host: i.e. the prophecy of a great host, whether *Edom* or *Ishmael* (see on xi. 3).

And he understood the thing, etc.: i.e. the explanation of the communication made to him in the last chapter; and that of the *Vision* which he had seen, i.e. chap. viii. See on the following verses.

2, 3. **In those days**: in the third year of Cyrus; the same *days* in which he lamented. The phrase **three weeks of days** indicates the difference between these weeks and the seventy weeks; which were of *years*.

I was mourning: he mentions certain things which he practised during those weeks; [in reference to] i. food; ii. drink; iii. scent. Of food he mentions **bread** and **meat**; of drink **wine**; and *the bread* he specifies as **pleasant**, since doubtless he must have eaten *some* bread; he explains that he did not eat fine wheaten bread, especially. But of *meat and wine* he says *it came not into my mouth*, since he neither ate the one nor drank the other at all. Probably he ate *bread* made of barley or coarse wheat with a relish of vegetables and grain; and perhaps *fruit.* Next he speaks of *oil* and *scent*, **neither did I anoint myself at all.** We know, too, that he must certainly have changed his costume and put on rough clothing and have shunned all amusement. All this is after the ordinary fashion of mourners. It remains to speak of the *fasting.* Some say that he fasted [in order to gain knowledge], as the angel says, *infra* ver. 10: supposing that fasting is one form of mourning, which is not improbable; so that he bound himself to continue mourning till God should reveal to him what He would of the affairs of the nation; similarly to the mourning which David enforced on himself till God revealed to him His will; Ps. cxxxii. 3. The saints of God could do this, knowing that God would answer their request favourably; the people of the Captivity cannot venture so far, but can only stand up and ask God concerning such things as persons like them can ask. We must explain the nature of the meat which Daniel abstained from eating. Let us state that it refers to *meat which was lawful to eat*, since he only abstained during these days from the four things to which in previous times he had been accustomed, and to which he returned after the revelation of what God pleased to reveal to him. As to food which had always been unlawful for him to eat, that cannot be included in the terms of the verse; nor can the word *meat* refer to the flesh of forbidden beasts, birds, and fishes. Nor again to the flesh of oxen and sheep, which is only made lawful after the performance of the conditions contained in the laws, as we have explained in the Commentary on the Pentateuch and the Book of Commandments which we have compiled. If any one ignorant of Hebrew ask, 'What flesh is that?' we answer, the meat of fowls, land animals, and fishes. If he ask again, 'How can you shew that בשר in Hebrew means "fish"?' We answer, בשר is a name for both fowl and fish, nor is there any distinction between fish and other animals. However, we can prove it by a text: Num. xi. 21, 'Thou hast said, I will give them flesh;' 22, 'Shall flocks and herds be slain for them? or shall all the fish of the sea be gathered together for them?' This shews that 'fish' are 'flesh' (בשר), no less than oxen and sheep. Then fowl are called so in the same chapter; ver. 33, 'While the flesh (i. e. the quails) was yet between their teeth.' Similarly fowls are coupled with beasts in Lev. xvii. 13, 14; and the same is indicated in the history of Noah. It is clear then that בשר is a name for *every* animal beyond question. Then those who allow meat during the Captivity cannot adduce this verse as evidence, especially as the altar of God was being employed, and sacrifices continually offered on it; for it had now been built a whole year.

4. This verse indicates that it was after the conclusion of the three weeks. So we learn that he began to lament on the third of the month. He tells us that he was walking on the bank of the Tigris, when this angel appeared to him. Observe that in the Vision he was not in reality on the bank of the river Ulai; he only saw this in a Vision, whereas this was seen by him waking, when he was standing in reality on the river's bank. He does not say at what point on the bank he was—Mosul, Babylon, or elsewhere. The source of the Tigris is above Mosul, and it flows into the Marshes.

5. **Uphaz** is the name of a place (Jer. x. 9).

6. This angel is not Gabriel, as some have thought, since he was already familiar with Gabriel; nor was his form so mighty and terrible; on the contrary, when he saw him at the end of his prayer he was not affected in this way at all, as we shall explain. Nor does he describe any of the angels whom he mentions as he describes this angel, owing to his fear and terror of him. We shall state what is necessary on this subject on ver. 13.

Then he describes the colour of his body: from his neck to his knees it resembled the colour of the blue stone; and his face, he says, was like the flashing lightning; and its colour red like the lightning. And his eyes, he said, were like torches of fire which sparkle to a distance. And his arms and legs, he tells us, were like the colour of burnished brass, i. e. yellow. And his voice was heard at a distance like the noise of

an army. All these things would frighten the spectator. And his garments were those of **authority,** girt up after the fashion of the warrior whose garments are tied in the middle. He had come to him from battle : *v. infra.*

7. Observe that he did not see the angel on the bank, but only in the air, above the river, raised above its surface, cp. xii. 6 ; and he tells us that he saw him in this terrible, frightening form.

For the men that were with us : indicating that there were people with him, and that he saw, but no one else. Now the words **I alone saw the Vision** already tell us that he alone saw it : what then is the purpose of the clause **For the men that were with me . . . ?** Answer : to indicate that these people, although they did not *see,* yet *felt* something, and that there fell on them a **quaking**; which possibly fell on them from the sound of his voice, so that they heard the sound, but did not see the figure. **They saw not the Vision** ; not, 'they did not hear.' On the contrary, when they did hear his voice, there fell on them a trembling, and they fled scared. Probably these were people who had gone out with him for some purpose not mentioned by the Scripture. Similarly when our forefathers heard the voice of God there fell on them fear and trembling, and they fled afar off (Ex. xx. 18).

8. In the previous verse he said, 'And I Daniel alone saw the Vision ;' in the present, **So I was left alone**; and there was none with me to keep me company.

There remained no strength in me : to stand.

And I retained no strength : to move.

My comeliness was turned in me into corruption : i. e. his face became yellow, as happens to people at the time of death.

9. **I was in a deep sleep** : he had swooned for a little.

10. **A hand** : i. e. the angel's hand, whose hand he saw, but not the angel moving it, so that he rose up from being on his face, and was on all fours ; not having strength to sit down or to stand.

11. He commanded him to do two things : first, to attend to what he should say to him, telling him that God had sent him ; secondly, to stand on his feet, that he might hear his voice. And he tells us that he did **stand,** yet not firmly, but was **trembling**.

12. **Fear not** : fear not that thy station in God's eyes may have been lowered, seeing that formerly in thy prayer the answer came to thee whilst thou wast praying, and this time three weeks are passed and no answer to thee. No. On the first day that thou didst commence to lament, thy words were heard, only I had an occupation that prevented me from coming to thee.

Thy words were heard indicates that he was also asking God to instruct him in that wherein he desired to be instructed ; and he adds that he is now come to tell him what God thought meet to tell him.

13–15. What prevented him from coming on the first day, he says, was his fighting with the Prince of Persia. The idea is that he fought with him till Cyrus died : when

Cyrus died he left him and came to Daniel. We shall supplement this so far as is necessary at xi. 1. As soon, he adds, as I had finished fighting with the Prince of Persia I came to tell thee what shall happen to thy people at the latter time; i. e. the time of the end of the four kingdoms.

For the Vision is yet for many days : i. e. the vision which thou sawest before relates to the latter time, i. e. to the end of the four kingdoms.

When the angel had proceeded thus far, his terror overpowered him, and he had no strength to stand, but fell on his face.

And I was dumb : there was no strength left in him to speak to him concerning his utterance ; he became dumb and could not talk at all.

16, 17. He saw an angel, resembling a man, talking with him; perhaps the angel's hand approached his mouth; cp. Is. vi. 6; Jer. i. 9. When the angel had approached him, his mouth was opened and he spoke.

Unto him that stood before me : the great angel who had addressed him. He said this by way of excuse : ' had it not been for the fright that came over me, and my strength failing, I had stood up as thou badest me.'

My sorrows are turned upon me : cp. 1 Sam. iii. 19.

For how can, etc.? i. e. I have no power to stand up to speak with such as my lord. My rank is not so high.

Straightway: since I met with thee, no strength nor motion has been left in me. Perhaps **breath** here means *reason;* so Job xxvi. 4; xxxii. 8.

18. When the hand touched him he spoke ; but there was no strength in him to stand : so the angel repeated what he had done, and approached him ; and thereupon he found strength to stand. The great angel was above the waters of the river : Daniel at first saw his hand, but nothing more. Afterwards he saw himself; and the angel talked with him familiarly, and now touched his lips, and now approached him; possibly took his hand and drew him up : **strengthened** him.

19. **Fear not** : spoken by the great angel ; meaning 'fear not for thyself ; rise up at once, and be comforted, and strengthen thy heart ; and hear what I shall tell thee.' And when he had heard his voice, his heart was strengthened, he having doubtless beforehand stood upon his feet.

20. **Knowest thou?** referring to his previous words (ver. 12). ' I have told thee already,' he says, ' why I am come ; and I must immediately return to fight with the Prince of Persia concerning the four kings which are left to Persia.' This is explained in what follows.

And when I go forth: i. e. I shall go forth from fighting with the Prince of Persia, and afterwards the Prince of Greece shall come. He does not tell what shall come after Greece.

21. **That which is inscribed in the writing of truth** : i. e. that which he had heard in the Dream which he wrote down (vii. 1). ' This,' he says, ' which is inscribed in the writing of truth has an inner meaning, which I will evolve for thee without further allegory.'

There is none that strengtheneth himself with me : there is none that helpeth me to destroy these kingdoms save Michael only.

Your prince : indicating that Michael is Prince of Israel, and that the angel conversing with him was demolishing the kingdoms with Michael.

Against these : either, the kings of Persia, who have just been mentioned ; or, the four kingdoms. These two angels were helping each other to put an end to all these kingdoms. The great angel does not state that he is prince of any one of the dominions. Perhaps Michael fought with the enemies of Israel only ; and this one with the ruler of every nation, whom he deposed, when the period of its sway was over.

XI.

1. Just as he had helped Michael to slay Cyrus, so he had helped him to slay Darius, or had killed him.

Here we must pause a moment and briefly state some necessary ideas on the subject of angels. We are not justified in setting aside the literal meaning of the Word of God or of His prophets, save where that literal meaning is hindered or precluded as being contradicted by *the reason* or by *a clear text*. In such a case it is understood that the first text requires an explanation reconciling it with the reason or with the other text ; the words having been used in some metaphorical or improper sense, as we have observed in a number of places in the Law and the Blessed Prophets. Ideas repudiated by *the reason*, are such as 'God descended,' 'God ascended,' etc. ; precluded by the reason, because, if we take the verse literally, it follows from it that God must be a material substance, capable of inhabiting places and being in one place more than in another, moving and resting, all qualities of created and finite beings, and He must possess these attributes. Such texts must therefore be capable of being explained away, and the term indirectly interpreted may be either the *noun* or the *verb*. The first is done in cases like 'and God descended,' 'and God ascended,' where we affirm the action of the person of whom 'ascending' and 'descending' are attributes ; only the person intended is the *Angel of* God, or the *Glory of* God or the *Apostle of* God, with the ellipse of a word. The second is done in cases like 'God was glad,' or 'God was sorry,' or 'God was jealous ;' all of which are accidents not to be predicated of the Immortal Creator. This phrase must contain a sense to be evolved in whatever way the words will allow. The language has employed in such cases metaphors and inaccurate expressions, because the application of the reason can point them out. Where one text is precluded by another, the one which admits of two or more interpretations must be explained away. Now no clear text of Scripture denies the possibility of God's having created angels ; nor does the reason reject it. Nor can their existence be rejected, whether we hold that they are accidents, or whether we hold that they are created and destroyed. For we find in the Scriptures many places in which angels are mentioned, and in two different ways. Sometimes they appear sensibly and are witnessed by persons waking, like any other visible object ; sometimes in dreams, and there too like other objects : instances of the first case occurred to Jacob, Moses, Balaam, Joshua, Gideon, Manoah, David, Nebuchadnezzar, Daniel ; of the second to Abimelech (as some think), Jacob, and Balaam. Their voices too have been heard without their being seen, as by Hagar, Abraham, Samuel, David. These all occur in our Chronicles, and there is no ground for rejecting these texts. It is known that nothing but *body* can be perceived by the sense of the eye : and that an accident cannot exist by itself. An angel therefore must be a *body*. Now a body cannot bring itself into existence, but must have a Creator to create it; and it is a thing which admits of persistence. An angel therefore being created must be capable of persistence ; and what is there to necessitate his annihilation ? If any one hold that an angel is only created for the moment, for the sake of a message or something similar, and that, when that is finished, there is no reason why he should endure,— what, we ask, indicates that he is created at the moment,—or created merely for the message or purpose which renders him for the moment necessary ? If you say: 'Then what has the angel to do besides delivering messages and similar tasks ?' We answer : To praise and glorify his Creator. Is not the prophet too chosen to deliver a message ? but nevertheless he is not created merely to speak. We find, too, in our accounts that angels *do* endure. Thus the Glory abode with the children of Israel nine hundred years ; and Daniel says of Gabriel, *and the man Gabriel, whom I had seen in the Vision at the beginning*, and there had elapsed between the two occasions a year. Nor can we suppose the second Gabriel was merely like the first, who had been created a year before and then destroyed ; for that would not entitle the second to be [called] the same as the first. Again, there are the words of this angel who is speaking to Daniel, who says : 'I have been some time in war, and am going to fight those who remain :' see also xii. 1. These verses point to their persistence : and after this discussion there may be a stop put to the assertions of those who maintain that they are created for a moment and annihilated. As for their orders, doubtless some are higher than others ; see our Commentary on Ezekiel, chap. i, and Ps. cvi. 1. Observe, too, that in this chapter he says of one **like the similitude of a man**, and tells us that he came near him, and was not afraid, whereas he was terrified and alarmed by the *great angel;* such things are common in our books ; and their powers are limited according as the Creator has given them. Observe that when Jacob wrestled with the angel, the angel was at the time unable to get rid of him (Gen. xxxii. 26). Though their forms be terrible, yet God has given the children of men power to behold them, save the great and mighty Glory which the blessed Apostle asked God to shew him, when He said 'thou canst not,' etc. (Ex. xxxiii. 20). This is a concise account of this matter ; we should gladly elucidate what we have said on this subject in other places ; it would not, however, be proper to introduce that subject in this place.

I stood up to confirm : the province is Michael's, wherein this angel helped him.

2. **After Cyrus came four kings :** sc. Ahasuerus (Mordecai's patron), **Artaxerxes the Less,** Darius the Persian ; these are the *three.*

And the fourth : i. e. Artaxerxes, patron of Ezra and Nehemiah.

Shall be far richer : he already told us that Cyrus got the treasures of the kings, and was exceedingly rich (Is. xlv. 3) ; and the same wealth is asserted of Artaxerxes in Esth. i. 4. In this verse he tells us that Artaxerxes was richer than all the Persian kings, and that he abode in his kingdom longer than the others, seeing that he reigned thirty-three years. Then he tells him that when he reaches the height of his wealth, his kingdom will terminate, and all will accrue to the king of Javan : **he shall stir up all.** This was not told in the *Dream,* nor in the *Vision,* but only here.

3. **And there shall stand up :** i. e. shall be established on the throne.

A mighty king : the one called in the dream 'a notable horn between his eyes :' i. e. Alexander ; called *mighty* because he took great cities ; his history is well known.

That shall rule : the Persians ruled three quarters, see on chap. viii. 4 etc., but Alexander all four (ii. 39).

And shall do according to his will : cp. ver. 19, of Nebuchadnezzar.

4. **His kingdom shall be broken :** the government was disturbed on Alexander's death. **And shall be divided :** with reference to the dispute between his generals, and the compromise by which each of the princes was to take one quarter of the globe ; the reason of this being his having left no son (**and not for his posterity**).

Neither like unto his government : in spite of these four holding the four quarters of the globe, they had no royal control or might like Alexander's.

For his kingdom shall be broken : the kingdom of the Greeks, to which belonged the four quarters of the globe, shall be shattered, dynasty after dynasty springing up on the death of these four, until 180 years were completed, according to the historical records.

And to others besides these : meaning that there arose after these a dynasty which discarded the traditions of its predecessors. These have been already mentioned in the words 'when sin is completed.' They were *sinners,* i. e. apostates, in respect of the traditions, [and usurpers] in respect of the government.

5. Observe that the kingdom was divided between four, each one taking a quarter, like those who were mentioned above. This is seen from the expressions *king of the north, king of the south* (which we shall clearly explain lower down) ; although of the four none are mentioned save the king of the *north* and the king of the *south.* Probably therefore the kings of the *west* and of the *east* remained quietly in their respective quarters, not seeking to acquire any other, and there was no war between them ; whence the Scripture does not mention them ; whereas it mentions the kings of the *south* and of the *north,* because they were engaged in eventful wars. Or possibly the kings of the west and east were in dependence respectively on the other two kings.

And of his princes: said to be one of the *princes* of the king who preceded him; the *king of the south* who preceded him being a Greek, and this one of the (latter's) princes. Otherwise, one of the princes of the *king of the north*, who rebelled and strengthened himself against the king of the north, which is likely, and is confirmed by the following verse.

He shall be strong above him: the king of the south above the king of the north.

A great dominion: his realm shall be greater and wider than that of any other sovereign; he being, in fact, the king of *Rome* (who is the king of the south), and this the first king who arose over them.

6. **At the end of years:** he does not say how many; certain years during which there was an understanding between the two; till the king of the north rebelled against the king of the south, on account of which the king of the south sent armies to the king of the north. It is like what happened to Sodom with Kedorlaomer, when they obeyed him for twelve years, then rebelled, and were assailed by him.

Shall join themselves together: for battle; cp. Gen. xiv. 3.

And the daughter of the king of the south: i. e. the whole of his host; compare the phrases 'Daughter of Egypt,' 'Daughter of Tyre,' etc.

To make an agreement: i. e. to desire him to deal peacefully with him again and continue in his previous allegiance; like what Sennacherib, king of Asshur, demanded of Hezekiah. Possibly he desired him to confess the former's faith, the king of the north being an idolater; to which the king of the north would not agree, but came out to fight the army of the king of the south; when the army of the king of the south could not stand before the king of the north (**but she shall not retain the strength of her arm**).

The arm is the *armies* of the king of the south, which shall flee before the king of the north, and afterwards capitulate (**but she shall be given up,** etc.).

She shall be given up refers to the army.

They that brought her to the captains of the host.

He that begat her to the general of the army appointed by the king of the south to lead the army, who went with it; the king himself not going with it, on account of one of two possible circumstances; either he despised the king of the north, and was assured in his mind that his army would rout the king of the north; or, perhaps, he was afraid lest, if he departed out of his realm, his affairs might become disturbed; whence he did not stir from his place.

And he that strengthened her in the times: referring to certain persons who were amongst his army by way of giving aid, but not actually belonging to his army, since he merely desired their assistance for money to be paid them; when they were required they went with his army, and afterwards returned to their place. Hence the phrase.

7, 8. The king of the south had no power to face the king of the north, but died defeated. After his death there arose there another king in his stead.

Out of a shoot of her roots : not his son therefore, yet one of the royal seed, and related to him ; a man of valour who took the command of the army and went with it, fearing lest there might overtake his army what overtook the former.

And he shall come unto the army : i. e. the army which had capitulated to the king of the north ; and when they see him arrived, they shall return to him, and thereupon he shall strengthen himself and shall come to the fortified cities of the king of the north, especially the capital city.

And shall deal with them : i. e. do battle with them, and prevail against them, and kill certain of **them**, i. e. of the soldiers.

Next he tells us how he shall take their idols, out of spite against them ; it is like what the king of Asshur did with the calves of Israel (Hos. x. 6).

With their princes : the king's lords and lieutenants.

The king did not fall into his hands, either, as some think, because he fled, or because he sent messengers, and agreed to give him what the previous king desired, as we explained in ver. 6 b. This is most probable to my mind. Now the king of the south did not accept these terms from the king of the north till after he had taken their idols with the whole of their treasures, that there might be no power left them, and the king of the north might be left very weak, and thereupon be compelled to absolute obedience to the king of the south.

9. The king of the north shall come under the sway of the king of the south, and after that the king of the south shall return to his land.

And he shall continue some years: i. e. after the death of the king of the north (cp. Gen. xxi. 21) ; signifying that he shall remain alive. The first king of the south then will die while the king of the north is alive ; then that king of the north will die during the lifetime of the second king of the south ; dying humbled and paying submission to the king of the south.

10–12. We know that the *first king of the south* began by being mighty, and was afterwards stricken : and that the king of the north was weak at first, and then prevailed against the king of the south, and afterwards is to be oppressed once more beneath the hand of the king of the south, and to die in that condition, his first state being weak, and his last state weak. Now he tells us that after his death his sons shall arise and take possession of the kingdom ; he does not tell us their number ; however they are governors, each having an army under him, one of them being chief in power with the others beneath him. And they said : ' Let us do as the second king of the south did, and let us take vengeance from him for our father ; ' and they all agreed thereto.

And they shall contend : he does not say for what : I imagine that they sent him messengers demanding that he should yield up the cities which he took from their father, or restore some of the tribute which he imposed upon him ; to this he did not consent : whereupon they collected an army and began to occupy city after city of the dominions of the king of the south, the king of the south not moving from his place for fear of them.

First he says **and his sons shall contend,** to signify that they sent messengers to the king of the south ; afterwards **and he shall come on and overflow,** referring to the one of them who was most illustrious.

And he shall return and contend : i. e. first he took certain cities of the king of the south, which came into his power ; but he did not venture to come to the capital of the king of the south ; yet when he saw that the king of the south did not stir from his place, he did venture, and assailed him in his capital ; **even to his fortress.**

Thereupon the king of the south was compelled to come out against him.

And shall fight with him, even with the king of the north : probably he directed his energies first against the armies, then against the king himself ; when the latter saw himself assailed he set up in his face a mighty army, to repel the king of the south or, if possible, to defeat him. Thereupon the king of the south becomes master of the mighty army gathered by the king of the north, and his heart is lifted up, and the king of the north flees by himself and returns to his city.

And he shall cast down tens of thousands : i. e. he took captive as many as he wished of the army of the king of the north, and slew a multitude of the soldiers and of others.

And there shall not prevail : i. e. no one shall be able to stand before him ; all shall flee before him. During a long period he shall be like this ;—I am inclined to think the KING of the SOUTH is meant, who burnt the Temple and carried our people captive ; from which time the Romans have been strong and their empire has prevailed, and has become a 'mighty terrible monster.' You must know that these wars covered many years, about two hundred ; the pronouns therefore refer not to individuals, but to the empire.

13. Probably this **king of the north** is not the same as the one who fled. He is to gather armies **more numerous than the former,** which were taken by the king of the south.

And at the end of the times, years (instead of 'at the end of years') refers to the prophecy of the seventy weeks. Or, it may mean after *the end of years* during which there was an agreement between them, made after the rout, and they obeyed the king of the south because of his power ; after the end of this period the king of the north shall collect these armies and assail the king of the south, *v. infra.*

14. In ver. 13 he said **at the end of the times, years :** now he goes back and tells us how in those times the power of the king of the south shall be great, and he shall collect mighty armies, whereas the king of the north shall be low.

The children of the breakers of thy people refers, it is said, to the followers of JESUS, said by the Christians to be the Messiah ; those followers who made the Gospel : their names are well known :

   i. Matthew the publican.

   ii. Mark the fisherman.

iii. Luke the physician, disciple of Paulus Abu-Shaoul.

iv. John, kinsman of Jesus, entrusted by him with certain powers.

These are called **children of the breakers of thy people** because they made a breach in the religion ; and doubtless multitudes of Israelites became Christians with them.

Shall lift themselves up : in that they got a great and mighty station, and a mighty name.

To establish : i. e. their purpose was to *establish the vision* in Jesus' favour, as is known from their profession in their gospels and records.

But they shall fall : if this refers to the followers of Jesus, it will mean 'they shall leave the religion of Israel;' if to the nation, then it means that Israel after this shall fall, being punished for the murder of God. How many Israelites will have been slain from that time till God deliver His people ! That then will be the meaning of **they shall fall** : signifying that the ruin of Israel was *by* them and *through* them. First we were ruined by our kings and false prophets, who were the cause of the cessation of our empire and of our captivity ; then these Christians have been the cause of our ruin and destruction during the Captivity; and some went astray at the beginning of the empire of the Little Horn, and also ruined us.

15. After the digression in which he introduces the history of Jesus and his followers, and what is to come upon us through them, he goes back and finishes what becomes of the king of the north after he has collected the armies. The words **so the king of the north shall come** are to be connected with **and he shall come on** in ver. 13 b. The king of the north is to come to the land of Rome and besiege the capital city and take it (**and take a well-fenced city**); i.e. *Constantinople.*

And the arms of the south : i.e. 'the many who shall stand up ' (ver. 14), great armies collected by the king of the south to help him.

His chosen people : hosts wherein he placed especial confidence. These, too, cannot stand before the king of the north, who slays multitudes of the hosts of the king of the south, while many more desert to him and help him ; *v. infra.*

16. **He that cometh unto him** : the deserters from the king of the south ; mighty men of valour, who will do the will of the king of the north, and open gates for him. He will make them governors in the territory of Rome, whereafter none of the countries of the king of the south shall stand before him. At that time the Romans will have spread over the land of Israel, and be in possession of it, especially of the holy city, having great hosts in it ; and the king of the north shall assail them with his armies, and shall remain in the land of Israel a long time, and shall slay a multitude of Romans (**and shall destroy with his hand**).

17. The king of the north shall attack the fortresses of the king of the south with his armed men.

And upright ones with him : (according to some) certain Israelitish *Scribes* etc. who shall be with him, and inform him of what is written concerning his invasion, whose words he shall believe **and do** thereafter.

The daughter of the women : the holy city, it is said ; signifying that he is to ravage certain places consecrated to the Roman worship, and their royal palace; maybe God will give him power over the king of the south, and let him deal thus with him, in return for what the king of the south did in the Second Temple, and with Israel ; so that this will be some consolation to His people.

Then he tells us that the king of the north will not stay in Syria, nor shall the country remain under his authority ; he shall turn away thence to another place, and the Romans shall be established there as before.

18. He shall invade the islands belonging to the king of the south: referring perhaps to the 'frontier-land,' sc. Tarsus, Cyprus, etc., which he shall conquer, slaying and plundering, not intending to remain in the territory of the south, but only to take reprisals for what the king of the south did to him. The king of the south had put to shame the king of the north by what he had done to him when he had assailed him *in his fortress :* so when the king of the north does all this to the king of the south, the *reproach offered* by the latter will be taken away. **A captain,** sc. the king of the north, **shall cause the reproach offered by him to cease.**

Yea, moreover, he shall cause his reproach to turn upon him : i.e. not only does he cause the reproach offered by him to cease, but in his turn he brings reproach upon the king of the south. The king of the south, who burnt the holy city, had not assailed the king of the north ; only after he had been assailed by the latter did he do as described to the latter's army. This king, on the other hand, invades his capital, kills his soldiers, takes many cities, and massacres their inhabitants ; thus doing more than the king of the south had done to him. Hence he says **yea, moreover,** etc.

The above has been an account of the relations between the king of the north and the king of the south, including three events :

i. and ii. The armies of the king of the south assail the king of the north.

iii. The king of the north assails the king of the south.

The first and second of these campaigns were won by the king of the south against the king of the north ; in the third the reverse took place. The king of the south conquered twice, the king of the north once. These three events took place during a long period, more than three hundred years, as we have explained above. The seat of the king of the north was in the province of Baghdad. This is the last war between the two kings.

19. After doing all this he shall return to Baghdad, his royal seat : and afterwards shall stumble in the place of his throne ; maybe some of his servants shall slay him, and the matter be concealed and not known about (**and shall not be found**).

20. **In his place :** i.e. the second shall sit in the place of the first ; had he not stated this, it might have been in another place. There shall sit then in his place another without vigour or victory or war. Two facts are told us about him :

i. **Causing the exactor to pass.**

ii. **Glory of the kingdom.**

With regard to the first, some scholars have asserted that he abolished the taxes, and that during his time there was no trouble, vexation or affliction imposed by him on the people. Other scholars assert that it is of him that it is recorded that he obliged the people to lock their doors at midday, and to occupy themselves with eating and drinking; the weak among them having supplies from the royal table; so that the time passed in eating, drinking, amusement, enjoyment, and the wearing of new and fine apparel. Whence the words **the glory of the kingdom.** He tells us however that his time will not be long (**within few days**); he shall perish without encounter or war. Those who know this history tell us that the Arabs seized the place while the people were engaged in eating and drinking. They seized the king and slew him. He was last of the *Magus* who reigned in Baghdad; from whom it was taken by the Arab kings, who still hold it.

21. **A contemptible person:** every king of these dynasties hitherto had possessed some spirit and generosity save this one, who had no sort of it. His story is well known, so we need not dilate on it.

He shall come with security: i.e. he shall enter city after city without war or siege, which his predecessors had used.

And shall obtain the kingdom by flatteries: i.e. his professed 'visions,' and the rest of what was described in chap. vii, 'the mouth that speaketh great things,' etc.; and in chap. x, 'understanding dark sayings.'

22. **And the arms of a flood:** great armies of the king of the north, and the armies of Rome also. They shall flee before him and be dispersed.

And with the prince of the covenant: said to be the ruler of Rome, compare ix. 26; called of the covenant because he had made a covenant with Israel, *ibid.* 27. Others make it refer to the *kings of Israel*, beneath whom the sons of David were afflicted.

23. **And after the league:** said to refer to a follower of the 'Man of Wind' (Muḥammad), Omar one of the 'ten.' He is to deal deceitfully with Israel, and others; their story is well known. He shall come up and become strong with a few helpers.

24. **With security** in verse 21 referred to the 'Man of Wind;' here it refers to Omar.

The fattest places of the province: the great cities wherein dwell the rich.

He shall do, etc.: in the way of conquest and massacre. His predecessors, he says, reached no such eminence as he.

He shall scatter among them prey, etc.: he himself was satisfied with meagre food, coarse raiment, and humble equipage. Whenever he took a city and plundered it, he relinquished the whole of the plunder to the soldiery, and took none of it for himself.

Prey may refer to men, whom he used to take captive; or to precious objects and instruments.

Spoil: garments.

Substance: beasts of burden, cattle and sheep.

Against the strongholds: certain fortresses in the province of 'Irāq, which belonged to the king of the north, which he took by plots and strategy.

Even for a time: till the end of his *progress;* when the time of his retrogression comes, his position will be reversed.

25. **And he shall stir up his power**: this means that the king of the south had made no preparations, while he had with him only the handful of men who were with him at the beginning of his career (**with a few men**, ver. 23) ; but it came to pass that fresh people became Moslems continually, so that his army grew great.

This battle was fought between Omar ibn El-Khaṭṭāb and the Romans in Syria. Omar, the historians say, entered Jerusalem, and the king of Rome made ready to fight with him, and they arrayed battle in the plain of 'Amwās, near Jerusalem. Omar is said to have had a **mighty army**, and for this reason the king of the south met him also with a mighty army, but the Roman army was greater than the Moslem, as is implied by the additional words in the text.

And he shall not stand: sc. the army of the king of the south. Indeed it took to flight as soon as they joined battle.

For he shall forecast: his army shall. When they saw the Moslem general approach they abandoned the king of the south; even his chosen youths who were fed from his table destroyed him : for they were not true to him in the war.

Thereupon the Moslems became masters of the Romans, and slew a vast number of them (**many shall fall down slain**); and the Moslems took the land of Israel from the Romans, and hold it to this day.

27. He said above **they set not upon him** (ver. 21); and indeed so long as he had not taken the holy city from the Romans he does not call him their king. Now they have taken it, he calls him so.

Both these kings: i. e. of Arabia and Rome.

Their hearts shall be to do mischief: i. e. they shall do some harm to Israel, each of them, in some fashion ; as it is well known that the Moslems and Christians do.

Against one table: to be referred, it is said, to Israel ; called **one table** because Edom and Ishmael eat each other's food. Compare ii. 43 with comm. There he spoke of their mixing in marriage ; no less do they mix in the matter of food ; Isaiah speaks of both, chap. lxvi. 17, where *they that sanctify themselves* are the uncircumcised, who profess *sanctity* and speak of *Saint* So-and-so, and how the time of sanctification is come, and have *offerings*, and profess that they have holy priests, and baptismal water, and consequently do not wash off pollution. As for the Moslems they do not hold that view, but do wash after pollution, and consequently are called by the prophet *them that purify themselves*. Consequently the uncircumcised use the word *sanctity*, and the others the word *purity*. *To the gardens* refers to the fact that both profess that the 'Garden' (i. e. Paradise) is for them, as is stated in their books and commonly declared by them. *Behind one in the midst* refers to the fact that they all agree that the

Law is superseded, and that another system has been delivered since, that system being a religion not to be superseded by another. So when Islām started, they said of the Law just what the Christians had said; further asserting that the Book of their founder had superseded the religion of the Christians with another. Then he informs us that the professors of sanctity eat *swine's flesh*, while the professors of purity eat *abominations and the mouse*. For although Islām forbids swine's flesh, still otherwise they do not abstain from eating the food of the uncircumcised, so that they may be said to eat at one table, whereas Israel form one table, since they eat neither swine's flesh nor abominations nor the mouse. From this point of view therefore the words **at one table** refer to Israel. If we can make *at one table* signify two things, one will be that they *sit* at *one table*, the other that they *lie* **against** God and His people.

It shall not prosper: i.e. Israel; their affairs shall not prosper, and they shall be afflicted and abandoned.

The end remaineth unto the time: i.e. until the end of the four kingdoms be accomplished; when Edom and Ishmael shall fail and turn back, and Israel prosper. The verse covers the long period from the rise of Islām to the end of the Captivity.

28. The speaker returns to complete what preceded. (In the preceding verse the ruin and death which were to fall on the king of the south were mentioned.) He informs us how the ruler of Islām will return to the place where his station was; this is said to have been Damascus, whither therefore he returned, with *great riches* plundered from the army of the king of the south.

And his heart shall be to hurt Israel; cp. ver. 27 a. The person alluded to is said to have been a bitter enemy of Israel (Omar ibn El-Khaṭṭāb).

And he shall do his pleasure in Israel by decrees which he proclaimed against them. These are the Jews established in the holy city. After this he shall return to his own city.

This was the battle which resulted unfavourably to the king of Rome at the holy city.

29. With this verse ends the account of what happened at the rise of the power of Ishmael. From this verse commences the notice of what is to happen at the close of their power. In the previous verse he said **the end remaineth unto the time,** signifying that when that time appointed came, and he arrived at the end of his career, he should **return, and come into the south,** i.e. enter into the Roman territory. This began some years ago in the western direction, when the king of the west, who is now the king of Egypt, sent armies into the Roman territory.

But it shall not be as the former refers to what happened at the rise of his dynasty: (1) his overthrowing three thrones (chap. vii. 5); (2) *supra* 25.

Or as the latter refers to what shall be explained on ver. 40. The first battles were all advantageous to Ishmael and against the king of the south. The last shall be all advantageous to the king of the south and against Ishmael. This intermediate battle shall be unlike either, and of an intermediate kind.

30. **There shall enter into it inhabitants of the desert and Cyprians** refers perhaps to their entering into his religion; or possibly under his rule.

And shall be broken: to be construed, not with *him*, but with the *people and countries;* every one of them shall be overthrown before him.

And shall have indignation against the holy covenant: the king referred to began by assailing Israel with injuries; then he left them; at the end he shall return to them. This is an event in the future. It has not yet come to pass.

He shall even return and have regard unto them that forsake refers to certain Israelites who abandoned the religion of Israel and entered into his religion, to whom he will shew favour. Evidently he will require them to abandon their religion: some will remain true to the religion of Israel, against whom he will be indignant. Others will abandon it, and enter his religion, to whom he will shew favour. We shall explain this at the end of the chapter.

31. He tells us first that he will fight with the king of the south (ver. 29); then the condition of Israel during his time; then he goes back to tell us what he will do with his people.

Arms: certain hosts which shall penetrate into their holy place, and do the following things:

i. **They shall profane the sanctuary, even the fortress**: i.e. the place mentioned in chap. viii. 11.

The term there used was 'cast down;' here, **profane**. The first signifies that he shall lay it waste, and raze it to the ground; the second, that their dead bodies shall be thrown into it, so that it shall become like a dung-pit or dirt-heap.

ii. **They shall remove the continual**: i.e. they shall put a stop to the *Hagg* (pilgrimage); men shall not go on pilgrimages thither thereafter, nor pray as was their wont, nor celebrate the tenth day according to their custom; it is called *continual* because the institution was perpetual; they never relaxed the *Hagg*. Compare viii. 11, except that here is added—

iii. **And they shall make the abomination desolate**: most probably referring to the images in that house (cp. 2 Kings xi. 8, and Deut. xxix. 17). These images were very ancient; he had not been able to remove them originally, so he removed them now. Reference is made to the same subject in Ps. lxxiii. 20. Observe that in the 'Vision' he mentioned several things collectively which here he separates. If the words **they shall make the abomination desolate** refer to the image itself, it must mean that it will be left fallen, after having been erect and protected; but if we refer them to its *place*, then the meaning will be that *place* will be left *desolate*, waste, unapproached; and this is alluded to by the prophet Isaiah in his prayer (xxv. 2), where the *palace* is the house, said to belong to *strangers* because there are in it these images, *never to be built for ever* because it is waste, and never to be rebuilt; if, thirdly, we refer it to its worshippers, it will mean that they will grieve at the ruin that has overtaken their sanctuary, even as Israel has grieved ever since ruin overtook *them*, and *their* sanctuary was laid waste.

32. A further explanation of the words **he shall have regard unto them that forsake**, etc.

He shall deceive them by soft, flattering words ; i.e. some shall go out from our people for certain worldly reasons, and shall take verses of the Scripture spoken concerning the Messiah which they shall divert to the temporal ruler, and shall interpret of him, explaining away the words *sabbath* and *feast*, ruining themselves and departing from religion. They are said to **do wickedly against the covenant** because they do wrong, and shake off the yoke of the law and the covenants of Israel.

But the people that know his God shall be strong refers to certain Israelites who shall understand the system of the temporal lord, and that he has a secret which many Israelites did not understand, and so perished. But some—scholars—shall investigate his religion, and see that it is false, and cling to the law, and act according to it, and not depart from the religion of Israel as others departed. The fulfilment of this began in the West many years ago, when many Israelites gave up their religion and adopted his ; as is well known. Those who do not give up the faith are called **the people that know his God.**

33. The **wise** are the same as the last.

Shall instruct many : i.e. they shall cause many Israelites to understand his system, and strengthen their hands in the religion of God, and shall not abandon the faith. Now when he sees that they do not enter into his religion, his wrath will become fierce against them, as was Nebuchadnezzar's against Hananiah, Mishael, and Azariah, so that he threw them into a fiery furnace. So will this prince deal with Israel ; some he will kill with the *sword*, others by *fire ;* some he will afflict by *captivity* or by *plundering* their slaves and property.

Days : the period of a year perhaps. Note the order :
1. **He shall have indignation ;**
2. **Arms shall stand ;**
3. **Such as do wickedly against the covenant.**

This shews that a *tribulation* shall come upon Israel before the devastation of the house : which the present verse explains.

They shall fall : the persons who follow the *wise.* The *wise* being spoken of in the following verse.

34. After saying that they should **fall**, he tells us that **when they shall fall they shall be holpen** ; not specifying *how.* Some have thought that God Almighty will raise up for them a Saviour like Esther the Queen. Others suppose they will be helped by God's destroying the official commissioned with their hurt.

But many shall join themselves unto them refers perhaps to the deserters ; this particular word being used of those who enter a religion ; cp. Is. lvi. 6. In spite then of God's helping those who fall ' by the sword and the flame,' many will adopt this man's religion, owing to the flattery which he will employ with them. With these **flatteries** compare *supra* 21. This prince then, too, has *flatteries* whereby he draws men into his faith.

35. He tells us first what will happen to the followers of the teachers, how they shall fall, but how God will help them and deal mercifully with them ; then what he will do with the wise themselves. They too, he says, will fall.

The terms **to refine and to purify** etc. are used of **the teachers**, but not of their followers, because the followers merely *follow* their predecessors, and when they see the teachers fall, their hands will be weakened. If the *falling* of the teachers be by sword and flame, they will say 'if God has delivered over our teachers, what can we expect ? ' Their hands will therefore be weakened, for they will say 'if our religion were true, God would not have delivered up our teachers, even as He did not deliver up Hananiah, Mishael, and Azariah.' If however *they shall fall* refer to their *leaving the faith*, like *supra* 14, of the disciples of Jesus, this will be worse than their death, for they will say 'had our religion been true, our teachers would not have departed from it, but would have remained in it, even as Hananiah, Mishael, and Azariah abode.' Therein shall be the test : since he that will stand, shall stand, and not be affected by what happens to the teachers ; whereas he whose faith is not good will depart from the religion. Hence he says to **refine and purify,** which words we shall explain on xii. 10. Then he states that this will happen to them and to the teachers when some time still remains before the end.

36–39. **Shall do according to his will** : possibly he refers to the empire generally, from the establishment of the state of Ishmael to the end of their history, in his account of the ten things beginning with **shall do** and ending with **divide for a price.** Or he may refer to the chief of these 'arms' who shall waste the sanctuary, and stop the *Ḥaǵǵ*. Both views are possible. Now we have already heard what he will do with Edom, Israel, and the sanctuary ; so he now goes back to tell us the general principles of his conduct.

(1) **He shall do according to his will** : compare what we said about the 'ram' and the 'he-goat;' it means that his commands are carried out, that he does what he pleases, that no one opposes his will, or makes head against him, owing to the might of his state ; and that he attains what he desires.

(2) **And he shall exalt himself and magnify himself above every god** : observe that in this chapter six *gods* are mentioned :

   a. **He shall magnify himself above every GOD.**
   b. **Shall speak marvellous things against the GOD OF GODS.**
   c. **Neither shall he regard the GOD of his fathers.**
   d. **Nor regard any GOD.**
   e. **He shall honour the GOD of fortresses.**
   f. **A GOD whom his fathers knew not.**

None of these except *b* refers to the Creator (cp. Deut. x. 17). The rest refer to deities other than Him. Of three of these it is said that he will not regard them, but magnify himself against them ; but two of them will be honoured by him (*e* and *f*). We are not told whether he will or will not serve the Creator, but merely that *he shall speak marvellous things,* cp. vii. 25. Why does he say of the *god of fortresses* that he will *honour* him, not *serve* him, and of all besides the Creator and *e* and *f* that he will not *regard* them? Most probably it means that he will profess to serve the Almighty Creator, but will say of him what is impossible. If it refer to the *kingdom* (i.e. the Caliphate) since its rise, the fact is shewn in their language and the popular belief; but if it refer to *this last*, then it is again a statement about the system which he will promulgate. Of the other deities he says **he shall magnify himself above all**; which does not mean that he shall *magnify himself* against the idols themselves, but against their worshippers; for he will revile their creeds.

Neither shall he regard the god of his fathers refers to the creeds of his fathers who served idols, if Pāsūl (Muḥammad) be meant; if *the last* be signified, it will mean that he will annul their present system, and in consequence ravage the house.

Nor the desire of women: Jerusalem, which the peoples and nations used to glorify. He arranged that it should no longer be the Qiblah, turning his back to it, and his face to the place whither they went on pilgrimage. If it refer to *the last king*, it will refer to the house whither the pilgrims went, which he will destroy. Very likely, however, the words *the desire of women* refer to a male image kept in their Qiblah; hence the words come between *the god of his fathers* and *any god*, indicating that it refers to a *special* idol.

Regard signifies *turn to;* observe this, because the word occurs three times in this passage (once in ver. 30, twice in this verse), and the meaning in all three is the same.

The god of fortresses: either the name of a particular idol, *Alāt* or *El-Uzzā* as some have thought—both are familiar—or some other; or the word *Mā'uzzim* may refer to a particular people of that name, mentioned again in ver. 39. They then will have a god and a religion which he will think fit to reverence and not to overthrow. This god he will **honour** merely; the other he will **honour with gold and silver**, etc.

And with pleasant things: i.e. handsome vessels (Ezra viii. 27).

And he shall deal with etc. may mean one of two things: (1) he shall war with them because they will not obey him; and those that submit to him and adopt his tenets will receive from him honour and gifts and promotion (**whosoever acknowledgeth him**, etc.); or (2) the last clause explains how *he shall deal with them*, viz. **whosoever acknowledgeth he will increase with glory**. Apparently, then, these *Mā'uzzim* have two creeds or two idols; one of which he shall uphold (ver. 38 a), but not the other (**with a strange god**). There will be a variety then in their creeds; and this king will approve of one idol to be worshipped, but not the other. We are told of three things that he will do with those who agree to his tenets:

a. **He will increase their glory**: referring to the wealth and office that he will bring them.

b. **He shall cause them to rule over many.**

c. He will give them lands; **he shall divide land for a price**, i.e. lands of high value; or it may mean that he will make this serve for a price, the price for discarding their faith and adopting his. And it is this which will ruin them 'that forsake the holy covenant;' when they see that all who adopt his faith are elevated to these stations, whereas those who will not assent to his tenets are slain or burnt. They will therefore abandon their religion; and thereby great multitudes of our people have been ruined, from the foundation of this empire till now; many, too, in the West have apostatised. As for Israel, when God shewed His wonders in Egypt and Sinai, the people ('the mixed multitude') believed in *their* religion for fear of the sword, but not in hope of promotion; and what God has enjoined on us in our Law is that if any one become a proselyte we are to feed him with our food as we feed the orphans or widows (Deut. xxiv. 19), but by no means to confer upon him eminent rank.

And he shall prosper (ver. 36) shews that he will succeed in all his doings, until the wrath of God against his people be ended; and after the reign of this dynasty there shall be no other; it is the last of the dynasties which shall oppress Israel.

40. **And at the time of the end** : this expression includes two things : (1) the *end* of the success of this dynasty; (2) the *end* of the indignation against Israel.

In the end then the tables will be turned; at the first appearance of the 'Little Horn' it warred with the king of the south and took from him three thrones, as we explained at vii. 24, viz. Syria and the capitals, and then took from the king of the north 'Iráq and Khorasán; and went on conquering and taking city after city (cp. ver. 24) up to the Caspian Gates. But when his success shall have come to an end, these two kings—of the north and of the south—shall turn against him (here *a* and *b*). Some portion of the operations of the king of the south has been realised in our time : I refer to certain battles wherein he has taken from the Moslems *Antioch, Tarsus, 'Ayn Zarbah* and that region; but more events are still to come. The king of the north however has not as yet done anything. He says of the king of the south that he shall *push at him*, because he is near him, and shall come from near Syria; of the king of the north that he shall *whirl against him*, because he shall come from near the Caspian Gates.

We promised that when we came to this verse we would explain the import of the phrases 'king of the north,' 'king of the south.' Many scholars suppose the king of the north to refer to the *king of Arabia*, because the latter took from the king of the north Baghdad, which had been the royal city of the Mágús. We shall shew how this difficulty can be solved.

You must know that the four kingdoms mentioned in the dreams of Nebuchadnezzar and Daniel are divided as follows. The first is a *world-empire;* now the rulers of the whole world are not named after any particular quarter, but after their chief city, e.g. 'king of Babylon;' not 'king of the east, west,' etc.; no such phrase can be found used of the king of the Chaldees, nor of the kings of the Medes and Persians, nor of Alexander, the first king of the Greeks. Only after his death, when his kingdom was divided among his four scholars (xi. 4), does he begin to speak of a 'king of the north' or 'of the south.' Now if the empire of Islám were in any one of the quarters—north or south—he might very well use of it the terms 'king of the north' or 'of the south.' As however that empire has seized countries in all four quarters, it cannot be named after any one of them. This principle is obviously correct. The king of Islām then can be neither. Hence he says the king of the south shall *push at him*, sc. at the *king* mentioned in ver. 36. If the king of the south *pushes at him*, *he* cannot be the king of the south. Similarly he says with reference to him that *the king of the north shall whirl against him*, i.e. come against him like a whirlwind; it is clear then that the king of Islām cannot be king of the north.

With chariots and with horsemen and with many ships: he does not specify which of the two shall come with them ; probably the king of the north will come to him *with chariots and horsemen*, while the king of the south does so on the sea *with ships;* cp. Num. xxiv. 24.

Observe *he shall come*, not *they;* which would have referred to both kings together, so that we should have supposed the two would assist each other against him. Now we should not know which *will come* from the words of Daniel; but this has been explained by another prophet, Joel son of Pethuel. He has written three chapters (commencing respectively at i. 2, ii. 1, and iii. 9) ; the first of which refers to Nebuchadnezzar, the second to the king of the north mentioned here (ii. 20 *I will remove far off from you the northern;* we shall presently explain how this shall be), the third to Gog.

The Islāmitic prince established at Baghdad—not the Abbaside—is from the north ; now they were originally unbelievers, but will be associated with the Abbaside Caliph ; and the chief of these *arms* will certainly take that city, sc. Baghdad, and they will be repulsed before him, and perhaps he will kill some of them; after which they shall rise up against those before whom they were repulsed, and make for Babylon, as the prophets foretold. See Isaiah xiii. 1, Jeremiah li. They say of them *they shall not regard silver or gold,* inasmuch as they will only desire to take vengeance for their sufferings at the hands of those who took their city, and shall gather together and come against them. They are referred to here in the words *and the king of the north shall sweep against him;* and the words *he shall enter into the countries, and shall overflow and pass through* indicate that he shall enter the realm of the king who took Baghdad from the hands of the Abbasides, and shall conquer the land of Babylon with the sword ; at his arrival a number of Israelites shall go out, directing their steps to the land of Israel; cp. Jer. l. 5. Then the king of the north shall direct his steps towards the territory of this king, and shall go out from Babylon to Syria, conquering every city he passes with the sword, it not being his primary intention to have a royal throne established for him, but only to destroy the cities that are under the sway of the lord of Islām. He will kill all whom he meets (**he shall stretch forth his hand also upon the countries**) ; and he is to come to the land of Israel (**he shall enter also into the glorious land**).

Shall be overthrown: i.e. most of the cities and villages in the land of Israel, and all the sea-coast.

But these shall be delivered out of his hand: Edom, i.e. Djebel-eshsharā, **Moab,** and a portion of the **children of Ammon.** We are not told the reason of this; he cannot pass them over through weakness, since these countries are not more powerful than Babylon and Egypt; rather he does not trouble himself about them, seeing that they have no state nor royalty nor wealth; he will not therefore regard them; many Israelites however will pass over thither (cp. Is. xvi. 4); and some have thought that they will pass over thither before this king; the Scripture moreover (Joel *l. c.*) shews that Israel will be in Zion at the time. Next he will pass over into the **land of Egypt,** that too being Islāmitic territory; and this is the only country which is said to be **plundered,** owing to the treasures and riches which it contains (ver. 43).

The Libyans and Ethiopians shall be at his steps : he will be *followed* at the time by certain Ethiopians and Libyans; or, perhaps, on his sojourn in Egypt he shall *destroy* the Ethiopians and Libyans, who are in Egyptian territory.

44. But tidings shall trouble him : when he comes to the western frontier of the province of Egypt, there shall reach him *tidings* from the east and the north, sc. of the entrance of Israel from the wilderness into Palestine, as we shall explain at length afterwards; and when they enter it from the wilderness they will conquer it with the sword, and their enemies shall be repulsed before them. When this reaches the king of the north, who will at the time be at the extremity of Egypt, he will return to Syria to **destroy and utterly make away with many,** i.e. Israel, who entered in large numbers. But when the news of his return reaches Israel, they will gather together on Mount Zion, and do what Joel says (chap. ii. 1 and foll.). This they will do at the time when he **plants the tents of his palace;** it is thought that he will pitch his tents at ʿAmwās; now between that place and Jerusalem are four parasangs; or else that he will encamp in the wilderness of Tekoa, which also is a vast plain. And when he spreads out his tents there, intending to come to them the next morning in Jerusalem, God will send His angel Michael, who shall destroy his entire army; they shall all die, and remain cast about and putrefying on the face of the plain till they decompose and stink (*v.* Joel *l. c.*). Thence we know that this section deals with the king of the north, and relates what will happen to Israel at his coming.

XII.

1. And at that time refers to xi. 40; and signifies the times specified in vii. 25.

Shall stand (instead of 'shall come' or some similar word) shews that the *standing* shall last three years and a half; and he *shall stand* for two purposes : (1) to put an end to the monarchies (*v.* x. 21); (2) to deliver Israel from certain calamities that are to befall them. Before Michael was called 'your prince;' here **the great prince,** shewing that he is a mighty angel.

And there shall be a time of trouble, such as never was since shews that there can have been nothing *like it* since the confusion of tongues; not that there has been nothing of the same *kind;* since there never have been wanting famine, sword, plague, sickness, poverty, and the other things found in the world, nor religious persecution either (we have seen Nebuchadnezzar require Hananiah etc. to worship the image he had made); it can only refer to a state like that which Oded the prophet described to king Asa, when 'there was no peace to him that went out,' etc. (2 Chr. xv. 8; cp. Zech. viii. 10). The chief source of these afflictions is that the 'Arms' will seek to take the kingdom of the Abbasides, coming from Babylon, as the learned tell us; and also that they will prevent the pilgrims from praying in Mecca, where they used to pray, and will destroy the remembrance of the Man of Wind; then the sword will come between them, and the 'Arms' will prevail against them, and will make mighty havoc among them; some of them will flee into the 'forest in Arabia' (Is. xxi. 13), hungry and thirsty; 'for they fled away from the swords.' The reason of their turning into that region is that they know it is impossible for them to return to their own cities because the *Conspirator* has already taken possession of them; they will take counsel therefore to flee to their kinsmen, who assent to their opinions, and to stay with them; these will come to meet them with food and water, that their souls may live. From that time civil war shall commence in Ishmael. The *Conspirators* however shall not get the empire, because their chief will require men to abandon their religion, a religion about four hundred years old, and indeed without any miracle, save the sword; the sword therefore shall fall among them, and at that time the sultan's courts shall cease, there shall be no longer a royal throne, nor business on the roads, nor police and guardians in the cities, no shops open, no merchants travelling, no rain falling from the sky, no husbandman or vine-dresser, no man with any possible means of subsistence. Then shall be the great famine and the great plague, with the sword; and then shall be accomplished the 'destruction and that decreed;' only a few men will be left, the cities shall be wasted and the roads desolate, the nation occupied with each other; then shall Israel flee out from among them to the 'wilderness of the nations.' To this condition do the words of the text allude. The king of the north shall come to Babylon, and the Israelites come out from Babylon into their own land before the great confusion. At that time there shall be an arousing in the land of Israel (?) before they depart (cp. Jer. li. 55):

Thy people shall escape: since the destruction will alight upon the Gentiles, as was said before; but from the addition **every one that shall be found written in the book** we see that not every Jew shall escape, but those that are written, and those only; not the wicked among Israel who did not 'repent at that time' (2 Chr. ii. 16 and Deut. iv. 30); those who repent shall survive; but those who do not repent shall perish by the sword by the hand of the enemy, or by the plague of God (Amos ix. 10).

Observe that Is. lxv. 10 uses the same phrase (*written*) of the works of the wicked, that is used of those of the righteous by Malachi iii. 16. Plainly the phrase here cannot refer to both good and bad, but must be interpreted as above. This is explained by Isaiah iv. 3, 'Every one that is written unto life in Jerusalem;' shewing that only those of them shall escape who are *written unto life;* adding afterwards, *when God shall have washed* away the filth of the daughters of Zion, indicating that the persons *written unto life* are those that are washed clean of filth and blood. [Of the others], those that are among the Gentiles shall fall by the sword ; those that do not perish by their hand, but go out with the people to the 'wilderness of the peoples,' shall be slain by God Almighty (Ezek. xx. 38). I cannot possibly give a full account of what will happen at that time, since that would require a book for itself; I have suggested in every book of the three portions of Scripture that I have explained as much as each passage allowed.

2. At that time many of the dead shall rise. **Many,** as in Est. viii. 17; not *all* the dead shall rise, but only *some;* we have explained this on Ezek. xxxvii. at length, and have said a little about it on Job xiv. 12; here let us add a little more. Let us observe, first, that he promises **the deliverance of the nation** (ver. 1) ; and then the resurrection of the dead ; indicating that the living and the dead both shall see the salvation. Now just as he divided the *living* into two portions, one to survive and one to perish, so he divides those that are to rise from the dead into two portions, one to **everlasting life,** and the other to **contempt.** Ezekiel has shewn that those who are to rise are people of the Captivity (xxxvii. 11), 'Behold, they say, Our bones are dried up, and our hope is lost,' which is not the condition of those who died under the monarchy. Similarly, Isaiah says (xxvi. 19), 'Thy dead shall live, awake and sing, ye that dwell in the dust,' which is to be compared with the phrase here, **them that sleep in dust of the ground** ; only there the prophet confined himself to the mention of the saints of the nation, whereas here he speaks of both classes together.

Shame and everlasting contempt : see Isaiah *ad fin.* : 'They shall look on the carcases of the men who sinned against the LORD ;' a description of those who died during the Captivity, having offended God by capital transgressions.

To shame and eternal contempt : **shame,** because they used to cast reproaches on the best of the nation, who sighed, and were troubled and vexed at what had befallen the nation and the house of God (cp. Ps. lxix. throughout), and would eat and drink and let their time pass in amusement and enjoyment, which God has forbidden us (Hos. ix. 1) ; nor was it sufficient for them that they did not do what God enjoined, but they must abhor those who obeyed Him, and reproach them for practising the Law, mourning and fasting ; hence, at the end of the Psalm quoted (ver. 22), he curses them ('Let their table before them become a snare,' etc.). Now when the Mount of Olives splits, and a vast gorge is formed between the halves, this gorge will become the place of punishment of these wicked ones ; and whenever there is a sabbath-day or a new moon, Israel will go out on the first day of the week or on the second day of the month to these prisoners, and see what has befallen them ; cp. Is. lxv. 15. These evil-doers used to reproach the saints wrongfully ; they shall *reproach* the evil-doers justly.

Contempt : when they hear their bitter cry, because of the pain of the fire and the bite of the serpents, for *their worm shall never die;* and **eternal,** because there is no end to it. Wherever the word *eternal* occurs there is no proof, intellectual or traditional, that there is an end ; on the contrary, reason makes it necessary that the punishment of the wicked shall be everlasting, without term. We must now observe that whenever the text has an intelligible expression with a possible literal meaning, it is not allowable to explain it away by abandoning that literal sense; it is necessary therefore that the words **those that sleep in the dust of the earth** must be taken literally, and must not be referred to the people of the Captivity, who, during that captivity, might be compared to the dead; especially as there is nothing in this chapter but what is to be taken literally. We are familiar with the fact that when there was the Vision, which Daniel saw, Gabriel interpreted it to him because it had an allegorical meaning; but when he came to the words 'two thousand three hundred,' etc., he said 'the vision is true,' meaning what we have there stated; similarly, at the beginning of this section, he said, 'I will tell thee the truth;' consequently the whole of this section is to be taken literally, so that this verse must be taken literally; nor is this refuted either by reason or tradition, as we have shewn. It stands besides in our records that God raised to life the child of the Shunammite, and likewise the dead man who touched the bones of Elisha; since, therefore, such a thing has happened and is no impossibility, that resurrection of the dead of Israel, which God has promised, shall be accomplished too. And since he says **these to shame and eternal contempt**, the state of the rewarded and of the punished alike shall be everlasting. God will raise the dead of the Captivity at the time of the Deliverance; the dead of the monarchy, on the other hand, when all the dead rise, to be rewarded or punished, which shall be at the *creation of the new heavens and the new earth*. Doubtless some great change will take place in this heaven and earth (see Is. xl. 26). Job refers to the same (xiv. 12): 'Till there be no more heaven they shall not wake.' It is well known among all mankind that the resurrection of the dead will take place when this takes place in the heaven and the earth (Job *l. c.*); the resurrection of the dead of Israel, however, shall take place before that. This is a mere fragment that we have given here; it was impossible for us to pass the passage without saying *something* about it.

3. He divides the living and the dead each into two companies, as we saw above. After that he says **the wise**, separating them from the multitude, to shew that their rank is higher than that of the rest of the nation. This all refers to those who will rise from the grave. The brightness of their faces, he says, will be like the colour of the firmament—marvellously bright, like the face of Moses. It is a light wherewith God will cover them, to shew their nobility, while at the same time they take pleasure in it.

They that turn the many to righteousness: those that turned mankind from error to religion. **The many**: so of the priests (Mal. ii. 6), 'And turned away *many* from iniquity.' They directed men to religion by teaching them the Commandments of Jehovah; and at the same time turned them from transgression by busying themselves with the Law of Jehovah, and praying God to direct them to the knowledge of His statutes. They are *those whose way is perfect*: their prayer is recorded and their words expressed in the twenty-two eight-lined stanzas; they are those who say to him that seeks instruction, *Ho, every one that thirsteth, come ye to the waters*. In Isaiah lii.

we are told that *by his knowledge shall my righteous servant justify many;* in that chapter the groaning of the *wise*, and his griefs, and his great knowledge and piety are recorded. These then are referred to in the words **the wise shall shine as the brightness of the firmament,** etc.

Like the stars conveys two ideas : (1) light ; (2) perpetuity and eternity ; it shall not be cut off for ever. This shall God do with them after he has shewn them the *salvation of Israel*, and the rebuilding of Jerusalem. They shall abide a while till they have seen the sight thereof, and then God will remove them to the place of reward. Maybe they will be with the angels above (cp. Zech. iii. 7), in return for their teaching Israel the Law, and turning them from their sins, and lamenting during the Captivity, and forcing themselves to grieve. Others than they engaged Israel in the study of traditions, and took their goods, and fattened their bodies with food and drink, and died merry, not doing their duty, but causing men to sin ; teaching them what would make God angry with them : unquestionably therefore their punishment will be far severer than that of their followers.

4. Hitherto the angel has been explaining what is to happen from the time at which he is speaking till the end of the world, as he said at the beginning of his discourse, **I have come to tell thee what shall be till the end of time.**

And thou Daniel close these words : i. e. leave them as they are. Do not ask for more to be revealed than has been told thee.

And seal the book : ' seal this book of thine at what has been told thee, and expect no more.' Nothing else could be revealed to him about the matter. Therefore he said this, shewing him that there was nothing left to be told him.

To the time of the end : shewing that it should not be revealed to any one till the end of the Captivity ; any one who professes to know the end of the Captivity is a deceiver.

Many shall run to and fro : i. e. the wise and the seekers of knowledge. This *running to and fro* may be of two kinds : (1) They shall run over the countries in search of knowledge, because scholars will be found in every region ; the seekers of knowledge, therefore, will go to and fro to learn from them ; this is expressed by Amos (viii. 12). This shall be at the beginning of their career ; when they seek so ardently, God will make revelations to them. (2) They shall *run to and fro* in God's Word like those who seek treasures, and thereafter **knowledge shall increase ;** knowledge of two things : (*a*) the *commandments;* (*b*) the *end*. God will not reveal the end until they know the commandments. They are the men that fear the LORD, who are *in possession of His secrets*, which cannot be had save by study and search and inquiry into the Word of God : compare the prayers *teach me, O LORD, the way of Thy statutes; open my eyes*. These and similar expressions shew the vanity of the profession of the *traditionalists* like *El-Fayyūmī*, who have destroyed Israel by their writings ; who maintain that the Commandments of God cannot be known by study, because it leads to contradictions ; so that we must follow the tradition of the successors of the prophets, viz. the authors of the Mishnah and Talmud, all whose sayings are from God. So he has led men astray by his lying books, and vouches for the veracity of any one who lies against God. He shall be punished therefore more severely than they, and God shall take vengeance for his people from him and them that are like him.

5. After Daniel had heard all that was said to him, without any other angel being with the one who had been addressing him,—when the angel had finished his speech, he saw two other angels, one with him in the region where he was standing, and the other on the other side.

Other two : this may indicate one of three things :

(1) That he knew that they were not the same angels whom he had seen in the 'Vision' (viii. 13), when one asked the other concerning that of which Daniel was thinking, and that other answered him ; as one of the angels here, too, asks the other *how long* etc., we might have thought they were the same ; the word **other** is therefore inserted to shew that this is not so.

(2) The word *other* may be intended to shew us that the author does not refer to the two angels already mentioned in this chapter (xi. 16, 18), but to two others ; in which case he will at this time have seen *five* angels ; two mentioned above and three here.

(3) The word *other* may be intended to prevent our thinking them the great angel with another ; by its insertion we know that there were *three* angels.

6. **And he said to the man** : i.e. *one* of the angels (not the plur., in which case we might have thought that both had asked him). *Which* of the two we do not know ; nor does he tell him the reason of his seeing the one who neither asked nor answered. Most likely the one who asked was standing on the other side ; while the one who stood with him was intended to allay his fears, or to bring Daniel to hear the question and the answer. Hitherto we did not know that the great angel was standing ; here he explains that he was standing in the air above the water, and not on the ground. He was not one of the angels who habitually descend from heaven to earth, having been sent by God for Daniel's sake only.

How long shall it be to the end of these wonders? The **wonders** are these *tribulations*, which shall come to pass at the last time. **How long?** what shall be their duration?

He answered just as Palmōni answered the first questioner (viii. 13). It was not the questioner's object *to find out himself:* for the angels know the mystery which is *closed up ;* he only asks that Daniel may hear the answer. If any one ask why he did not give this reply without a question, we answer that possibly the angel *would* not have given it unless questioned, seeing that the matter is one of the great mysteries.

7. Notice, too, that he does not answer without an *oath*. The angel, he says, swore an oath, to shew that there can be no alteration ; for it is a period of great length. This oath was not for *Daniel's* sake, but for Israel's, the Israel

that shall be in the time of tribulation. The force of this oath is marked by two things: (1) He raised *both* hands: now an oath with both hands raised is the most forcible kind; cp. Gen. xiv. 2, and 'I have raised my hand,' said by the Creator in a number of places. (2) He swears by the name of God; the most powerful oath, there is none more powerful (cp. Jer. xxiv. 26).

By him that liveth for ever: the Blessed Creator lives eternally. The Hebrew word חַי means (1) *living*, e.g. Gen. vi. 19; (2) as a substantive, *life*, e.g. by the life of Pharaoh, *ibid*. xlii. 16. Here it must be interpreted as (1).

He swore **that it shall be for a time, times, and a half**; exactly the same as the period mentioned in vii. 25.

Here we will collect the passages wherein the *times* connected with the *end* are mentioned. They are eight in all.

(1) Is. xvi. 14. *Within three years, as the years of an hireling, and the glory of Moab shall be brought into contempt.*

(2) Is. xxi. 16. *Within a year, according to the years of an hireling, and all the glory of Kedar shall fall.*

(3) Dan. vii. 25. *And they shall be given into his hand until a time, and times, and half a time.*

(4) Dan. viii. 14. *Unto two thousand and three hundred evenings and mornings.*

(5) Dan. xi. 33. *They shall fall by the sword and by flame, by captivity and by spoil, many days.*

(6) The present passage.

(7) *Infra* 11.

(8) *Infra* 12.

Of (1) (three years) we know both the beginning and the end. It *begins* when 'Moab comes to his sanctuary to pray, and is not able' (ver. 12), i.e. *when the pilgrims desire to pray according to their wont, but are prevented by the Arms*, as we have explained above; it *ends* when 'the glory of Moab is brought into contempt' (ver. 14), i. e. when they become feeble and few in number, 'small and of no account' (*ibid.*), 'with no *ruler*' at their head (*ibid.*).

(2) Commences when 'those that would pray' flee into the forest in Arabia (Is. xxi. 13; *v. supra*), and ends when 'all the glory of Kedar shall fall;' when no 'glory' shall be left to Kedar, and their mighty men shall be few. This is one of the above three years; when *one* of those years is passed their glory shall fall; at the end of the *three* it shall be brought into contempt; i. e. no glory shall be left them at all.

(3) Means, as we have said, either that the time which he shall take about his work in Ishmael and Israel is a 'time, times, and half a time;' or that Israel shall be in the hands of this Conspirator till that period be left till the end; most probably, in my opinion, this person, who is said to be about to put a stop to the pilgrimage and

to destroy the house, and to overthrow the religion of Israel, will continue to do so till that period commences, when he will cease and perish, 'be broken without hand;' so that it does not refer to the duration of his power. Rather, when his reign is over, that period will commence; and when that period commences, the *tribulations* will commence (*v. supra*); and when it ends, they will end. This may be seen from the expression here, it shall be for a time, times, and a half; and when they have made an end of breaking in pieces the power of the holy people, all these things shall be finished. It is clear, therefore, that the tribulations will begin when the times begin, and end when they end.

(4) The *two thousand and three hundred* have already been shewn to be 1350 days; the author says they end when *holiness shall be justified;* their beginning is not told us. Most probably the *tribulations* shall remain upon Israel from the time of the king who shall destroy Mecca and throw the religion of Israel down to the ground for *two thousand and three hundred mornings and evenings :* for one year out of this they shall *fall by the sword,* etc. ; but at the end of the period *holiness shall be justified,* which is the opposite of *truth being cast on the ground.* This may mean either that Elias will appear, or that Israel shall enter their land from 'the wilderness of the Gentiles.' Probably, part of the 2300 falls in the time of the Arms, and part in the 'time and times;' since in them Israel shall depart into 'the wilderness of the Gentiles' (*v. supra*). It is clear, therefore, (1) that *they shall fall by the sword* before the *times;* (2) that part of the 2300 falls in the time of the Arms and part into the general sum of the *times.* Now we have shewn above that עַד means a single time, and that עִדָּנִין refers to periods *more than one,* not necessarily two. Most probably this period is the same as that mentioned in ver. 11, *ubi vide.*

Breaking in pieces the power of the holy people refers to the tribulations which fell on Israel during these years. Observe that there is a time when tribulation shall be on Israel only, and a time when tribulation shall be on the whole world. See Jer. xxx. 5, where *we have heard a voice* refers to the news which shall reach Israel, cp. Is. xxiv. 16 ; and *fear and not peace* refers to tribulations which shall be common to the whole world ; cp. Is. *l. c.* 17, Jer. *l. c.* 6, 'Wherefore do I see every man with hands upon his loins,' followed by (ver. 7), 'it is even the time of Jacob's trouble.' Which last may indicate one of two things : either what will happen to Israel in the time of the Arms, mentioned above, which will be a *time of trouble,* or what will happen to them after they have entered their land from the 'wilderness of the Gentiles;' in which case it will refer to three events :

(*a*) What will come upon them from the 'northern,' see on xi. 44.

(*b*) The tribulation mentioned in Ps. lxxxiii, which refers to the 'tents of the Edomites and Ishmaelites.'

(*c*) Gog, the last tribulation that shall befall them.

The order of tribulations then will be—(1) in the time of the Arms ; (2) from the northern king ; (3) from the 'tents of Edom ;' (4) Gog. During all these years the purification shall go on ; cp. Zech. xiii. 9.

8. Daniel says, 'I heard the voice of the angel saying "for a time, times,"' etc., but **I did not understand.** He did not understand three things :

(*a*) He did not understand the length of a מוֹעֵד (*v.* on vii. 14): עֵדָן, עֵת, מוֹעֵד all three mean the same : a עֵת may be the twinkling of an eye, an hour, or anything more, e. g. years. The words *for a time* therefore conveyed no indication of a *definite period*.

(*b*) He did not know when these *times* commenced.

(*c*) The word *times* conveyed no notion of the *number* of times.

And I said, O my lord : as much as to say 'I do not understand what thou sayest :—if thou canst tell me, what will be the end of these things?' The angel answered two things, (*a*) his question *what shall be the end?* (*b*) his saying *I did not understand* (though the angel did not hear this last).

9. **Are shut up** : cp. viii. 26, 'shut up the vision;' only that was said to Daniel, and would not prove that no one else understood them; whereas the words 'for they are shut up and sealed' indicate that they are hidden *from the children of men.*

Till the time of the end : till then they are closed; thereafter they shall be revealed.

He adds that at that time many **shall purify themselves** ; indicating that the end shall not come till after the purification of the nation from the transgressors.

Here we must pause a moment. Let us observe that there are certain texts which contain signs, the occurrence of which is to indicate the expected deliverance. These signs are of two classes; one consisting of the action of the nation, the other of the action of God. The first consists in our returning to God, the second in many things which we shall recount. As for our returning to God, it is mentioned in the following passages : Deut. iv. 30, xxx, Hos. xiv. 2, Jer. iii. 14. Only they will not return to God till after great afflictions, as has been said before in this chapter, ver. 1. Cp. Is. lix. 20. Some of the Jews have been misled by Is. lix. 16, 'And he saw that there was no man,' fancying that Israel perhaps would not repent, and the deliverance come to them without repentance. This is an error; could the deliverance come without repentance, God would not have delayed it all this period. We can only say that the people of the Captivity at the end of this last dynasty are divided into two classes : a good class, who will seek knowledge and strive thereafter, and will multiply fasting and lamentation, and put on sackcloth, and grovel in ashes, humiliating themselves, and asking God to deliver His people ; and a class sunk in transgression, submerged in the commission of capital offences, at the same time abhorring the pious sect, and accusing them and looking upon them as hypocrites, excommunicating them and driving them away, because they will not assent to their doctrine, nor adopt their faith. As for the first sect, they are those whose conduct is described in Is. lviii. 2, 'yet they seek me daily and delight to know my ways,' where the author complains of wrong being committed in dealings and judgments between them and their poor, which they do not redress, and that they do not care sufficiently for the weak; see the chapter throughout. But to the great section, the mass of the nation, he says, ' Behold the LORD'S hand is not shortened that it cannot save ; but your iniquities have separated between you and your God; for your hands are defiled with blood,' down to 'yea, truth is lacking' (ver. 15). It is to this verse that the words ' He saw that there was no man' refer. The words ' therefore his arm brought salvation unto him ' are a prophecy of tribulations which shall befall these evil-doers till certain of them repent, and the rest perish ; that the former words refer to the whole nation is in the highest degree improbable. To the first sect he says, ' Hear the word of the LORD, ye that tremble at His word;' where he tells them that their brethren hate them and revile them, saying at the same time, 'God is pleased with us, and for our sake the redemption will come ;' in which they are deceived. This, then, is a partial account of what has been told us about their return to God, after which the redemption will come. A partial account, too, has been given on ver. 4. Let us now explain what will be the course of Israel's conversion to God, what will be done by their chiefs and what by the mass of them.

The chiefs will turn to the Law at the time when they have come into the most miserable state of poverty and straitened circumstances, and their enemies among the nation and the great sect are most numerous.

They and their followers are the *people whose way is perfect*. The great sect will wane, those who follow the sayings of their predecessors ; one after another will confess, till the two thousand three hundred begin. At the time of the demolition of the thrones of the dynasties, when the people are merged in the *tribulations*, the doctrines of the chiefs of the Jews shall be exploded, as well as their authority ; and the enemy, the temporal lord, shall seek them out. At that time it shall become clear to the multitude, who accept their authority, that the truth is with the sect, and that by it the redemption shall come. They will return to the Law and abandon the tradition of those who cling to the books of their ancestors; and then God shall no longer delay the redemption. This we have fully and satisfactorily explained in the Commentary on Canticles ; it would be too long to repeat it here. This is what we are told about *our* action : what is told us of *God's* action may also be divided into two parts. One refers to our condition prior to the redemption at our repentance ; this is recounted in Deut. xxxii, where it is said that ' the LORD shall judge His people,' and that God shall take vengeance for His people upon their enemies, and restore them to forgiveness when they are at the height of their trouble, and none of them has any power : 'when He seeth that their power is gone,' which refers (1) to the weakness of poverty ; (2) to the fact that there are no royal ministers among them, as there were when they had judges, governors, etc., who attended to their affairs, so that they became poor after having been rich in respect of rulers, and rich in merchants, and resigned their possessions : *v.* Zech. viii. 10. This is the meaning of *their power is gone ;* to which is added, 'and there is none shut up or left at large :' i. e. none of them has power to bind or loose any more. The second refers to the condition of the Gentiles: *ibid.* 35, 'Vengeance is mine, and recompense;' indicating that so long as the affairs of the Gentiles are well regulated, we shall remain in our distress, and in the continuation of our Captivity; but when they begin to be reversed, their distress shall come, and they shall perish quickly, 'for the day of their calamity is at hand.'

There are three signs of salvation: when they appear, the wise shall feel confident of redemption. Hence he says **they are sealed and closed till the time of the end** : when the end approaches it shall be revealed. God in His mercy has seen fit to hide it from them; because, if they had known how long the Captivity was to last, multitudes of the people would have perished [apostatised]. He left them therefore in hope, expecting the deliverance: one after another will be converted, and God's anger will cease. And when the time comes, these signs will appear, and they shall know that the time is come at last; they will cling to their faith and not abandon it, save a few, as we said above.

10. **Many shall purify themselves** : the people are divided into three classes, excluding a fourth, as I shall now explain. He said above (xi. 35) **to refine them and to purify** ; that is here repeated, to shew that it is to be at the time of the end. **Purify** literally means *winnow* or *sift*, e. g. *grain* from *chaff, stones, earth;* cf. Jer. iv. 11 ; or as the money-changer separates the good Dirham from the bad, or clears the good from the bad mixed up with them. The meaning is: there are among the people some who are good and repentant, who are the wheat; and also wicked ones who eat unlawful food, and change sabbaths and festivals, commit abominations, and do not repent. God therefore will distinguish between them by destroying the bad, some of whom will perish by the sword, others by pestilence; *v. supra*, and compare Ezek. xx. 38, Amos ix. 10. As yet we have two classes, the perfectly righteous, and the completely wicked. Now he says **and shall whiten themselves**, with reference to a class who are intermediate in religion, who keep the commandments, but not perfectly, being like a garment which has got marks of foulness, which requires that those stains be got rid of. So it must be washed; cp. Is. lxiv. 5. When the tribulations come near, they will discard the sins that are about them; cp. Jer. ii. 22. These are a stage below those of whom it is said **they shall purify themselves**, the latter being perfectly righteous, whereas these are intermediate. These are descriptions of the people who will come out of the great sect.

And be refined : a description of the great sect themselves, who are compared to silver or gold mixed with *dross*, i.e. the doctrines which they have inherited from their fathers, so that they assent to what their chiefs tell them, and confess it. They therefore shall undergo tribulations; God will *refine* them, so that they shall discard these doctrines and return to the Law of Jehovah. This describes their state shortly before the appearance of Elijah, as we have explained elsewhere (i.e. in the Psalms).

But the wicked shall do wickedly : i. e. those that do wickedly against the covenant (xi. 32). They are the portion to whom I alluded on the words 'they shall purify themselves.' He means they shall transgress more and more; **and not understand**, i. e. pay no regard to that which is written in the Book of God, in which case they might have turned to God, or might never have abandoned His religion; they are the people who *allegorise the text*, as we said before.

But they that be wise shall understand : they shall turn to the Book of God and understand its contents, and know that what God said in His Book has come to pass. Understanding that, they will make Israel understand it, who will then cling to the Law and throw off the sins that are upon them; *they shall be strong and do exploits* (xi. 32).

11. The angel now explains to him what he did not understand in ver. 7 (*v. supra*); shewing him that **a time and times** refers to twelve hundred and ninety days; that **a time** is restricted to a year, and **times** to two years and no more; and that **a half** is something less than a year; further that this sum of four years all but a fraction commences *from the time that the continual shall be removed. The continual* has now been mentioned three times, of which the first is—

viii. 11. ' It took away from him the continual, and the place of his sanctuary was cast down.'

There he did not state who does this; later on he says that it is to be done by certain rulers, *arms from him* that *shall stand up* (xi. 31), where he adds that 'they shall profane the sanctuary and make the abomination desolate.' Which last he repeats here, to shew Daniel, and us too, that the *times* commence from the time of the removal of the *continual;* and that at the end of the twelve hundred and ninety days the tribulations shall be ended. This he explained to Daniel, and taught him what he did not know. Now we must give the reason why he says *a time, times, and a half*, with the word *time* once in the singular and once in the plural, instead of saying *three times*. We will answer this question as best we can. These times being *years*, as we have said, begin with the time of *the removal of the continual;* Isaiah's *three years*, as we said, are identical with the *time and times;* at the end of one year of these three, Isaiah tells us, 'the glory of Kedar will cease, and his warriors be few;' that year is therefore the *time*, which is distinguished here as the first year of the three, wherein 'the whole glory of Kedar shall perish;' the other two years (or *times*) will be of one tenor, viz. in them 'the glory of Moab' will be finally 'brought to contempt.' Isaiah does not speak of the *half-year*, because it is in the time after the fall of Ishmael : probably 'half' is an approximation merely, being really more than half, and lasting from the time of the conquest of Babylon by the king of the north till Israel enter Palestine from the ' wilderness of the peoples,' after which the king of the north shall perish. Next, it is clear that *as the years of a hireling* refers to lunar years; this will make the three years thirty-six months, or a thousand and sixty-five days, which will leave out of the twelve hundred and ninety days two hundred and twenty-five, which make *half a time*, as we have said, the word יצח in the Hebrew language being sometimes used for an exact half, sometimes for slightly more or less, as we shewed from Isaiah. Here it is rather more; and during this half-time there will be an excitement in the world caused by the king of the north, starting from the time when Ishmael is destroyed and left without a chief. He will go out from Babylon till he perishes in the land of Israel, as we have explained at xi. 44.

12. These days are not the same as those mentioned above, nor are we told when they are to commence, nor when they end. They do not come within the days of the kingdoms. The person who **waits** must already have got into the *time, times,* etc.; he will then count them, knowing that they are a short period, which will [soon] end, when he will be freed from the *tribulations,* and then he shall come to these thirteen hundred and thirty-five days. These persons are the good, *whose way is perfect,* and their followers. This has been noticed by Moses in Psalm xc. At the end of that psalm he says 'with long life will I satisfy him;' some people will doubtless die during the *time and times;* hence he says **blessed is he that waiteth and reaches,** since not every one that waits will reach. Most probably they begin from the destruction of the king of the north, when Israel will begin to prosper and their power to increase. In them will be the second gathering of Israel, prophesied by Jeremiah (xxxv. 9). In those days the Messiah will appear and Israel shall be secure.

At the end of those days Gog shall come, and God shall deal vengeance upon him; that will be on the last day of the thirteen hundred and thirty-five. After Gog shall be the reign of the Messiah over the people of the whole world. The thirteen hundred and thirty-five are separated from the latter, because in them there will be some troubles, though they will be after the consummation of the monarchies, and most of what we expect will come to pass in them.

13. He said above (ver. 9) *go Daniel,* without saying *whither.* Here he explains this: go, i.e. pass away, thou and Israel in thy sorrow to thy grave, as the rest have passed away till the **time of the end.**

And thou shalt rest: sc. in thy grave; cp. Is. lvii. 2. We do not know where that grave was; most probably in Babylon, as he did not go up to the Second Temple, as seems clear; since, in the third year of king Cyrus, he was in Babylon; whereas the people had gone up in Cyrus' first year.

Thou shalt stand: i.e. rise from the grave.

In thy lot: either (1) the place of the reward which he had earned; or (2) the land of Israel, wherein he had a *lot;* so that he is to live a long time at the time of the redemption, and rejoice in the sanctuary of the Almighty, and the reunion of the nation. After this God shall take him alive to the place of reward among the angels.—I prefer the second view.

Then he tells him *when* he shall rise to be rewarded; **at the end of the days:** i.e. most probably at the end of the thirteen hundred and thirty-five days God shall raise him up and bring him to his *lot;* and at that time, too, shall be that resurrection of their dead which God has promised: 'Behold, I will open your graves, and cause you to come up out of your graves, O my people' (Ezek. xxxvii. 12); and then, too, He will shew them what He has promised (cp. Ps. cvi. 4).

Let us ask God Almighty to bring this near in our days and yours; not to deny us or you abundant knowledge of His Book, revelation of His secrets, and attachment to His faith; to sanctify His sanctuary, and shew us its restoration; *for the sake of His great name, and His abundant mercies.* Amen.

We have explained this chapter in accordance with what we have heard from the teachers of the Captivity, or read in their books, so far as those theories seemed probable. God will forgive and pardon any slips or errors, in His goodness and gentleness. We shall now follow this with a statement of the views of others about these times and the end, that any one who cares to know them may do so. The scholars who preceded Joseph ibn Bakhtawī explained the 2300, 1290, and 1335 as *years;* the Rabbanites, too, spoke of the *end*, and fancied that from the third year of Cyrus to the *end* would be 1335 years; the term is passed some years since, so that their opinion has been disproved, and that of their followers; similarly El-Fayyūmī explained it years, and has been proved false; he had however some marvellous inventions with reference to *the time and times.* He was answered by Salmon ben Jerucham; whom we need not in our turn answer, since his term is past and the end not arrived. Certain of the Karaites, too, made the 2300 years date from the exodus from Egypt; that term too is past years ago, and their prophecy not come true. Salmon ben Jerucham, in his Commentary on Ps. lxxiv. 9, denied that it was possible to ascertain the *end;* but on Ps. cii. 14 he offered a date which is passed and falsified. He agreed with many others in interpreting the 2300 and 1290 as days, but differed about the interpretation of the *time of the removal of the continual,* which, he thought, meant the *destruction of the Second Temple.* Benjamin Nahawendī agreed with him in the latter point, but differed from him about the days being days and not years. Benjamin took a separate view in believing that they were years. Salmon ben Jerucham referred the 1290 to the three and a half spoken of in chap. x. 27 ('for the half of the week he shall cause the sacrifice and the oblation to cease').

Each of the commentators has taken a different line, and all have gone wrong in making the days years. Benjamin Nahawendī, indeed, made the 2300 date from the destruction of Shiloh, and *from the time of the removal of the continual* from the destruction of the Second Temple; this leaves still some 400 years; but this is a delusion.

All these theories are confuted by two facts:

(1) Their inventors profess to know the *end*, whereas the Scripture says that the matter is *closed and sealed;* any one therefore who professes to know it before *the time of the end* is professing what cannot be true.

(2) They make the days years. Now we know that where he speaks of *weeks of years* he expressly distinguishes them from *weeks of days;* consequently none of the three sums mentioned (2300, 1290, 1335) can be years. All must be days. The one commentator who made them days supposed the three periods to follow one upon the

other ; i. e. he made the 2300 the first *time*, the 1290 the second, the 1335 the third. He fancied there was no statement of the number of days of the *half-time;* he suggested that it might be half the first *time*. Assuredly this is more probable than the views of the others.

We have now given the views that seem to us clear or probable. Let us now ask God to pardon any slips or errors; for what we have given is not any positive opinion, but merely a probability. The Almighty himself has said that *the words are shut up and sealed till the time of the end.* At that time it shall be revealed at the hand of the wise; *the wise shall understand.* God Almighty, in His mercy and loving-kindness, bring near their realisation. Amen.

GLOSSARY.

———◆———

أسعا *now* for الساعة Is. xlviii. 7; spelt اسعد MS. 2474, p. 46ᵃ.

اسفيدروية (Pers.) *tin* MS. 2472, p. 17ᵃ اعنى اسفيدروية כלי חרש كل ما يشاكل.

اَلَّى (ii) for ولد. Is. lix. 4 (הוליד) تاليد.

اللهم *quod si* MS. 2468, p. 106ᵃ يقول القائل اللهم *quod si dixerit aliquis.*
اللهم MS. 2468, p. 5ᵃ. ومعنى اللهم يلحق عارض لا ياكلون MS. 2467, p. 84ᵃ لا يعلم باذ ثم بئر.

أَنْ MS. 2473, p. 85ᵇ اوّل عجنة ان بعجن (the classical language would here have used no particle). Ibid. 64ᵃ من اى موضع ان ندخل. Comm. on Is. ix. 4 كل شى, فى جبل ان يشرف منى Ps. lxi. 2 ان ياخذون منهم, where ان may be kept (omitted by Bargès). MS. 2468, p. 188ᵃ.

أنطة Lat. *antes* (?). For האיל 1 Kings vi. 31.

اَوّل (ii) and (v) تاوّل *to equivocate* MS. 2500 (Comm. on Kings, p. 191ᵇ) حتى اودّيكم اى الرجل الذى تطلبونه وتاوّل فى هذا القول. Used often in this book and elsewhere of 'explaining away' texts of scripture, miracles, etc.; see pp. ١٠. 15, ١٢. 15, ١٢٢. 2, ١٢٨. 6. Compare تاويلات p. ٢٢. 11, 13.

اَوّل امس *nudius tertius* (שלשם) Ex. xxi. 36.

اَوّلة fem. of اول Fleischer, *Kl. Schr.* i. 336; Comm. on Prov. (Paris), p. 4ᵃ فذكر اللفظتين الاولتين. Here, p. ١٢٦, n. 1.

ايس (Syr. ܐܝܬ) Dan. iii. 15 ايسكم etc. Used apparently only in translations.

بادان MS. 2468, p. 199ᵇ هى كلانس بادان ككلانس القضاة... המנבעות.

بادهنج Comm. on Amos ii. 12 وهى البادهنجات بعضها بيوت الصيف.

بنرى 1 Kings xxi. 10 for בני בליעל الرجلين البتريّين. Compare بترة *contumacia* (Vullers s. v.).

بختت (iii) مباختة *trying his fortune* MS. 2500, p. 159ᵃ.

n

[II. 3.]

بدر رحم‎ Ex. xxxiv. 19 for פטר‎ بدر‎.

برّ‎. برّا الی‎ *foras* Ps. xli. 6 (BARGÈS).

برط‎. ابرط‎ Num. xiii. 20 (השמנה הוא אם רזה)‎ دقيقة ام ابرط هل الارض وايش‎.

برماورد‎ MS. 2467, p. 44ᵇ reckoned among articles of food نار الی تحتاج لا‎.

بَسّ‎ (Persian) *only* MS. 2478, p. 22ᵃ بس للجادّة يكون ان جوازی التخصيص اوقع‎.

بُسْطل‎ *architrave* (ἐπιστύλιον) MS. 2500, p. 42ᵇ البسطلات هی اساقف‎.

بطش‎ *practice* Ex. xxxv. 25 (חכמת לב בידיה)‎ البطش حاذقة‎.

الباطش‎ is *the immediate actor*, as opposed to الآمر‎, while التولدات‎ are actions accomplishing themselves when once started, e. g. if a man shoots an arrow and dies before it hits the mark. MS. 2467, p. 186ᵃ.

بعر‎ (vi) *to trample down* Is. v. 5 for לבער‎ للتباعر‎. Comm. ibid. سياجه ازيل انا‎.

יבער‎ for يبعر‎ Ex. xxii. 4 يتباعروه حتی; ويتباعروه للكرم يثبوا‎.

بعرق‎ *to shake* Comm. on Is. xxix. 7 الممالك هذه تتبعرق ان بعد‎.

بلط‎. ابلوط‎ explanation of בן שמן‎ Is. v. 1 تنبت الغروس فيها غرس اذا الذی جيد قوية اشجارها‎.

بنى‎ (v) المتبنّد‎ for נסס‎ Is. x. 18.

بنك‎ (v) Spec. p. 22. 15 المتبنكة الشجرة‎ (BARGÈS : *Arbor firma*).

بور‎ (ii) for בוקק‎ Hos. x. 1 مبورة‎.

تَكْتَنج‎ (Pers. تَخْت‎) for קרשים‎ Ex. xxvi. 15 (תכאתג)‎.

تَقَن‎. تقانة‎ *skill* Comm. on Prov. xiv. 1 etc.

تَمّ‎ *to be possible* MS. 2472, p. 16ᵇ له يتم ما منها ياكل ان عليه اوجب انما‎; كذا يفعل ان لفلان تم ان‎; here, p. ١٣٧. 26 etc. (Classical.) MS. 2500, p. 157ᵃ اكله‎;

ثَقَة‎ for נאמן‎ Is. xlix. 7, here, p. ١٢. 17 dual ثقتان‎ Comm. on Is. viii. 1, plur. ثقات‎.

ثَمَّ‎. ثَمّ انه‎ 'il y a,' *there is* here, p. ٣١. 19.

ثَنوية‎ *dualists* here, p. ٧٢. 12.

جاب‎ (for جاء ب‎), impf. يجيب‎, infin. اجابة‎. With additional ب‎ e. g. Is. xli. 2 العالمين رب‎. Cant. p. ٣٥ᵇ. 5. به يجيب‎

لم يكن لهذه الحجارة جباس بل كان وجه للحجارة من ‏MS. 2500, p. 44‎[a] جباس

‏p. 44‎[a]‎., داخل البيت مثل وجهها من خارجه

جرّ. والمجرّ ‏עבר‎ زمان *and so on, and thenceforth* Comm. on Is. lxiii. 8 مصرים والمجرّ.

جزر *to decree* (Heb. ‏גזר‎) ‏MS. 2467, p. 73‎[b] ‏MS. 2474,‎ الى ان جزر عليهم. ‏p. 63‎[a]‎.

جزل *to rob* (Heb. ‏גזל‎) Comm. on Is. lviii. 6 من ظلم الناس وجزلهم.

جالوث *captivity* (Heb. ‏גלות‎). Plur. جواليث Comm. on Is. lvi. 10. Rel. adj. جالوثيّ here, p. ‏١٣٨‎. 12.

جار (v) *to become a proselyte*, ‏גר‎, Cant. p. ‏١١٦‎[b] ult. تجيّروا فى زمان الاباء.

جوئى rel. adj. from ‏גוי‎ ‏MS. 2467, p. 202‎[b]‎.

جوز (v) *to marry* (for ‏זוג‎) David b. Abr. s. v. ‏אור‎.

حتى. لحتى for ‏למען‎ Is. v. 19. Compare here p. ‏٣٥‎. 15.

حجّ. محجوج *a responsible person* ‏MS. 2467, p. 6‎[a] etc.

حرس *an incantation* ‏MS. 2475, p. 23‎[b] ليس ينفعه حرس.

حرف. حرّاق plur. حرّاقون for ‏שרפים‎ Is. vi. 2.

حرى. فبالحرى *scarcely* here, p. ‏٧‎. 10; compare in the sense of فاحرى ان Spec. p. 15. 11 *nedum ut sit* ولم ياتوا بحجة محتملة وبالاحرى ان تكون واجبة *necessaria* (BARGÈS: *ubi potissimum firmis erat opus*).

حط. حطيط *the lowest depth* (‏حضيض‎?), here, p. ‏١٢‎. 8.

حكر. حاكور ‏MS. 2472, p. 148‎[a] ‏שדה עיר‎ وهو حاكور يكون فى المدينة او بستان.

حكم (viii) Comm. on Is. lxv. 8 ‏כאשר ימצא התירוש‎ يريد به اذا احتكم العنب نص محكم here, p. ‏١١١‎. 21. وجاء من يفسده.

حاز. احازة for ‏אחזה‎ in Translation of Numbers (MS. 2473).

حال (iv) *to declare impossible* Comm. on Is. ii. p. 211‎[b] لما كان كثير فى الامم تحيلوا حدث العالم.

خدّ. خدود plur. for ‏מזוזות‎ Is. vi. 4, and passim.

خرق (vi) *erupit aqua* Comm. on Is. xxx. 25.

خزق *a spot on a garment* MS. 2468, p. 5^b ما مثل خزق وقع فى ثوب.

خَصّ. خاصّ for אַף Is. lxiii. 8 etc.; for רק Is. vi. 1.

خوخ Comm. on Ex. xxvii. 8 فعلى هذا الاصل يكون عمل له حيطان بما يدور وبينهما חכוך שׁביה בבואטי للحمام MS. 2468, p. 144^a.

دابة (Pers.) *a nurse*, plur. دايات Comm. on Is. lx. 16.

دغم. مدغم *ambiguous* MS. 2500, p. 155^b فاجابه מיכיהו בכלאם מדגם.

دقل Comm. on Is. xxxi. 23 תרן اسمه فى العراق دقل.

دلج (iii) for שָׁחַר Hos. v. 14 etc.

دلف for דלף Ps. cxix. 28.

دلقف *to couple* for חִבֵּר. Ex. xxvi. 3 مدلفقة (חֹברת).

دمسمون for באושים Is. v. 2.

دوامس *a course of bricks*, etc. (δόμος) MS. 2500, p. 35^a اشار به الى دوامس خشب معمولة بين دوامس الحجارة.

ديدب *to watch* Hos. ix. 8 مديدب. Prov. xv. 3 فى كل موضع عينى اللّه مديدبة *read* مدريبة. Regularly in Psalms for Heb. צפה.

ذهب. وذاهب *and onwards* MS. 2472, p. 14^a من اليوم الثامن وذاهب.

راس. راس المال *capital*, dual راس المالين MS. 2468, p. 23^b.

راى. ترى ما .. ام ترى *whether—or.* MS. 2467, p. 56^a.

رت plur. رتوت for Heb. פר passim. BARGÈS on Ps. l. 9; the meaning was noticed by EICHHORN, *Einleitung ins A. T.* i, 519.

رجراجى *liquid* passim; MS. 2472, p. 26^a وقال فى الدم لا تاكلوا معما انه رجراجى.

رسانينق for נטיפות Is. iii. 19. (VULLERS: رستينه 'vox dubia.')

ركس plur. ركوس Cant. i. 17; see BARGÈS ad l.

رمل (ii) *viduam fecit* Comm. on Is. x. 3. (v) ترمّل *status viduae* Comm. on Is. lxi. 10.

رام *to wish* with الى MS. 2468, p. 188^a لا يثبت له ما رام الى اثباته.

ريزنع (Pers. ريزه) Comm. on Num. xxii. 30 فعل لا تفعل اعدم البهائم وريزغها.

ريزة *a socket* (?) MS. 2468, p. 114^a (of the 'rings' of the ark) انها فى ريزات مضروبة فى جنب الئارון.

رِیش الدלויות هى الريش التى اذا *a tap* (for water) Comm. on 1 Kings vii. 29 دیرت خرج الماء فيها يغلق وبها يفتح. MS. 2500, p. 50^b.

زرغن Comm. on Is. xix. 3 אשת בעלת אוב פזרغنت عليه.

زعر نפשה מרה לה for نفسها زعرت لها 2 Kings iv. 27. (v) Here, p. ١١٧. 23.

زغم for זעף here, p. ٩. 13. (v) Frequently for זעם.

زلع *to draw* water يزلع منه الماء كما يزلع من البرك MS. 2500, p. 49^a.

زودن Comm. on Is. xxix. 21 سماهم لۇ من حيث انهم يحبون الزودنة والاكل.

سبسب (ii) *to overhang* for סרח Ex. xxvi. 12 bis.

المستور. ستر *the poor* Comm. on Prov. xiii. 23 etc.

سخف *contumely* for קלון Prov. ii. 34. (iv) به اسخف *he insulted him* MS. 2500, p. 157^b.

سفر. سافور for שופר Ps. xlvii. 5 etc.

سقبلبيات (Syr.) for תהפכות Prov. ii. 14 etc.

سقف Comm. on Prov. xii. 5 الكلام المسقف الذى يحتمل الوجوه الكثيرة; ibid. p. 64^a يسقفون كلامهم.

سقلاطبين for אטון Prov. vii. 13.

سقم (ii) (from استقام) *to make straight* Is. xl. 3; مسقم for מישר 1 Kings vi. 35.

سلف for החליק Prov. ii. 16.

سوى. مستوى (for مستويا) *directly* here, p. ١٩. 14.

شبه. شبهة *a false religion* Spec. p. 17. 11 واقاموا لۇ شبهة. (BARGÈS: *statuam in honorem eius erigunt.*)

شثل for שתל, مشثول Ps. i. 3, xcii. 13 (BARGÈS); شثول *surculi* Ps. cxxviii. 3.

شفكره for סנורים 2 Kings vi. 18 etc., David b. Abr. s. v.

شا *whether* Ex. xl. 22 (MS. 2468, p. 204^b), شا אהרון ام غيرة, MS. 2472, p. 74^b شا كان مرجوم او غريق, here, p. ٥٥. 14; Spec. p. 18. 8.

صنع واى شى كان للملكة فيه صنع كان لۇ فيه الثلث, here, p. ٥٥. 8.

ضرع Ps. xxxii. 4 انقلب ضرعى *conversus est humor meus* BARGÈS, ibid. p. 59, n. 3.

طغس (ii) *to despise* Comm. on Ps. xxii. 5 (HOFFMANN).

طلخم for התקדר 1 Kings xviii. 45; (ii) for קדרות Is. l. 3. Often spelt طلخم or ضلخم BARGÈS on Ps. xxxv. 14.

عبرانة Num. xiii. 23 العبرانة التى كانت فيها العنقود. MS. 2474, p. 62^b.

عزل *section* MS. 2472, p. 25^b وفى ذكره نبلة وطرفه بعزل مفرد.

علج. علاج *the process whereby any food is changed from its natural state*, and *the result of that process;* see Appendix; MS. 2472, p. 104^b لم ينفع اخراج الالات. Here, p. ١٢. 14 etc. والعلاج من البيت.

علق (v) تعلق *an excuse* MS. 2475, p. 5^a.

علم. عالم *a large number* here passim; in Spec. p. 15. 8 the correction عظم is unnecessary.

عمل with على اعمل على *to intend* here, p. ٥٥. 8; *to suppose* MS. 2468, p. 185^a ان لا تقع الهنحة على غير الحيوان.

عهس for עוד Num. xxii. 30 מעוֹדך for من عهدك, passim in Isaiah. Sometimes written عاد, whence EICHHORN wrongly supposed it to be a transliteration of the Heb. עוֹד.

الغاريسبة *the Pharisees* here, p. ١٩. 13, = the Rabbanites, רבנים, as the Sefer ha-'osher interprets; the Karaites are similarly called 'Sadducees.'

فنج *extent.* See here, pp. ٣٣. 5, ٣٧. 17.

فريرة (for فريضة? yet derived by Jephet himself from ما يفرز) for תרומה for Ex. xxv. 1 etc.

فسبغة *perquisite* Comm. on Is. xxxii. 6 لهم فسائق ياخذوها من الموسر والمعسر; فسيقة الرئيس ibid.

فقم *to grin* Comm. on Ps. xxii. 8 (HOFFMANN).

فلذ (Pers.) *cacare* Comm. on Ex. x. 21 حتى ان كل واحد فلذ فى مكانه; فلاذات for מחראות in 2 Kings x. 27; فلاذة for צואה Is. xxviii. 8; cp. FLEISCHER, *Kl. Schr.* i. 169.

فنطاس for פטיש Is. xli. 6, in Comm.: من شان الذى يضرب الصفائح الكبار ان يضربها بالفنطاس.

فاف fut. يفيف (Weiterbildung of فى?) *to take refuge* here, p. ٤٥. 14.

قرمط (ii) for Heb. התקשר 2 Kings ix. 14 etc. Hence it appears that the קשרים mentioned passim here are the Carmathians.

قصن. جعل قصده من *to take note of* here, p. ٣٨. 21; Comm. on Prov. vii. 10 (p. 34^b).

قطع Prov. iv. 15 اقطع المادة من *pass away from.* Perhaps however we should read الماء; Spec. p. 18. 18 قطع الماء من أصله *he allows no compromise.* (BARGÈS: ' h. e. interpretatione non egent verba.')

قفان (for قبان) passim, Prov. xvi. 8 etc.

قهر *a he-goat* (caper?) שעיר העזים Lev. ix. 3 ; here, pp. ٨١. 18, ٨٣. 7, etc.

كبس لا يفزع عن عدو *to surprise* here, p. ١٢٢. 16. Comm. on Prov. iii. 24 مفחד פתאם يشير به الى الكبسات; ibid. (يكبسه read) يكسبه.

كرتم (ii) *to be vexed* here, p. ١٣. 4 etc.; Ps. lxxii. 4; cf. ሕᎣᎀᎁ:

كنس (vii) *to gather together* MS. 2468, p. 89^b انكنست من جميع النواحى.

كون (v) see here, p. ١١. 7.

كيمية common form in MSS. (e.g. 2468, p. 197^b bis) for كمية; perhaps by false analogy from كيفية.

لاشيبة (for لا شى?) Ps. cxix. 119; 'ex comment. videtur hac voce innui *scorias,*' BARGÈS.

لصف prep. for Heb. אצל Prov. vii. 8, here, p. ١٠٩. 2.

ليس with suffixes لسنى for لست Ex. xxiii. 7, ليسه Lev. xi. 39, here, p. ٢٢. 15.

منتيبة (or rather مثيبة) for מתיבה plur. مثائب Cant. p. ٧٣^b ad fin.

مشمش (مشّش) for גרם Num. xxiv. 8.

مشى. Here, p. ١٥٢. 10 مشى على أصله *he took a separate view;* see also p. ١٣٢. 20.

معنية for מעניח Ps. cxxix. 3 (probably corrupt).

مماخايجة see here, p. ٥٢. 9.

نبيلة for נבלה Ps. lxxix. 2.

نثّ *queri* BARGÈS Ps. lv. 2, 17; Is. liii. 8.

نجل (ii) *complanare* for פַּנּוּ Is. xl. 3 ; Ps. lxxx. 9.

نظر (iii) with عن *to answer for* Is. xli. 21 تناظر عن نفسها حتى هاتوا معظماتكم, here, p. ١٨. 2.

نقص *deficient* (adj.), here, p. ٩٩. 11.

نهد. نهدة *suspiritus* BARGÈS on Ps. xxxviii. 9.

ناق *to give light* for האיר Ex. xxv. 37; Comm. on Ex. xl. 38 (MS. 2468, p. 206ª) الاش تنيق بالليل.

ه for أ before hemza; Ex. xvii. 7 هايس, MS. 2500, p. 191ª; here, p. ٢٣. 3. Baiḍāwī on Sūra iii. 59.

هبج *to strike* Comm. on Prov. xviii. 6 ؛ الهبج والضرب for מהלמות Prov. xviii. 6, 8.

هلم. وهلم *and onwards* MS. 2468, p. 104ᵇ اليوم السابع وهلم.

هَمّ *also* MS. 2475, p. 13ᵇ בלק ايضا يقول كان وهم. Comm. on Prov. p. 110ᵇ فلو كان اذا تزوج هم هو לא טוב, here, pp. ١٧. 4, ١٢٣. 9. EICHHORN l. c.

هوان Ex. xxvi. 19 for אדנים.

واحد here, p.٢٥.15 للواحد سبعة for חד שבעה; see NÖLDEKE, *Syr. Gram.* p. 166.

وخر (ii) for اخر (ii) MS. 2467, p. 129ª bis.

ورب (ii) توريب *obliquity* MS. 2500, p. 42ᵇ.

ولد (v) see بطش.

ولف (ii) for الف (ii) here, p. ٨٨. 1.

يوما *ever* here, p. ١٩. 2. Comm. on Prov. xiii. 5 ولا يخجل يوما.

ERRATA.

Page ١٨, line 5 فيتعدى بروحك: read فى تعذيب روحك.

P. ٢٥, ١١ بثبت: read بثبت.

P. ٢٨, ١٠ ينتظر: read ينتظر.

P. ٣٠, 2 بلفظ: read بلفظ.

P. ٦٨, ١9, 20 غير (على): read (على) غير.

P. ٧٠, ١4 يعنى: read يعنو.

P. ٨٣, 2 وشركائه: read وشرقاء ٥.

P. ٨٧, 2 ארבע to be read twice as in MS.

P. ٨٨, 9 مذا: read هذا.

P. ٩٠, 5 قيل: read فيل.

Ibid. 20 عرف: read عرّف.

P. ٩٣, ١ يسرائيل: read بسرائيل.

Ibid. 20 فرحماته: read ورحماته.

P. ٩٨ n. والداه: read والدوه.

P. ١١١, ١ الأربعت: read الأربعة.

P. ١١٢, 23 مخلوقا: read مخلوقا.

P. ١٣٣, 15 وخمسة ماية يوم: to be corrected as in translation.

P. ١٣٦, ١. The second كثيرين is a copyist's error of الاشرار.

For the 'Index,' to which reference is made in the notes, substitute 'Glossary.'

APPENDIX.

Page ۴ line 13. The missing words are supplied in the translation. Twenty-two years are given to Evil-Merodach by Jephet in the passage cited from his Comm. on Jeremiah on p. ٥٢, n. 4; compare too the calculations on p. ١٣, l. 16.

P. ۹, l. 1. The passage referred to is in Cod. Brit. Mus. Or. 2468, fol. 169ᵃ and following:

ولذلك يضيف هذا الذبائح الى المعبودات كما قال וזבחו לאלהיהן وقال ויאכלו זבחי

מתים فكل من يقرب לעבדה זרה هو עובד עבדה זרה وكل من اكل من اكل الذبائح

فهو اكل זבחי מתים ليكنه دون זובח לאלהים وهى منزلة ثانية غير انه قد ساوا

النص بين اوכל ذبائح الנוים واכل خبزهم وشارب خمرهم ونعلم ذلك من قصة

דانيال اذ جعل פתבג המלך ויין משתיו منزلة واحدة كما قال וישם דניאל על לבו אשר 5

לא יתנאל בפתבג המלך وبين משתיו فجعل الלחם والיין תחת الנואל ويجب ان تعلم

انه لم يحرم الיין من جهة انه נסך للمعبود اذ من عادات الكتاب ان يضيف

الذبائح والخمر المرسوم לעבדה זרה اليها كما بيّنّا اينفا وهاهنا اضافه الى الملك

كما قال מפתבג המלך ויין משתיו فصارت ذبيحة الנוים وخبزهم وطبيعهم وشرابهم

منزلة واحدة فى باب التحريم فجميع الرجراجيات والمستخرجات تحريم واحد فى باب 10

التحريم والטמא لقوله فى فصل الשרצים وכל משקה אשר ישתה בכל כלי יטמא والיין

هو واحد منها وكذلك قال فى الמנע נוגע בכנפו אל לחם ואל הנזיד ואל היין ואל כל מאכל חגי ב׳ יב

היקרש فقد ساوا الله تمّ بين المعالجات كلها فى قبولها التحريم والטמא ليس

بينها فرق فقد غلط الذين زعموا ان خمر الנוים اسور وغيره מתר فاطلق معالجات

الנוים وهى حرام لا شك اذ لا يجوز من דانيال ان يخاطر بروحه ويجرّد نفسه للموت 15

فى شى غير واجب الا ترى قول המלצר וחיבתם את ראשי למלך ثم من قوله ויתנו

לנו من הזרעים ונאכלה ומים ונשתה علمنا انه طلب שלא דבר נשתנה מבריחו للحبوب

والماء فاما ما تغيّر عن خليقته ودخل فى حد العلاج فحرام اכלه من الנוי ولو كان

انما يحرم خبز الנוים من جهة تلويث زهومة الذبيحة لقد كان لا يحرم الخمر ثم قد كان

يمكنه ان يامر للخباز الا يلوّث طعامه بزهومة فهذا طرف ذكرناه فى هذا الموضع ◆ 20

U 2

شرح سفر دانيال

للمعلّم الفاضل

מר׳ ורב׳ הש׳ המשכיל הגדול המעוז המגדל
יפת הלוי בן כג״ק מר׳ ורב׳ עלי הלוי נ״ע

المعروف

بابى علىّ حسن البصرىّ تغمّده الله بالرحمة والرضوان

طبع

فى المطبعة المدرسيّة فى مدينة اوكسفرد

سنة ١٨٨٧ المسيحيّة

◊ شرح سفر دانيال ◊

فهرست ¹اعلم ان كان سبب نسب هذا السفر الى سيّد دانيال عليه السلام دون غيره
السفر ²(ما) كان فيه ³ذكر اخباره ونبوّته° ⁴وهو يشتمل على° احد عشر فصلا ◊
⟶ الفصل الاول ما كان من خبره وخبر رفقائه وهم حننيا ميشائيل وعزريا⁵ من
امتناعهم عن ⁶اكل طعام° الملك وما وصلوا اليه من فضيلة المنزلة فى ما ⁷يديمهم 5
الملك له° من تعليمهم لغة ⁸الكسدانيّين وخطّهم وحكمتهم على ما تضمّنه
الفصل ◊

الفصل الثانى ما كان من المنام الذى رآه الملك ونسيه وطالب للحكماء
بالمنام وتفسيره وما كشفه سبحانه وتعالى الى السيّد دانيال من المنام حتى وصل
10 الى المنزلة العالية ◊

الفصل الثالث خبر الصنم الذى اقامه (بختناصر) وطالب الناس بالسجود
له وما كان من خبر حننيا ميشائيل وعزريا وما اوصلهم الملك اليه من المنزلة
الجليلة بعد ذلك ◊

الفصل الرابع ذكر المنام الذى رآه الملك ولم ينساه وطالب للحكماء بتفسيره
15 ولم يقفوا عليه حتى فسّره دانيال عليه السلام ◊

الفصل الخامس ذكر ما لحق الملك من خروجه عن جملة الناس وكونه مع
الوحوش سبع سنين ◊
وهذه للخمسة فصول جرت فى ملك نبوخذناصر◊

---

¹ Introduction in B P X only. B P commence with Heb. and Arab. of ver. 1, then
proceed נסב הדא אלי דניאל. In X the Heb. and Arab. of ver. 1 follow the words
X. אכבארה ודכרה ונבותה. ² Obliterated in X; מן חית B P. ³ אלפצל (sic) אולה
B P אלאכל וטעאם D X; אכל טעם ⁶ في. Prob. ⁵ והדא אלכתאב ינמע ⁴ B P.
(ex corr.). ⁷ ידמה אלמ' X; ידומה אלמלך BD; ידימהם אלמלך לה (partly
obliterated) P. ⁸ אלכסדאני codd.

Line 14. ينسه.   18. Cp. WRIGHT, *Ar. Gr.* ii. 265.

[II. 3.]   A 2

فهرست الفصل السادس ما كان من خبر ¹ابن ابنه بلشاصر فى اخراجه اوانى بيت

السفر الله عز وجل وشرب الخمر فيها وما اظهره الله تعالى من الخطّ على الحائط بالمجلس

حتى التمس الوقوف على ذلك وسائر ما جرى الى ان قتل الملك ۰

الفصل السابع ما جرى لدانيال فى ملك الفارس من المنزلة الجليلة وما احتيل

5 عليه حتى طرح فى جبّ السباع ۰

الفصل الثامن ذكر المنام الذى رآه دانيال عليه السلام فى معنى الاربع ممالك

وتفسير ذلك ۰

الفصل التاسع ذكر החזון الذى رآه فى معنى الثلث ممالك على الشرح الذى

تضمّنه الفصل ونظر ذلك ﴿فى السنة الثالثة﴾ من ملك بلشاصر ۰

10 الفصل العاشر يذكر فيه صلواته وما كشفه الله اليه من خبر בית שני ۰

الفصل الحادى عشر يذكر فيه ما اوراه الله تعالى ²الملك وشرح له سائر ما

تعلّقت به نفسه من خبر הקץ ما جاز عند³ ٭ ٭ كشف له على ما تضمّنه الفصل ۰

واذا جمعنا السنين التى تضمّنها هذا السفر يكون جملتها سبعا وستين سنة ٭ ٭

٭ ٭ ٭ ٭ ٭ ٭ ٭ ٭ ٭

تقضى منها سبع سنين ملك يهوياقيم على ما نشرحه فى كلامنا ههنا تبقى من

15 ذلك ثلث وستون سنة ⁴وسنة [سنين] לדריוש המדי وثلث سنين לכורש הפרסי يكون

جملة ذلك سبعا وستين سنة ۰

۰⁵الفصل الاول۰

شرح السفر فى سنة ثلث لملك يهوياقيم ملك يهونا جاء نبوخذنناصر ملك

فصل ¹ بابل الى يروشالايم وحاصرها ۰

فاسوق ¹ اعلم ان ملك يهوياقيم منقسم ⁶على ثلثة اقسام ⁷اربع سنين كان تحت

21 طاعة ملك مصر والثانى ⁸ثلث سنين ﴿كان﴾ تحت طاعة ملك بابل° كما قال

---

¹ אבן D only; cett. om.   ² للملك codd.   ³ Prob. add. ات (اللہ تبارك).
⁴ وסחה codd.   ⁵ X has אול אלפסוק מן הדא יכתב.   ⁶ אלי B.   ⁷ Prob. add. الاول.
⁸ תחת מאעה מלך בבל ג סנין B P.

Line 2. وشربه.   11. ارآه.   13, 15. تكون.   14. يقضى (cp. Fleischer, Kl.
Schr. i. 265).

فصل ١   وملك [1]⟨والثالث كان ملكا براسه ثلث سنين⟩   ויהי לו יהויקים עבד שלש שנים

فاسوق ١   بابل مشغول فى خروجه فى عمل [2]الشرق فى هذه الثلث سنين فلمّا تفرّغ قليلا غزاه

ملك ب. كد. ا   فى السنة العاشرة من ملكه وحاصره بجيشه وفتح البلد واخذه واجلى معه قوم مع

بعض اوانى بيت الله كقوله فى صدر هذا السفر ❖ ⟨قال⟩ בשנת שלש ولم يقل

بשنة العاشرية لملكوت יהויקים لمعنى وهو انه كان اوّلا تحت يد ملك مصر ثم صار من ٥

تحت يد ملك بابل ومضى له سبع سنين فلمّا عصى على ملك بابل وصار ملك

براسه لا يدى طاعة لاحد الملوك قال بשنת שלש لملكوت יהויקים מלך יהודה فجعل

هذا التاريخ مردود الى وقت كان ملك براسه ❖ * [3]يرى على ما قلنا من انقسام ملك

يهوياقيم على ثلثة هو ان ملك مصر اخذ يهواحاز اخو يهوياقيم وودّاه الى مصر

 د ه ب. لو. د   وجعل مكانه يهوياقيم كما قال וימליך מלך מצרים את אחיו وعلمنا انه

السنة ١١   اقام تحت طاعة ملك مصر اربع سنين وان ملك ⟨ملك⟩ بابل فى السنة

يرم كه. ا   الرابعة من ملك يهوياقيم كما قال הדבר ونحو فعرّف ان اوّل ملك

نبوخذناصر هو السنة الرابعة ليهوياقيم وفى تلك السنة حارب ملك بابل عسكر

ملك مصر الذى كان مقيم على شاطئ الفراة كما شرح ذلك ירמיהו عليه السلام

ملك ب. كد. ا   وعند ذلك حصل الشام تحت يده كما قال ולא הוסיף ونحو فحصل يهوياقيم تحت طاعة

١٦   ملك بابل فى السنة لخامسة من ملكه ❖ وقال בא נבוכדנצר מלך בבל ירושלם

ויצר עליה [4]اعلم انه لم يكتفى [5]بان يغزوه بعسكر جاء هو بعسكره ولو خرج اليه

يهوياقيم لم يحاصر البلد لكنه لم يدى اليه طاعة وغلق ⟨الباب⟩ فجلس فى الحصار

فظنّ ان ملك بابل يضجر وينصرف عنه فاقام محاصر [6]البلد حتى فتحه كما قال

٢١   [2]فسلّم الله بيده يهوياقيم ملك يهونا وطرفا من اوانى بيت

الله وجابهم ارض الشنور بيت معبوده والاوانى [7]ادخلهم بيت

⟨خزانة⟩ معبوده ❖

[8]إما ان يكون فتح البلد بالسيف على راى قوم وإما ان يكون فتحوا [9]له وهو

---

[1] B. אלשרף.   [2] והדא אלד סנין wanting; the codd. giving instead والثالث ... سنين.   [3] Prob. وما يدلّ.   [4] לאנה עלם codd.   [5] בעסכר אן זונה codd.   [6] אלבאב codd.   [7] ארסלהם Heb.   [8] אנמא Heb.   [9] M².

Line 3. قوما.   5. من redundant.   6, 8. ملكا.   8. مردودا.   9. اخا, واتّاه.   14. مقيما.   17. يكتفي.   18. يوّدّ.   21. وجاء بهم.

فصل ١ الاقرب لانه لم يذكر ١قتل اصلا وقد ذكر ان يهوياقيم مات خارج يروشالايم فايما ان

فاسوق ٢ يكون عذّبه فمات او قُتل او يكون هو قتل نفسه ❖ وقوله ויביאם ארץ שנער שנער يشير

به الى ثلث الاف ونيّف اجلاهم ملك بابل وهم المذكورين فى اخر سفر يرمياهو

ירמ' נב. כח بقوله זה העם אשר הגלה נבוכדראצר בשנת שבע יהודים ❖ وعرّف انه ادخل

٥ الاوانى الى خزانة اوانى بيت معبوده وهذه الاوانى ٣لم يذكر عددها ولا اى شى هى

ذهب او فقّة او نحاس وهى لا محالة دون الاوانى التى اخذها مع يهوياخين لقوله

וד"ה ב. לו. ז فى ذلك עם כלי חמדת בית ייי ונו' ولم ٤يستخدمها بل تركها مصونة على جملتها

M² def. لانه | لو فعل ذلك لم يمكّنه الله [بل] كما لم يمكّن بلشاصر من ذلك بل اثّر فى

ذلك اثرا كبيرا كما سنشرح ذلك فى فصله ❖

M² ٣ وقال الملك لاشفناز ٥رئيس خدمه ٦لاجابة من بنى يسرائيل

١١ ومن نزرّيّة الملك ٧ومن البطارقة

٤ ٨ناشئة ليس فيهم شى من العيب وجميلى المنظر ومرشدين

فى كل حكمة وعارفى المعرفة ومفهمى العلم واللذين فيهم طاقة

للوقوف فى هيكل الملك ولتعليمهم الخطّ ولغة الكسداديّين ❖

١٥ ٩عرّف انه امراجلّ خدمة الذى كان تحت يده المنجليين من يسرائيل ان يختار

M² def. من جملتهم غلمان هذه صفتهم ولم يذكر عددهم فلزمه ان يتامّل | ١٠حال من يوجد

بهذه الصفة وياخذه اليه ١١اينما كان قليل ام كثير❖ وقال מבני ישראל ليس هو

من نزرّيّة الملك ولا من اولاد الروساء وهم من عوامّ الناس وليس يفكر بانه من العوامّ

M² بعد انه | بهذه الصفة المذكورة ليدلّ ان ليس يعيب اهل الفضل نقص حسبهم ❖

---

¹ Heb. קבל. ² Om. M². ³ Om. Heb. ⁴ Heb. יתחדם בהא ⁵ אלריים לכדמה
⁶ Heb. מן אלאנבלי ; M²: من البطارقة ومن الاجلى. ⁷ M². للاجابة. ⁸ The
rendering in Heb. is different : נלמאן אללדאן ליס פיהם עיב וחסאן אלמנטר—ומפהמי.
(D לתעלימהם) ולעלמהם—ולדאן קוה פיהם ואלדאן. אלמערפה. ⁹ Corrupt in Heb. ערף אנה
. ¹⁰ Prob. كلّ. D. אנה אמר ; B מן אמר אנל כדמה אלדי כאן תחת ידה מן ישראל
¹¹ Prob. اتّما.

Line ١. قتالا, فى خارج. ٣. المذكورون. ١٥. المنجلون. ١٦. غلمانا.
١٧. قليلا ام كثيرا.

فصل ١ وامر [١]بأن يأخذ احسنهم لانه يقبح ان [٢]يقف فى مجلس قبيح [٣]السحنة بل من

فاسوق ٣ كان حسن التخاطيط [٤]وله ملح وروعة٥ ٠ وقوله ومشכילים בכל חכמة ليس هذه

لِلحكمة حكمة التورا من طمא [٥]وطהور وقرابين اذ ليس [٦]يريد ذلك الملك وانما اراد

به عُقلاء فى سائر الضروب التى للعقل فيها مدخل وما يتعلّق بذلك من الاداب ٠

٥ وقوله ויدعי דעת الاقرب فيه انها من جنس علوم سليمن عليه السلام فى ضروب

الفلسفة فلم تخلوا امّة بنى يسرائيل من اصولها وكانوا يعلّمون اولادهم ذلك مع

ولِلحكمة ٠ وقوله كونهم فى [زمان] لِلجهل والفساد لم يخل من بينهم اهل العلم [٧]

ومبيني מדע يعنى [٨]انهم يهتدون لتعليم غيرهم علمهم اذ ليس كل عالم بحسن

يعلّم ٠ [٩]فاختار [١٠]كل من [١١]اجتمعت فيه هذه لِخصال وهذه الاوصاف المحمودة فاذا

M² def. كان هذا فى ذلك الزمان [١٢]فاخرى | ان يكون فيهم صبيان [ان يكونوا] بهذه الاوصاف ٠

١١ وقوله ואשר כח בהם يعنى كون فيهم جلادة للصبر على الوقوف قدام الملك ويصبرون

عن التنخّع والبصاق وما شاكل ذلك ٠ [١٣]وامر بان يعلموا لِخطّ واللغة حتى يكتبون

بها ويتكلّمون بها لانهم ما كانوا يعرفون خطّهم ولا لغتهم ٠ ولولا ان اشفناز هذا

كان فيه كثرة هذه الامور ويقف عليها [١٤]لم يامره بذلك ٠ وكان غرض الملك فى اخذ هولاء

M² الغلمان الموصوفين بهذه الاوصاف شيين | [١٥]احدهما رغبته الى اهل العلم كما رسم الملوك

١٦ الفضلاء ان يربون منهم العلماء والثانى يفتخر عند الامم بان عنده اشرف الامم ٠

---

[١] ان ;M² ¹ [٢] وאמר באן יכום חסאن .Heb ² [٣] M² corrected لِلحسنة [٤] .Heb
الله עקל ואدب ;B (!) ولة אלبחאסنة ;X אלبحסنة ;P אלبحסنة ;D אلסحנה ;السحنة ⁴
יעני פיהם הדו M² ;וطهר .Heb ⁵ [٥] ירי .Heb ⁶ [٦] אلحכמא .Heb ⁷ [٧] הדו .Heb ⁸ [٨]
לתעאלים פאן לים כל מن יערף אלעאלם .etc פערף אنה יכתאر Heb ⁹ [٩] .M² Om ¹⁰ [١٠]
اجتمعت ¹¹ [١١] M² ;هذه الاوصاف المحمودة M² ;انثمע BP ;ינثמע DX ;אنثמע
;فبالحرى .Prob ¹² [١٢] .X D הذה البצائל (X אلبצائל) وهذه الدلائل المحمودة BP ;المحمّ'
.cp. Dozy, s.v. ¹³ [١٣] ואما codd. ¹⁴ [١٤] M²

لم يامر يعرفوها . . .

انغا من امران احدهما رغبة ــ الامم (?)

[١٥] The Heb. have instead אحרהמא אנה עלם בפצ'ילתהם ואنהם מן אلעאلم בכلאף כל
امة من الدنيا والثاني ليתבאהא בדلך عند קומة (BP קوم) פי אن פי هيכلה אشرف
הדה אלامة.

Line 6. تخل. 11. Cp. WRIGHT, Ar. Gr. ii. 242. 12. يكتبوا. 13. يتكلّموا.
16. يربوا; but cp. FLEISCHER, Kl. Schr. i. 81.

فصل ۱ ۰ وارزقهم الملك رسم يوم بيومه من طعام الملك ومن خمر

فاسوق ۵ مشروبه ¹ولتربيتهم ثلث سنين وعند ²انتهائها ²يقفون قدام الملك۰

لم يكن ³قصد الملك فساد دينهم⁴ كما فعل⁵ في ⁶قصة الصنم الذي اقامه ⁷وانما
اراد ان تربوا ابدانهم وتحسن الوانهم باعتدال الغذاء فجعل جرايتهم مثل طعامه°

M² def. ومشروبه اجلّ طعام واجود مشروب | ۰ ⁸وذكر انه ثلث سنين يرتّيهم حتى يدخلون الى
٦ الملك حسان البدن واللون وقد عرفوا لخطّ واللغة وسائر ما يطلب منهم ۰

۰ فكان فيهم من بني يهونا دانيال ورفقاوه ۰ ז

[وقصد] ذكر هذه الاربعة من اجل انهم امتنعوا من طعام الملك وسائر ما وصلوا
اليه وقد كان فيهم مزرع الملاخة ولم يذكرهم الكتاب ولو كانوا هولاء الاربعة مزرع
١٠ الملاخة لقد كان قال ويهي بهم مزرع الملاخة ويذكر حسبهم وهذا ⁹يدفع قول من قال

ישע' ל"ט. ז. (في) ومبنيخ اشر يناو ممخ (انه) يشير به الى هولاء ۰

وجعل لهم رئيس الخدم اسماء وجعل لدانيال بلطشاصر
ولحننيا شنرخ ولميشائيل ميشخ ولعزريا عبين نغو۰

عرّف ¹⁰انه لقّبهم باسماء كسدانيّة ولعلّها اسماء جليلة لان بلطشاصر هو اسم
ה.ו. معبود بختناصر كقوله له دي شمه بلطשצר כשם אלהי وعلى مثل ذلك القول في
١٦ الثلثة ايضا ۰

فجعل دانيال على قلبه انه لا يتلوّث بطعام الملك وبخمر
مشروبه وطلب من رئيس الخدم ان لا يتلوّث۰

كانه الزم نفسه انه لا ياكل من طعام الملك ولا يشرب من مشروبه ولو بلغ به
٢٠ الامر ما بلغ فخاطر بنفسه مثل ما خاطر في الصلوة وكما خاطر حننيا ميشائيل
وعزريا في انهم لم يسجدوا للصنم ۰ ولا يجوز ان يخاطر بما ليس عليه في ذلك وزر

---

¹ ולתרתיבהם B P X.　² נהאיתהם Heb.　³ אלמלך קצד Heb.　⁴ עליהם add. Heb.
⁵ דלך add. Heb.　⁶ באב Heb.　⁷ Heb. ואנמא כאן מראדה
add. B P] מא דכרה אלמלצר] אן תתרבא אבדאנהם ותחסן אלואנהם באלאעתדאל פי גדאהם
פנעל גדאהם מן טעאמה.　⁸ Prob. وقصد.　⁹ ירפע B.　¹⁰ אנה K only; cett. om.

Line 4. تربو.　5. يدخلوا.

كما قال بعض من لا لـه دين وقد ذكرنا الرّد عليـه فى موضع الفرض • وقال לֹא فصل ١
ولم يقل יֹאכַל لمعنى وهو انه لا يأكل علاج عينـه طاهرة وقد تلوّث בְּטֻמְאָה فاسوق ٨
ولم يفرق بين الطعام الذى فيه ذبائح الدماء وبين الشراب ولعلّه لم يكون لحم
حيوان حرام فى الاصل وليس للخمر عينه محرمة وانما حرّم لانه علاج الدماء ولو سلم
من كل تلويث للحرام وذلك انه جعل النبيذ هو الاصل وامتنع من ان يأكل ما ٥
يمازجه للحرام • وهذا שַׂר הַסָּרִיסִים هو اشفناز • كانه قال يا سيّدى ما احبّ ان
تطعمنى وتسقينى ما لا يصلح واجابـه بجواب ايّسه من ان يعطيـه سواله فى ذلك •

• وجعل الله دانيال لفضل ولرحمات قدام رئيس الخدم •

قولـه לְחֶסֶד וּלְרַחֲמִים جمع فيه وقتين * * وهو הַחֶסֶד وهو انه قد افضل عليـه
من اشياء كثيرة اختصر ذكرها والثانى فى وقته هذه وهو הָרַחֲמִים (وهو) انه ١٠
لم يبطش بـه ولم يوذيـه ولم يظهر ذلك للملك بل اعتذر اليـه كقولـه

١٠ فقال رئيس الخدم لدانيال انا خائف من سيّدى الملك
الذى وصف طعامكم وشرابكم الذى لما يرى وجوهكم متزعّمة من
الغلمان الذين مثل طربكم فتوجبوا قطع راسى للملك •

عرّفه انه ليس ينكر ذلك الّا من خوفه على نفسه من الملك عند ما يبعث ١٥
يطلبهم فى كل وقت يريد يتاَمّل حالهم فاذا نظر وجـه غيرهم ونظر وجوههم مخالفة
لوجوه غيرهم فاذا استقصى عن ذلك وعرف ما جرى من تغيّر غذائهم فيعود اللوم
عليـه وهم لا يعذلون • قال כְּדִבְרֵיכֶם لان العلماء لهم طرب وسرور لان العلم
ينحف للجسم ويهلكه • וְחֹבְחֶם مثل חֲבֹלָתוֹ חוֹב יָשִׁיב •

יחזק׳ יח׳ ז׳

١١ فقال دانيال الى القهرمان الذى وكّل رئيس الخدم على ٢٠
دانيال ورفقائـه •

لما لم يجيبـه שַׂר הַסָּרִיסִים الى ما طلبـه منـه وقد كان الزم نفسه ان يستقتل على

---

¹ Prob. فى.   ² אלֹה B.

Line 2. علاجا.   3. يكن.   11. يوُذِوِ.   13. الذى for فإنّ (cp. HABICHT,
Epistolae, p. 53, n. 92*).   22. يجِبـّه.

[II. 3.]   B

فصل ١ ذلك فتلطّف بان قال للرجل الذى تجرى جرايتهم على يده حتى يفعل ذلك هذا

فاسوق ١١ معهم وبجرّبهم كما سنشرح ذلك فى ما بعد •

ــــــــ

١٢ جرّب الان عبيدك عشرة ايّام ويعطونا من البزور وناكل وماء ونشرب ١ •

١٣ ويتراؤن بين يديك منظرنا ومنظر كل الغلمان الاكلين طعام الملك وكما ترى اصنع مع عبيدك •

جرّبنا عشرة ايّام وهى مدّة يسيرة ليس كاد ان يتكوّن فى مجارى عادات الناس حتى يقرب الامر ولا يبعد ٢فعل ذلك •

١٤ وسمع لهم (قبل قولهم) هذا القول وجرّبهم عشرة ايّام •

١٥ وعند انقضاء عشرة ايّام راى منظرهم حسن وسمينى البدن من جميع الغلمان الاكلين من طعام الملك •

عرّف انه قبل منهم ما التمسوه ثم افتقدهم بعد ذلك فنظرهم اعبل واحسن من غيرهم الذين كانوا ياكلون طعام الملك و(يشربون) شرابه • هذا من فعل البارى تعالى الذى جعل فى الحبوب ما يسدّ مسدّ اللحم وكذلك فعل فى الماء واما اولئك الذين لم يفعلوا ما فعل دانيال واصحابه اما لانهم ٣تاوّلوا فى انهم ٤معذّورين وان لم يمكنهم مخالفة السلطان او لانهم لم يفكروا فى حلال وحرام ارسل الهزال فى ابدانهم ولم يعبلوا • دلّ ذلك ٥على ان٥ اللّه تقع عانى باوليائه المستقتلين على فرضه • وقوله ومقتاة يمام عشرة عرّف انه لمّا نظر انهم قد زادوا فى الحسن والسمن دام على ذلك مدّة ثلث سنين •

١٦ وكان القهرمان حامل ٦طعامهم وخمر مشروبهم ومعطيهم بزور٦ •

انتفع هو ٧بالجرايا واخذها اليه ولم يعلّم ذلك لاشفناز بل كان يفعل ذلك سرّا •

١ نשرב codd. ² Perh. فى. ³ תולו codd. ⁴ מעדודין .codd., scr معذورون.
⁵ לאן K X; text B P. ⁶ אלטמעאמהם K. ⁷ באלגראה B; באלגרא P X; text K.

Line 5. وليترآء. 10. حسنا. 17. عان. 20. بزورا.

فصل ١   اعلم ان פַּת בַּג يجمع خبز ¹وادم وهذه الكلمة تنقسم كلمتين פת בג خبز² ²وادم

فاسوق ١٦   وهو لخبز واللحم وبدله זרענים • ³فكانوا ⁴ياخذوا حنطة للخبز وحبوب اخر ⁵يطبخونها

مثل عدس وارز وحمّص وباقلى ويشربون الماء ولا شكّ فى انهم ياخذون حبوب غير

متلوّنة وماء من النهر فى آنية ⁶نظيفة كما يريدون •

١٧   وهؤلاء الغلمان اربعتهم اعطاهم الله معرفة ورشد⁵ بكل خطّ

وحكمة ودانيال ⁷فاهم بكل وحى واحلام •

كانوا ⁸بالوصف الذى ⁹ذكره من لحكمة فزادهم الله ¹⁰تقع فى هذه الايام ¹⁰حكمة

زائدة بكل خطّ وكل فلسفة ¹¹يعرفونها للحكماء ¹²والكسدانيّين فاما دانيال فقد

زاد عليهم بامور ¹³الاهيّة من تفسير كل حزن ¹⁴لان ¹⁵الכשדים لم يقفوا على ¹⁶المنام •

ولم يتعذّر ذلك على دانيال فكان حننيا ¹⁷وشركاؤه فاضلين وكان دانيال افضل ١٥

منهم • والكل من مقصد ¹⁸البارى عز وجل كقوله נתן להם مثل قوله יהב חכמתא ב. כא

לחכימין وقال כי יוי יתן חכמה •   משלי ב. ו

١٨   وعند نهاية الايام الذى قال الملك لادخالهم انخلهم رئيس

الخدم قدام ببختناصر •

١٩   ¹⁹فتكلّم معهم الملك فلم يجد من جملتهم مثل دانيال ²⁰حننيا ١٥

ميشائيل وعزريا ووقفوا قدام الملك •

----

¹ Om. B.   ² וְאָדֶם B.   ³ K X; פכאנה B P.   ⁴ Om. B P X; ins. K.

⁵ יסבכונהא B P X; text K.   ⁶ שיפה B = נציפה (P).   ⁷ פהם K P X; פַּהֶם B.

⁸ אלוצף B.   ⁹ דכרהם codd.   ¹⁰ בחכמה codd.   ¹¹ יערפוהא B P.   ¹² אלכסדאנין

B P X; text K.   ¹³ אלאהיא K X; text B P.   ¹⁴ אן B P.   ¹⁵ כסדים B P.

¹⁶ מנאם B P.   ¹⁷ ואצחאבה B P.   ¹⁸ אללה B P.   ¹⁹ פכלם B P.

²⁰ ורפקאה B P.

Line 1 (1st). خبزا وادما.   2. وحبوبا, ياخذون.   3. حبوبا.   5. ورشدا

8. والكسدانيّون.   13. التى.

فصل ١ ٢٠. وكل خطاب حكمة فهم الذى طلب منهم الملك ١وجدهم

فاسوق ٢٠. عشرة اضعاف على كل الفلاسفة والسحرة الذين فى كل ملكه •

عرّف ان عند ما انقضت الثلث سنين الذين امر الملك ان يتربّون فيها
ويتعلّمون للخطّ واللغة ادخل بهم שר הסריסים اليه فاخذ الملك يمتحنهم فى باب (باب)

٥ من العلوم فلم يجد فى الغلمان ٢اليهود مثلهم ٣والى اليهود اشار بقوله מדלם°
وذاك بما تقدّم القول ان الله تعالى رزقهم قرائح صافية • ثم عرّف انهم كانوا افضل من
حكماء الملك عشرة اضعاف اما ان يكون عدد بالحقيقة ٤وذاك بحيث ان الملك
احضر كل حكمائه عنده بحضرتهم وامرهم بان يسالوا بعضهم بعض وهو يسمع ما
يجرى بينهم فى كل باب وباب ولا شكّ فى انه كان حكيم يبصر الكلام ويقف على ما

١٠ يجرى فى انهم ٥يفوقوا على كل حكمائه عشرة اضعاف فى سعة العلم ولعلّ كان
فى حكمائه من يعانى علمه طول عمره الى ان شاخ فلم يبلغ منزلة هؤلاء الاربعة •
٦كل ذلك° ليشرّف الله تعّ اولياءه الذى كانوا قد ٧نزلوا الى للحطيط وانهم قد
تمسّكوا بدينه ولم ٩يلدّذوا انفسهم باكل للحرام بل اكلوا للحبوب • وحصل عند الفلاسفة
توسوس ١٠بضد اللحمان° ١١فالوديل لمن اكل طعاما ملوّث باللحرام وعلاج الدنس وقد نجّس نفسه

١٥ واخرجها ١٢من القدوسيّة وابعدها عن الله تعّ ويتاوّل بالوان وياكل المحرّمات ويشرب
اشربة الدنس وفيها الשקוצים والרמשים وليس فرق بين للخمر وبين سائر الاشربة لان
كلهم مسكّم ولا يجوز لاحد فى للجالوث ان ياكل علاج من ١٣يعلم انه غير ثقة فى
ما يعانيه فى باب العلاج ١٤فطعامه للحرام والطمى ١٥وفى مثل هذا° قال אל תשקצו

ויקרא כ. כה את נפשותיכם وقال الولّى عليه السلام יראו את יוי קדושיו •
תה' לד. י.

٢٠ ٢١. وكان دانيال الى سنة احدى لكورش الملك •

اراد انه كان فى ملك السلطان الى سنة احدى لكورش وهو وقت اطلاق يسرائيل

<hr>

١ ונדרהם X; cett. וונדרהם. ٢ יהוד K. ٣ Om. B. ٤ ודאת B P. ٥ יקפו B P.
٦ (omitting כל) B P. ודלך ٧ זלו ונזלו B P. ٨ Sic. ٩ ילתדו B. ١٠ Om. B P.
١١ פאליל ואלעויל B P. ١٢ ען B P X; text K. ١٣ יסלם B. ١٤ פי מעאמה codd.
١٥ ופי מתלהא B P.

Line 3. يتربوا, اللواتى. 4. دخل بهم, ويتعلموا. 7. عددا. 8. بعضا.
9. حكيما. 15. يفوقون. 12. الذين. 14. ملوّثا.

للصعود الى بيت المقدّس لعمارة القدس فاعتزل عن العمل وتفرّد ¹للزهد وايضا انه   فصل ۱

كان قد شاخ ۰ واما رفقاؤُه فلم يذكر لهم خبر بعد قصّة الصنم ۰   فاسوق ۲۱

---

۲ ۱ وفى السنة الثانية من ملك تبوخنناصر حلم ببوخنناصر

احلاما وتكرّنمت روحه وسنته نكوّنت عليه ۰

كما قلنا فى سنة ثلث يهوياقيم للملك ان ليس هو اوّل ²الملك على ظاهر 5

القول كذلك هذا ايضا ليس هو ³اوّل للملك° لأن دانيال هو الذى فسّر المنام فهو

لا محالة مردود الى وجه ⁴آخر فقال قوم انها السنة ⁵الثانية لـגלות יהויקים وهو بعيد

لان دانيال لم يحصل له رتبة الا بعد ثلث سنين لقوله ולנדלם שנים שלוש ומקצתם

יעמדו לפני המלך فدلّ ذلك على انه ⁶جازهم بعد ثلث سنين وقال قوم انه ⁷مردود

الى خراب القدس كانه لم يحسب له ⁸ملك الّا بعد ان ملك يسرائيل وليس هذا 10

بعيد والذى يقرب متّى انه بعد ان ملك على الدنيا باسرها لقوله ובכל די דירין

בני אנשא חיות חיות ועוף שמיא ومن المعلوم انه فتح بيت المقدّس قبل ان يفتح صور ב. לח

وفتح صور قبل مصر ويقرب ان فتح مصر فى س|نة ⁹ثلاثين من ¹⁰ملكه والدليل على M

ذلك قول يحزقال عليه السلام ولا تحسب اربعيم سنة وقال بي כה امر يوی אلهים כט. יא

M def.

مקץ اربعیم سنة اקבץ את مצریم من העمים اשر |¹¹نפוצו שם وقد كان حكم اللّه كט. יג

تقع على سائر المنجلين انهم يبقوا على ما هم عليه تمام السبعين سنة الذى جعله 16

نبوخذناصر وولده وولد ولده لقوله ועבדו הגוים האלה את מלך בבל שבעים שנה فليس יرم' כה. יא

يرجع منهم احد الى بلده الّا بعد ان تتمّ السبعون سنة ففتح مصر آخر الفتوح

لان لم يقم به احد الملوك غير فرعون | فيكون قوله ובשנת שתים למלכות נבוכדנצר M

---

¹ באלוהד K X; text B P.   ² מלכה codd.   ³ לאול למלכה codd.   ⁴ יוכר B.

⁵ אלראבעה K.   ⁶ גזאהם B P; גזאהם K X; perh. اجازهم.   ⁷ מרדודה K X; text B P.

⁸ אלמלך K.   ⁹ סתת ותלאתין Heb.   ¹⁰ מלכה לקו סידנא Heb.   ¹¹ M after a

lacuna (from the word אשר) proceeds: לا قابل التى سنة السبعين فى ملكهم الى يرجعوا

اسرايل ولا غيرهم فعلمنا انه فتح مصر اخر ما فتح من البلدان لانه لم يقاس ملك بابل

.غير ملك مصر فيكون الخ

Line 2. خبرا.   10. ملكا.   11. بعيدا.   16. يبقوا ان.

فصل ۲ هى سنة ¹اثنين وثلاثين من ملكه بعد خراب القدس ثلثة عشر سنة۰ وفى هذه
فاسوق ۱ السنة نظر سيّد يحزقال صورت הבית وذلك انه ²فتح بيت المقدّس واحرق القدس۰ فى
السنة السابعة عشرة من ملكه فاذا كان نظرة المنام فى سنة اثنين وثلاثين من ملكه
كان قد مضى لخراب ³القدس ثلثة عشر سنة ويكون نظرة المنام فى سنة ⁴اربع عشرة
5 [من ملكه] ۰ وقال חלמות وهو منام واحد لا اكثر ⁵فالذى نقول فيه انه ⁶قال
חלמות من حيث ان فى المنام ⁷خمسة معانى ⁸وهو انه يقتضى ⁹خبر ارבע מלכיות
وخبر دولة يسرائيل ومثله قوله فى ¹⁰المنام الذى رآه يوسف عَم على חלומותיו ועל
בראשית לז.ה דבריו قبل ان ¹¹يرى المنام الثانى وذلك ايضا ¹²من حيث ان المنام الاوّل يقتضى
ثلثة معانى احدها והנה אנחנו מאלמים אלמים בתוך השדה والثانى והנה קמה אלומתי
10 والثالث והנה תסובנה אלומתיכם وعرّف انه تكرّمت روحه بحيث انه انتبه ونسى
المنام ¹³وطلب ان يذكر اى شى رآه فلم يذكره اصلا ثم رجع نام ¹⁴كما قال۰ ושנתו
נהיתה עליו اعلم انه فرق بين منام فرعون وبين منام نبوخذناصر بوجهين احدهما
שם מא. ח هو ان فرعو نظر منامه آخر الليل كما قال ויהי בבקר ونبوخذناصر راى منامه ¹⁵وهو
بعْدُ ليل۰ كقوله ושנתו נהיתה عليه ۰ والثانى هو ان فرعو ذكر منامه ونبوخذناصر
15 ¹⁷نسى منامه ۰ والسبب فى ذلك هو ان منام فرعو صحّ عن قرب ومنام نبوخذناصر
¹⁸بعد لم يتمّ ۰ وذاك لموضع ما تمّ منامه عن قرب لم ينسيه ¹⁹الله تَعَ المنام
ونبوخذناصر لموضع ما كان منامه ما يتمّ الّا بعد مدّة طويلة انساه الله تَعَ اياه۰
حتى اذا قيل له المنام كان ذلك دليل على صحّة تفسيره ۰

²فقال الملك ²⁰لادعاء بالفلاسفة ²¹والمشعونزين ²²والسحرة
20 والكسدانئيّين لاخبار الملك منامه ²³وجاؤا ووقفوا قدام الملك ۰

---

¹ Om. Heb. ² För القدس—فتح Heb. have אכרב אלבית. ³ אלבית Heb.
⁴ אלארבע Heb. ⁵ פאלרד B P. ⁶ فقال M. ⁷ خمس M. ⁸ وهى M.
⁹ Om. Heb. ¹⁰ فى منام يوسيف M. ¹¹ ראי Heb. ¹² Om. Heb. ¹³ פטלב Heb.
¹⁴ בקו Heb. (passim). ¹⁵ من M. ¹⁶ פי תוסם אלליל K; והו בעד אלליל P X; وهو ليل M;
codd. B. והו בעיד ליל ¹⁷ انسى M. ¹⁸ אלי אלאן K. ¹⁹ اياه—الله om. M. ²⁰ لادعى
M. (?) ²¹ المسودين M. ²² والسحار M. ²³ وjو Heb.; وجوو M.

Lines 1, 3. اثنتين. 1, 4. ثلث عشرة. 6, 9. معانِ. 16. ينسيهِ. 18. دليلا.

هؤلاء הכשדיא لهم ¹حكمة يدّعونها فلم ²تبق طبقة تتكلّم على كشف السرّ فصل ٢
³على ضرب ما اِلّا ⁴ودعاها وطالبهم ان يخبروه المنام الذى نسيه ۰ فاسوق ٢

٣ فقال لهم الملك حلم حلمت فتكرتمت روحى لمعرفة المنام ۰

⁵كان مراده منهم ان يخبروه المنام لقوله فى الفسوق ⁶المتقدّم להגיד למלך
חלמותיו ۰ ٥

٤ ⁷وخاطبوا الكسدانيّين مع الملك بالارمنيّة ايها الملك الى
الدهر عيش قل المنام لعبيدك ⁸والتفسير نخبر ۰

يمكن انه قال لهم ⁹بلغة غير لغة الارمنيّة ¹⁰חלם חלמתי هم بلغة الارمنيّة°
فخاطبهم هو بعد ذلك بلغة ¹¹الارمنيّة كما خاطبوه ¹²هم ۰ ¹³قالوا ¹³قل انت المنام
حتى نخبر تفسيره° ولم يقولوا° ليس نقدر على اخبارك بالمنام ۰ ١٠

٥ مجيب الملك ¹⁴وقائل الكلمة متّى نهبت ان لم تعرفونى
المنام وتفسيره ¹⁵اعضاء تعملون ودوركم صوافى يجعلون ۰

قال اوّلا طالبتكم بالمنام ¹⁶فاذ لم ترضون بذلك فانا اطالبكم بالمنام ¹⁷وتفسيره
¹⁸جميعا فان كنتم لا تعرفونى المنام ¹⁹وتفسيره ²⁰تبضعون قطع اى يقطع° ²¹لحمكم
وتصير منازلكم بما فيها صوافى للسلطان ۰ ١٥

---

¹ הכמא most Heb., misunderstanding حكما. ² Om. Heb. ³ وعلى ضرب M
and some Heb. ⁴ ודעאהם Heb. ⁵ وكان M. ⁶ Om. Heb. ⁷ حاطبوا M.
⁸ وتفسيره M. ⁹ בגיר Heb. ¹⁰ Om. Heb. ¹¹ מערופה Heb. ¹² Om. Heb.
¹³ يقولوا—قل om. Heb. ¹⁴ וקאל Heb. ¹⁵ איצא Heb. ¹⁶ ואד Heb.
¹⁷ والتفسير M. ¹⁸ Om. Heb. ¹⁹ After وتفسيره Heb. ins. תערפון. ²⁰ קטמעאן תקטע
Heb. (cp. A. E. ad h. l. ויפת אמר תעשו קטיעות קטיעות). ²¹ لحسكم P; חסכם K X;
לאסכם B.

Line 3. حلما. 6. الكسدانيون. 7. عِش. 12. يجعلون, تعملوا. 13. ترضوا.
14٠. لم تعرفونى, تبضعوا, قطعا. 15. صوافى.

فصل ٢ ۷ وان ۱انتم المنام وتفسيره تخبرون عطايا ۲وجوائز وعزّ ۳كبير

فاسوق ٦ تتسلّمون من قدّامى لكن المنام وتفسيره خبّرونى ۞

ـــ

۴قال لهم ان كنتمْ تعرّفونى المنام وتفسيره اهب لكم خلع ودنانير وجوائز جليلة
ومراتب جليلة تحصل لكم لكن بعد ان تخبرونى بالمنام وتفسيره ۞ لـمّا سمعوا
5 وعيده ووعده ولم يجدوا ۵مخلّص اعادوا قولهم ثانية مثل الاوّل كما قال

۷ اجابوا ثانية وقالوا المنام يقول الملك لعبيده وتفسيره نخبر ۞ | M def.

۶قالوا نحن ثابتين على قولنا الاوّل انّا نضمن تفسيره ولم يقولوا انّا لا نقدر
على اخبارك المنام ۞ لـمّا ۷راهم انه اوّلًا طالبهم بالمنام من غير ان ۸يعدهم
ويتواعدهم رجع طالبهم بالمنام وتفسيره ووعدهم فلـمّا اعادوا القول ۹بالتفسير ولم يقولوا
10 ليس نقدر على ذلك قال لهم قول اخر ۞

۸ مجيب الملك وقائل من يقين عارف انا ان الوقت انتم
مشترين (او بائعين) من حيث الذى نظرتم الذى نهبت متّى
الكلمة ۞

۹ الذى ان كان المنام لم تعرّفونى ۞ ۞ ۞ ۱۰واحدة وكلمة كذب
15 وفساد تواقفتم عليها للقول قدّامى حتى الذى الوقت يتغيّر
لكن المنام قولوا لى واعلم ان تفسيره تخبرونى ۞

قوله עדנא אנתון يعنى تمشّوا وقتكم وتتوهّمون انى امسك عن مطالبتكم بـه
وتتركونى مكروب الفكر وروحى ۱۱تتضرّب ولا تفكرون وذاك من حيث نظرتم المنام

──────────

۱ Perh. كنتم. ۲ Om. Heb. ۳ Om. B P. ۴ קאל להם אן M ; B P وان كنتم
כנתם תערפוני אלמנאם ותפסירה אהב לכם בעד אן الخ ; K X omit the whole par. (as
far as بالمنام). ۵ אלכלאץ Heb. ۶ קאל K X ; text B P. ۷ ראיהם codd. ; the
passage is mutilated. ۸ יועדהם K. ۹ בלא תפסיר codd. ۱۰ ואחרה om. B P ;
something like فان حكمهم has fallen out. ۱۱ תצטרב B P.

Line 1. ثابتون ۰۷. ۰۲ تتسلموا. ۰۳ خلعا. ۵. مخلصا. ۶. يقل. ۷۰ ثابتون.
etc. نظرتم ان ,حيث ان ,بائعون ,مشترون .۱۲ قولوا .۱۵ يتوعّدهم .9
تمشّون .۱۷۰

فصل ٢

ذهب متّى وليس اذكره وقوله حدה היא דתכון يعنى [1]حكم واحد وليس وليس افرق بينكم

فاسوق ٩

[2]فلا يتوهّم احد انى اعفو عنكم ولا عن احدكم وقيل ان كلكم قد اتّفقتم على شى

واحد وهو ان تقولوا قل المنام ونحن نفسّره ولا تخبرونى بالمنام ♦ وقوله [3]ומלה

ושחיתה يعنى به انكم ان لم تقولوا لى المنام فَهَمْ تفسيره لا تقولون [4]لى وانما

تقولون نحن نفسّر المنام مدافعة حتّى يتغيّر الوقت يعنى يندفع عنكم ما تواعدتم

به [5]لكن قولوا لى المنام فاذا قلتم المنام علمت منه انكم تقولون تفسيره ♦ اعلم

ان هذه הזדמנתם من لغة [6]זמן وحرف الدال° زائدة فيه يعنى انكم جعلتم هذا

الوقت مخالف لما كنتم تقولون لنا انكم تقفون على السرائر ♦ وذلك ان نبوخذناصر

كان يسمع منهم يقولون انهم [7]يقفون [اى° يصلون الى الوقوف] على مثل هذا

١٠

الجنس ولولا ذلك ما كان يطالبهم به ولم يقتلهم الّا بحيث انهم قبل هذا الوقت

كانوا يدّعون ذلك وفى هذا الوقت عند ما احتدث عليهم مطالبته ولم يجدوا الى

ذلك سبيلا قالوا مرّة بعد مرّة قل المنام حتى نفسّره [8]ولم يقولوا اتّا غير واصلين الى

ذلك وانما يذهبوا الى انه قد يعرف المنام [9]ويطالبهم ب(ما) ذكره او يكون لم يرى

منام اصلا ويطالبهم بما [10]لم يرى ♦ ولذلك قال لهم ומלה כדבה ושחיתה فلمّا سمعوا

١٥

منه هذا القول الاخير [11]اضطرّوا الى ان يكذّبوا انفسهم فى ما كانوا يدّعونه من انهم

يكشفون السرائر ♦

١٠ اجابوا الكسدانيّين قدام الملك يقولون ليس ايس انفسنا ولا

انسان على الارض الذى [12]منام الملك يقدر على الاخبار من حيث

الذى كل [13]ملك كبير وسلطان كلمة مثل هذا [14]لم يسال لكل

٢٠

فيلسوف ومشعون وكسدانىّ ♦

---

[1] Prob. حكمكم.   [2] פלם K X; text B P.   [3] כדנה K X; text B P.

[4] Om. K X; text B P.   [5] לא כן codd. After به B P add הדמין תתעבדון.

[6] מן לגה זמן חרוף אלדאל codd.   [7] يقفم اى only K.   [8] ולא codd.

[9] P X. בדכרה K; ויטאלבהם במא לא ירא או יכון—ויטאלבהם: [10] לא ירא X.

[11] אמרדו B P X; text K.   [12] Prob. أمَرَ.   [13] אלמלך B P X; text K.   [14] ליס

B P X; text K.

Line 4. Cp. Index s.v. هم.   5. توعّدتم.   7. زائد.   8. مخالفا.   13. يذهبون,بر.

14. بر,منامها   17. الكسدانيون   17. Cp. Fleischer, *Kl. Schr.* i. 148.

[II. 3.]   C

فصل ۲   اعلم ان لم يستجرئ احد على مخاطبة الملك غير الكسدانيّين لانهم كانوا اقرب الى

فاسوق ۱۰ الملك من الكل وهم ¹يناظرون عن الكل ²فقالوا ايها° الملك نحن نصدقك القصّة

ــــــ لا تظنّ ان واحدا من الناس يقدر على كشف ³هذا السرّ لا نحن ولا غيرنا فلا

تشغل قلبك بشى من ذلك ولا تطالبنا بمحال ولا تتوقّم عتّا انّا نقف على

٥ شى من ذلك ⁴واتّا نطلب بذلك مدافعة الوقت ⁵فيتعدّى بروحك° ثم احملنا

على العدل هل احد من الملوك الذى سبقك ⁶طالب حكماءه° بهذا الشى الذى

تطالبنا به ۰

۱۱ والكلمة ⁷التى الملك مطالبٌ بها عزيزة فى الوجود واخر ليس

ايس الذى ⁸يخبرها قدام الملك لكن الملائكة الذى ليس سكناهم

۱۰ مع البشريّين ۰

⁹وادى شرح القول قالوا ⟨איתי ואחרן⟩ לא איתי ويلوح لى انهم قصدوا دانيال ورفقاءه انهم

يدّعون مثل ذلك ثم احالوا على الملائكة فقالوا فى الفاسوق الاوّل לא איתי אנש על

יבשתא ويشيرون به الى حكماء اليهود وقالوا ¹⁰ليس يقف على ذلك غير الملائكة

فانصفنا ولا تطالبنا بمحال ۰

۱٥ ۱۲ من حيث هذا الملك قطب وجهه وغضب كثيرا وقال لابادة

كل حكماء بابل ۰

۱۳ والسنّة خرجت والحكماء مقتولبن وطُلب دانيال ورفقاوه

للقتل ۰

בנס תרגום זעף ۰

۲۰ لما راى انهم كاشفوه واتّسوه حرد وامر بقتل كل من حضر منهم فى بابل وعلى انه

يحضر غيرهم من المتفرّقين فى غير بابل بعد قتل هؤلاء ويسمع ما عندهم ۰ وقوله

ובעו דניאל וחברוהי להתקטלה دلّ على انهم لم يكونوا حاضرين معهم فى كل

פי תעדיב ⁵   .وانما Prob. ⁴   .הדה codd. ³   .פקאל איה K. ²   .נאטרין K. ¹

רוחך codd. ⁶   .מאלבו חכמאהם K. ⁷   .אלדי codd. ⁸   .יכברוהא codd. ⁹   P X; ואדי

ואדי B K.   ¹⁰ Prob. add.   .ههنا

Line 3.   .واحدا 6.   .الذين 9.   .الذين 11.   .آدى 17.   .مقتولون

المخاطبات ¹التى جرت بين الكسدانيّين وبين الملك وذاك من حيث انهم .لم فصل ٢
يدّعوا يوم قط انهم يقفون على ²السرائر كما كانوا يدّعون هؤلاء وانما حكماء فاسوق ١٣
بابل قالوا نحن وغيرنا مشتركين فى اخذ ارزاق الملك فلِمَ نُقتل نحن دونهم
يقتلون هم ايضا فلما ارتفع الخبر الى دانيال بادر وجاء الى سيّاف الملك حتى
استكشف الحال منه ودخل الى الملك وساله فى ³المهلة وضمن له ما التمسه من ٥
الحكماء ❖

١٤ حينئذٍ دانيال رقّ ⁴الراى والامر الى اريوخ كبير السيّافين
الذى للملك الذى خرج لقتل حكماء بابل ❖

١٥ مجيبٍ وقائل لاريوخ كبير السيّافين الذى للملك على ما
نا السنّة مسرعة (وقيل متنقّحة) من قدّام الملك ⁵حينئنٍ الكلمة عرّف ١٠
اريوخ لدانيال ❖

אֱדַיִן ماخوذ من אז مثل ومن אֱדַיִן וְעַד כְּעַן ❖ עֵטָא يوخذ من עֵצָה ❖ מְהַחְצְפָה عزرا ה. י.
قيل من لغة الفارسيّة يقال للوقيح חֲצִיפָא ❖ عرّف ان دانيال رقّ الراى والتدبير الى
اريوخ بعد ما ساله عن كشف القصّة مستوى واخذ رايه وامره فى ان يدخل الى
الملك يسله فى المهلة ام لا يدخل اليه خوف من حرد السلطان فلا يمهله ويامر ١٥
بقتله فلمّا علم اريوخ ان الملك يمهله ولا يستعجل عليه اشار عليه بالدخول ولعلّه
استاذن له حتى دخل اليه وساله فى المهلة واجابة الملك الى ذلك وكان السيف يعمل
فى حكماء بابل اوّل ⁶فاوّل ولعلّه ابتدى فى افضلهم ❖

١٦ ودانيال دخل وطلب من الملك ان يعطيه وقت والتفسير
لاخبار الملك ❖
    ٢٠

قوله וֹפִשְׁרֵהּ ليس يريد به انه يقول التفسير دون المنام فانه ⁷لا يفسّره من لا

---

¹ B. אלניאב ואלאמר ואלראי   ² codd. אלדי   ³ K. אלמסלה   ⁴ D. סאיר אלסראיר
⁵ Om. D X P (suppl. in marg.); ins. B.   ⁶ codd. פי אול   ⁷ לם D K X; text B P.

Line 2. يوما.   3. مشتركون.   4. يقتلوا.   8, 9. الذين.   14. Cp. Index
19. وقتا.   18. ابتدأ، اوّلا فاوّلا.   15. خوفا.   مستوى s.v.

فصل ٢ يقف على المنام ١اصلا وانما يفسّره من بعد وقوفه على المنام وتفسيره٠ ٠ فالذى
فاسوق ١٦ طلب الملك من حكمائه المنام وتفسيره ضمنه دانيال للملك وذاك من حيث
انه لاح له وقوى فى نفسه وغلب فى ظنّه ان ربّ العالمين سبّ ٢انساه
المنام ليكذّب حكماء بابل ٣ممّا كانوا يدّعونه ويكشف ذلك لدانيال ليشرّف
٥ امّته التى تعبد الاله لحقّ الذى هو مورى المنامات وهو كاشف الاسرار لا غيره
سبّ وقع ٠

١٧ حينئنٍ دانيال الى بيته مرّ ولحننيا ميشائيل وعزريا رفقائه
عرّف الكلمة ٠

كانه عرّفهم ايش السبب فى القتل وما ضمنه للملك ٠

١٠ ١٨ ورحمات للطلب من قدام الاه السماء على كشف هذا السرّ
الذى لما نا يبيدون دانيال ورفقاءه مع بقيّة حكماء بابل ٠

كانهم قاموا ٤الاربعة يدعون الى الله ويطلبون منه الرحمة فى ان يكشف هذا
السرّ ٥حتى لا يقتلون مع غيرهم ٦لانهم علموا ان لا يتركون ويقتل غيرهم٠ خاصّة
مع ضمان ذلك دانيال للملك ٠

١٥ ١٩ حينئنٍ لدانيال فى منظر الليل السرّ كشف حينئنٍ دانيال
بارك لاله السماء ٠

لمّا لم يكن فائدة فى كشف السرّ لاربعتهم وكان الواحد منهم يقنع كشفه
لدانيال الذى هو مقدّمهم لا سيّما ولم يطالب الملك ٧لكل حكماء بابل تعريفه
M المنام بل لو اخبره واحد منهم عفا عن الكل | الا ترى ان دانيال قال للسيّاف
٢٠ لحכימי בבל אל תהובד ٠ ثم عرّف انه لما كشف الله تع له ذلك سبّح الله تع على
ذلك واعلم انه اورى لدانيال المنام الذى نظره الملك وهو صورة الصنم وانقطاع الحجر
من لجبل ودقّ الصنم وحمل الريح ترابه وما صارت لحجر جبل عظيم ٠

---

١ ארבעתהם DK, omitting the rest. ٢ נשׂאה K. ٣ Prob. فيما. ٤ ارבעתهם
P X; text B K. ٥ Om. B. ٦ Om. B. ٧ لכל ואחד מן P X; text B K.

Line 5. مرئى. 13. s. يقتلوا. 22. حبلا عظيما.

۲۰ مجيء دانيال وقائل ليكون اسمه الذى للالاه ¹مبارك من
الدهر والى الدهر الذى الحكمة والجبروة الذى له هى ۰

۲۱ وهو مغيّر الاوقات والازمنة مزيل الممالك ومقيم الممالك معطى
الحكمة للحكماء والمعرفة لعارفى ²الفطنة ۰

۲۲ هو كاشف العميقة والمنسترة عارف ما فى الظلمة والنور عنده⁵
منحـل (³وقيل ساكن) ۰

۲۳ ⁴لك يا الاه ⁵ابائى انا شاكر ومسبّح الذى اعطيتنى الحكمة
والجبروة والان عرّفتنى الذى ⁶طلبناه منك الذى كلمة الملك
عرّفتنا ۰

اعلم انه عرّف انهم طلبوا من الله تع ⁷ان يكشف لهم السرّ⁸ حتى لا يقتلون ١٠
مثل غيرهم من حكماء بابل وعرّف ان دانيال شكر الله تع على ما كشف له
السرّ ولم يذكر شكره على خلاصهم ⁹من القتل⁰ اذ كان ١⁰قدّوش הַשֵׁם فى ¹¹نفسه اعظم
من خلاص ارواحهم ومع ذلك فانه اذا انكشف السرّ ¹²قد نجوا⁰ من القتل لا
محالة ۰ ثم انه شكر الله تع عزّ وجلّ حسب ما يوجبه معنى المنام فقال דּי
חכמתא ונבורתא من حيث انه رزق⁰ حكمة لم يقف عليها غيره كما قال דּי ١٥
חכמתא ונבורתא יהבת לִי فقال له للحكمة على احد ¹³معنيين إما ان يكون اراد
¹⁴به وهو للحكيم للجبار وإما ان يكون اراد⁰ به هو معطى للحكمة وللجبروة لمن يريد كما
قال فى ¹⁵للحكيم כי ¹⁶יוי יתן חכמה وقال فى القوّة הנותן לך כח ¹⁷وقال הנותן ליעף
כח ۰ ثم قال והוא מהשנא עדניא ¹⁸וזמניא اراد بقوله עדניا فصول السنة ¹⁹وهى

משלי ב. ו
דברים ח. יח
ישע׳ מ. כט׃

---

¹ مبرك M. مبّرك; B K X. ² المعرفة M. ³ او M. ⁴ Om. X. ⁵ ابائى M.
⁶ طلبنا M. ⁷ Om. M. ⁸ الدى حتى P. ⁹ Om. (apparently) M. ¹⁰ قدّوش,
معانيין or معنيان Heb. ¹¹ كشف السر Heb. ¹² تخلصوا Heb. ¹³ الشيم M.
(معانيين B); M. معناين ..... ¹⁴ Om. B. ¹⁵ فى للحكيم M. ¹⁶ ﻻ M. ¹⁷ Om. M.
¹⁸ Om. X. ¹⁹ Om. P M.

Line I. مباركا, ليكن. ١٥. يقتلوا.

فصل ٢   קר וחם וקיץ וחורף واراد [1]بقوله וזמניא الليل والنهار وليس يقدر على ذلك غير الخالق

فاسوق ۲۳ تَعَ ❖ ثم قال מהעדא מלכין ומהקם מלכין لانه مالك العالم كله يُملك من يريد ويعزل

من يريد وقدّم מהעדא على ومهقم מלכין من حيث انه [2]تقدّم الملوك [3]في العالم

קהלת א. ד [4]منذ [5]ملك [6]نمروذ بعد الطوفان وهذا يشبه قوله דור הלך ודור בא ❖ ثم قال יהב

٥ חכמתא لحكماء على ما تقدّم به القول وهو العقل والتمييز الذى به يفوقون بنى ادم

على الحيوان وبه [7]يفوق [8]بعضهم بعضًا فعرّف ان حكماء العالم وفهماءهم لم يصلوا

الى ذلك من [9]ذات انفسهم وانما الله تَعَ اعطاهم للحكمة والمعرفة ❖ وقوله הוא גלה

עמיקתא يقصد به [10]الى علم الغيب [11]ومثله باشياء هى فى عمق لا [12]يوصل اليها او

שע מו   شى مستور خفيّ لا يعلم به [13]وهو [14]كمعنى מגיד מראשית אחרית ويحتمل ايضا انه

١٠ اراد به يكشف عمّا فى ضمير الناس الذى لا يقف عليه غير خالق القلب والكلى

ירמ יז   وهى مستورة عن كل احد وهو عارف بها كما قال אני יוי חוקר לב בוחן כליות ❖

وقوله יודע מה בחשוכא وهو مستور ايضا عن بنى ادم لان حاسّة البصر لا تبصر فى

الظلمة وخالق الظلام والنور والنور [15]يعرف ما [15]هو فى الظلام كما [16]يعرف ما [16]هو فى النور

קלם יב   وكما قال الوليّ عليه السلام מן חשך לא יחשיך ממך وغرضه فى ذلك هو لما كان عارف

١٥ للخفايا [17]علم [18]ما نظره للملك وكشف لدانيال ❖ ثم بعد ان ذكر هذه الخمسة ضروب

التى هى مشاكلة لمعنى المنام وما يتعلّق به من [19]قوله די חכמתא וגבורתא [20]فهو

ما رزق دانيال منها واما تغيّر الازمنة [21]فهو ما غيّر [22]الاوقات [23]على يسرائيل وغيرهم

[24]وذلك لما تضمّن هذا المنام ازالة [25]ملك واقامة ملك وكذلك كشف الاسرار قال لك

אלה אבהתי ويشير به الى الاباء والاجداد الذى اختار الله تَعَ بهم وفضّلهم وفعل مع

٢٠ دانيال ذلك لانه من اولادهم فسبّح الله تَعَ على ما رزقه من للحكمة والجبروّة حتى

وصل الى تلك المنزلة [26]الجليلة قبل ان يرى نبوخذناصر المنام [27]وهى مدّة

---

[1] P only; cett. om.   [2] Heb. קר עדם; perh. تقادم.   [3] فى M P; cett. من.

[4] Heb. מתל   [5] Heb. אלמלך   [6] نمروذ M P; cett. אלנמדוד; M adds فى عالم.

[7] Heb. יפוקון   [8] B. בעץ עלי בעץ.   [9] Heb. דואת   [10] Heb. אלי עאלם; X. אלי עלם.

[11] M. ومثلها   [12] M. يصل   [13] M. وهى   [14] Heb. במעני   [15] M. يكون

[16] Om. M.   [17] Heb. עאלם   [18] Heb. במא   [19] add. Heb. מעני   [20] M. وهى;

cett. והו   [21] codd. وهو   [22] Heb. אלוקת   [23] على M P; cett. האל

[24] M. وكذلك   [25] Prob. ممالك.   [26] Om. M.   [27] Heb. והו

Line 5. بنو.   19. الذين.

اثنين وعشرين سنة منذ حصلت له منزلة عند الملك الى هذا الوقت ✦ ثم قال   فصل ٢

وكعن هودעתני די בעינא מنك يشير به الى ما كشف ¹سرّ الملك كما قال די מלת מلכا فاسوق ٢٣

²فكانه ذكر ما فعل معه منذ ³وقف قدام الملك الى هذه الحال ثم ذكر ما فعل معه

فى هذه القصّة واشرك معه رفقاءه فى هذه القصّة دون ما سبق له فى الزمان كقوله די

בעينا منك يعنى انا ورفقائى ومثله قال ⁴ههنا הודעתנא ليعرّف انه وان كان له كشف ٥

دونهم فان ذلك لجماعتهم من حيث ⁵ان الكل طلبوا للقتل والكل صلّوا وتضرّعوا

كما قال ورحمين למבעא وتمام القول | ✦ ثم بعد ان سبّح اللّه تع على ذلك مضى الى   M def.

اريوخ ولم يلبث لانه قد سبق الضمان بذلك وهو انه اجّله الملك ⁶الى وقت°

محدود ويمكن انه طلب منه يوم واحد لا اكثر ⁷فلمّا قاموا فى الصلوة اربعتهم اتّفق

ان دانيال عفى فراى المنام فانتبه مسرور وعرّف ذلك لرفقائه فسبّحوا هم ايضا للخالق ١٠

تع ولعلّه قام ليلا من وقته الى الملك ليسرّه بذلك فيهدى الناس من قلقهم ومن

خبطهم لانه لا شكّ فى ان البلد ⁸ارتجّ بقتل للحكماء فيبقى البلد بغير حكماء وهو

من اكبر المصائب على البلد ✦

٢٤ من حيث هنا دانيال دخل الى اريوخ الذى وكّله الملك

لابادة حكماء بابل نهى وكذى قال له لا تبيد حكماء بابل ١٥

ادخلنى قدام الملك والتفسير للملك اخبر ✦

عرّف انه للوقت مضى الى اريوخ وذلك لشيين احدهما ⁹ليخلو عن قتلهم

والثانى ليدخله الى قدام الملك ✦

٢٥ حينئنٍ اريوخ بسرعة ادخل دانيال قدام الملك وكذى قال له

قد وجدت رجلا من الجالوث من اليهود الذى التفسير يخبره٢٠

¹⁰للملك ✦

قوله די השכחת גבر والملك عارف بدانيال لا محالة هو انه ردّ لقول للحكماء يورى ان

---

¹ מن מנאם Heb.   ² وكانه M.   ³ וقت וקופה Heb.   ⁴ Om. M.

⁵ Om. M.   ⁶ לוقת P.   ⁷ פכמא B D.   ⁸ ארתהג D P Q.   ⁹ ליכلו codd.

¹⁰ אלملك B K P.

Line 1. اثنتين.   9. يوما واحدا.   15. مسرورا.   15. ثبّدَ.

فصل ٢ من اولاد الجالية ¹الذى هم۰ عند الحكماء نقص ذليلين هوذا يعرف

فاسوق ٢٥ هذا السرّ ۰

٢٦ مجيب الملك وقائل لدانيال الذى اسمه بلطشاصر ²هايبسك

قادر لتعريفى المنام الذى نظرت وتفسيره ۰

٥ قد ضمن للملك انه يخبره بالتفسير عند الاجل ولم يكن الملك متيقّن بذلك

فقال هل تقدر على ذلك وهو ان تخبرنى المنام وتفسيره لننظر ما تقوله وذكره

فى هذا الموضع الاسم الذى كنّاه به שר הסריסים من حيث انه جليل [فذكره

بالاسم الجليل] ۰

٢٧ مجيب دانيال قدام الملك وقائل اى السرّ الذى الملك مطالب

M² به ليس احد من الحكماء والمشعوذين والفلاسفة والقطّاعين | قادرين

١١ لاخبار الملك به

٢٨ اّلا ايس الله فى العلو كاشف الاسرار ³وعرّف للملك نبوخذناصر

ايش الذى ⁴يكون فى اخر الزمان منامك ومناظر راسك ⁵على فراشك۰

هنا هو ۰

١٥ قوله عن حكماء بابل وغيرهم انهم ⁶ما يقدرون على ⁷كشف السرّ ⁸ليس اقامة

عذر لهم وانما قصد الطعن على كل من يدّعى من حكماء الامم علم الغيب وقد اخبر

فى ما بعد انه لم يعلم السرّ من نفسه وانما للخالق تعّ كشفه وعرّف ان الله ⁹جلّ

---

¹ אלי תם ‎.B K. ² הא סַף ‎X. ³ מערף ‎Heb. ⁴ סיבון ‎Heb. ⁵ Om. Heb.

לים יריד אקאמה ‎Heb. ⁷ לא ‎For seqq. in Heb.: מא טאלבהם אלמלך ‎Heb. ⁸

עדר להם ואנמא כאן קצדה פי דלך תכדיב כל מן ידעי אנה יצל אלי דלך מן אחד

אלצרוב אלדי ידכרונהא חכמא אלאמם וסיקול בעד הדא אנה הו איצא לם יקף עלי דלך

מן גהה נפסה ואנמא אלכאלק כשף לה ה פי אלמנאם לא גיר תם ערף אלך‎. ⁹ Heb.

אללה תע כשף דלך אלסר‎.

Line 1. ذليلون, الذين. 3. هل انت (cp. Index s.v. ه; FLEISCHER, Kl. Schr.

i. 147). 5. متيقّنا. 15. ليس هو.

ذكره هو كاشف الاسرار ¹لمن يريد° لانه هو ²يورى المنامات لبنى ادم ³وقال ان اللـه فصل ٢
اعلمنى بما خطر ببالك ممّا يكون فى ما بعد° وقوله חלמך וחזוי ראשך قال فاسوق ٢٨
⁴انك لم تطالب الّا بما رايت وهوذا اخبرك المنام فتذكره وتعلم انى لم ازد ولم
انقص منه° ٭

٢٩ انت ايها الملك افكارك ⁵صعدت وانت° على فراشك° ⁶ما ⁷ما ٥
النى يكون ⁸بعد هنا والنى هو° كاشف الاسرار °عرّفك ما
يكون° ٭

¹⁰ذكر اوّلا شى ليس هو من المنام وليس هو مما نسيه الملك وهو قوله انك قبل ان
تنام وتنظر المنام افكرت فى ما يكون بعد هذا الوقت من ملكك الذى قد بلغ الى
العلوّ والنهاية ومن ياخذ الملك بعدك فلمّا سبق ذلك فى فكرك واردت ان تعلم ذلك ١٠
عرّفك كاشف الاسرار ما يكون بعد ذلك لتعلمه فتعلم ان الملك لمن يثبت من سائر
الممالك ٭

٣٠ وانا ¹¹فليس ¹²من حيث ان° فيّ حكمة افوق بها على جميع
الاحياء هنا السرّ كشف لى ¹³لكن من اجل ¹⁴ان التفسير للملك
يعرّفون وافكار قلبك تعرف ٭

¹⁵اراد انى لم اعلم هذا السرّ بحكمة وجدت فيّ اختصت بها من سائر (الناس) ١٥
كما يتفاضل العلماء فى اجناس العلوم ولم يذكر الوجه الاخر ¹⁶اكثر من قوله ان اللـه

---

¹ אלדי יוריה M²; corr. from Heb.   ² All but ى obliterated in M²; Heb. לם יזל.
³ Heb. וערף אן אללה תע אראד פי איראה הדא אלמנאם ליערפה מא סיכון מן הדה
⁴ Differently אלדולול אלתי תקום פי אלעאלם פאוראך הדא אלמנאם לתעלם מא יכון
worded in Heb.   ⁵ Om. Heb.   ⁶ צערו add. Heb.   ⁷ איש Heb.   ⁸ Om. Heb.
⁹ Heb. קד ערפך אלשי אלדי סיכון   ¹⁰ Instead of this paragraph (suppl. from Heb.)
M² has: اراد ان للخالق تعالى اعلمه ان ملكك وملك من يقوم بعده من دول الامم لا
¹¹ Heb. ל ם.   ¹² فى M².   يثبت شى منها الا دولة امته فقط التى ذلت فى زمانه ٭
¹³ לאבן P; الا cett. Heb.   ¹⁴ אלדי Heb.   ¹⁵ From اراد to غيرهم (p. ٢٦, l. 3) is
differently worded in Heb.   ¹⁶ Suppl. from P.

[II. 3.]   D

فصل ٢ كشف الّتى ١ذلك ٢لتعلم ما يكون وما قد افكرت فيه واردت ان تقف عليه٥ والذى
فاسوق ٣٠ اراده الله اوّلا فى ايرائه المنام ليعلم صحّة ما يدّعونه يسرائيل ان الملك ٣يهيب اليهم
دون | ٤غيرهم من الامم وان ملك نبوخذناصر يبطل وينتقل الى غيره ممن هو دونه
فيزداد غمّه ويعرّفه ايضا ان الذى يذكرونه يسرائيل ان الله تعّ يكشف لهم سرائر لا
٥ يقف عليها غيرهم حقّ والذى حكماؤه ان ليس يقف على هذا السرّ احد غير
الملائكة ان الله تعّ قد عرّفه لدانيال وان الله تعّ خلّص دانيال ورفقاءه من القتل
وانهم خلّصوا غيرهم من حكماء بابل من القتل كما تقدّم القول لֶחֲכִימֵי בָבֶל אַל
תְּהוֹבֵד ❖ ولا شكّ فى ان عند ما كان يفسّر المنام حضر جماعة يسمعون كلام دانيال
وعند قوله انك افكرت قبل ان تنام فى ما يكون بعد الملك قال كذى كذى كان وهذا ايضا
١٠ سر كشفه الله تعّ له ❖

٣١ انت ايها الملك كنت ناظرا وانا صنما واحدا كبيرا صنما ٥مركبا
جليلا وبهاءه زائدا قائما حنزاءك ومنظره فزع ❖

وصف الصنم باربعة اوصاف احدها كبره وهو طوله وعرضه وارتفاعه وذاك لطول
٦مكثتهم وعظم شانهم والثانى ترتيبه وهو قوله דְּכֵן رب وهو استواء دولتهم ونظام
١٥ ملكهم والثالث حسن منظره لان كل واحد منهم كان له عساكر والرابع هيبة وخوف
لان كل دولة لها هيبة وخوف وخوف وخاصّة على يسرائيل ❖

٣٢ هو الصنم راسه من ذهب جيّد صدره وذراعيه من فضّة
امعاؤه ووركه من نحاس ❖

٣٣ ساقيه من حديد رجليه بعضها من حديد وبعضها من حزف ❖

٣٤ ناظر كنت حتى انقطعت حجر لا بايادى وضربت الصنم على
٢٠ رجليه الذى الحديد والنحاس ودقّتهم ❖

٣٥ حينئذٍ اندقّوا جميعا الحديد والنحاس والذهب وصاروا مثل

---

¹ قولك M²; corr. from Heb.   ² لتعلم—عليه om. M²; suppl. from Heb.
³ يهسب M² (perh. يُوهِبُ). לָהֶם דִּין גֵּירֵהֶם (אֱלֹהִים לֵיס הו לֹדֵרהֶם P) Heb.   ⁴ See
note 15 on preceding page.   ⁵ Prob. مدكنا; cp. inf. vii. 19.   ⁶ مدهبهم X; text B etc.
Line 11. صنم etc.   17. وذراعاه.   19. ساقاه, رجلاه.   20. ناظرا, بايادى.

فصل ٢ موص من انادر الصيف وحملهم الربيع وكل اثر ما وجد لهم
فاسوق ٣٥ والحجر التى ضربت الصنم صارت جبلا عظيما كبيرا وملئت كل
الارض •

٣٦ هذا المنام وتفسيره نقول قدام الملك •

٥ حكى له المنام على ما نظره الملك وهو يشهد بذلك ثم قال وهوذا نفسّره لك لان
كل حكمائه لا يصلون الى تفسيره لا محالة كما لم يصلوا الى تفسيره[ة] منامه الثانى •

٣٧ انت ايها الملك ملك الملوك الذى الاه السماء اعطاك ملكوت
قويّة وعزيزة وصلبة •

٣٨ وفى كل موضع الذى ثم ساكنون الناس حيواناة البرّ وطائر
١٠ السماء سلّم بيدك وسلّطك على كلهم فانت هو الراس الذهب •

٣٩ وبعدك نقوم ملكوت اخرى ادون منك وملكوت ثالثة اخرى
التى تتسلّط بكل الارض •

٤٠ وملكوت رابعة نكون صلبة مثل الحديد من حيث ان
الحديد[1] راضّ كل هذا ندقّ وندرّض •

١٥ ٤١ والذى نظرت ارجله واصابعه بعضها من حديد وبعضها من
نحاس ملك منقسم يكون ومن اصل الحديد يكون فيها من حث
الذى نظرت حديدا مختلطا بخزف الطين •

٤٢ واصابع الارجل منها حديد ومنها [2]خزف من طرف الملكوت
نكون صلبة ومنها نكون منكسرة •

٢٠ ٤٣ والذى نظرت حديد مختلط بخزف الفخّار مختلطين يكونون

---

[1] After الحديد K B add צח מן אלחדיד.   [2] כזף P; פכהר cett.

Line 7. ملكوتا قويّا آلخ (cp. FLEISCHER, Kl. Schr. i. 173).   11. اخر, ويقوم, etc.
16. ملكا منقسما.   20. حديدا مختلطا.

فصل ۲ بنسل الناس ولا [لكون] ملتزقين يكون هذا مع هنا هكنى الحديد
فاسوق ۴۳ غير مختلط مع الخزف ❖

شرح فى تفسير المنام شيا من اوصاف ¹الصنم لم يشرح ذلك فى المنام وهو انه
قال רגלוהי מנהן פרזל ומנהן חסף وشرح فى التفسير רגליא ואצבעתא على ما نشرح
5 معناه ❖ وقوله ומלכותא חסנא ותקפא اما חסנא فلكثرة عساكره واما תקפא فلبطشه
واما ויקרא فلكثرة المال والعدد وطاعة الناس له ❖ وقال ובכל די דירין فعرّف ان
جميع بنى ادم تحت طاعته حتى ²ان الوحوش والطيور تحت سلطنته بمعنى انه
يفعل ما يشاء فيهم اذا وقع بهم وقال بعض الناس انه قصد الى كونه معهم فى
السبع سنين التى اقام معهم وهو يبعد من حيث ان هذا وصف للحال وليس هو
10 على شى ينتطر وقال سيّد ירמיהו עם ונם את חית השדה נתתי לו לעבדו وهى هيبة
כו. ו. وقعت له فى قلب الوحوش ³والطيور وقال اخر انه يشير بذلك الى سكّان البوادى
والجزائر المنقطعة ❖ فقال سيّد دانيال عم فلموضع ما قد حصلت فى هذه المنزلة
وانت اوّل الاربعة ممالك واجلّهم ⁴כנת الراس الذهب للجيّد ⁵هذا تفسير الراس ومن
يقوم بعدك ملك هو دونك كقوله ארע מנך اعلم ان ארע هو مشتق من ארעא وهو
15 استعارة يعنى ⁶ان الارض تحت الانسان ❖ وقال فى هذه المملكة الثانية אחרי لان
دينهم مختلف وسننهم غير سنن الكسدانيّين ولم يشرح ذلك ولم يطنب فى صفة الدولة
⁷الثالثة ⁸لكنه اكتفى بقوله انها ادون من الفقّة ❖ وقال די תשלט בכל ארעא ليفرق بين
الملك الثانى وبين الملك الثالث لان الملك الثانى ملك ثلث جهات العالم والثالث ملك اربع
جهات العالم ⁹وسنستوفى هذه الشروح كلها فى تفسير منام سيّدنا دانيال عليه السلام ❖
20 ثم ذكر الملك الرابع فمثّله بالحديد لا لمعنى انه دون النحاس لكن من اجل صلابته كقوله
תקיפא כפרזלא ولان هذا الملك ¹⁰يدقّ العساكر كما ¹⁰يدقّ الحديد الذهب والفقّة
والنحاس ❖ قال מהדק וחשל כלא وهو انه سحق الممالك الذى كانوا فى زمانه كما سنشرح
ذلك فى באדין דקו כחדא وهذا هو ملك الروم قبل ان يقوم ملك العرب ❖ وجعل
الراس الملك الاوّل والصدر والذراعين الملك الثانى والبطن والافخاذ الملك الثالث وجعل

---

¹ אלמנאם codd. ² P only; cett. om. ³ ואלטאיר or ואלטיר codd. ⁴ אנת B.

⁵ K only; והו cett. ⁶ Prob. كانّ. ⁷ אלתאניה codd. ⁸ لאנה codd.

⁹ וסיסתופא codd. ¹⁰ תדק codd.

Line 14. ملكا.

22. التى كانت.

فصل ٢ فاسوق ٤٣

[1]اوّل الساقين الملك الرابع قبل ملك العرب ◆ ولم يقل فى الملك الرابع אחרי كقوله فى [2]الثانى والثالث° من حيث ان اصل ملك الروم يونانيّين كما سنشرح ذلك فى בשנת שש למלכות בלשצאר ◆ ثم قال ודי חזיתא רגליא ואצבעתא فقوله רגליא يقصد بها الى مشط الرجل ثم ذكر [3]الاصابع واخبر ان رجلى هذا الصنم ⟨واصابعه⟩ تشبه [4]رجلى بنى ادم واصابعه رجلين وعشرة اصابع بل يشبه ان الصنم يشبه بنى ادم بقامة منتصبة وصلبه واوراكه وساقيه ورجليه واصابعه واعلم انه جمع الرجلين والاصابع بقوله רגליא ואצבעתא من حيث انهم من جوهر الحديد والفخّار جميعا كقوله מנהון חסף ומנהון פרזל ◆ فالحديد هم الروم والفخّار هم العرب وذلك ان الروم ملكت قبل العرب بماية سنين ثم ملك العرب وملك الروم مقيم كما هو مشاهد فى زماننا هذا ◆ ومثّل ملك العرب بالفخّار اذ ليس لهم كما للروم من القوّة ولا بطش كبطش الروم ◆ فقوله מלכו פלינה هو من وقت ملك العرب الذى كان الملك للروم وحدهم ثم ملك العرب معهم ◆ وقوله ומן נצבתא די פרזלא ليورى ان هذا الحديد المختلط مع الفخّار ليس هو من غير الحديد المتقدّم بل هو منه ◆ وتفسيره هو ⟨ان⟩ ملك الروم مقيم مع ملك العرب وانما [5]يشاركه العرب فى الملك فلذلك قال ומן נצבתא די פרזלא להוא בה ◆ وقوله מערב בחסף טינא ليس يريد [6]اختلاط ممازجة كاختلاط الذهب مع الفضّة لان هذا لا يصحّ فى جواهر الحديد والفخّار لكنه كاختلاط الحنطة مع الشعير وما جرى مجراهما وهو ⟨ان⟩ بعض مشط الرجل حديد وبعضها فخّار ◆ وذاك لطول المشط ◆ وكذاك القول فى الاصابع ايضا ◆ وقوله فى الاصابع מנהון פרזל ומנהון חסף يشبه ان هذا الحديد ليسه من الروم لكنه شرح فى العرب فقط ◆ فقال فى [7]تعبير ذلك מן קצת מלכותא תהוא תקיפה ומנה תהוה תבירה فإما ان يكون اراد به اوّل امرها كان [8]صلب على ما نشرح ذلك فى موضعه [9]من هذا السفر واخر [10]امرها يكون ضعيف وعلى هذا التفسير يجب ان يكون اوّل الاصابع المتّصلة [11]بمشط الرجل ⟨من⟩ حديد واخرها من فخّار ◆ وإما ان يكون قصد به الى ملك [اولاد] قوم من اولاد الصاحب يكون لهم قوّة وقوم اخر تبع يكونون دونهم

1 האלי P; om. cett. 2 אלתאניה ואלתאלתה codd. 3 אלאצבע codd. 4 רגל BP(KX?). 5 שארכוה codd. 6 אכטלט B. 7 תג״יר codd. 8 צלב PQX; צלם BK. 9 פי מוצעה בקולה פי הדה BKX; text P. 10 אמרה codd. 11 מע משט P.

Line 2. يونانيّون. 9. سنة. 19. ليس. 21. صلبا. 22. ضعيفا.

فصل ٢ مثل الفخّار ٠ وقوله ודי חזיתא פרזלא מערב בחסף טינא ليس عاطف على اختلاط

فاسوق ٤٣ الاصابع اذ لم ينصّ عليها بلفظ مערב وانما قال منه פרזלא ومنه חסף وانما هذا

يرجع الى اختلاط الرجلين المقول فيها כל די חזית פרזלא מערב בחסף טינא وهو

اختلاط الروم والعرب فعرّف انه كما انهم اشتركوا فى الملك كقوله ملכו פלانه فانهم

يختلطون فى باب الزيجة والولد فليس منهم من ينكر ذلك كما ينكروه اسرائيل

فلذلك قال ايضا متعارضين لهن בזרע אנשא لان المسلمين لا ينكرون ان يكون لهم

زوجة على دين النصرانيّة ولا يكره النصارى ان يعطيَ زوجة على دين الاسلام ٠

وقوله ولا ل>ה<ون دבקין דنה عم דنه بحيث انهم يخالفونهم فى اصل الدين لان هولاء

يقولون بالواحد فقط ويعتقدون فى عيسى بن مريم انه بشريّ وهولاء يعتقدون

انه خالق السماوات والارض كما هو مشهور من دين النصارى وكذلك القبلة

والوان كثيرة يطول شرحها ٠ فلذلك قال ولا להון דבקין דنه עם דنه ٠ وبيّن ذلك

بقوله הא כדי פרזלא يعني كما لا يختلط الحديد مع الفخّار ٠ الى ههنا انتهى

وصف الصنم ٠ وتفسيره وهي اربعة ممالك تقوم فى الدنيا وَاوّلها هى التى خرّبت

القدس واجلت الاّمة عن ديارها وبعدها ملك الفرس وهى امرت ببنى البيت

واطلقت المرور اليه وابذلت المال والنفقة والقرابين من مالها والثالث هو ملك

اليونانيّة لم تجلى الاّمة ولا خرّبت ديار لكن قد لحق الاّمة منها اذاً كما تواترت

ذلك اليهود فى كتبها واخبارها وان كانت كتب الانبياء لم تشرحه ٠ واما الدولة

الرابعة فقد اجلت اسرائيل كما عملت الاولى وزادت على ذلك فى البغضة والاذاء

واما العرب فلم تفعل كما فعل غيرها من الجالوث والخراب لكنها قد اذت فى الذل

والهوان والدين٠ وغير ذلك مما سنذكر طرفا منه فى منام سيّد دانيال عليه السلام

ونبوّته ٠ وجعل كل هذه الدول مضمومة بعضها الى بعض اذ ليس فيها صاحب حقّ

وان اختلفت ايضا مذاهبها وجعل كلها قطعة واحدة وبعد ان ذكر تفسير الصنم

ذكر تفسير الحجر التى انقطعت من الجبل فكسّرت الصنم ٠ وقال

١ ואלאולד codd.   ٢ وبعتقدون—وهولاء om. X; text B P Q.   ٣ ישו B; בن مريم

om. B; text P Q.   ٤ ممא P Q X; text B.   ٥ משאהד B X; text P Q.

٦ ובעצהא B.   ٧ והו B.   ٨ תתוארת codd.   ٩ נלת codd.   ١٠ ممא B X;

text P.   ١١ ואלאדני P only; ואלדין cett.; prob. ואלהואן ואלرين, i.e. والادناء.   ١٢ Om.

P X; ins. B.

Line ١. عاطفا.   ٣. فيهما.   ١٦. تجل, ديارها.

 ٤٤ وفى ايّام هؤلاء الممالك يقيم الاه السماء ملك الذى لا ينبين فصل ٢
للابد وملك لشعب اخر لا تنترك تدقّ وتفنى كل هذه الممالك هى فاسوق ٤٤
ثابتة الى الدهر ٠

٤٥ من حيث الذى نظرت ان من الجبل انقطعت حجر لا
بايادى ودقّت الحديد والنحاس والخرف والفضة والذهب الالاه ٥
الجليل عرّف الملك ما يكون وحقّ المنام وثابت تفسيره ٠

مثّل الاربع ممالك بصنم مصنوع ومثّل ملك اسرائيل بحجر انقطع من جبل لان
ملكهم ¹ازلىّ فاما ان يكون الامّة واما ان يكون المسيح الذى هو منهم او من ولد
داود عمّ ٠ وقال فى المنام انها دقّت رجلى الصنم وهو انهم يدقّون اذوم ويسماعيل ٠
ثم قال באדין דקו כחדה بحيث ان ناموس كل مملكة مقيم الى زمان ملك المسيح ١٠
وقوم منهم ايضا ٠ فعرّف انها تدقّ يسماعيل واذوم وتتلف بقايا الثلث ممالك
المتقدّمة هم ونواميسهم كقوله תדק ותסף כל אלין מלכותא ٠ واورى الفرق بين هؤلاء
الاربع ممالك وبين ملك المسيح وهو ان كل مملكة من هذه الاربع ممالك بطل ملكها
وسلّم الملك الى غيرها وهذه المملكة ليس تبطل ولا تسلّم الى غيرها ٠ ولم يذكر فى
الصنم ان اللّه تعّ اقامة كما ذكر فى ملك المسيح كقوله יקים אלה שמיא لانهم ذليلين ١٥
قليلين واللّه تعّ هو الذى يقيمهم من التراب وينزل غيرهم من العلوّ لانه عز وجل
انزل بهم من العلوّ كقوله השליך משמים ارض תפארت ישראל ورفع دولة غيرهم كقوله איכה ב. א
הרים קרן צריך وكذلك يفعل فى المنتظر ²يرفع شان يسرائيل ويذلّ الدول كقوله מי שם ב. יז
כיו המנביחו לשבת ٠ واورى اللّه تعّ [فى] هذا المنام لنبوخذناصر لانه اوّل الممالك תהל׳ קיג. ה
واعظمها ليعرّفه ³وكل مملكة ⁴تقوم بشرف يسرائيل وما يكون منها فى اخر الزمان ٢٠
وان كل دولة ستبطل عند دولتها فلا ⁵تظنّ واحدة منها انها دولة تثبت وانه سبيلهم
ان لّا يذلّوها لانها تحت الادب لا غير فلما لم يفعلوا ذلك كان اللّه عز وجل ساخط
عليهم ومعاقبا لهم وفى ذلك ايضا حسّن الصبر لامّته لما تعلمه من بطلان هذه الدول
وثبات الدولة لها وخشوع الامم بين يديها فهو ⁶العزاء الكبير لها ٠ وقوله וייב

---

¹ אצלי P Q X; text B.   ² ברפע codd.   ³ ולכל codd.   ⁴ יקום codd
⁵ יטן codd.   ⁶ אלעזר B.

Line ١. مملكة etc.   ٥. بايادو.   ١١. وقوما.   ١٥. ذليلون etc.   ١٧. نزل بهم.
٢٢. ساخطا.

فصل ٢ חלמא ומחזון פשרה يعرّف ان ليس هذا المنام عن تخييلات ولا عن شغل فكر الذى قد

فاسوق ٤٥ يرى الانسان بالمنام ما كان يعانيه ويفكر فيه ويراه وليس له تفسير ينتظربل هو منام

قصد الله تعالى اراءه اياه ٠ وقوله ומחזון פשרה يعنى ان هذا الذى فسّرته صحيح

وليس له تاويل غير ما قلناه ٠

٤٦ حينئنٍ الملك بختاصروقع على وجهه ولدانيال سجد وهديّة

٥ وقرابين قال للصبِّ له ٠

لما اعتقد انه فى دانيال ١شىء من٠ الالهيّة على ما ترى النصرانيّة فى المسيح

جعله موضع الالاه فوقع على وجهه وسجد له وامر ان يقرّب له القرابين كما ٢تقرّب

الالاه ولم يذكر انه قرّب له فيقرب فيه ان دانيال منعه عن ذلك ٠

٤٧ مجيبٍ الملك وقائل لدانيال من يقين حقّ ان الاهكم

١٠ هو الاه الالاهات مولى الملوك وكاشف الاسرار حتى قدرت على

كشف هذا السرّ ٠

٤٨ حينئنٍ سمّى الملك لدانيال ٣جليلى (او معلّمى) وعطايا كبار

كثيرة اعطاه وسلّطه على كل مدينة بابل وكبير الروساء على كل

١٥ حكماء بابل ٠

قوله מן קשט يحقّق ان الله هو الاه الالاهات كقوله הוא אלה אלהין وان من اجل

ذلك وصل دانيال الى علم هذا السرّ ٠ ثم انه سمّاه ٤רב وجعل نفسه تلميذا له او

غلاما له كقوله רב ٠ ثم انه ٤برّه بعطايا كثيرة جليلة كما ٥ضمن الكسدانيّين מתנן

ונבזבה וגו' وزاده شى لم يذكر لاولئك بالشرح وهو انه جعله سلطان على مدينة بابل

٢٠ وجعله رئيس على كل حكماء بابل ٠

٤٩ ودانيال طلب من الملك حتى وكّل على عمالة مدينة بابل

لشنرخ ميشخ وعبين بنغو ودانيال فى باب الملك ٠

كما بلغ الى رتبة جليلة لم يجُزْ عنده ان يبقون رفقاؤه بغير رتبة جليلة فاما هو

---

١ שיין codd. ٢ יקרב codd. ٣ אלידליל P. ٤ ברא B. ٥ Prob. ضامن.

Line ١٣. כבارا. ١٩. سلطانا, شيئا. ٢٠. رئيسا. ٢٢. ل redundant. ٢٣. يبقوا.

فحصل فى باب الملك لا على انه بوّاب لكنه ينظر فى امور الناس من جنس ما كان   فصل ٢
يعمله يوسف فالاسم للملك والامر والنهى لدانيال عمّ ۞   وتقدّم المدوّن ذكر رتبة رفقائه   فاسوق ٤٩
لما سيذكرو من بعد ذلك ۞

الى هاهنا انتهى الفصل الثانى' ثم اخذ¹ فى الفصل الثالث ۞

٣ ۱ بختناصر الملك عمل صنما نهبا ارتفاعه ستون نراع ²فتته ٥ ٥
ست ³انرع اقامه ⁴فى بقعة دورا فى مدينة بابل ۞

٢ وبختناصر الملك بعث لجمع الامراء والروساء والعمّال واصحاب
الشرط والجهابنة والكتّاب واهل العلم والفقه وكل سلاطين المدن
لداشن الصنم الذى اقام بختناصر الملك [وكانوا وقوف حذاء الصنم
الذى اقام بختناصر] ۞

٣ˉ حينئن كانوا مجتمعين الامراء والروساء والعمّال واصحاب
الشرط والجهابنة والكتّاب واهل العلم والفقه وكل سلاطين المدن
الى داشن الصنم الذى اقام بختناصر الملك وقائمين ⁶قدّام الصنم
الذى اقام بختناصر ۞

٤ ومنادى ينادى بالقوّة لكم ⁷قائلون ايها الشعوب والامم ١٥
واللغات ۞

٥ فى الوقت الذى تسمعون صوت قرن البوق والصفّارة والقيثار
والعود والناى والصرناى وكل الوان الات الملاهى (او الغنى) تقعوا
وتسجدوا لصنم الذهب الذى اقام بختناصر الملك ۞

¹ After اخذ B X add יְדַכֵּר.   ² Sic; cp. ܨܠܡܐ.   ³ דראע K Q; אדרע cett.
⁴ פי בעד בקעה B K; דורה all.   ⁵ Verse 3 om. Q X; supplied in the marg. of P; it
had been omitted (except the last clause) in the archetype of Hebr.; the corrector of
P translated it afresh with אלדי ב׳ אלמ׳ אקאמה.   ⁶ קדם codd.   ⁷ קאילון K P Q;
קאילין cett.

Line 3. مِن redundant.   5. ذراعا.   9. وقوفا.   15. مناد.
[II. 3.]   E

فصل ٣   ٦   ومن لا يقع ويسجد فى تلك الساعة يرمى الى ¹وسط اتون

فاسوق ٦   النار الوقيدة ٠

<hr>

٧   من حيث هنا فى الوقت كما كانوا سامعين كل ²الشعوب
صوت قرن البوق والصقارة والقيتار والعود والناى وكل انواع [الـ]الات
الملاهى (او الغنى) واقعين كل الشعوب والامم واللغات ساجدين
لصنم النهب الذى ³اقامه بـختناصر ⁴الملك ٠

٨   من حيث هنا فى الوقت تقدم رجال كسدانيين وغمزوا
باليهود ٠

٩   اجابوا وقائلون لبـختناصر الملك ايها الملك عيش للابد ٠

١٠   البس انت الملك جعلت امرا ان كل انسان الذى يسمع صوت
قرن البوق والصقارة والقيتار والعود والناى والصرناى وكل انواع
الات الغنى يقع ويسجد لصنم النهب ٠

١١   ومن الذى لا يقع ويسجد يرمى الى وسط اتون النار
الوقيدة ٠

١٢   ايس رجال يهود الذى وكلتهم على عمالة مدينة بابل وهم
شنرخ ميشخ وعبين نغو اولائك الرجال لم يجعلوا امرا من جهتك
ايها الملك على انفسهم لالاهك غير عابدين ولصنم النهب الذى
اقمت غير ساجدين ٠

١٣   حينـئـن بـختناصر بغضب وحرد قال لاجابة شنرخ ميشخ
وعبين نغو حينـئـن اولائك الرجال جيبوا قدام الملك ٠

<hr>

¹ P only; om. cett.   ² סעוב P.   ³ P only; cett. אקאם.   ⁴ P only; cett. om.

Line ١. يُرْم.   ٥. واقعون.   ٧. كسدانيّة.   ٩. عش.

١٤ مجيب بختناصر وقائل لهم احقًّا يا شنرخ ميشخ وعبين‌نغو   فصل ٣
لالاهى ليسكم عابدين ولصنم الذهب الذى اقمت غير ساجدين ⚬   فاسوق ١٤

١٥ الساعة ابسكم عتيدين فى ٢ الوقت الذى تسمعون صوت قرن
البوق والصفارة والقيتار والعود والناى والصرناى ‹وكل انواع الغنى›
تقعوا وتسجدوا للصنم ١الذى اقمت٠ وان كان لا تسجدون فى ٥
الوقت ترمون الى وسط اتون النار الوقيدة ومن هو الالاه الذى
ينجيكم من يدى ⚬

١٦ اجابوا شنرخ ميشخ وعبين‌نغو وقائلون للملك ليس نحن
محتاجين على هنا قولا لاجابتك ⚬

١٧ ٢فان ايس الاهنا الذى نحن عابدين قادرا لينجينا من ١٠
اتون النار الوقيدة ومن يدك يا ايها الملك ينجى ⚬

١٨ وان كان ٣لم ينجينا فمعلوم يكون عندك ان لالاهك ليس
نحن عابدين ولصنم الذهب الذى اقمت غير ساجدين ⚬

١٩ حينئن ٤بختناصر امتلأ حرد وقالب وجهه تغيّر على شنرخ
ميشخ وعبين‌نغو مجيب وقائل لاشعال الاتون للواحد سبعة حتى ١٥
نظر لاشعاله ⚬

٢٠ ولرجال جبابرة القوّة الذين فى جيشه قال لكتف شنرخ
ميشخ وعبين‌نغو لرمى الى اتون النار الوقيدة ⚬

---

¹ Om. P X; text B.   ² כאן B.   ³ לא codd.   ⁴ אלמלך X; om. P; text B.

Line 2.   12. ينجينا.   15. لبسنا.   12, 8. عابدوه.   5. تقعون وتسجدون.   لستم.
فمعلوما.   14. حردا.   15. See Index, s.vv. حتى, واحد.

٢١ حينئذٍ اولائك الرجال كتّفوا بسراويلاتهم [1]خفّاتينهم
[2]وطيالستهم ولباسهم ورميوا الى اتون النار الوقيدة ٠

٢٢ من حيث هنا الذى قول الملك [3]متّقِمٍ والاتون اشعل فضل
اولائك الرجال الذى حملوا لشنرخ ميشخ وعبيندنغو قتلهم شرار
النار ٠

٢٣ واولائك الرجال ثلاثتهم شنرخ ميشخ وعبيندنغو وقعوا الى
وسط اتون النار [4]مكتفين ٠

٢٤ حينئذٍ بختناصر الملك نهل وقام بدهشة مجيب وقائل
لندمائه اليس ثلاثة رجال رمينا الى وسط اتون النار مكتّفين
مجيبون وقائلون للملك يقينا ايها الملك ٠

٢٥ مجيب وقائل ها انا [5]ناظر اربعة رجال محلّلين سائرين فى
وسط النار وشىء من الفساد ليس فيهم ومنظره الذى للرابع شابه
للملائكة ٠

٢٦ حينئذٍ تقدّم بختناصر الى [6]باب اتون النار الوقيدة مجيب
وقائل شنرخ ميشخ وعبيندنغو عبده الذى للالاه العالى اخرجوا
وتعالوا حينئذٍ خارجين شنرخ ميشخ وعبيندنغو من وسط النار ٠

٢٧ ومجتمعين الامراء والعمّال وندماء الملك ناظرين لاولائك
الرجال الذى لم تتسلّط النار بجسمهم وشعر راسهم لم يتشيّط
وسراويلاتهم ما تغيّرت ورائحة نار ما [7]صعدت فيهم ٠

---

[1] כפיטאנהם many MSS.   [2] וטילסאתהם codd.   [3] מתקמה codd.   [4] מכחפין B P X;
מכפתין D K.   [5] Om. B D K.   [6] Om. B K; add in marg. D.   [7] זאלת P X; text B etc.

Line 2. ورموا.   3. فضلا.   4. الذين.   16, 17. خارجون etc.   18. الذين.

٢٨ مجيب بختناصر وقائل تبارك الاههم الذى لشنرخ ميشخ فصل٣
وعبين‌نغو الذى ارسل ملكه ونجا عبده الذى اتكلوا عليه وكلمة فاسوق ٢٨
الملك غيّروا وسلّموا اجسامهم حتى لا يعبدون ولا يسجدون لكل
الاه لكن لالاههم ◦

٢٩ ومتى اجعال امرا الذى كل شعب وامّة ولغة الذى يقول ٥
غلط على الاههم الذى لشنرخ ميشخ وعبين‌نغو اعضاء يُعمل
وبيته صوافى يُجعل من حيث ان ليس الله اخر الذى يقدر
لخلاص مثله ◦

٣٠.١ حينئن الملك انجح لشنرخ ميشخ وعبين‌نغو فى مدينة
بابل ◦ ١٠

هذه القصّة جرت لبختناصر وكان لحننيا ميشائيل وعزريا فيها مدخل ٢فدوّنت
لنا لما فيها من النفع الكثير ◦ اوّل ما يجب ذكره هو ما الذى حمل بختناصر على
عمل هذا الصنم فنقول فى ذلك انه لما تمكّن العالم فعل هذا الصنم ونادى المنادى
(ان) من لا يقبل ويسجد يُرمى لاتون النار ◦ فاذا فعلوا ذلك بان طاعتهم له وقبل
ان يصيروا تحت ملكه لم يمكنه ذلك ◦ وقد كان له معبود اخر يعبده كما سيقول ١٥
لالهى לא איתיכן ◦ فقد تمّ له مراده اذا بان ان الكل سجدوا له غير اليهود الذى
ذكر الكتاب ◦ وذكر ارتفاعه وفتحه وقوله פתחה فيه ٣[فتح] ٤طوله وعرضه ◦ واقامه
ببقعة دורה لانها تسع عالم من الناس يقفوا فيها ◦ وجعل ارتفاعه ستين ذراع
حتى يرونه من بُعْد حتى يسجدون اليه من كل ناحية ◦ ولم يقيمه قبل ان يجمع
الناس وانما صنعه اوّلا ثم بعث وجاب الناس من كل مدن العالم فلما حصلوا فى ٢٠
بابل اقامه وامر بالسجود له ◦ وجاب الاجلّاء ولم يجيب الرعيّة اذ ذلك متعذّر
٥ويخرب العالم ولا يسعهم المكان ايضا وانما جعلوا هولاء للجائين خلفاء لهم يضبطون

---

¹ Verse 30 om. B. ² פדוונהא B K; פדוינהא P X. ³ Om. P. ⁴ צׂולה X;
text B etc. ⁵ Prob. فيخرب.

Line 2. الذين. 3. يسجدوا,يعبدوا. 6. غلطا. 18. عالما,يقفون,ذراعا.
19. يروة,يسجدوا,يقمه. 21. يجىّ ب. 22. للجايئون.

فصل ٣   المواضع ¹التى كانوا فيها الى ان يرجعون ◇ وعرّف انهم جاءوا عند ما ارسل اليهم

فاسوق ٣٠   ولا يتخلفوا فبان من ذلك طاعتهم له ◇ فلما اجتمعوا الى بابل عمل للصنم دعوة

فكانهم يجتمعون ويسجدون له وبعد ذلك ياكلون ويشربون ولم ياكلوا قبل السجود

فكانه ذبح الذبائح واستعدّها لهم ◇ ثم عند ما اجتمعوا اقام اصحاب الملاهى

5 بالاتهم فلما ثبتوا قدام الصنم امر المناديين يطوفون فى الناس وينادون ويقولون

معاشر الناس كونوا على حذر ولا تغفلون عن السجود للصنم اذا ما سمعتم صوت الات

الملاهى يقع كل واحد على وجهه ساجد للصنم وانه اى انسان لم يسجد فى الوقت

يُلقى ²فى اتون النار ◇ وهذا يدلّ على انه قد بنا اتون نار عظيم حتى ان خالف

انسان يطرح الى النار وليس بدّ من ان قد جعل قوما من قِبَلِه يطوفون فى الناس

10 الذين جاءوا من البلدان حتى ينظرون هل خالف احد او ³لم يخالف ◇ ثم عرّف

المدوّن ان كل من حضر سجد عند ما سمع صوت الات الملاهى غير هؤلاء الثلاثة

المذكورين وبجب عند ذلك احد قولين إما ان يكون اراد من الناس ان يتركوا

دينهم ويعبدوا غير معبودهم او يكون اراد منهم طاعتهم فقط ◇ فلمّا بعُد ان

يكون اراد منهم ان يتركوا معبودهم اذ الأديان كانت مقيمة كل امّة تعبد معبودها

15 وجب ان نقول انه اراد منهم طاعة لا غير ◇ والكلام فى كل يهوذيّ كان فى بابل هو

ان الملك لم يطالب بذلك العوامّ وانما طالب اصحاب السلطان والاجلّاء واما غيرهم

فلا ◇ ولو لم يكون حننيا ميشائيل وعزريا من اصحاب السلطان كما تقدّم به

القول لم ⁴يحضرهم فى الجملة ولم يلزمهم السجود ◇ فاما الكلام فى دانيال عمّ فلم

يراد منه السجود للصنم لانه كان ارفع طبقة لانه كان عنده مقام المعبود كقوله

20 ומנחה וניחחין ◇ وهؤلاء الذين غمزوا بهم هم غلمان الملك الذى امرهم ان يجعلوا

قصدهم من الناس ◇ وقوله לאלהך לא פלחין يقصدون به المعبود الذى كان يعبده

قبل ان يوقف الصنم ◇ وعرّف انه عند ما قيل له عنهم انهم لم يسجدوا للصنم

امتلأ حرد وتغيّر لونه * * * ◇ وإما ان يكون من حيث ⁵وقع الخلاف منهم و[اما]° اذا

---

¹ אלדי codd.   ² אלי P.   ³ לם P; לא cett.   ⁴ יחצרוהם P X (ex corr.);

text B.   ⁵ יקע P X; אלכלאף B K; אלכלאﬡ P Q X; ואנמא K P X; ואנמא B Q;

something apparently is lost.

Line 1. يرجعوا.   2. ولم.   5. المنادين.   6. تغفلوا.   7. ساجدا.   8. عظيما, يلق.

15. ينظروا.   17. يكن.   19. يُرّد.   20. الذين.   23. حردا.

فصل ٣   انكشف ذلك لغيره تنقص هيبته ولولا ذلك لم يصعب عليه وهو قريب في نفسى

فاسوق ٣٠   وتشوّش عليه ما اراده ولعله لم يتمّ חנכת צלמא ❖ فامر باحضارهم واخذ يعاتبهم

لعلهم ان يعتذرون بعذر ما فلا يتنقّص عليهم سرورهم ❖ وقوله כען הן איתיכון

עתידין يريد به هل الساعة سمعتم الندى او ليس قد تقدّم الكاروز به ولعله قال

هذا القول حتى يعتذرون بشى ليعلم الناس انهم لا يستحقّون به وقد فات وقت 5

السجود لانه انما اراد من الناس يسجدون له فى وقت سماعهم صوت الات الملاهى ❖

فلم يردّ للجواب منهم[1] على سبيل العذر بل كاشفوه فلذلك وجب عنده ان يفعل ما

فعله ❖ وقولهم לא חשחין يريدون به ليس بنا حاجة الى ان نقيم لنا عذرا كما

لعلك تومّى اليه واما قولك ומן הוא אלה فيجب ان تعلم ان معبودنا قادر على

خلاصنا من اتون النار الذى تهوّل علينا به على وجوه[2] كثيرة وان انت اومیت الى 10

قتلنا على وجه اخر اتون النار فهو ايضا قادر على ذلك ❖ وقوله והן לא ليس

يريد به وان كان لا يقدر فيكون ذلك مناقضة لقولهم יכיל לשיזבותנא وانما اراد به

وان لم ينجينا[4] لانه ليس يتركنا بيدك من حيث انه لا يقدر ❖ وليس نعبده

ليخلصنا من عذاب[5] الدنيا وانما نعبده لنتخلص من عقاب الاخرة ويحصل لنا

الثواب[6] فتكون[7] تعلم ان الذى قيل لك عنّا حتّى لم نعبد معبودك[8] وصنمك ولا[9] 15

نعبده ايضا فى ما يستانف ❖ وهذا القول قالوا له بحضرة العالمين الذين كانوا قد

سجدوا للصنم ❖ وهذا القول[10] يعلم منه انه لا يجوز السجود للصنم وان كانوا غير

معتقدين عبادته ❖ واصله من التوراة وهو قوله לא תשתחוה להם ולא תעבדם[11] وانה שמות כ. ה

ثم[0] دار اخرى للجزاء غير هذه الدار لانه اذا لم يكن ثم دار اخرى بعد هذه الدار

فأى شى[0] يتقونه[12] حتى لا يسجدون للصنم واى شى يرجونه حتى يبذلون انفسهم للنار 20

وكذلك دانيال طرح نفسه للجبّ الذى فيه السباع ❖ وقولهم והן לא يدلّ على ان[13]

يجوز عندهم ان اللہ תّﺢ يترك عبيدَه ان يعذّبون ويقتلون بيد الكقار ليجازيهم

---

[1] P after منهم ins. אהדא.   [2] C. בתרה.   [3] C. ירידו.   [4] C; לם לא most MSS.
[5] C. עידאב.   [6] C. תואב.   [7] codd. פיכון.   [8] C. נעבוד.   [9] cett. ולם; ולא C.
[10] most MSS.; מנחם יעלם מנה C. מנהם יעלם מנה   [11] C. ותם.   [12] C. יתוקונה.
[13] B (om. انه) cett. (يدل على انه ومن قولهم)

Line 3. يتعذروا.   5. يعتذروا.   8. عذرا.   ١٠. اومأت.   13. ينجنا.
٢٠. يسجدوا etc.   22. يعذبوا etc.

فصل۳ على ذلك فى دار الاخرة وقد وقفوا على كل هذا ولم يفعلوا ۰ وامر بان يطرح من

فاسوق۳۰ الحطب اضعاف ما كان يطرح للواحد سبعة تهويلا عليهم ليرجعوا ويخضعوا ولم

يبالوا بقوله ولم يفكروا فيه ۰ ثم عرّف انه امر بكتفهم بثيابهم ففعلوا كما امر

الملك ۰ פטישיהון خفاتينهم ۰ וכרבלתהון ازرهم ۰ ולבשיהון يمكن انها عمائمهم

5 او مشدّات لان كان زيّهم زيّ العمّال ۰ ۱ورموا بالمنجنيقات لان ۲اتون النار۰ عالى

مرتفع ۳عن وجه الارض ۴فرموا الى راس الاتون ولم يلقوا من باب الاتون لانه اراد

تهويل القصّة وليشاهد ذلك العالمين الوقوف [اذ ۵حلقوهم] عن بعدٍ من موضع

عالى ۰ ولعله ربما كل واحد ناحية الواحد بعد الاخر كانه طرح اوّلا حننيا ۶ليرتعد

الاثنين فلم يبالوا وطرح الثانى ولم يبال الاخر۷ ۰ ثم اخبر المدوّن عن الذين رموهم

10 ان وهج شرار النار قتلتهم وذلك بحيث ان الجمار ارتفعت عند وقوعهم عليها وصعد

منها وهج عظيم فلحقهم ۸حماء النار فتلفوا ۰ وكان نبوخذناصر واقف على الموضع

العالى ۹اذ القوهم بالمنجنيق مشرف على لاتون وليس كان دخان يصعد يحجب عن

نظر الاتون فرآهم واذاهم ۱۱ماربّين جائمين فى النار ۰ فذهل من هذا ودهش كقوله

תוה وقم وقال ما قاله لندمائه فإما ان يكون كانوا معه حاضرين ولم يروا ما رآه لان

15 الله تعً حجب عنهم كما جرى لدانيال عند نظره للملاك فلم ينظره غيره كما

سنشرحه فى موضعه فلم ينظروا لا الملاك ولا الثلثة وإما ان يكون نظر ندماؤه

الثلثة ولم ينظروا الملاك ۰ فقال הלא גברין וגו' يعرّفهم انه ناظر ما ليس هم ناظرين

۱۲كان استخبر اوّلا منهم ليعلم هل هم ناظرين ام لا فقال اليس رمينا ثلثة لا اكثر

فقالوا نعم فقال ها انا ناظر اربعة اشخاص ۱۳لكن الرابع يشبه الملائكة ۰ ولا شكّ

20 فى ان الثلثة هم شذرخ ميشخ وعبيذنغو ۰ ثم لما رآهم سائرين وجايمين فى الاتون

وليس يخرجون من الاتون قال فى نفسه هؤلاء لو اقاموا ما اقاموا لم يخرجوا حتى

---

۱ ورمو C; פרמו cett. ۲ אלאתון C. ۳ עז C; עלי cett. ۴ The MSS. in
this chapter have רמיו for רמו passim. ۵ القوهم חלקוהם codd. (B C K P Q X), scr.
۶ ליתדע Q; לירתדעו B C K X; לירתדעו P. ۷ After الاخر, מנחם ins. by some MSS.
۸ חמא C K Q X; חמו P; חמאת B. ۹ אלדי codd. ۱۰ נאר B K. ۱۱ מאריין C.
۱۲ לבנה codd. ۱۳ לאכון C.

Line 5. عالٍ. 7. العالمون. 8. عالٍ. 9. يبالا، الائنان. 11. واقفا.
12. مشرفا. 13. مارّون جايمُون. 18. ناظرون.

كانهم فى بستان يتنزهوا فيه ✦ فقرب نحو باب الاتون يسالهم الخروج من الاتون فصل ٣
لانه لا طريق لهم من بابه وكانهم يورون ان الذى يخرجهم هو ولا يخرجون الا فاسوق ٣٠
بامره ✦ فقرب من باب الاتون وقال لهم [1]اخرجوا تعالوا[0] فعند ذلك خرجوا ولا شك
فى ان الملاك كان معهم الى ان فارقوا الاتون لانه مهما هو معهم ليس يلحقهم شى
من اذاء النار ✦ وعند خروجهم لم يكونوا عرايا بل كانت ثيابهم تسترهم وهى ٥
سراويلاتهم دون كل ثيابهم لانه ذُكر سراويلاتهم دون غيرها فبقّى للخالق فاعل
المعجزات سراويلاتهم فقط [2]لتسترهم وليبين المعجز ايفا ان بعض الثياب احترقت
وبعضها لم يحترق ✦ فاما اجسامهم فقد اخبر انه لم يتعلق النار بشى من جسمهم
اصلا حتى انه فى ظفر يدهم او [3]رجلهم [4]الذى ليس [5]فى ذلك [6]ضرر كثير[0] لم يتاذون
منه ✦ واما شعرهم فلم يتشيط كما من شان الشعر يتشيط من يسير من النار اذا ١٠
قرب منها ✦ ثم عرّف ان [7]رائحة النار لم تشمّ منهم ولا من سراويلاتهم وليس
ذلك [8]عجيب من افعال البارى القادر تعّ لانه هو جعل حاجزا بين النار وبينهم
بلطائف هو قادر عليها ولم يجعل للحاجز بين النار وبين ثيابهم سبحانه فاعل
[9]المعجزات دون المخلوقين كقولـﮥ لعاوشه נפלאות גדולות לבדו ✦ وهذا يبطل دعوى القائلين ההלי׳ קלו. ד
بدفع المعجزات وينكرون ذلك ✦ [10]فاظهر الله تعّ هذا المعجز العظيم فى زمان بُختناصر١٥
كما اظهر معجزاته فى مصر ودفع بذلك مذاهب الحرطمים حتى اذعنوا وقالوا אצבע שמות ח. טו
الهים هو ✦ فعند ما شاهد ذلك بختناصر وسائر اصحابه امنوا بفعل للخالق وعند
ذلك سبّح للخالق وقال بريך אלההון די שדרך מישך ועבד נגו ومنذ ساعة كان قولـﮥ لهم ו"ן
هو الله אלה די ישיזבינכון من يدى ✦ وقال די שלח מלאכיה ושיזב لعبدوهی لانه شاهد
الملاك سائر معهم والله تعّ بعث الملاك ليحقّق عنده ان ذلك من افعالـﮥ ولا من ٢٠
افعال غيره ✦ وقولـﮥ ושיזב لعبدوهی די התרחיצו עלוהי يورى انهم تخلصوا بما
اتّكلوا عليه ولم [11]يفكروا فى ما [12]تهدّدهم به كقولـﮥ ומלת מלכא ✦ وقولـﮥ נשמיהון די לא
יפלחון ולא יסגדון يعنى سلّموا اجسامهم للنار كل ذلك حتى لا يعبدون غيره ✦ ثم

---

[1] תעאלו אכרנו C.   [2] לסתרתהם C P X; text B.   [3] רגליהם most MSS.
[4] Om. C   [5] פיהא B; פיה C Q X; פי P.   [6] אלצרר אלכתיר codd.   [7] אראיה Q;
ראיחה B.   [8] ענב C Q.   [9] אלענאיב P Q.   [10] פאטהאר B.
אראייח C; ראיחה B P.   אראיח X; יכפרו C; יפכרו [11]
[12] יתההדדהם C.   [12] יהדדהם B; כאן יהדדהם P Q X;

Line 9. يتاذوا.   12. عجيبا.   20. سائرا.   23. يعبدوا.

فصل ۳ قال ومنى شم طعم فامر ان يبطل مجالس النظر فى ذكر المذاهب الذى يطعن بها على

فاسوق ۳۰ مذاهب الموحّدين كقوله دى يامر شلو على الههم دى שדרך מישך ועבד נגו وانه كل

من طعن عليه كان يبعض يعنى يقطع جسمه ويجعل ماله صوافى للسلطان ❖

ثم قال دى לא איתי אלה אחרן فجزم انه ليس فى كل الاهات الامم من يقدر على

5 خلاص عبيده من البلايا والعقوبات مثله ❖ وعند ذلك اخبر¹ بما فعل معهم بعقب

ذلك فقال הצלה وهو انه زاد فى مرتبتهم ²وجلالهم ❖ وقد يسل الناس عمّا تقدّم من

قول بختنصر فى الوقت الذى فسّر له دانيال ³فيه المنام من קשט دى الههم وتمام القول

فيقول⁴ ⁵اليس هذا القول يدلّ على انه امن بالله تع وبعجائبه فكيف فعل ⁶بهم

ذلك° وقال ومن هو اله دى ישיזבנכון מן ידי ❖ للجواب فى ذلك هو انه ليس هو

10 باعجب ممّا ⁷شاهدت آباونا من ⁸عجائب الله° تع ومخاطبته لهم على طور سينى

وبعد ايّام يسيرة عبدوا العجل بتاويلات ادخلوها فى ما قد شاهدوا فاحرى ان يجرى

مثل ذلك من بختنصر الكافر فكانه فى الوقت يتحقق ثم يرجع عنه بضروب من

التاويلات الفاسدة ❖ ولا شكّ فى ان الله تع ⁹يعاقبه على رجوعه⁹ ⁱ⁰وادخال الشُبَه

على نفسه ¹⁰ ❖ كملت القصّة الثالثة فى ما ذكره من خبر الصنم وما كان من اخبار

15 حننيا ميسائيل وعزريا ❖

ثم اخذ فى القصّة الرابعة

۳۱ بختناصر الملك بعث الى كل الشعوب والامم واللغات السكّان
فى كل الارض سلامكم يكثر ❖

¹¹هذه كتب كتبها° بختنصر الى ¹²كل اهل° العالم بعد تقضّى السبع سنين التى

20 جرت عليه وهو مع الوحوش فعند ما رجع اليه عقله¹³ ¹³وعاد الى ملكه كتب الكتب

وشرح فيها القصّة اوّلها אתיא ותמהיא واخرها ودى מהלכין בגוה ❖

---

¹ אלמדרן add. C.   ² ואנגלאלהם codd.   ³ פי codd. (B C K P Q X).   ⁴ אלדי
added in most MSS. after يقول (not C).   ⁵ ליס C; ليس most MSS.   ⁶ دلك بهم C P.
⁷ שאהדוה B.   ⁸ אפעאל P; ענאיב א׳ אפעאל א׳ X; om. عناיب אפעאל אללה B C Q;
⁹ عاقبه Prob.   ¹⁰ ואدכל C P.   ¹¹ هذا كتاب كتبه Prob.   ¹² כל אהל C;
אהל כל cett.   ¹³ ועד C.

٣٢ الايات والبراهيين التى عمل معى الالاه العالى حسن عندى للاخبار • فصل ٣ فاسوق ٣٢

قوله اתיא ותמהיא يشير الى ما جرى عليه فى السبع سنين ١وسنشرحه فى موضعه • وقوله שפר קדמי هو ما وجب عليه ان ٢يذكره للعالمين ولا يغفل عن ٣به ٤وبسطه ٥وشكر ٦الله تَعَ على ذلك •

٣٣ ایاته كم هى كبار عظيمة وبراهينه كم هى صلبة ملكه ملك ٧الدهور وسلطانه مع جيل وجيل •

قوله אתוהי يشير به الى ايات تقدمت من افعال الله تَعَ والى ما هو ٨دائم ٩موجود فاورى انه مومن بها وليس يدفعها كما تدفعها الفلاسفة • وقال מלכותה מלכות עלם وفى ذلك شيئين احدهما انه ١٠باقي لا الى نهاية والثانى فاعل ما يراه فى عالمه ١٠ وسلطانه على الكل فى اختلاف الاعصار والازمنة كقول المسيح מלכותך מלכות תה׳ קמה. יג كقول المسيح כל עולמים •

٤ • انا بختنناصر ١١سالى كنت فى دارى وغَض فى هيكلى •

عرّف انه راى هذا المنام فى وقت كان هادى ولم يعرض له سفر والعالم انطاع له طاعة كاملة لا عدوّ ولا مناصب وامورہ واسبابه جارية على نظام كما يحبّ ومعنى ١٥ ורענן בהיכלי سلامة جسمه وحسنه بخلاف ما كان عليه فى اوقات ١٢معاناته للحروب فى استقامة احواله •

٢ منام نظرت فافزعنى وافكار (او خواطر) على فراشى ومناظر راسى يدهشونى •

---

١ מוצעהא . . וסנשרחהא codd.   ٢ ידכרהא B C.   ٣ נתה B ; נתה C P Q X ; בתהא
٤ Om. C P Q X ; ins. B K.   ٥ ואלשכר C P Q X ; text B K.   ٦ ללה C.
٧ אליהוד B K.   ٨ דואם D X ; text B etc.   ٩ Om. C D P X ; ins. B etc.
١٠ באקי B ; אלבאקי cett.   ١١ סאל K X etc. ; סאל B ; סאיל C ; סאלי C   ١٢ מעאנאתה P Q X ;
מעאנאתה B K.   מעאנאדתה C.   Probably we should transpose, reading בכלאף كما يحبّ
ما كان عليه فى اوقات معاناته للحروب ومعنى ורענן בהיכלי سلامة جسمه وحسنه
فى استقامة احواله.

Line 10. شيَّان ,باقي.   13. ساليا ,وغَضّا.   14. هادئا.   18. مناما.

فصل ۴   عرّف انه نظر منام وحصله ولم ينساه كما نسى المنام الاول فلما انتبه ¹واذاه

فاسوق ۲   فازع° ويتجد ايضا انه حكاية حاله وهو ناظر المنام وهو ²سامع صوت الملائكة נَدُو

אِילَנه وقوله והרהרين על משכבי وصف حاله بعد ان انتبه انه كان يفكر فى ما

رآه ويدهش ويتحيّر وليس يقف على تفسيره ۰

۵   ۳ ومنى ³اجعال امرا لادخال قدامى كل حكماء بابل حتى

تفسير المنام يخبروني ۰

۴ حينئذ دخلوا الفلاسفة والسحرة والمشعونين والكسدانيّبين

والقطّاعين والمنام قائل انا ⁴قدامهم والتفسير غير ⁵معرّفين لى ۰

اعلم انه لم يبعث الى دانيال ويحضره ويساله عن تفسير المنام وقد كان حاضر

۱۰   معه فى بابل وبعث الى حكماء بابل اوّلا لمعنى وهو انه لما طالبهم بالمنام الاول

قالوا دفعة بعد ⁶الاخرى قل المنام وعلينا تفسيره فلما راى هذا المنام وعلم ان

تفسيره صعب جدّا اراد ان يحكيه ⁷لحكماء بابل على اختلاف طبقاتهم حتى اذا عجزوا

عن تفسيره بان عندهم. وعند الناس نقصهم وبعد ذلك يبعث خلف دانيال ويحكى

له المنام بحضرتهم ويفسّره باب بيمين ⁸فضيلته كما بان فضل يوسف ثم

۱۵   عند ما عجزوا حكماء مصر عن تفسير منام فرعون وقرّوا ⁹الكل له بالحكمة كقول

נראˈ מאˈלח فرعون הנמצא כזה ۰

۵ وفى الاخرة دخل قدامى دانيال الذى اسمه بلطشاصر ¹⁰كاسم

الاهى والذى روح الالاه القديسين فيه فقلت المنام قدامه ۰

۷ يا بلطشاصر ¹¹اكبر الفلاسفة الذى انا علمت ان روح الالاه

۲۰   القديسين فيك وكل سرّ غير ممتنع منك نظر منامى الذى نظرت

وتفسيره قل ۰

---

¹ ואראה פזע all except C.   ² יסמע C D P.   ³ שגעל B; אנַאל D.   ⁴ קדאמכם

فضيلته … فضل ⁸   codd. على חכמא ⁷   دفعة D. ⁶   מערופין B. ⁵   codd.

P. באלכלאה .add וقروا After ⁹   יבין, יבאן, באן between as also ,vary .codd the

¹⁰ באסם codd.   ¹¹ اكبر obliterated in K Q; om. B.

Line 1. بابا بابا.   7. والمشعوذون etc.   9. حاضرا.   14. ينسه, مناما.

فصل ٤ عرّفهم انه سمّاه بلطشاصر باسم معبوده لما فيه من רוח אלהין קדישין فشرّفه

فاسوق ٦ بذلك وقوله כשם אלהי قال قوم ان مع هذه القصص التى جرت كلها كان يعبد

الاصنام على ضرب من ضروب التاويلات او لسياسة ملكه لانه ان اظهر للناس انه

على مذهب اليهود لزمه الشرائع وسقط وكان يانف [1]عن انتقاله عن معبوده

فهو يعظّم الاه السماء ولا يترك دينه او يكون قوله כשם אלהי على ما كان [2]قديما

يعبده° قبل ايمانه بالله عز وجل ٠ وقوله די אנה ידעת هو على ما تقدّم من

المنام الاوّل الذى انكشف له السرّ ٠ وقوله וחזוי חלמי די חזית ليس يريد به قل

المنام وتفسيره مثل الاوّل لانه قد حكاه بين يديه وانما يريد به انا اقول المنام

الذى نظرت وانت فسّره ٠

٧ ومناظر راسى على فراشى كنت ناظر وانا شجر فى وسط

الارض وارتفاعه عظيم ٠

٨ شجر كبير وصلب وارتفاعه يبلغ الى السماء ومنظره الى دهاية

كل الارض ٠

٩ ووورقه حسن وثمره كثير وغذاء الكل فيه تحته تفيف حيوانة

البرّ وفى اغصانه يسكنون طيور السماء ومنه يغتنون كل البشر٠

١٠ ناظر كنت فى مناظر راسى على فراشى وانا بملائكين من

السماء [3]نزلا ٠

١١ منادى بقوّة وكنى قائل اقطعوا الشجر وقصّصوا اغصانه اقلعوا

[4]اثره وبنزروا ثمره حتى [5]تنون الحيوانة من تحته والطيور من

اغصانه ٠

١٢ غير ان اصل عروقه اتركوا فى الارض وبالقيين الذى من حديد

[1] Prob. مِن.   [2] יעתקד קדימא B K.   [3] נאזל codd.   [4] אתרה codd.
[5] Prob. تَنيذّ.

Line 10. ناظرا.   16. ناظرا.   18. مناوٍ.

فصل۴ ونحاس فى كل البرّ وبندى السماء ينصبغ ومع الحيوانة قسمه فى
فاسوق ۱۲ عشب الارض ◦

۱۳ عقله من الناس يغيرون وقلب الحيوانة يعطى له وسبعة
اوقات ۱يبتدلون عليه ◦

۵ ۱۴ بقطع الملائكة القول وقول الملائكة المسلة من اجل ان
يعلمون الاحياء ان متسلط العالى بملك الانسان ولمن يريد يعطيها
واسفل الناس يقيم عليها ◦

۱۵ هذا هو المنام الذى نظرت انا الملك بختنناصر وانت بلطشاصر
قل تفسيره من حيث ان كل حكماء ملكى غير قادرين لتعريفى
۱۰ تفسيره وانت قادر الذى روح الالاه القديسين فيك ◦

۱۶ حينئذٍ دانيال الذى اسمه بلطشاصر اطرق (وقيل استوحش)
ساعة وافكاره يدهشونه مجيب الملك وقائل يا بلطشاصر المنام
وتفسيره لا يدهشوك مجيب بلطشاصر ۲وقائل يا مولاى المنام
لشانيك وتفسيره لاعدائك ◦

۱۵ ۱۷ الشجر الذى نظرت انه كبير وصلب وارتفاعه يبلغ الى السماء
ومنظره الى كل الارض ◦

۱۸ وورقة حسن وثمره كثير وغذاء الكل فيه تحته تاوى حيوانة
البرّ وفى اغصانه يسكنون طيور السماء

۱۹ انت هو الملك الذى كبرت وصلبت ۳وجلالتك كبرت◦ ووصلت
۲۰ الى السماء وسلطانك الى نهاية كل الارض ◦

۲۰ والذى نظر الملك ان الملائكة نزل واحد منهم من السماء وقال

اقطعوا الشجر وافسدوه غير ان اصل عروقه اتركوا فى الارض وبقيبن   فصل۴
من الحديد والنحاس فى كلا البرّ وفى ندى السماء ينصبغ ومع   فاسوق ۲۰
حيوانة البرّ قسمه الى ان يتبدلون عليه سبعة اوقات ◦

۲۱ هنا هو التفسير وقطع العالى هى وصلت على مولاى الملك ◦

۲۲ ولك طاردين من بين الناس ومع حيوانة البرّ يكون سكناك
وعشب مثل الثور يطعمونك ومن ندى السماء صابغون لك وسبعة
اوقات ¹يتبدلون عليك حتى تعلم ان متسلط العالى فى ملك الناس
ولمن يريد يعطيها ◦

۲۳ والذى قالوا من ترك اصل عروقة الشجر ملكك ثابت (لك)
حتى تعلم ان متسلطين الاه السماء ◦

عرّف انه عند ما حكا له المنام وقال له ان غيرك من حكما بابل لم يقدرون
يفسرونه وانت قادر عليه لما فيك من حكمة الله فقُل تفسيره وذكر ان دانيال
اطرق ولم يبتدئ بتفسيره حتى قال له الملك ما قال له لم يكن ذلك تحيّر من
دانيال فى تفسيره لانغلاقه عليه وانما كان يفكر فى ما [كان] يلقى الملك(به)اذ لم
يحسن (ان) يلقاه بالتفسير لما فيه مما ينال الملك وفكر فى انه لا يحسن ان يطالبه
يطالبه فى تفسيره ولا يقول فراى ²من الصواب° ان يطرق الى ان يقول الملك ويطالبه ◦
ولشدّة فكره فى ذلك كان لونه يتغيّر فعند ما رآه الملك بهذه الصورة قال له لا
يهوّلك المنام ولا تفسيره ظنّ ³عنه انه يحتاج فيه الى فكر كبير فاجابه دانيال بانّه
لم يكن سكوته عن تفسيره من حيث هاله وانما هو من جهة الملك ولولا ذلك لقد
كان بادر بتفسيره للوقت ◦ وقوله חלמא לשנאך على طريق التحمّل والتحاسن ولانه
لا يحسن ان يلقاه الا بمثل ذلك فزعم قوم انه كان غرض دانيال اعداء الله تع وشانئيه
واحدهم بختناصر ◦ ثم اخذ يقسم المنام على ثلثة اقسام ويفسّر له كل قسم منها
مفرد ◦ اما ما رايته من كبر الشجر وصلابته وعلوّه وما فيه من الغذاء لكل الحيوان

---

¹ יבתדלון P X; text B.   ² אן אלצ׳ D P X; text B K.   ³ מנה codd.

Line 3. يتبدلوا.   6. وعشبا.   9. Cf. FLEISCHER, *Kl. Schr.* i. 294.

۱۵. متسلطون.   11. يقدروا.   13. تحيّرا.   23. مفردا.

فصل ۴ وسكناهم فيه وتحته فانه علوّ الملك وبلوغه الى نهاية العالم ۞ وقد بقي شي لم يفسّره
فاسوق ۲۳ وهو تفسير فاسوق وعفيه שפיר وאנבה שגיא فالمراد في עפיה שפיר حسن عساكره واولاده
وتفسير وانבה שגיא هو كثرة المال الذى جمعه من البلدان ۞ وتفسير ومزون לכלא בה
هو ارزاق ۞ وقوله תחתוהי תטלל חיות ברא البادیّة ۞ وتاويل الطاير هم الذين جاءوا
5 اليه من كل بلد وحصلوا في ملكه واستكثّوا تحت ملكه ۞ وقوله ومנה יתזין כל בשرا
يقرب فيه ما انتفع الناس من الكسب بعد ان استقرّ ملكه ۞ ثم ذكر الباب الثانى
وهو ما سمعه من كلام الملائكة קרא בחיל ۞ واعلم ان هذين الملاكين الواحد منهما
كان في العلوّ وهو القائل גדו אילנא وهو المسمّى עיر وهو ارفع طبقة من القديس فاما
القديس هو السائل العير ان يبقّى عروق الشجر في مكانه كقوله בגזרת עירין פתגמא ۞
10 قوله בגזרת עירין هو قوله גדו אילנא وقצצו ענפوهי وقوله ומאמר קדישין שאלתא هو وانه
سأله ترك עקر שרשוהي ۞ وقال اوّلاً עיר وקديש وقال بعد ذلك עירין وקדישين فعرّف
انهم كانوا جماعة فدلّ ذلك على ان جماعة (من) העירין امروا גדو אילנא وجماعة
من القديسين سألوا في بابه وهذا اوراء الله ليعلم ان الأمرين جميعا بامر الخالق عز
وجل وهو ما يلحقه في نفسه وبقي الملك له الى ان يعود من البرّ ۞ ومعنى גודو
15 אילנא هو اخذه من بين الناس ۞ وقوله וقצצو ענפوهي هو انقطاع عساكره منه ۞ وقوله
ברם עקr שרשوهي سنشرحه من بعد ۞ وقوله ובאסور די פרזל ونحש هو كونه [في ما
بين الوحوش] في تلك المدّة كانسان مقيّد لا يقدر ينبغ ولا يجي بل هو مقيم مع
الوحوش ۞ وقوله בדתא די ברא يريد انه ياوي في الموضع الذى ينبت للحشيش
والعشب ليغذو منه وانه يكون من جملة للحيوان الذى ياكل العشب وليس يكون
20 من الوحش المفترس ۞ وقوله ובטל שמיא هو كونه ليل ونهار تحت الندى ليس
لكن يستكنّ فيه من الندى ۞ وقوله לבבה מן אנשא هو زوال عقله منه وحصوله
مسلوب التمييز الذى كان له ۞ واعلم انها ثلثة اشياء هي على ظاهرها وهي עשבא
כתורין ومثل שמיا יצבע ولבבه מن אנשין يשنون وغير ذلك كله له تاويل ۞ وقوله
وשבעה עדנین יחلفون עלوהي ذهب قوم على انها سبعة فصول ليكون جملة ذلك دون
25 السنتين وقال قوم انها سبع سنين وهو اقرب كانه طالت مدّته وذلّه للخالق تع ۞
وعرّف ان كل ذلك نزل به ليعرف ان الملك لله تع وانه يعطيه لمن يريد ولو انه

---

¹ Om. P.   ² יהרב B; יהרב ידהב X.   ³ الموאضع B.   ⁴ Prob. السماء.
Line 20. ليلا ونهارا.

احقر الناس كقوله ושפל אנשים יקים עליה وهذا يدلّ على انه كبر قلبه وليس الناوه   **فصل ۴**

فذلك الله حتى يتحقق ان الله تعّ سلطان فى عالمه ويعمل ما يشاء فيه وقد شرح   **فاسوق ۲۳**

ذلك فى الفصل الذى بعده ۰   ثم ذكر ¹(القسم° الثالث° كقوله° ודי אמרו فقال والذى

سمعت يقال اتركوا اصل عروق الشجر المراد فيه هو ان الملك باقى لك وليس ينتقل

منك كقوله מלכותך לך קימה ۰   ثم بعد ان فسّر له المنام اخذ يشير عليه بما لو كان 5

استعمله ²لم يتمّ° له ذلك ۰   فقال

۲۴ ³لكن ايها الملك راىى يحسن عندك وخطاياك فكّ بالعدالة
ونوبك برؤف الضعفى فان نكون مهلة لسلوتك ۰

هذا يدلّ على انه كان يجور على الناس كقوله فيه الحمس كم لمته רשע وتقول الامّة

حمסى ושארי על בבל فلعله كان يصادر الناس او رسم رسوم هى جور ۰   وقوله بمحن عنين 10

يدلّ على قساوة قلبه على الضعفى وقال قوم انه قصد به الى امّة ישראיל الضعيفة

لانه كان حنق عليهم دون غيرهم وهذين ذنبين عظيمين من الكبّار يعاقب الله

تعّ عليها فى دار الدنيا كما اهلك דור המבול من اجلها كقوله כי מלאה הארץ חמס

מפניهم وكذلك سدوم وعمورا وكذلك اهل نينوا قبل ان يتوبون كقوله ומן החמס אשר

בכפיהם ۰   وقوله הן תהוה ארכא לשלותך يعنى يدفع الله عنك (البلاء) الى وقت وهذا 15

كما دفع البلاء فى زمان بحזקיاهو ۰   عرّف انه يلحقه ذلك من اجل ظلمه واقتداره

فان لم يفعل ذلك دفعه الله تعّ عنك فيكون בגזרת עירין ان كنت مقيم على جملة

ذنوبك ۰

۲۵ كل ذلك وافى على بختناصر الملك ۰

ليس هذا الفاسوق قول دانيال للملك وانما هو قول المدوّن عرّف ان بختناصر لم 20

يقبل ما اشار به عليه فلذلك نزل به تفسير المنام كقوله بعده

۲۶ لانقضاء ¹اثنى عشر شهرا على هيكل الملك الذى فى بابل
كان ساىر۰

---

¹ אלתלתה codd.   ² לחם P Q; ליחם D K X.   ³ אן B; om. cett.

⁴ אתנאעשר P X.

Line 4. باقٍ.   ۱٥. رسوما.   ۱۲. وهذان etc.   ۱۳. اجلهما,عليهما.

۱۴. تابوا.   ۱۷. مقيما.   ۲۳. ساىرا.

   [II. 3.]   G

فصل ٤ ٢٧ مجيب الملك وقائلًا اليس هذا بابل الكبيرة التى انا بنيتها
فاسوق ٢٧ لدار الملك بصلابة قوّتى ولعزّ بهجتى ٭

ليس هذا القول فقط كان سبب ما نزل به بل كان على ظلمه وتعدّيه مقيم واجّله
اللـه سنة منذ وقت نظره المنام فلما لم يتُب وانصاف على ذلك هذا القول فلم يمهل
5 اللـه عليه اكثر من ذلك ٭ وهو انه اتفق انه طلع الى سطح ١القصر فاشرف على
المدينة ونظر حسن بناتها فقال هلا دا هيا בבל רבתא ودلّ هذا القول على انه
جدّد بناءها كما يريد لتكون له دار الملك وكان كل عُدَده فيها فلذلك قال בתקף חסני
וליקר הדרי ٭

٢٨ بعد الكلمة فى فم الملك حتى وقع صوت من السماء لك قائلين
١٠ بنختناصر الملل ان الملك قد زالت عنك

٢٩ ولك طاردين من الناس ومع حيوانة البرّ ماواك عشب مثل
الثيران يطعمونك وسبعة اوقات ²يتبدلون عليك حتى تعلم ان
متسلط العالى فى ملك الناس ويعطيها لمن يريد ٭

هذا الصوت الذى سمعه من السماء يحتمل انه لم يسمعه غير بختناصر فقط
١٥ ويحتمل انه سمعه الناس وهو اعظم ليعلم الناس ذلك ٭

٣٠ فى الوقت الكلمة تمّت على بختناصر وطُرد من الناس وعشب
مثل البقر ياكل ومن ندى السماء جسمه ينصبغ حتى كثر شعره
مثل شعر ³النسورة واظفاره مثل مخاليب الطبور٭

ينبغى ان يكون كما سمع هذا القول النازل من السماء حصله ثم زال عقله عنه
٢٠ ووقع من قصره ومرّ تائه على وجهه وهداه الخالق الى البرّيّة ولم ينضبط وخاصة
خبره كان مشهور وكان دانيال ذكر لهم ذلك فلم ⁴يتعلقوا به ٭ ⁵وقوله עד די שערה
כנשרין רבה فدلّ ذلك على طول المكث وهى سبع سنين ٭

---

¹ קצרה D P X ؛ text B. ² יבתדלון Q X ؛ text B etc. ³ So all (B D P Q X):
so too MS. 2467, p. 132 a (ad Ex. xix. 4). ⁴ יתעקלון D Q X P (corr. in marg.)؛
text B. ⁵ Prob. واما قوله.

Line 3. مقيما. 9. قائلون. 11. طاردون، عشبا. 16. وعشبا. 20. تائها. 21. مشهورا.

٣١ وعند نهاية الايام انا بختناصر رفعت عينى الى السماء وعقلى   فصل ٤

يعود علّى وللعالى باركت ولحىّ الدهر سبّحت وبجّلت الذى   فاسوق ٣١

سلطانه سلطان الابد وملكه مع جيل وجيل ♦

٣٢ وكل سكّان الارض كلاشى محسوبيين وكمراده فاعل فى

١جيوش السماء وسكّان الارض وليس ايس من يضرب ٢بيده ٥

ويقول له ايش عملت ♦

عرّف انه كما تققّت שבعה עدنין رجع عليه عقله فنظر نفسه بين الوحوش فى

البرّيّة وشاهد حال جسمه وكبر شعره وطول ٣اظفاره فتحقّق ان تمّ عليه ما قيل له

فعند ذلك رفع عينيه الى السماء وقال ما قال ♦ وقال מלכותה מלכות עלם وשלמנה

لانه ملك بنى ادم وسلطانهم زائل منقضى ♦ وقوله وכل داري ارעא ليعرّف ان ١٠

كبيرهم وصغيرهم غير محسوبيين بشى لانهم منقضين منصرفين ومع ذلك فهذا

قول فى عوامّ الناس على اغلب امرهم فاما الانبياء ٤والصالحين فهم عماد العالم فان

كان اومى بختناصر الى الموت وتقّى اجل الناس فيجب ان يكون قولا عامّا وان كان

قصده فى المرتبة والقدر فليس يدخل الانبياء والصالحين فى ذلك ♦ وقوله وכמצביה

עבד בחיל שמיא يمكن انه يشير به ٥الى الملائكة ويمكن انه يشيربه° الى المنيرات ١٥

التى تنكسف ٦وتسودّ وتتساقط° ♦ وقوله وداري ارעא يمكن [ايفا] انه قصد به الى بنى

ادم فانه مميت ومحيه وموريش ومعشير وبحتمل ايضا انه يدخل فيه سائر للحيوان ♦

وقوله ولا ايתי די يمحه بيده يجمع فيه חיל שמיא وداري ارעא وقوله يمحه بيده

يعنى يضرب على يد الله وبجوز انه اراد به يضرب على يد نفسه ٧حذرا على الله

والاوّل اقرب فقال لا يقدر احد من חיל שמיא وداري ارעא يمنعه عن مراده ولا يقدر٢٠

ايضا ان ينكر عليه فعله ويقول له ايش هذا الفعل الذى فعلت وهو قبيح وهذا نظير

قول ومى يامر לو مה تعשה وذكر ذلك لانه يشبه معناه الذى لم يقدر يرّد فعل الله   קהל ח. ٦

عن نفسه ولا يقدر ان ينكر عليه فعله لانه عادل فى فعله وقد نصحه دانيال ولم يقبل

فاستحقّ جميع ما جرى له ♦

---

١ ניש X; text B etc.   ٢ עלי ידה X; text B etc.   ٣ אטאפירה P.   ٤ ואלצלחא P.

٥ الى—بـ° om. DX; ins. B etc.   ٦ Om. DP.   ٧ חרדא or חרדא codd.

Line 4. محسوبون.   10. منقضي.   11. منقضون etc.   12. والصالحون.

14. والصالحون.

فصل ٤ سوق ٣٣

٣٣ فى ذلك الوقت معرفتى علىّ تعود والى عزّ ملكى وبهجتى وبهائى يعود علىّ ولى يطلبون ندمائى واجلّائى وعلى ملكى رتّبت وجلالة كثيرة [1]زيدت لى ❖

قال فى ما تقدّم ומנדעי עלי יתוב ليلحق به ולעלאה ברכת ثم رجع اعاده ليعرّف انه رجع فسكن فى ملكه وبهجته وانه قد قال له دانيال מלכותך לך קימה فعرّف انه ليس بدّ ان يرجع الى ملكه ❖ وقوله ולי הדברי ורברבני יבעון هو ان دانيال كان يعدّ الاوقات فلمّا تمّت امر العسكر والاجلّاء ان يخرجون خلفه ويتفرقوا فى طلبه حتى وجدوه يطلب العمارة فاخذوه وردّوه ❖ وقوله ורבו יתירה עّرف انه لم ينقص عندهم عندما حلّ به البلاء بل زادوه هيبة وعزّ وكان ذلك من حيث انه عدل فى الناس وترك الظلم والفساد والاقتدار فجعل له الهيبة فى قلوب الناس وزاد فى قدره وجلالته ❖ ولم يذكر الكتاب كيف جرى احوال الناس فى هذه السبعة اوقات بلا ملك راتب فقال قوم ان دانيال كان يدبّر الملك وقال قوم ان ولده اويل جلس الى رجوع الاب ❖

٣٤ الان انا بختنصر [2]مسبّح ومشرّف° ومبجّل لالاه السماء الذى كل افعاله حقّ وسبله دين والذين سائرين فى الاقتدار قادر [3]للتسفيل ❖

كانه قد تلا عليهم هذا الفصل من اوله الى ههنا فى كتب نفذت اليهم فختم ذلك بان قال انا مسبّح ومرقّع لملك السماء فعرّف انه مسبّح الخالق جلّ ذكره على سائر افعاله ❖ وهذا اخر ما كان من خبر نبوخذناصر ❖ ثم اخذ يذكر خبر بلشاصر وهو ابن ابنه ولم يذكر خبر ابنه اويل مروذخ لان لم يجرى منه كما جرى من ابيه ولا كما جرى من ولده بلشاصر وانما ذكر من خبر اويل مروذخ ما فعله بيهوياخين ملك يهوذا من الجميل فلقد كان [4]أَخْيَرهم ❖

---

[1] וזואת B. [2] משרף ומסבח K X; משרּף ומסבּח D. [3] ללתספל codd.
[4] אברהם D K; אברהם B; حاشية واما اويل مروذخ اقامة سلطنته اثنين وعشرين سنة وذلك مذكور فى اخر سفر يرمياه من كلام الشارح ז״ל ❖ P. See Appendix.

Line 7. يخرجوا. 9. عزّا. 15. سائرون. 20. يجرِ.

فصل ٥
فاسوق ١
بلشاصر الملك عمل ¹طعام ²كثير لاجلّائه الف وبحذاء الالف
شارب خمرا ٠

اعلم ان بلشاصر ملك ثلث سنين على التقليل ولم يعمل هذه الدعوة الّا فى
اخر الوقت لقوله فى اخر هذه القصّة בה בלילא קטיל ولم ينكر الكتاب المعنى الذى
من اجله عمل هذه الدعوة اصلا لكن يمكن ان يكون عدّ السبعين سنة الذى كان
الله تعّ جعلها لهم فلمّا راى ان قد تمّت السبعون سنة والملك باقى بحاله عمل هذه
الدعوة سرورا بذلك وظنّ ان جميع ما قيل انه ساقط ومن اجل ذلك استجرى على
اخذ الات بيت الله التى كان ابوه نبوخذناصر قد صانها ولم يتبدّلها ولما راى بلشاصر
انه قد تمّت السبعون سنة والملك باقى قال هذه الالات لى وليس ثم رجعة ثم اخذ
يستبح معبوداته لتحقّق بها فاستعجل فى ذلك وهى كانت احد اسباب عطبه ٠ ولم
يدع فيها غير الاجلّاء وغلمانهم وتباعهم وعرّف انهم كانوا الف نفس ٠ وقوله לקבל
אלפא חמרא عرّف انهم كانوا فى مجلس وكان هو حذاءهم يشرب ٠

بلشاصر قال فى ³ريا الخمر لاجابة اوانى الذهب والفضّة التى
اخرج جدّه من الهيكل الذى فى يروشالايم ⁴ويشرب بها الملك
واجلّاؤه وسريّانه ووصائفه ٠

حيننّ ⁵جابوا اوانى الذهب الذى اخرجوا من الهيكل الذى
لبيت الله الذى فى يروشالايم وشربوا بها الملك واجلّاؤه سريّانه
ووصائفه ٠

⁴شربوا الخمر وسبّحوا لالاه الذهب والفضّة والنحاس والحديد
والخشب والحجر ٠

⁶قوله בטעם חמרא قيل فيه انه اراد به ان السكر حمله على ذلك ولو كان صاحى
لم يفعل ذلك بل كان يتوقّف عن اخراجها والشرب فيها وقيل انه اراد به انه عندما

¹ טעאם אלמלך all (B D K P X). ² Prob. كبير. ³ ראי codd.
⁴ ويشرب—om. D P X; ins. B. ⁵ ניבו D X; text B etc. ⁶ קולה D;
בכّ cett.

Line ı: طعاما etc. 6, 9. باقي. 7. استجرأ. 16. التى. 21. صاحيا.

فصل ۵ لذّ له لخمر اراد ان يشرب باوانى بيت اللّه وهى الّت يصلح ان يُشرب فيها مثل

فاسوق ۴ كعارات وكفوت وما شاكل ذلك ۰ وقال فى الفاسوق الاول مאני דהבא וכספא ولم يذكر

الفقّة فى الثانى إما ان يكون اختصر ذلك لانه اذا جيبت الذهب فلا محالة ¹انه

جيب٥ الفقّة ايضا او يكون امر باجابتها وبعد ذلك اراد الذهب دون الفقّة ۰ وعرّف

5 انهم سبّحوا ²الاء الاصنام٥ ولم يسبّحوا للخالق سبّ استخفاف بانفسهم وراوا انهم

قد تمكّنوا من اوانى بيت اللّه تع ۰ ³فعند ذلك وافى للّذ الذى حدّه اللّه تع ۰

۰ فى الوقت خرجت ⁴اصابع يد انسان وكتبوا حنآء القنديل

(وقيل ⁵الممخائبجة او ⁶الصقة) على الشيين الذى على حائط هيكل

الملك والملك ناظرككّ يد كاتبة ۰

10 من قوله ⁵۵ يدא يدلّ على انه راى ككّ ظهرت ولم ير الذراع ولا الشخص وقد راى

ח.ذ. سيد يحزقال عمّ يد فقط كقولة וישלח יד ومثله دانيال بعد هذا يقول והנה יד נגעה בי

٦.ذ. وهى يد ملاك لا غيره ۰ وقوله על נברא ⁷די כתל היכלא يقصد به الى الشيد الابيض وكان

للخطّ اسود٥ ⁸فبان ذلك٥ ونظر الملك دون غيره ⁹ممّن كان فى المجلس كما راى

نبوخذناصر حننيا ميسائيل وعزريا والملاك دون غيره ۰

15 ٦ حينئن الملك بهآؤه ¹⁰تغيير عليه وافكاره يدهشونه وعقد ظهره

منحلّين وركبه هنه لهنه ضاربات ۰

لما شاهد هذه الاتّة داخله داخله رعدة وفزع فمن كثرة رعدته تحلّلت خَرَز صلبه وركبه

تضرب واحدة الاخرى ۰

٧ منادى الملك بقوّة لادخال المشعونين والكسدانيين

20 والقطّاعين ۰

---

¹ אנה נאב (or אנא) codd.   ² לאלאה אלצנם דהב P; לאלאה אלדהב D.   ³ After

تع most MSS. ins. לה (not B D).   ⁴ אצבע codd.   ⁵ אלממכאינה codd.;

perh. المخارجة (cp. VULLERS, s. v.)   ⁶ אלפצה B D.   ⁷ די כתבא כתל all

(B D K P Q X).   ⁸ פבאן ביאן B; פכאן ביאן D.   ⁹ ממא B D K.   ¹⁰ תניירו

codd.

Line 5. استخفافا.   10. ككّا.   11. يدا.   16. منحلّة.   19. مناد.

مجيب الملك وقائل لحكماء بابل كل انسان يقرا هذا الخطّ فصله   فصل ه
وتفسيره يخبرني يلبس الارجوان وطوق الذهب على عنقه وثلث   فاسوق ٧
فى الملك يتسلط •

للوقت استدعى بهولاء ليعرّفوه لخطّ وتفسيره وضمن لكل من قرا وعرّف تفسيره
ان يلبسه ثياب الملك ويطوّقه بطوق الذهب ومنادى ينادى بين يديه ان له فى ٥
الملك ١ثلثا وهذا من جنس ما فعل فرعون بيوسف عَمّ غير ان ذلك ولّج الامور
اليه ولم يجعله شريك فى الملك وهذا عمل على انه ٢على اىّ شى حصل له من لخراج
كان له ثلثه واى شى كان للملك فيه صنع كان له فيه الثلث • ولم يقل بختناصر
جدّه لمن قال له المنام وتفسيره مثل ما قال وانما ضمن له ٣العطايا ولجوائز
والمراتب فى غير الملك ٤لعلمه ان هذا الباب اعظم من ذلك فى نفسه وما لحقه من ١٠
الهول ولخوف والهلع •

٨ حينئذٍ داخلين كل حكماء الملك وما كانوا قادرين على قراة
الكتاب ولا على تفسيره لتعريف الملك •

لم يكن لخط ليس موجود مثله فى يد الناس بل كان موجود ٥شا كان عبراني
او غيره من لخطوط لكن لجواب فيه انه لم يكن منظوم حرف الى حرف وانما كان ١٥
٦مقلوب مثلا حروف منه الألف قبل النون والنون قبل المّيم وكذلك سائر لحروف
التى لاربع ٧كلمات كان فيها تقديم وتاخير فلم ٨يفطنوهم بذلك فكان اذا نظموها لم
يثبت لها كلام مفهوم وكيف تفسيره ٩واراد ان يمرض قلبه بذلك حتى اذا قراة دانيال
دون غيره وفسّره له امكن ان يخاطبه بما خاطبه به على راس الملا ويعرّفه جنايته
وقبيح فعله على ما تقدّم القول به فى راس الفصل • ٢٠

٩ حينئذٍ الملك بلشاصر مندهش عظيم وبهاؤه تغيّر عليه واجلّاؤه
متحيّرين (او منشوّشين) •

---

١ תלתה codd.   ٢ Perhaps spurious.   ٣ אלעטאיא X.   ٤ Apparently something
is lost.   ٥ Or شاء? Cp. Index.   ٦ מקלב X; text B etc.   ٧ Prob. الكلمات.
٨ יפטנו הם BX; prob. يفطنوها.   ٩ Perh. وكاد.

Line 2. ثلثا.   5. ومنادٍ.   7. شريكا.   12. داخلون.
14. موجودا twice.   عبرانيا.   15. حرفا, منظوما.   16. مقلوبا.   21. عظيما.
22. متحيّرون etc.

فصل ٥ كان يؤمل ان حكماؤه يقفون على ذلك ويعرّفوه تفسيره فلما لم يقفوا عليه زادت

فاسوق ٩ دهشته وتغيّر لونه ولا يبعد انه كان يرى اليد وغيره لا يراها ومن اجل ذلك كانوا

متحيّرين ومتشوّشين اذ يقول يا قوم هوذا ارى يد عظيمة التى كتبت هذا والزمع هوذا يعثرنى •

١٠ الملكة من اجل اسباب الملك واجلّائه الى بيت المشرب دخلت اجابت الملكة وقالت ايها الملك عش للابد لا يدهشوك افكارك وبهاؤك لا يتغيّر عليك •

هذه الملكة هى جدّته زوجة بختناصر كانت تعرف هذه الامور من اوّلها • وقوله لمדבל מלא מلכه اشار به الى ما لحقه من الرعدة والزمع وتغيّر ديباجة وجهه وتحيّر

١٥ اجلّائه وما لحقهم ايضا من جهة الملك حتى انه انقلب سرورهم الى مثل هذا الحال • فاوجعها قلبها عليه لانه ولد ولدها وقد نزل به هذا البلاء وفزعت عليه ان يموت من الزمع الذى داخل قلبه وانه لا ¹يهدى من به قوة ان يقرا° عليه هذا الخطّ ويقف على تفسيره •

١١ ابس رجل فى ملكك الذى روح الاله ²القديسين فيه وفى

١٥ ايّام ابيك الرشد والعقل وحكمة كحكمة الاله وجدت فيه والملك بختناصر جدّك كبير الفلاسفة والمشعونين والكسدانيّين والقطّاعين نصبه جدّك الملك •

١٢ من حيث الذى فيه روح فضيلة ومعرفة وعقل مفسّر المنامات واخبار ضروب النوادر ومحلّل العقود وجدت فيه هو دانيال الذى

٢٠ الملك سمّى اسمه بلطشصار الساعة دانيال يقرا والتفسير يخبر •

عرّفته ان عنده فى المدينة دانيال يقرا له هذا الخط ويفسّره له ليزول (عن) ما لحقه • ثم اخذت تصف له من حكمة دانيال وانه فوق كل ³حكماء ابيه الذى كان افضل

---

¹ لا يهدى حتى ياتى من B; perhaps لא יהדא מא בה או יקרא ² אלקדים P X; text B. ³ codd. חכמת or חכמה.

Line 3. يدا.

حكمائه ليتحقّق في نفسه ان دانيال يقف على هذا وعلى ما هو اعظم منه ۞ فصل ٥
والاشبه في هذه القصّة ان دانيال ما كان يدخل عليه ولا يعرف اصلا وذلك ان دانيال فاسوق ١٢
كان غائب عن بابل في هذه السنة كما سنبيّن ذلك في بשنת שלוש למלכות בלשאצר
המלך وبعد ذلك رجع الى بابل ويقرب في ذلك انه قصد المجيّ الى بابل لهذا المعنى
بتوفيق من الله تعّ ۞ ثم انها وصفت دانيال له ليعرفه ويعرف محاله ۞ فوصفته ٥
في الفاسوق الاول باربعة اشياء وهى רוח אלהין ونهيرو وשכלתנו وحكمة כחכמת אלהן
وفي الفاسوق الثاني ذكرت بعض الاربعة بمثل ذلك اللفظ [1]وبعضها بتغيّر اللفظ ۞ والاشبه
فيه هو ان רוח יתירא هو [2]بمعنى רוח אלהין קדישין وان מנדע هو شرح قوله חכמה
כחכמת אלהן وשכלתנו مثل الاول واما מפשר חלמא ואחוית אחידן ומשרא קטרין فهى
تفصيل نהيرو وذلك ان لفظة نهيرو يتّجه ان يكون تفسيره מא رشد مثل العبرانية وبّجه ١٠
انها نور في لغة الارمانيّة ونهورا עمه שרא ومعناها انه يظهر الاشياء لخفية التى كانها
في الظلمان فتظهر فيوقف عليها ۞ فقوله רוח יתירא لما فيه من الالهام المعدوم جنسه
من حكماء بابل ۞ واما المندע فهى العلوم الفلسفية كما جرى في تفسير ومשכילים
בכל חכמה ۞ واما ושכלתנו فهى علم الاستنباط ۞ مפשر חלמין يشير الى المنامات
المعبة مثل ما جرى له في تفسير الشجر ۞ واما ואחוית אחידן ومשرא קטרin فليس ١٥
ذلك منصوص في ديوانه لكن ذلك في كلام الفلاسفة نوادر يضعونها كلام مبنى على
اغراض من جنس قول شمشون עם لכם חידה ۞ واما ומשرא קטرin فهو كلام
يظنّ انه من جنس واحد والحكيم يفصل بعضه من بعض ۞ وعرّفته ان جدّه جعله
فوق كل حكمائه من حيث اجتمعت فيه هذه الاوصاف وانه سمّاه باسم معبوده هَمْ
من اجل ذلك ۞ فقالت من كان معه هذا الرجل (لم) يلحقه ما لحقك الساعة ابعث ٢٠
خلفه فانه يجيء ويقرا ويفسّر وينزول شغل قلبك ۞

١٣ حينئنى דانيال ادخل قدام الملك ۞ مجيب وقائل لדانيال
انت هو دانيال الذى من اولاد الجالية من اليهود الذى جاب
الملك جتى من اليهود ۞

لم تذكر له الملكة ان دانيال من اليهود فيمكن انه سال عنه للحاضرين فاخبروه ٢٥

---

[1] בעצה codd.   [2] מעני P X ; text B.

Line 3. غائبا.   16. منصوصا.

فصل ٥ بذلك ۞ وليس هذا القول من (بلشاصر) استنقاص بدانيال فى مثل هذا الحال التى
فاسوق ١٣ هو عليها لكن لما كان خبر اليهود مشهور بالنبوة وعلوم الالهية قال له هذا القول ۞

١٤ وسمعت عنك ان روح الالاه فيك والرشد والعقل وحكمة فاضلة
وجدت فيك ۞

٥ ١٥ والساعة دخلوا قدامى الحكماء والمشعونين ليقرون هذا الخط
وليخبروني تفسيره فلم يكونوا قادرين على تفسيره للاخبار ۞

١٦ وانا سمعت عنك انك تقدر على التفاسير لتفسر والعقد لتحلل
الساعة ان كنت تقدر على قراة الخط وتفسيره لتعريفى ثياب ارجوان
تلبس وطوق ذهب على عنقك وثلث فى الملك تتسلط ۞

١٠ قال فى الفاسوق الاول دִי רֹוּחַ אֱלָהִין ונהירו ושכלתנו وزاد فى الثانى פשרין הם على
رسم ما قالت الملكة ۞

حينئذٍ مجيب دانيال وقائل قدام الملك عطاياك لك يكونوا
وجوائزك اعطى لقوم اخرين غير ان اقرا الخط للملك والتفسير ۞ ۞

لم يقبل منه شيا مما ذكرو لاشياء احدها لم يكن راغب الى برّه لانه على غير
١٥ استواء وهو جهله [1]وتقحّمه والثانى انه شى [2]يزول للوقت والثالث لئلا يقال انه فسّر
ذلك لمعنى ما ياخذه ۞ فقال له ليس اقبل منك شى فان اردت ان تهب فهب لغيرى
لمن تختاره وانا اقرا لك الخط واعرّفك تفسيره وهو مرادك وبغيتك لا غير ۞

١٨ انت الملك الالاه العالى الملك والجلالة والعزّ والبهجة اعطى
لبختناصر جدّك ۞

٢٠ ١٩ ومن [3] ۞ ۞ الجلالة التى اعطاه كل الشعوب والامم واللغات

---

[1] רבותא om. ;BDK ;ותקדّمה BK; ותקדّימה D. [2] חול B. [3] ומן רבותא
PQX; prob. كثرة.

Line 1. استنقاصا. 2. مشهورا. 5. المشعوذون ليقرّوا. 9. ثلثا. 13. أعطى.
14. راغبا.

كانوا مضطربين وفازعين من قدّامه الذى كان هاوى كان قاتل فصله
والذى كان هاوى كان ضارب والذى كان هاوى كان مرفّع والذى فُسوق ١٩
كان هاوى كان مسفّل •

٢ وعند ما شمخ قلبه وروحه تصلّبت للاتّقاح حطّ من كرسىّ
ملكه والعزّ زال منه •

٢١ ومن بين الناس طرد وقلبه مع الوحوش جعل ومع حمير
الوحش ماواه عشب مثل الثور يطعمونه ومن ندى السماء جسمه
ينصبغ حتى علم ان متسلّط الالاه العالى بملك الناس ولمن يهوى
يقيم عليها •

قدّم هذه المقدّمة ليعرّفه ان ليس هو باجلّ من جدّه الذى بلغ فى الملك والعزّ
والهيبة والخوف منه ما لم يبلغ هو فلما اتّقح ولبس ثوب الاقتدار ذلّه البارى ذلّ ليس
بعده ذلّ فقد رفع المتسقّلين وسقّل المترفّعين وقتل الملوك الكبار وعمل سائر ما كان
يريده ولم يقدر احد يخالفه ويدفعه عن مراده •

٢٢ وانت ولده بلشاصر لم تسفّل قلبك الذى هنا كل عرفت •

٢٣ وعلى مولى السماء ترفّعت ولاوانى بيته جيب قدّامك وانت
واجلّاؤك سرّيّانك ووصائفك الخمر شاربين بهم ولالاه الفضّة
والذهب والنحاس والحديد والخشب والحجر الذى غير ناظرين
وغير سامعين وغير عارفين سبّحت ولالاه الذى نسمتك بيده وكل
سبلك لم تبهّج •

قوله ١٦ כל די דנה ידעת يدلّ على ان بلشاصر عرف كل ما جرى على جدّه فقد كان
سبيله ان يتادّب بذلك • ثم عرّفه ان اخذه لاوانى بيت الالاه انه اقتدار عليه واستخفاف
بنفسه • ثم ان دانيال نظر الى المجلس ومن فيه من الناس ونظر الالات التى لبيت

_____

فصل ٥ الآلاء وان قد شربوا فيها وعرّف انهم سبّحوا معبوداتهم ولم يبجّلوا الله تعّ كما يستحقّ

فاسوق ٢٣ وسبّحوا الاصنام الذى لا فعل لها بل هى تماثيل وصور فقط كقوله ١٦ لۀ חזית ٠ ثم

بعد ان عرّفه نقص معبوداته وجهله وتجاسره قال له ومن اجل ذلك بعث من كتب

هذا الكتاب ٠

٥   ٢٤ حينئنٍ من قدامه ارسل كفّ يدٍ وكتب هذا الكتاب ٠

٢٥ وهذا الخطّ الذى رسم عدد عدد وزن وتكسيرات ٠

٢٦ هذا تفسير الكلام عدد عدّ الله ملكك ووفاها ٠

٢٧ وزن وزنت بالميزان ووجدت ناقص ٠

٢٨ تكسير كسرت ملكك واعطيت لمادى وفارس ٠

١٠   عرّف ان من اجل ما تقدم من فعله وجّه ملاك حتى كتب هذه الاربعة كلمات ثم

وآلّف هذه لخمسة عشر حرف علم وقال מנא מנא دفعتين الواحدة عدد السبعين

ירמ כו. ٦ سنة الذى جعلها الله تعّ لنبوخذناصر وولده وولد ولده كقوله ועבדו אתו וגו' والثانى

هو ١ملك بلشاصر فعدّ لهم ثلث ملوكٍ و[عدد] السبعين ⟨سنة⟩ فلما تمّت لم يبق

لهم٢ ٠ وفسّر תקל תקילת يعنى انه من كان ناقص لا يوخذ الا ما كان وافى وهو عقله

١٥   وحكمته ودينه وسائر احواله وذلك انه قد كان فى ابيه وجدّه بعض لخصال المحمودة

وليس فيه هو شى من ذلك بل كل احواله ناقصة ٠ وفسّر פרסין تكسيرات وجعله مثل

الشى الذى يكسر فلا يبقى فيه شى ينتفع به [وهو تلف كل من كان يعضده فى

ملكه وقتله ولذلك قال פרסין بلفظ التكثير] وانما قال פרסין على معنى تلفه وهو قتله

وبعد ذلك تلف من بعده كل من كان عاضد ملك الكسدانيين ⟨ولذلك قال פרסין

٢٠   بلفظ التكثير⟩ ٠ ثم عرّفه انها تنتقل الى مادى وفارس ٠

٢٩ حينئنٍ قال بلشاصر فالبسوا لدانيال ثياب الارجوان وطوق
النهب على عنقه ونادوا عليه ان يكون متسلّط على الثلث فى
الملك ٠

---

¹ Om. B.   ² B adds תלת מלוך ועדד אלכלאם; perh. add. ملك.

Line 2. التى.   ١١. علما, حرفا, ألّف.   ١٢. التى.   ١٤. ناقصا, وافيا.
٢٢. متسلّطا.

لم يكن بدّ من ان يفعل ما قد ضمنه ولم يمكن دانيال مخالفته وعلم ان هذا فصل ه
ملك زائل •   فاسوق ٢٩

—|·••|·—

٣٠ فى تلك الليلة قُتِل بلشاصر الملك الكسدانيّ •

علم داريواش ان يقول دانيال قول ثابت وان الملك لمادى وفارس وليس يبعد ان
دانيال عرّف داريواش ان الملك له دون غيره فجسر على قتله او يكون بعض غلمانه ٥
قتله اذ الكتاب لم يذكر قاتله من هو •

٦١ وداريواش المادى تسلّم الملك وله اثنتين وستين سنة •

قوله קבל מלכותה يريد انه تسلّم الملك من الكسدانيّين كقوله بعد هذا אשר המלך
על מלכות כשדים ولم يذكر كيف تمّ له الملك وكيف اقعد فى بابل على كرسيّ الملك
وعرّف انه كان له[1] * * * * فى السنة التى اجلى بختنصار يهوياخين ملك يهوذا ١٠
ولد داريواش ليعرّف ان فى سنة عمل ما عمله فى يروشاليم وكان فتح كبير فى تلك
السنة اقام اللّه تبع عليه من يتسلّم الملك منه فمن اجل ذلك ذكر تاريخ سنينه فى
وقت تسلّم الملك من الكسدانيين ولما لم يكن لغيره من ملوك الدنيا ولا من ملوك
يسرائيل ايضا[2] من يفيد منه معنى [فهو] فى تعريفنا كم له وقت ملك لم يذكر
لنا ذلك •   ١٥

٢ حسن قدّام داريواش واقام على كل الملك ماية وعشرين اميرا
حتى يكونون فى كل الملك •

٣ وارفع منهم ثلاثة بطارقة الذى دانيال واحد منهم [من الثلاثة]
حتى يكون هؤلاء الامراء يعطون لهم الامر ولا يكون الملك متانى •

عرّف ان داريواش علم ان الملك مستوى بيده وليس يحتاج الى سَقَر حتى يحارب ٢٠
من يناصبه فجعل هؤلاء الماية وعشرين اميرا لكل واحد بلد من البلدان يجعل له
فيه واحد من تحت يده وهو مقيم عنده فى المدينة وجعل الثلاثة סרכין يرجعون الى

———————————

[1] Supply ان ما يفيد منه سنة ٦٢ ملكه وقت. [2] מן DQX; מן אן BP; prob. ما.
Line 4. قولا etc. ٢٠. مستوٍ. ١٧. يكونوا. ٧. اثنتان وستون. ٢١. بلدا.
٢٢. واحدا.

فصل ٦ قولهم وامرهم وجعل هولاء المابة وعشرين حتى يدبرون المملكة ولا يحتاج الملك الى

فاسوق ٣ التعب فى سائر الامور وهذا من جنس ما فعله فرعون الذى جعل يوسف يدبّر المملكة

وهو مترفه ليس له غير الاسم فقط ۰

٤ حينئذٍ هنا دانيال كان مشترف على البطارقة والامراء من حيث

٥ ان روح فاضلة فيه والملك كان مدبّر (او محتال) لاقامته على كل

الملك ۰

يونה א. ٥   עשית מעל אולי יעעשת האלהים לנו אבדו עשתנותיו ۰ جعل الثلثة فوق المابة

תהלים קמ٥. ٦ وعشرين وجعل دانيال الذى هو واحد من الثلثة فوق الامراء وفوق البطارقة حتى لا

يفعل واحد منهم شى الا عن رايه وامره وعرّف انه فعل ذلك من حيث فيه רוח יתירה

١٠ فليس يلحقه عجز ولا يلحق رايه وامره فساد ۰ ثم عرّف ان الملك كان هوذا يحتال

فى ان يبطل اولائك ويجعل دانيال وحده كانه لم يتمّ له من اوّل شى ان ينصب دانيال

بل علم ان هذا الباب يحتاج الى تلطّف فجاء الى [١]اصحاب الدولة الكبار فلم يقلعهم

عن [١]المدينة للجليلة حتى استوى له الملك فلما استوى له الملك اخذ فى تدبير وحيلة

حتى ينزعهم قليل فقليل فلما حسّوا هم بذلك اخذوا فى الحيلة عليه ليقلعوه عن

١٥ الملك اصلا كقوله

٥ حينئذٍ البطارقة والامراء كانوا طالبين شى من العلل للوجود

لدانيال من جهة الملك وكل علّة وفساد لم يكونوا قادرين للوجود

من حيث انه ثقة وكل غلط وفساد ما وجدت عليه ۰

عرّف ان البطارقة مع الامراء اتّفقوا على كلمة واحدة وذلك من جهة الحسد الذى

٢٠ داخل قلوبهم منه فقالوا ان الملك انما رقّعه علينا لجودة رايه فنعمل كل حيلة حتى

يصحّ عند الملك زلل وتقصير به ويزيله عن الملك اصلا فعرّف انهم طلبوا زلل ولم يجدوا

وقال עלה ושחיתה فالعلة هو ظلم الناس وשחيתה فساد فى معنى الملك وفى تضييع

المال ۰

---

¹ Prob. المرتبة.

Line ١. يدبّروا.   ٤. مشرّفا etc.   ٥. روحا.   ١٤. قليلا etc.

٢١ (2nd). زللا.

٦ حينئنٍ اولائك الرجال قائلين ليس نجد لدانيال شى من العلل لكن وجدنا عليه فى سنّة الاهه ٥

عرّف انه لما اّيسوا ان يجدوا عليه طريقا من جهة الملك قالوا نصل الى مرادنا فيه فى معنى عبادة ربّه وقد كان مرادهم وغرضهم فى ذلك (لا) انهم يقدروا ان [لم] يظهروا عليه انه مفيّع شى من دينه لكن من طريق اخرى ٥

٧ حينئنٍ البطارقة والامراء ارهجوا (وقيل تزاحموا) على الملك وكنزى قائلين له داريواوش ملكا الى الدهر عيش ٥

٨ نشاوروا كل بطارقة الملك والروساء والامراء والخدماء والعتّال لتثبيت امر الملك لتصليب رباط ان كل من يطلب طلبة من كل اللّه ومن الناس الى ثلاثين يوم لكن منك ايها الملك يرمى الى جبّ السباع ٥ ١٠

٩ الان ايها الملك تثبت الرباط وترسم الخطّ حتى لا يتغيّر مثل سنّة مادى وفارس التى لا تزول ٥

١٠ من حيث هنا الملك داريواوش رسم الخطّ والرباط ٥

قولهم אתחיעו عرّف انهم اجتمعوا [1]وتجادوا فى ما يكون فيه ضبط الملك للملك ١٥ حتى يطيعوه الناس وانه كذى يجب ان يُعمل وان لم يفعل الملك ذلك تشوّش عليه الملك والزموا ذلك انفسهم حتى لا يتمّ لدانيال عبادة اللّه تع الذى هو غرضهم ولم يعرف الملك غرضهم فيه وهذا من دقّة حيلتهم عليه ولو عرف الملك ذلك لم يرض برأيهم ولا قبله ولا طرح ولا خطّة ٥ ثم انهم قالوا له ادع خطّك حتى يقرا على الناس فى الاسواق وفى الجموع حتى لا يخالف احد من الناس ٥ وجمعوا فى قولهم ١٦ دל ٢٠ אדש كل متديّن بدين من سائر الاديان ولم بخصّوه بدين غير دينهم ذلك لدقّة حيلتهم حتى يتمّ ذلك على دانيال ٥ وجعلوا ذلك مدّة ثلاثين يوم حتى تطول المدّة

Lines 1, 7. قائلون.   7. عش, الملك.   15. يوما.   12. يرسم, ريثمت.

22. يوما.

فصل ٢ وهى غاية ما كان عندهم ان [لا] يبقوا بلا عبادة الاههم ولو لم يجُزّ ذلك فى دينهم
فاسوق ١٠ لم يرسمه ❖ ومنعوا ان يطلب احد من احد حاجة كما لا يطلب من الاه ولم يكن
الغرض غير الاله ❖ وفعلوا ذلك حتى لا يفطن احد غيرهم بما قصدوه ❖ ثم استثنوا
بالملك لشيين احدهما هو لا بُدّ من ذلك والّا تلف الناس بظلم يجرى من الناس
5 بعضهم على بعض وحوائج تعرض لهم فليس بُدّ من ذلك والاخر جعلوا الملك فوق
كل الاه ليعظّموا شانه وكل ذلك ليوروه ان بهذا الامر ينضبط له الملك وينتظم ❖ فلما
رآهم قد اتّفقوا على ذلك ظهر له انّه لم يفعل ما قد اتّفقوا عليه تشوّش عليه [1]ففعل
ذلك ❖ ولم يوخذ راى دانيال فى ذلك [2]لانه اظهروا ان هذا ليس هو من تدبير
المملكة الذى لدانيال فيه مدخل اصلا ❖

10 ١١ ودانيال كما علم ان الملك قد رسم الخطّ دخل الى بيته وكان
له كوّى مفتوحة فى غرفته حنِاء يروشالايم وثلثة اوقات فى اليوم
هو بارك على ركبه ومصلّى وشاكر قدّام الاهه من حيث انه كان
كنى فاعل من قبل هذا الوقت ❖

يمكن ان دانيال وقف على ما كان فى نفسهم وقصدهم انه هو الغرض دون الناس
15 كلهم وهو يقف على ما فعله الملك ولم يذكر للملك وولّج الامور الى خالق الكلّ ❖
وذكر الكوّى لانهم اشرفوا منها عليه وكبسوه واذا هو يصلّى ❖ وقال نكد يروشلم
ليس يريد به ان الكوّى مفتوحة نكد يروشلم [3]وانما [4]المراد كان الوقوف حذاء يروشالايم°
وهى القبلة ❖ وقال دل كبل دى هوا ليعرّف ان ليس هو شى ابتداً به فى هذا الوقت
فدلّ ذلك على انه دائماً كان يفعل هذا وانه امر واجب لا يجوز ان يدفع ان وهذه
20 الثلاثة اوقات يقرب انها عرب وبكر وظهرين ولما قال برك عل بركوهى علمنا انه من شرط
تلّيم צה. ١ الصلوة وكذلك قوله בואו נשתחוה ונכרעה נברכה לפני יוי עושינו :

١٢ حينئذٍ اولائك الرجال ارهجوا ووجدوا دانيال طالب ومتضرّع
قدّام الاهه ❖

---

¹ Prob. add. الملك. ² Prob. لانهم. ³ وانما ... يروشالايم om. BDK.
⁴ P. אלנרש.

Line 12. مصلّي.   13. فاعلا.   22. طالبا etc.

فصل ٦   لا شكّ فى انه قد حسّ بمجيّتهم لينظروه فلم يقطع صلوته بل اقام على جملته
فاسوق ١٢   فنزلوا عليه وهو يصلّى وهؤُلاء الرجال هم الامراء والبطارقة ❖

١٣ حينئذٍ تقدّموا وقائلون للملك على رباط الملك البس رسمت
ان كل انسان يطلب حاجته من الاه وانسان الى ثلاثين يوما لكن
من عندك ايها الملك يرمى الى جبّ السباع [1]مجيب الملك وقائل
يقينا الكلام كسنّة مادى وفارس التى لا تزول ❖

قوله ‏ڧاۧ‎ מلחۚ‎ يعنى كذى هو لا يجوز لاحد ان يتعدّى ذلك وانه كل من تعدّى
يرمى الى جبّ السباع فلما سمعوا هذا القول من الملك وحصّلوا عليه قوله قالوا
بعد ذلك ❖

١٤ حينئذٍ اجابوا وقائلون قدام الملك ان دانيال الذى [2]هو من
بنى الجالية من اليهود لم يجعل على نفسه [3]امرا من جهتك[3]
والرباط الذى رسمت وثلثة اوقات فى اليوم طالب طلبته ❖

قولهم מן בני‎ גﻟﻮﺗﺎ‎ استحقار به ويعنون بذلك انه من احقر الناس وقد رفعته على
الجميع وقد خالف ما رسمت وحلّ ما ربطته على الناس وارادوا من الملك [ان يقول]
بعد هذا القول ان يامر بطرحه الى جب السباع ❖   ١٥

١٥ حينئذٍ الملك كما سمع هذا الكلام عظيم صعب عليه ومن اجل
دانيال جعل حيلة لتخليصه والى وقت دخول الشمس كان
[5]مكالف لتخليصه ❖

كما سمع قولهم ان الذى خالف ما جرى هو دانيال تيقّن انهم عملوا الحيلة عليه
فاخذ يحتجّ لدانيال وهو ان ليس يدخل فى جملة من [5]منعناه لانه هو مدبّر الملك ٢٠
وانما كان غرضنا غيره فهذا الكلام وما جانسه كان يقول لهم الى مغيب الشمس

[1] מן נחחך‎   [2] Om. C.   [3] מנִיב‎ P Q D (corr.); פֵֿנִיב‎ X; פֵנִיב‎ K; פֵֿינִיב‎ B D.
   C אמרא‎ [4] Perh. متكلفا.   [5] מענאה‎ B K.

Line 16. عظيما.

فصل ٦ كان مخالف لقولهم ¹ومحتجّ عنه وقد زعم قوم انه كان يقول لهم لم يعلم دانيال
فاسوق ¹⁵ بما كتب ولو سمع ²بذلك لم يخالف ما رسمناه فلما جاء ³وقت المغيب قام يصلى
فلم يمكن الملك يحتجّ له بشى •

١٦ حينئنٍ اولائك الرجال ارهجوا على الملك وقائلون للملك اعلم
٥ ايها الملك ان ستّة لمادى وفارس ان كل رباط وتثبيت الذى يثبت
الملك ليس يجوز تغيّر ذلك •

غرضهم فى هذا القول انه ان كان لا يطرح دانيال الى جبّ السباع فقد بطل ما
كان ⁴من رسم مادى وفارس وان جاز ان يبطل ذلك فى دانيال جاز فى غير ذلك
وهذا باب يتّسع ويكون فى ذلك فساد وغرضهم فى ذلك انه ان غيّر⁵الملك رسومهم
١٠ عموا عليه لانه لا سبيل لهم ان يملك عليهم من ⁶غيّر رسومهم •

١٧ حينئنٍ قال الملك وجابوا داينال ورموه الى جبّ السباع
مجيب الملك وقائل لدانيال الاهك الذى انت عابده على الدوام
هو يخلّصك •

⁷كان قول داريوش مخالف لقول بختناصر لان بختناصر قال ومن هو الههكن وني'
١٥ لان هذا كان يامن بالله نعّ انه قادر على خلاصه على ضرب من ضروب المعجز وبختناصر
لم يامن بانه قادر على ذلك • والقوم الذين طرحوا اولائك الى الاتون قتلهم وهج
⁸النار لقربهم منه وهؤلاء الذين طرحوا ⁹دانيال الى جبّ السباع لم يلحقهم شى من
ذلك لبعد السباع عنهم • فقال داريوش لدانيال فى وقت طرحه الى السباع لا شكّ
فى ان الله الذى تعبده على الدوام هو ينجيك من السباع لانه قادر على هذا ولا يتم
٢٠ لهؤلاء الذين احتالوا عليك مرادهم فيك •

١٨ وجيبت حجر واحدة وجعلت على فم الجبّ وختمها الملك
بخاتمه وخاتم اجلّائه لالّا يتغيّر مران بدانيال •

¹ ויחתני C; אחתני cett. ² דלך C. ³ Om. C. ⁴ Om. C. ⁵ Ins. C D
only. ⁶ ינייר C. ⁷ Ins. C only. ⁸ אלנאר K D (in ras.); אלאתון cett.
⁹ לדניאל C.

Line 1. مخالفا etc. 14. مخالفا.

يمكن ان هذا الجبّ له باب ادخلت السباع منه [1] ولم تم ضوْ يطرح لهم منه اللحم   فصل ٦

حتى ياكلون اذا لم يطرح لهم انسان وكان من شان هولا اذا استوجب الواحد القتل   فاسوق ١٨

طرحوه الى السباع لياكلوه وكان رسم بختناصر يقتل بالنار وغيرهم بالسيف ۞   وقوله

דִי לָא חֲשַׁלְנָא לְבַד יعنى [2] ۞ انهم اذا نظروا ان السباع لم توذيه طرحوا هم عليه

حجر وقتلوه لانهم قد كاشفوه وعلم الملك ان اللہ تعّ يخلّصه فعل ذلك ولولا ذلك   5

لم يختم للحجر الذى على راس البٔر ۞

١٩ حينئنٍ نهب الى هيكله وبات مشتوى والات الملاهى ما

انخل قدامه ونومه نفرت عليه ۞

فسروا מות חרנום צלי אשׁ يعنى احترق قلبه على دانيال ومنع الغنى والفرح ولعظم

شغل قلبه به كثرت افكاره فى بابه فنفرت سنته ولم ياخذه النوم الى الفجر ۞   10

٢٠ حينئنٍ الملك فى وقت السحر يقوم بشمعة وبسرعة الى جبّ

السباع نهب ۞

٢١ وعند قربه من الجبّ صرخ بصوت شاقّ مجيب الملك وكنى

قائل لدانيال يا دانيال الالاه الحىّ الالهك الذى انت عابده على

الدوام البس قدر على خلاصك من السباع ۞   15

٢٢ حينئنٍ دانيال تكلّم مع الملك ايها الملك للدهر عيش ۞

٢٣ الاهى بعث ملاكه وغلف فم السباع ولم يفسدونى من حيث

ان زكوة وجدت لى ۞ ۞ ۞ وايضا قدامك ايها الملك فساد لم

افعل ۞

قام عند الفجر لتعلّق قلبه به ثم نادى اليه ليسمع كلامه فيطيب قلبه بسلامته ۞   20

وقول دانيال אלהי שלח מלאכה [3] تفسيره على مسموعه انه بعث اللہ تعّ [4] بملاك

---

[1] codd. יפסרה   [2] Perh. add. يخشى.   [3] all; perh. ايضا ولم تم خو.

[4] B. بالملاك.

Line 2. ياكلوا.   3. طرحه.   4. توذه.   5. حجرا.   7. مشتويا.

16. عش.   18. فسادا.

فصل ٢ يتخلصه كما بعث الى حننيا ميسائيل وعزريا و(قوله وسגד פם اريوتא) هو انهم كانوا

فاسوق ٢٣ جياع ولم يجعل لهم سبيل لاذائه ٠ وقوله די קרדמوהי זכו يشير الى سائر افعاله

——•——— الصالحة بينه وبين الله تعّ وايفا لما تقدّم من قوله דל קבל די מהימן הוא ٠ ثم قال

وאף קרדם מלכא חבולא לא עבדת ليورى انه لم يفعل شى يستحقّ من اجل ذلك ان

٥ يعمل به ما عمل به ٠

٢٤ حينئذٍ الملك كثيرا طاب له وقال ليصعدوا دانيال من الجبّ

ولم يجد فيه شى من الفساد من اجل انه وثق بالاهه ٠

دلوا اليه حبال كما جرى فى امر يرميا عمّ ٠

٢٥ وقال الملك حتى جيبوا الرجال الذى غمزوا بدانيال ورموا

١٠ الى جبّ السباع هم وبنيهم ونساؤهم ولم يبلغوا الى ارض الجبّ

حتى نسلّطوا بهم السباع وكل عظامهم سحقوا ٠

هولاء الرجال هم المايه واثنان وعشرون التى دبّروا عليه وكل من ظهر منه عداوة

دانيال لحقوا بهم واولادهم وحرمهم الذى كان حكمهم فى سنن الفارس ان يلحقوا

الاولاد والنساء بالرجال فعمل على رسمهم او يكون نساؤهم واولادهم الكبار اظهروا من

١٥ السرور بذلك وعداوة دانيال فاستحقّوا ذلك عند الملك ٠ ويقرب فيه انهم كانوا

يطرحوا قوم بعد قوم بعدّة السباع [1]وتناول كل واحد من السباع واحد من الناس

فاذا راوهم قد اكلوه يخرجوا غيرهم الى ان اكلوا الكل ٠ ورجع دانيال الى تدبير

الملك وحده كما كان يدبّر المَلِك قبل ذلك كما تقدّم القول به [2]كقوله עשيת ٠ وليس

بدّ من ان [3]يكون تمّ ما رسم الملك فى كتابه الى ان تمّ ثلاثين يوما غير (على)

٢٥ دانيال ونظرائه من عباد الله عز رجل ٠

٢٦ حينئذٍ داريَاوش الملك كتب الى كل الشعوب والامم الذين

سكّان فى كل الارض يكثر سلامكم ٠

٢٧ من قدامى اجعال امرا ان كل من هو فى سلطان ملكى

---

١ וينאول codd.　　　² וקولה codd.　　　³ יכان B.

Line 2. جياعا, سبيلا.　　　8. حبالا.　　　١٥. وبنوهم.　　　16. توما.　　　19. ثلاثون.

يكونون ¹مضطربين وفازعين من قدام الاه دانيال الذى هو الالاه   فصل ٦
الحىّ الثابت الى الدهر وملكه لا ينفسد وسلطانه الى النهاية ♦   فاسوق ٢٧

٢٨ منجى ومخلّص وفاعل الايات والبراهين فى السماء وفى
الارض هو الذى نجا دانيال من يد السباع ♦

فعل داريوش كما فعل بختناصر بعد رجوعه من البّريّة الى ملكه من انفاد ٥
الكتب بما جرى له لانه وجب عنده [من] تعظيم للخالق جل ذكره ونىّ معجزاته وامر
الناس بالخوف منه لانه هو الالاه الباقى الذى لا يزول ملكه وسلطانه النافذ ويخلّص
وينجو من يريد ♦ وقوله ٱעَבﬧ אﬨ‬ין ותמّהין בשﬦאָﬡ ובﬡﬧ﬏גּﬡ يعنى به ايات فى جنود
السماء من الكسوفات وغير ذلك (و)فى الارض من جنس ما جرى فى قصّة دانيال
ورفقائه وقد شاهد ذلك داريوش وعلمه ♦ ثم عرّفهم ان دانيال طرح الى ²جبّ السباع ١٠
فلم يوّذوه ولا شكّ فى ان الناس قد علموا بما فعلوا المّاية واثنين وعشرين رجل حتى
طرحوا الى السباع ³واعزلوا ونصب غيرهم ⁴خلفاءهم ♦

٢٩ ودانيال هذا انجح فى ملك داريوش وفى ملك كورش
الفارسىّ ♦

يعنى كان على الملك والرياسة كما تقدّم القول فى تفسير וﬓﬔ﬩ דﬕﬡﬓ ע﬩ שﬓﬨ אﬖﬨ ١٥
ﬓ﬒﬙ﬨגּ ﬓﬗﬓ﬒ ♦

وهذا وصف ما جرى لنبوخذناصر وبلشاصر وداريوش ♦ فاما اخبار كورش ومن
قام بعده من ملوك الفارس فقد ترجمه سفر عزرا عمّ ♦

١٠ فى سنة احدى لبلشاصر ملك بابل نظر دانيال مناما
ومنظر راسه على فراشه ♦ حينئنٍ كتب المنام اوّل الكلام قال ♦ ٢٠

قد كان وقف على ما تضمّنه منام بختناصر من اربع ﬓﬖ﬒﬒ﬓ على ما شرحه لكن
وقف بعد ذلك على شروح هى اوسع من ذلك شى منها فى هذا المنام الذى راه وشى

---

¹ ﬗﬔﬨﬓ﬒﬒﬒ ﬒﬒ﬖ﬒﬒ codd.   ² Ins. P only.   ³ ﬒﬒ﬖﬗ﬒﬒ ﬒ﬓ﬒ﬗﬓﬓ﬒ ﬒﬒גּ﬒ ﬒﬒﬒ﬓ﬒ﬓﬓ﬒ codd.
⁴ P. ﬒﬒﬒ﬓ﬒ﬓ﬒ Q; ﬒﬒ﬓﬗ﬒ﬓ﬒

Line 11. وائنان وعشرون رجلا.

فصل ٧ منها فى الفصل الذى بعده وهو בשנת שלש למלכות בלשאצר وشى منها فى سنة احدى

فاسوق ١ لكورش وشى منها בשנת שלש לדריוש جملة ذلك خمسة فصول ۞ فاما منام بختنصر

وهذا المنام الذى نظره دانيال فهما يجمعان ذكر الاربع ممالك واما הٮٮٮ فليس

فيه ذكر الملك الاول بل يذكر فيه الثلثة ممالك واما الفصل الرابع فيذكر فيه خبر

5 בית שני مجمل ويذكر فيه ما فعلت الروم ببيت المقدس وهو الملك الرابع واما الفصل

للخامس فانه يتضمّن شرح ما يجرى من اخبار ملوك اليونانيّة والروم والعرب وساٮر

القصّة على ما سنشرح ذلك بعون الله تعّ ۞ وهذه الاربعة فصول التى حكاها سيد

دانيال عمّ تنقسم ۞ قالاول منها هو ما راه فى المنام والثانى بحازون والثالث والرابع

كان منتبه وراى الملائكة وخاطبوه ويدلّ ذلك على زيادة رتبة فى النبوة ۞ وكشف

10 الله تعّ ذلك لدانيال دون غيره لشدّة احتراقه على مصائبنا وتعلّق قلبه بما يجرى

علينا ١وارادة الوقوف على المدّة كم تكون ولذلك سمّاه איש חמודות ۞ وقوله הלמא כתב

ذلك لانه اراد ان يكون مثبوت فى جملة اخبارنا التى كتبتها الانبياء عمّ ۞ وقوله

ראש מלין אמר قيل فيه ان ذكر عيون المنام المُعوّل عليها وقيل انه اراد به اوّل ما

قال فى الكتاب ענה דניאל كما هو مكتوب يعنو على ما هو فى هذا السفر كذا

15 كان لئلا يظن انه كان شى مكتوب فاختصره ٢لان الانبياء عمّ قد يكتبون البعض

ويختصرون عن البعض كقوله فى اخبار الملوك ויתר דברי פלוני:

٢ مجيب دٯٮبٯل وقائل كنت ناظر فى مناظرى مع الليل وانا

اربع رياح السماء مقفرة للبحر الكبير۰

٣ وانا اربع حيوانات كبار صاعدات من البحر متغيّرات هنه۰

20 من هنه۰

عرّف انه راى اربع رياح ٣هاٮجة البحر الكبير وهو البحر المحيط وعند هيجانه

صعدت منه هذه الاربع حيوانات وهذا يدلّ (على) انه راى فى المنام انه واقف على

شطّ البحر حتى صعدت منه هذه الاربع حيوانات ۞ ثم اخذ يذكر وصف حيوانة

حيوانة من هذه الاربع حيوانات ۞

---

١ ואראד codd.   ٢ לבן P Q; לאן cett.   ٣ הינת or הינה codd.

Line 5. مجملا.   9. منتبها.   12. مثبوتا.   15. مكتوبا.   17. ناظرا.

۴ القدّاميّة مثل الاسد واجنحة النسر لها كنت ناظر حتى نُتفوا فصل ٧
اجنحتها ورفعت من الارض وعلى رجلين مثل الانسان اقيمت فاسوق ۴
وقلب الانسان اعطى لها ٠

۵ وانا بحيوانة اخرى ثانية شابهة لدبّ والى جانب واحد
اقيمت وثلثة اضلاع فى فمها بين اسنانها وكذى قائلين لها قومى
كلى لحما كثيرا ٠

۲ بعد هنا كنت ناظر وانا اخرى لها مثل النمر ولها اجنحة طائر
على صلبها واربعة رؤوس للحيوانة وسلطان اعطى لها ٠

۷ بعد هنا كنت ناظر فى مناظر الليل وانا بحيوانة رابعة فرعة
وهيوبة وصلبة فاضلة واسنان حديد لها كبار اكلت وسحقت ١٠
والبقية برجليها رفست وهى متغيّرة من كل حيوانة التى سبقتها
وعشرة قرون لها ٠

۸ متفرّس كنت فى القرون وانا بقرن صغيرة صعدت بينهم وثلثة
من القرون المتقدّمة انقلعوا من قدّامها وانا عينين مثل عينين
الانسان فى هذا القرن وفم متكلّم بالكبار ٠ ١٥

يجب ان نبيّن لاى معنى مثّلت الممالك بالحيوان فمرّة ¹تمثّل بالخيل كقوله
وهנה ארבע מרכבות وهى اهليّة وقد مثّل بعد هذا ملك الفارس بكبش ومثّل ²ملوك וכו׳ וכו׳ ח
اليونانيّة بعتود فنقول انه مثّل الاربعة ممالك بخيل من حيث ان لها للحرب فلما كان
كل واحدة منها حارب غيرها مثّلها بالסוסים ٠ ومثّل بختنصر مرّة بسبع ومرّة بنسر
فمثّله ³بسبع ونسر وهو اعظم الطائر المفترس وكذلك السبع اعظم الوحش المفترس ٢٠
فلذلك لم يكن فى ארבע מלכות اعظم منه ولا اشدّ منه باس وكذلك مثّله بالذهب

---

¹ ימתל codd.   ² Perh. ملك.   ³ Perh. بالنسر only.

Lines 1, 7. ناظرا.   13. متفرسا.   14. عينىّ.   21. باسا.

فصل ٧ وهو اجلّ من الفقّة وفى النسر ايضا طيران وعلوّ وكذلك كان بختناصر كقوله فيه

فاسوق ٨ هنה כעננים יעלה וכסופה מרכבותיו ووصفه اخر ان עוף ואין כושל בו ❖ وفى السبع

يرם' ד. יג
ישע' ה. כד
משלי ל. ל

ايضا قوّة عظيمة وانه لا ينهزم كقوله ולא ישוב מפני כל فمثّلة فى هذا الفاسوق بالشيئين

جميعا اعنى بالسبع والنسر كقوله كאריה وقال ונפין די נשר وهى عساكره الكبّاز ❖

5 وقال חזה הוית يعنى فى ما كنت اراه بهذه الصورة الهائلة حتى رايت واذا قد انتفت

اجنحتها حتى لم تقدر تطير وتأويله هو ان انقطع سفره وغزواته وتأويل ونطילת من

ארעא هو ما لحقه فى السبع سنين وهو قوله ומן אנשא טריד ❖ وقوله על רגלין כאנש

הקימת ולבב אנשא هذا وصف حاله عند ما رجع اليه عقله فوحّد الله تعّ وترك الظلم

والتعدّى ورجع الى ملكه وازداد رفعة عمّا كان قبل ذلك ‹كقوله› ורבו יתירא הוספת' לי ❖

10 فوصف بختناصر وحده ولم يذكر حال اولاده اذ لم يكن لهم حال تُذكر اعنى جبروة

وفتح بلد بل هى للحال التى ورثوها من بختناصر فقطّ ❖ ثم وصف للحيوانة الثانية

انها تشبه الدبّ وذلك لجهلها لانهم قوم ثنوّية جهال ❖ وقوله ולשטר חד قيل انه فى

ظاهر امرها انها صعدت اعزلت ناحية وهو ما ذكره من فعلها مع يسرائيل وهو

ما فعله داریباوش مع دانیال وما فعله كورش ودارياوش الفارسيّ وارتحششتا مع يسرائيل

15 وكذلك احشويروش بعد قصّة هامان ❖ وقوله ותלת עלעין بفمه هو انهم ملكوا ثلث

جهات الدنيا وقد شرح ذلك بقوله فى ما بعد ראיתי את האיל מנגח ימה وצفונה ונגבה ❖

ד. ח

وقوله وكن אמרן לה קומי אכלי בשר סניא هو قول هامان ام على המלך טוב יכתב لابدم

אסת' ג. ט

وتمام القصّة ولم يذكر انها اكلت من حيث انه لم يتمّ ذلك فى يسرائيل بل انعكس

على اعدائهم ❖ ووصف ما تفعله ملوك الفارس ولم يذكر من ملوك كשדים غير

20 نبوخذناصر وحده كما تقدّم به القول ❖ ثم ذكر للحيوانة الثالثة فمثّلها بنمر والنمر

اصغر من الدبّ وكذلك فى الفصل الاخر مثّل ملوك الفارس بكبش ومثل ملوك اليونانية

يرם' ה. ו

بعتود وهو اصغر من الكبش ومع ذلك فان النمر يلازم ابواب البلدان كقوله نמר

שקד על עריהם واعلم ان النمر هو كل ملوك اليونانية ❖ وقوله ולה גפין ארבע די עוף

هو اربع تلامذته اعنى ¹ذى القرنين كما سنشرح ذلك فى الفصل الاخير عند قوله

וبעמדו תשבר מלכותו ותחץ לارבע רוחות השמים ❖ وقوله ושלטן יהב לה هو المشهور

יא. ד

26 من اخبار ¹ذى القرنين ❖ باثر دنה ثم ذكر للحيوانة الرابعة ولم يمثّلها بحيوانة

معروفة كما مثّل غيرها باسد ودبّ ونمر وذاك انه لم يكن لها مذهب واحد ولا

---

¹ דן codd.

ستّة واحدة فلم يعرف لها دانيال صورة حيوانة ¹تمثّل بها لكن ذكر لها خوف وفزع   **فصل ٧**

وهيبة وهى وصف ملك روم وكما شرحنا فى قوله وכחפרזלא די מרעע כל אלין תדוק **فاسوق ٨**

ותרע ✧   وقوله ושנין די פרזל לה هو טיטוס הרשע وامثاله الذى كانوا يغزون البلدان **وתרע**

ويقتلون لان الوحش يدق باسنانه وانيابه كقوله אכלה هو قتله ومدقة هو الذل ✧

وقوله ²משניה هو تغيّر الرسوم وكثرة الاذى ✧   وقوله وקרנין עשר לה هى عشرة كراسى ٥

كما سنشرح ذلك فى قوله עשרה מלכין יקומון ✧   وقوله משתכל הוית בקרניא فذلك

لعظمها فكان ³يتفرّس فى عظمها ✧   ونظر واذا بعد ذلك قد صعدت هذه القرن

الصغيرة فى ما بين العشرة قرون فلما حصلت القرن الصغيرة بينهم القيت من

قدامها ثلثة قرون وبقين سبعة قرون فهذه القرن الصغيرة بينهم ✧   ثم عرّف ان

لهذه القرن الصغيرة عينين تشبه عينين الناس وان لها فم يتكلم بكلام كبار لم ١٠

يذكر ما هو وسنذكر ذلك فى ומלין לצד עליא ימלל ✧

٩ ناظر كنت حتى رُموا الكراسى وقديم الزمان جلس لباسه

مثل الثلج الابيض وشعر رأسه مثل الصوف النقّى كرسيّه شرار النار

بكرة نار مشتعل ✧

١٠ نهر من نار (وقيل ضياء نورٍ) منقطع وخارج من قدامه الف ١٥

الوف يخدمونه وربوة ربوات قدامه يقومون الحكم جلس والكتب

فتنحوا ✧

هذه الكراسى الملوك التى تقدم ⁴ذكرها ✧   وقوله ועתיק יומין هو ملك ليحاكم   **ن. ذ.**

الامم يوم القيامة وفيه قال اסף עם יבוא אלהינו ואל יחרש אש לפניו תאכל ✧   فعرّف **ההל'**

انه طرح له كرسيّ من نار وان بكر الكرسيّ نار تشتعل لان الملائكة العلويّة اجسامهم ٢٠

نار وكذلك كراسيها من نار ✧   ثم اورى ان نهر من نار خارج من قدام الملك يعاقب

به العصاة ✧   وقوله אלף אלפין ישמשונה ذلك لانه ملاك عظيم من الملائكة كالسلطان

---

¹ ומתל codd.   ² הי codd.   ³ יתפרס corr. P in marg.; יפתרס cett.

⁴ דכרה or דכרהם codd.

Line 10. تشبهان, عينيّ, فما, بيكلّم.   12. ناظرا.   21. نهرا.

[II. 3.]   K

فصل ٧ العظيم الذى يقف قدامه عالم من الغلمان ❖ وعرّف لاتى معنى جلس على الكرسىّ
فاسوق ١٠ ووقف بين يديه هذه الغلمان فقال دِינَה יְתִב וְסִפְרִין פְּתִיחוּ وهو محاكمة الامم على ما
كفروا به كقوله وامر ايه איה אֱלֹהֵימוֹ צוּר חָסָיוּ בוֹ ❖ وقوله וְסִפְרִין פְּתִיחוּ ذاك من اجل
ان لهم ذنوب طويلة وافعالهم محفوظة عليهم كقوله הֲלֹא הוּא כָּמוּס עִמָּדִי وذلك ان
٥ فى مجارى عادات الناس ان يدونون ما يحتاج اليه بعد دهر ¹لألا ينساه فتكلم على
منهاج العالم ومثله قوله فى افعال الاشرار הִנֵּה כְתוּבָה לְפָנָי ومثله قال فى عمل
الصالحين וַיִּכָּתֵב סֵפֶר זִכָּרוֹן לְיִרְאֵי יְוֹי וּלְחֹשְׁבֵי שְׁמוֹ وقال יִמָּחוּ מִסֵּפֶר חַיִּים ❖ وقد قال
عن محاكمة الله للامم على فعلهم بيسرائيل الظلم كقوله וְקִבַּצְתִּי אֶת כָּל הַגּוֹיִם וְהוֹרַדְתִּים
לְעֵמֶק יְהוֹשָׁפָט وحسن ان يذكر يوم المحاكمة بعقب فراغ اربع ملكيات ليورى ان بعد
١٠ انقضاء ملكهم عليهم حكومة ومطالبة ودينونة وان افعالهم محسوبة عليهم ❖

١١ ناظر كنت حينئذٍ من اجل صوت القرن المتكلمة ناظر كنت
حتى قتلت واهلك جسمها وسلّمت لوقيدة النار ❖

رجع يذكر ما يكون من الحيوانة الرابعة فعرّف انه كان سبب هلاك هذه الحيوانة
الكبيرة هو ما كانت تتكلم به القرن من العظيم وان كان قد امهل الله تَعَ عليها
١٥ دهر طويل فان لكل مهلة انتهاء فيكون قد جاء الوقت ❖ وقوله קְטִילַת חֵיוְתָא ثم
قال וִיהִיבַת לִיקֵדַת אֶשָׁא فقوله קְטִילַת يريد به قتل ملوكهم وتلف عساكرهم ❖ وقوله
וְהוֹבַד גִּשְׁמַהּ الاقرب فيه بطلان عباداتهم ونواميسهم فلا يبقى لهم بيعة ولا موضع
قبلة ويتّجه ايضا قطع ذكر עשׂוּ من الدنيا ❖ وقوله וִיהִיבַת مطالبة الاخرة وهى ניהִנֵּם
الذى المراد بهذا الاسم على موضع الدينونة ❖

٢٠ ١٢ وسائر ²الحيوانات ²ازيل سلطانهم ³ومهلة بالبقى° اعطبت
لهنّ الى وقت وزمان ❖

بعد ان ذكر تلف الحيوانة الاخيرة ذكر زوال الثلاثة الممالك التى تقدّم ذكرها وهذا
من جنس قوله فى الصنم ان الحجر ضربت الصنم على رجليه فانسحقت عند ذلك سائر

---

¹ לאלא P only ; אלא cett.   ² דיל C.   ³ ומהלא באלבקא C.

Line 4. ذنوبا.   5. يدوّنوا.   11. ناظرا.   15. دهرا.

الدول كقوله באדין דקו כחדא كما شرحنا ذلك فى موضعه ۞ وقوله וארכה בחיין הו ان   فصل ٧
مذهبهم وبقاياهم موجودة مع دولة غيرهم ونماويسهم ۞ وقوله ועד זמן ועדן يريد به فاسوق ١٢
الى انقضاء [1]الدولة الرابعة ועדן هو دولة يسرائيل فان ليس يتلف بقايا الدول   ———
ونماويسهم الا عند ظهور دولة المسيح عَمّ ۞

١٣ ناظر كنت فى مناظر الليل وانا مع سحب السماء مثل ابن ٥
آدم كان جائ والى قديم الزمان وصل وقدامه قرّبوه ۞

مثّل المسيح بانسان بخلاف الاربع ملכיות التى مثّلها بالوحش لمعناين احدهما
لانه חכם يعرف ربّه والثانى لانه سلطان على الكل ۞ ثم قال עם ענני שמיא لان اللذ
تقع بعث به ويشاهدونه الناس كما يشاهدون الغيم ۞ وعرّف انه وافى الى الملك
الذى جلس ليحاكم الناس وعرّف انه قدّمه اليه وقرّبه اليه ثم عرّف انه سلّم اليه ١٠
[2]اللذ الملك كقوله

١٤ وله سلّم السلطان والعزّ والملك وكل الشعوب والامم واللغات
له يطيعون سلطانه سلطان الدهر لا يزول وملكه لا ينتقل ۞

ذكر له ثلاثة الفاظ שלטן ויקר ומלכו فاما השלטן فهو بطشه باعدائه [3]ومن لا يطيعه
واما ויקר فهو مجيّهم للسجود له فى كل חג סכות [4]والهدايا النفيسة واما ومלכو فهو١٥
جلوسه على كرسيّ الملك واخذ للخراج وكتب الكتب والتوقيعات باسمه وخاتمه ۞ ثم
عرّف ان سلطانه لا ينقضى كما انقضى ملك هولاء الممالك ولا ينفسد ملكه كما انفسد
ملك غيره ۞

١٥ تكرتمت روحى انا دانيال فى [5]وسط الغمد ومناظر راسى
يدهشونى ۞

هذا وصف حاله بعد ان انتبه فلحقه كما لحق بختناصر وغيره عند ما لم يقف
على تاويل المنام وهذا عجيب ان يكون دانيال ما وقف على ذلك وهو מפשר חלמין

---

[1] דולה codd.   [2] אללה add. C, om. cett.   [3] ובמן C.   [4] Prob. بالهدايا.
[5] וצם codd.

Line 5. ناظرا.   6. جايئا.   7. لمعنيين.

فصل ٧ فرجع نام ونظر ملائكة وسألهم عن تفسير ذلك ¹وهو ايفا° انه راى فى المنام كانه
فاسوق ١٥ كان تكرتمت روحه وانه قد اندهش مما رآه وانه جاء الى الملك الواقف قدام الملك
الكبير للجالس على الكرسىّ يسئله عن تفسير المنام • وقوله بنوه ندنه قلبه الذى
د״ה א. כא. כו هو مقام الغمد للسيف لان ندنه مثل ويشب חرבو אל ندنه •

5 ١٦ نقتّمت الى واحد من الملائكة الوقوف ويقيين اطلب منه
على كل هذا فقال لى وتفسير الكلمة يعرّفنى •

قال وאמר لי ثم قال وפשر מלאיה فيقرب فيه انه اراد بقوله وאמר لا ما ذكره فى
معنى ارבע חין وقوله وפשר מלאיه يشير به الى قوله ממلל רברבن وقد بيّن ذلك كقوله
וملן لעד وقول اخر وهو ان قوله وאمر لא يشير الى قوله אلين حيותא רברבתא وقوله
١٠ وפשר מلאيه يشير الى قوله אדن צבית ليצבא وتمام القول •

١٧ هولاء الحيوانات الكبار الذى هم اربعة اربع ممالك يقومون
من الارض •

١٨ ويتسلمون الملك قديسين العالى وينتحلون الملك الى الدهر
والى دهر الدهور •

15 جاء بقول مجمل ولم يبسط له شرح الاربع حيوانات وهذا من جنس ما فعله يوسف
ودانيال فى تفسير المنامات ياتون بقول مجمل وهو فتح الموضع المنغلق والمنعقد •
وفسّر الاربع حيوانات اربع ممالك وفسّر البحر الارض ولم يفسّر ارבע רوחی שמيא •
وهذه الارياح هى حركات من عند الله فعند ذلك قامت هذه الدول • وقوله ويקבלون
מلכותא يشير الى כבر אنש אתא وגו' ولم يحتاج دانيال ان يسل عن الثلث حيوانات
٢٠ اصلا بل احتاج ان يسل عن الرابعة كقوله

١٩ حينئذٍ هويت الوقوف على الحيوانة الرابعة التى كانت متغيّرة
من كلهم فزعة فضل اسنانها حديد وظفرها نحاس اكلت وسحقت
وما بقى برجلها رفست •

---

¹ Perh. ويتجه ايفا.

فصلا .22   يحتج .19   Line 5. ويقينا.

٢٠ وعلى القرون العشرة التى فى راسها والاخرى التى صعدت فصل ٧
ووقعت من قدامها ثلثة وقرن ١مدكّن مرتّب وعينين لها وفم متكلم فاسوق ٢٠
بالكبائر ومنظرها افضل من ٢رفقائها ♦

٢١ ناظر كنت وانا القرن ٣المدكّن التى عملت الحرب مع القديسيين
وقدرت عليها ♦

٢٢ الى ان جاء قديم الزمان والحكم اعطى ٤لقديسيين العالى
والزمان دنا والملك انتحلوا القديسيين ♦

عرّف انه سأل عن اربعة اشياء احدها عن تفسير الحيوانة وعظمها واسنانها
وظفرها واكلها والثانى عن حال العشرة قرون والثالث عن حال القرن (الصغيرة)
وعينيها وانها كبرت على العشرة قرون والرابع حال القرن فيما رآها تحارب القديسيين
وتغلبهم وهذه كلها لم يقف عليها وقوف مستوى وفى مسئلة دانيال للملك اشياء
زائدة عمّا ذكرها فى نظرة المنام وهى اربعة اشياء احدها מפרה די נחש والثانى
والثالث דכן וחזוה רב מן חברתה والرابع עבדא קרב עם קדישין ولم يسلو
عن الاربعة ٥فواسيق وهى חזה הוית עד די כרסו والثانى נהר די נור والثالث
באדין מן קל والرابع ושאר חיותא لانه ٦قد وقف على معناها ♦ فلما سأل عن هذه
المسائل اجابه عنها فقال

٢٣ كذا قال ♦ الحيوانة الرابعة ملك رابع يكون فى الارض التى
ينتغيّر من كل الممالك وتأكل كل الارض وتدوسها وتسحقها ♦

٢٤ والعشرة قرون من تلك المملكة عشرة ملوك يقومون واخر يقوم
بعدهم وهو ينتغيّر من المتقدمين وثلثة ملوك يسقّل ♦

---

١ מרכן codd.   ٢ רפקאתהא codd.   ٣ אלמרכן codd.   ٤ X. לְקַדִּישִׁין
٥ פוסיק P; פסוקים cett.   ٦ קד ins. P; om. cett.

Line 4. ناظرا.   11. وقوفا etc.

فصل ٧
فاسوق ٢٥

٢٥ وكلام فى جهة الخالق العالى يتكلم ولقديسيين العالى ١يبلى
ويؤمل لتغيير الازمنة والسنن ويسلّمون بيده الى وقت واوقات
ونصف وقت +

اعلم انه قال فى هذه الرابعة משֹניה وقد قال فى الاربعة שנין דא מן דא فى
5 صورها كما ٢ذكر صورة كل واحدة وجعل هذه الرابعة متغيّرة فى معانى ذكرها وهو قوله
דחיל֗א ואימתני وايضا فى ان اسنانها من حديد وظفرها من نحاس ٣وعن قوله ايضا
אכלה ומדקה וגו' وقوله ותאכל כל ארעא وهو انهم لما اخربوا בית שני واجلوا الامّة
زادوا فى السلطنة على سائر الناس + وفى العشرة قرون עשרה מלכין هى عشرة كراسى
كانت للروم على كل كرسى صاحب + وقوله ואחרן יקום אחריהן يريد بعد ظهور العشرة
10 قرون يقوم بعد سنين وعرّف انه صعد بين العشرة قرون يعنى فى توسط ملكهم فاخذ
من عملهم ثلثة كراسى فقال قوم ان هذه الثلثة كراسى هى اسكندرية وبيت
المقدس وعكّا + وقوله فى القرن الصغيرة והוא ישנא מן קדמיא هو فى معنى نفسه
وانه صعد الى السماء واجلسه ٤عن يمينه٥ وما جرى هذا المجرى ٥مما لا يمكن ذكره

תהל' עג. ם

وهو مشهور معلوم ٦ليس بنا احاجة الى شرح ذلك٥ وفيه قال שתו בשמים פיהם وهذا
15 شرح وفم مملل רברבן + ثم بيّن معنى עבדא קרב עם קדישין ויכלה להן فقال
ולקדישי עליונין יבלי ٧وهو اسقاط قدرهم وذلهم وتمأهم فى كل باب وفن فى امر الدين
والدنيا فوق ما تقدّم ولباس الغيار ولا يقدر يتكلم اذا شُتم وطُعن على دينه ولا يقدر
يتكلم ولا يمشى على يمينه ولا يتقدم على شراء بضاعة يلتمسها بما غلا وما جرى
هذا المجرى٥ + ثم زاده الملك شى لم يسل عنه وهو قوله ויסבר להשניא قال ויסבר
20 להשניא ولم يذكر انه يغيّر عليهم وانما يؤمل ولم يتمّ له ذلك من حيث ان اللّه
عز وجل يمكّنه من ٨ذلّتهم ودقّهم فى امور دنياهم ولا يمكّنه من تبطيل مذهبهم +

<hr>

١ תבלי PQX; יסקט cett.   ٢ דכר P; דכרה cett.   ٣ Perh. وفى.   ٤ عن
ימינה P; עלי ידה most.   ٥ מא codd.   ٦ Ins. PQ; om. cett.   ٧ PQX: اسقاط
قدرهم وذكرهم وجاههم فى كل باب وفى معنى الدين اولا ثم فى امور دنياهم فوق
ما ذلتهم الدول المتقدمات من لباس الغيار وما يجرى [נרי] مجراه مما يطول شرحه
+ ثم زاده.   As above B K.   ٨ Perh. ذلّهم.

Line 1. وكلاما.   5. معانى.

فصل ٧
فاسوق ٢٥

وقوله زمن ודת هى ايام الاقداس سبت وعيد ❖ وقال להשניה ولم يقل لבטל لانه ليس
يبطلهم بالكلّيّة لكنه يرجو (ان) يغيّرها بان يلزمهم ان يعملوا اعمالا هى حرام
عليهم فعلها فى ايام السبوت والاعياد واما الدت فيمكن انها القبلة وضروب من
العبادات مثل قول هامان ואת דתי המלך אינם עשים يشير¹به الى ما امر من الركوع

است ג. ח
٥

والسجود لهامان او يكون يشير الى يمي פורים وما جانسها من السنن التى بيد
يسرائيل ولم يشرح لنا ذلك على التمام ❖ وهذا الذى ذكره من ולקדישי עליונין يبله
هو دائم على يسرائيل واما ייסבر فيمكن ان كان منه طرف عند اول ظهوره واكثره
يكون فى عت צרה كما سنشرح ذلك فى الفصل الاخر بعون الله تعّ ❖ وقوله ויתיהבון
بيده עד עדן ועדנין ופلג עדן يحتمل انه اراد به الى ان يتمّ له עדן ועדנין ופلג עדן

١٠

وهى مدّة ملكه من اوّل ما يملك الى اخر ملكه واما ان يكون يريد به يجرى على
يسرائيل منه هذه الצרה التى تقدم ذكرها اعنى ייסבر להשניה زمنين ודת مدّة עדן ועدنين
ופلג עדن ❖ واعلم انه قال עדן وهو وقت واحد ثم قال ועدنין وهو لفظ ربيم وليس
يدلّ على وقتين دون ثلثة وما فوق ذلك وكذلك قال ופلג עדן هو مثل חצى الذى لا يدلّ
على نصف على التحرير بل هو كسر الشى المقول فيه עדן وغيره مثل قوله חציו שרף

يسّا' מד. يו
يג. ז

במו אש لقوله ויתרו לתועבה עעשה وكذلك قوله فى ما بعد כי למועד מועדים וחצי
فهذا هو ذلك لا غيره ونحن نشرح ذلك هناك ونذكر كلام العلماء فيه ونذكر ما يقرب

١٦

عندنا فيه ان شاء الله تعّ ❖

٢٦ والحكم حلس (او رتب) وسلطانه يزبلون لاستئصال ولابادة
الى النهاية ❖

٢٠ قوله דינא يתيב يقرب فيه انه اشار به الى قوله דينא יתיב וספרין פתיחו ليعرف انه
عند نهاية עדן ועדנין ليس يبقى لاحد ملك غير ملك الله بل يحاكم الامم على
فعلهم كما تقدم بذلك القول ❖ وقوله ושלטנה يشير الى ازالة الملك الذى تقدم
ذكر فعله بيسرائيل من قوله ולקדישי עליונין يبله وتمام القول ❖ وقوله יהעדن اما ان
يكون يشير به الى يسرائيل على الاصل المقول على الصنم ומחת לצלמא וגו' او الى

٢٥ ²القשרים وهم הזרועים كما سنبيّن ذلك فى الفصل الاخر ❖ وقوله עד סופא ليورى ان
ليس يكون لها رجعة كما يكون ليسرائيل ❖

---

¹ Ins. Q only.   ² See Index.

فصل ۷ ۲۷ والملك والسلطنة والجلالة التى للممالك تحت كل السماء
فاسوق ۲۷ سلّمت لشعب قديسى العالى ملكه ملك الدهور وجميع السلاطين
له يطيعون ويجتمعون ۰

قال די מלכות اذ كان فى العالم ممالك غير ممالك الروم والعرب فعرّف ان كلها
٥ تطيع ملك الله تع الذى هو ملك امّته ومسيحه ۰ وعرّف ان ملكهم لا يزول كقوله
يشع' ط. ١ عن دولة المسيح لمربה המשرה ولשلوم אין קץ נו وقوله יהי שמו לעولم وقد اتّسعت
תהל' עב. יז الانبياء فى هذا الباب فى عدّة مواضع ۰ واعلم ان قوله קדيشى עليونين فى هذا الفصل
يحتمل ان القديسين يسرائيل وעليون هو البارى على ما يقول فى هذا السفر الهه
الهة فلمّا كانوا يسرائيل קديشين لربّ العالمين ¹جائز ان يقول קديشى עليونين
١٠ ويجوز ان يكون עليونين مقول على اسرائيل لان الله تعّ جعلهم עليونين كقوله ولتחتך
דبر' כו. יש עليون על כל הגويم ۰

۲۸ الى ههنا نهاية القول انا دانيال كثيرا افكارى يدهشونى
وبهائى يتغيّرون علىّ والكلمة فى قلبى حفظت ۰

قوله עد כה סوفא يعنى هذا آخر كلام قيل لى فعند ذلك اخذنى الفكر فى ما
١٥ نظرت ۰ وقوله ומلاها بلבي نطرت يعنى حفظت ما فسّره لى حتى اسل عنه كانه
كتب المنام للوقت كقوله באدין חلמه ولم يكتب التفسير ۰ فهذا ما جرى له
فى سنة احدى لبلشاصر ثم اخذ يذكر ما جرى فى سنة ثلث فقال בשنת שלש ۰

۱ ۸ فى سنة ثلث لملك بلشاصر الملك نظرا نرايا لى انا دانيال
بعد الذى نرايا لى فى الابتداء ۰

٢٠ المعنى انه كتب المنام بلغة الارمنية وكتب هذا بلغة القدس قيل فيه انه راى
ذلك المنام وهو فى بابل وهذا نظره فى שושن הبيره ولم يكن مع الملك وهذا يدلّ على
ان دانيال غائب عن بابل الى שושن הبيره ولم يذكر ايش السبب فى ذلك وقيل انه
لما راى المنام غاب عن البلد الى ان تمّت السبعين سنة لبابل فرجع من اجل

---

¹ Perh. جاز.

Line 10. مقولا.   18. نظر.

فصل ٨   وقوله ❖ وكان الحزن رآه فى שושן הבירה فى اوّل السنة او فى توسّطها ❖   دارياوش ❖

فاسوق ا   على يدلّ الاوّل القول كان وان رآه الذى المنام الى يشير בתחלה אלא הנראה אחרי

ذلك بعد يكن لم انه (على) ليدلّ אלא הנראה אחרי قال فانما ذلك بعد هذا ان

❖ الممالك هذه معنى فى حزن او חלום

٢ فنظرت فى ¹المنظر وانا فى نظرى وانا فى سوس الجوسق ٥
الذى فى خوز المدينة ورايت فى المنظر وانا كنت على دهر اولى ❖

هو انه ينظر ما ينظره ²فى المنام° وهو ينتبه فيحاضر اشياء يراها وليس هى فى
الحقيقة مرئيّة فقال دانيال رايت هذا الحزن وانا كنت فى שושן הבירה ورايت فى
الحزن ³كاّنى واقف على نهر اولى كما راى بحزقال وهو فى بابل كانه فى بيت المقدّس ❖
ירמ׳ י. ה   وهذا نهر الدجلة على كان الآخر الفصل وفى שרשיו ישלח יובל על مثل نهر אובל
النهر اعنى אובל אولى فيه قولين إما ان يكون اسم النهر אولى مثل نهر פרת وإما ١١
ان يكون אולى اسم سقع او مدينة مثل نهر מצרים ❖

٣ فشلت عينى ونظرت وانا بكبش واحد واقف قدام النهر وله
قرنان والقرنان شامختين والواحدة شامخة اكثر من الثانية
والشامخة صاعدة فى الاخرة ❖   ١٥

٤ نظرت الكبش ناطح عربيّة وشرقا وجنوبا وكل الحيوانات ليس
يقفون قدامه وليس مخلّص من يده وكان يعمل برضائه وكبر ❖

٥ وانا كنت متفطّن حتى قد وافى قهر الماعز من جهة الغرب على
وجه كل الارض وليس دانى بالارض والقهر له قرن لها منظر بين
عينيه ❖   ٢٠

٦ فوافى الى الكبش صاحب القرنين الذى كان واقف قدام النهر
وحاضر اليه بحدّة قوّته ❖

---

¹ אלמנאם codd.   ² Om. X.   ³ ואנא כנת ins. B.

Line 11. قولان.   16. ناطحا.   19. دانيا.

[II. 3.]   L

٧ ونظرته قد دنا بجنب الكبش فتمرمر البه وضرب الكبش وكسّر

قرنيه ولم تكن فى الكبش قوّة للوقوف قدامه والقاه الى الارض

وداسه ولم يكن مخلّص للكبش من يده ٭

٨ وقهر الماعز عظم جدّا وعند عظمه انكسرت القرن الكبيرة وصعدت

5 أربع قرون لها منظر فى موضعها الى أربع جهات السماء ٭

٩ ومن الواحدة منهم ظهرت قرن واحدة من الصغيرة وعظمت

فضل الى الجنوب والى الشرق والى الشام ٭

١٠ وعظمت الى جيش السماء وطرحت الى الارض من الجيش

ومن الكواكب وداستهم ٭

15 ١١ والى رئيس الجيش عظم ومنه افرز الدائم والقى محيا

مقدسة ٭

١٢ وجيش تسلّم مع الدائم بجرم وتلقى الحقّ الى الارض

وتعمل وتنجح ٭

١٣ وسمعت واحد قديس متكلّم فقال الواحد القديس لفلمونى

15 المتكلّم الى متى هذا المنظر الدائم والجرم مستوحش اجعال

والقدس والجيش مداس ٭

١٤ فقال لى الى مساء وصباح الفين وثلث مائة يوما يعدل

القدس ٭

ينبغى ان نعود الى الفصل بشرح ظاهره اوّلا ثم نتبع ذلك بتفسير الملاك لهذا

20 الـחלם ونجمع بين الفصلين كما عملنا فى المنام ٭ عرّف انه رأى فى الـחלם [1]كأنّ

كبش عظيم واقف عند شطّ النهر وان طلعت له قرن واحدة اوّلا ثم رأى [2]كأنّ اخرى

---

[1] באן codd.   [2] באן codd.

Line 7. فضلا.   14. واحدا etc.   21. كبشا etc.

فصل ٨   كان وحوش ¹ ثم عرّف انه رای وان الثانية أكبر من الاولى وان الاولى طلعت من بعد الاولى

فاسوق ١٤   يتقدّم من واحد كل ينطح واذا شرقيّة من النهر لان نواحيه ثلث من به التقوا

اليه من الوحوش وانه لا يلقى حيوانة الا ²وعمل بها ما يريد ولعله رای هذه الحيوانات

عظام مسبعة وبعد رای ان كل الحيوانات قد تلفت ولم تثبت بين يديه وبقى وحده

٥ [رای] كانه الارض من يدنو ولم بسرعة المغرب ناحية من اليه القهر هذا اقبل قد

سائرٌ فى الهواء وقيل ايضا انه لم يكن من الوحوش واحد دانى فى الارض لخوفهم من

هذا القهر ورای ³كان له قرن لها منظر كبير فى وجهه بين عينيه ورای انه قصد الى

الكبش فلما رای الكبش ⁴فزع ولم يتحرّك من مكانه فوافاه القهر بسرعة وحدة وهو

واقف على شط النهر فلاصقه لعله يبادر بحركة او ينطحه بقرنيه واذا بالكبش قد

١٠ انخذل ثم عرّف انه كان القهر מחרמר لمعنى وهو انه كان يرى الوحوش والحيوانات

قد انهزموا من بين يديه واختبوا وان الكبش واقف مكانه لم يهرب منه تزعّر من

ذلك وقصد الكبش وقتلة ويشبه ان القهر لم يؤذى احد من الوحوش اذ لم يقفوا

بين يديه فلما وقف الكبش جاء اليه فصدمه ونطح قرنيه بقرنه الكبيرة ولم يكن

فى الكبش من القوّة ما يقاومه فطرحه الى الارض وداسه ثم رای ⁵كان ثم عبّار طريق

١٥ يرون ما ⁶فعله القهر ولم يخلّصوه فلم تكن فيه قوة ليخلّص[ه] نفسه ولم يجد

احد يخلّصه فقتله ✦ ثم عرّف ما كان من القهر فعرف انه كبر جدّا وارتفع وان عند

ما عظم رای وان القرن الكبيرة قد انكسرت بغير ان يكسّره وحش او انسان كما

كسّر هو قرن الكبش ✦ ثم رای ان بعد (ان) انكسرت صعد له اربع قرون بدلها ولم

تكن هذه الاربعة ملتصقة ⁷الواحدة بالاخرى بل رای ان كل واحدة فى جهة ⁸ ✲ ✲ ✲

٢٠ اليسار وواحدة فى حاجبيه فوق راس الانف والاخرى فى راس لجبهة كقوله לארבע רוחות

השמם ✦ ثم رای ان ظهرت قرن واحدة من وسط واحدة من الاربعة وهى التى عن

صُدغه اليمين وهو قوله ومن האחת מהם יצא קרן ✦ وقوله מצעירה عرّف ان الواحدة

من الاربعة التى صعدت منها كانت اصغر الاربعة ورای ⁹كان هذه القرن التى صعدت

كبرت وزادت على ارتفاع الاربعة قرون ورای كانها تميل مرّة الى ناحية لجنوب ومرّة

٢٥ الى المشرق ومرّة الى ناحية ארץ ישראל ✦ ثم رای ¹⁰كانها قد صعدت الى جنود السماء

---

¹ באן codd.   ² וימעל X.   ³ באן codd.   ⁴ Perh. فزع غير.   ⁵ באן codd.

⁶ יפעלה B D.   ⁷ אלואחד הי codd.   ⁸ Perhaps supply ⟨من لجهات فى جهة

באנהא ¹⁰   ⁹ באן codd. كان واحدة فى جهة اليمين وواحدة فى جهة⟩ اليسار

codd.; and so passim.

فصل ٨ فطرحت من جنود السماء وقوله ﯨﯨﺑﺎ השמים يقرب فيه انه يشير الى كواكب البروج

فاسوق ١٠ وقوله ﯨﻣﻦ הכוכבים يشير الى بعض السبعة كواكب السيّارة اعنى زحل وشرقاءﮦ ٭ وراى

كانها داست الكواكب فى الارض ٭ ثم راى ١كان القرن دخلت الى رئيس الجنود

واعظمها ولم يذكر ان القرن عملت شى بِرئيس الجيش اكثر من قوله הגדיל فقطّ ٭

5 ثم قال وﻣﻤﻨﻮ הורם התמיד كانة كان لرئيس الجيش مكان فى الارض يتردّد اليه فمنع

عنه وان الركن الذى ٢له القى الى الارض وخرب ٭ وراى ٣كان بعض الجنود ٤التى لم

تدوسها القرن تسلمت مع الموضع الذى كان ٥يتردّد اليه القرن ٭ وسمّى القرن פשע

من حيث انه راى فى الﺣﺰﻦ ان القرن قد حادت عن الموضع وارتفعت ٭ وراى كانها

وافت ٦الى قوم ٩ يتكلّمون بالحقّ فالقتهم الى الارض وزجّتهم وانها تثبت ولم يجى من

10 يكسّرها ٭ فلما راى هذه الامور راى ملكين ٧واقفين بحذائﮦ فسمع احدهما يسل الاخر

עד מתי ولم يكن سواله ليعلم هو وانما كان سواله ليسمع دانيال يُعلم ذلك من

قوله بعده וﯨﯨﺎמﯧ אﲦﯨ עﯨ עﯨﯨﺑ בﲭﯧ ولم يقل וﯨﯨﺎﯨﯧ אﲦﯨﯤ كانه علم الملك ان دانيال

يريد ان يقف على ذلك كما اراد الوقوف على معنى المنام لكنه قدر هو ان يتقدم

الى تلك الملائكة كقوله ﱏﯧﺑﲭ עﯨ ﲭﯧ وهذه الملائكة لم يستجرى ان يسلهم ٨قال الواحد

15 للاخر عمّا يحتاج دانيال ان يسل عنه ولم يسل عن جميع ١٠الﺣﺰﻦ لانه قصد الى ما

يحتاج ﯨﺸﯧﺎﯩﯤ الى معرفته ٩مما يكون فى اخر الزمان وهو ﱝ ﯩﯧﯤ אﯧﲭﯦ מﯤﲭﯦﯨﯤ : قوله

וﯨﺸﲦﯦ אﲦﯨ ﱝﯨﲭ وهو السائل عﯧ ﲦﯧ הﲭﯧﯤ התמיד وقال ﯤﯗﯨﲦﯧﯦ המדﲥﯨ فعرّف ان

ﯗﯨﲦﯧﯦ هو المجيب ولم يذكر اسم السائل من هو من الملائكة كما لم يذكر اسم كثير

من الملائكة ٭ وقال السائل עﯨ ﲦﯨ ﱏﯧﲭﯦ يريد الى متى يدوم هذا الذى يفعل هذه

20 المذكورة فى الفاسوق وهى ثلثة اشياء احدها ﲦﯧ والثانى ﯅ﲭﯤ والثالث ﯨﯨﺑﺎ فجا للجواب

עﯨ עﯨﯨﺑ בﲭﯧ ونحن نشرح ذلك فى ما بعد ٭

١٥ وكان عند نظرى انا دانيال المنظر ابتغيت فهم وانا واقف

حنآئى مثل منظر رجل ٭

<hr />

١ ﯨﺎﯨ codd.   ٢ Ins. ﯩﯧﯤ (ﯩﲭﯤﮦ) B.   ٣ ﯨﺎﯨ codd.   ٤ אﲦﯦﯤ codd.   ٥ תﲦﯧﯦﯦ

codd.   ٦ אﲦ קﯧﯨ X; אﲭﯧﯨﯨ cett.   ٧ ﯨﺎﯗﯨﺎﯨ X.   ٨ Perh. ﯤﲭﲥ and الاخر.

٩ ﯨﺎ codd.

Line 22. ﯦﯤﯨﺎ.

١٦ وسمعت صوت انسان بين النهر فنادى فقال يا جبريال فهّم   فصل ٨

لهذا الانسان المنظر الذى رآه ❖   فاسوق ١٦

١٧ فجاء لصق وقوفى وعند مجيّه انبهرت ووقعت على وجهى

وقال لى افهم يا ابن ادم فان ¹الى وقت° الحقّ هذا المنظر❖

١٨ وعند تخاطبه معى انسبت على وجهى الى الارض فدنا بى ٥

واوقفنى على وقوفى ❖

عرّف انه نظر ثلثة ملائكة وسمع كلامهم وسمع صوت واحد ولم يراه وذكر اسم
اثنين وهما פלמוני ונבריאל ولم يذكر اسم الاثنين فدلّ ذلك على ان دانيال لم يسمع
من الملائكة الاُوّلين اكثر من المسلة وذلك لعظم هيبتهم وكان נבריאל قريب من صورة
الناس فانس اليه ❖   وعرّف انه لم يبتدى נבריאל من نفسه بل لما سمع غيره يأمره ١٠
بتعريف دانيال ذلك فبعد ذلك جاء الى دانيال وعرّفه ذلك ❖   وهذا يدلّ على ان
الملائكة وقفت كلها على ذلك ويمكن ان الملك الذى ²سمع صوته اعظم هيبة من
الاثنين المتقدّمين اعنى السائل والمجيب ❖   ثم عرّف ان عند مجيّ جبريال اليه انبهر
من هيبتهم ثم وقع منسبت على وجهه ❖   وقوله הבן בן אדם כי לעת קץ החזון يعنى
تحتاج الى معرفة ذلك لانه يذكر فى اخره ما يكون فى اخر للجالوث ❖   وقال ויעמידני ١٥
על עמדי كانّ شجعه واوقفه ❖

١٩ وقال ها انا معرّفك ما سيكون فى اخر ³الزغم ان لوقت النهاية
(او الحقّ) ❖

ثم اخذ يذكر جوامع ما رآه فى الחזון فقال

٢ الكبش الذى نظرت صاحب القرنين ⁴هم ملوك ⁵ماداى   M

وفارس° ❖   ٢١

قال هذا القول جملة ⁶وينبغى ان نعود ⁷على التفسير كما فعلنا فى غيره ❖   قال

---

¹ אלוקת X؛ אלוקת cett.   ² סמעה codd.   ³ אלזם X.   ⁴ Om. M.

⁵ מאדאי وفارس M, but not consistently.   ⁶ ينبغى codd.   ⁷ אלי M؛ على Heb.

Line 7. يَرَهُ.   9. قريبا.   14. منسبتا.

فصل ٨ فى ¹الحزن ان القرن الواحدة اصغر من الاخرى وهى التى صعدت اوّلا وتاويل ذلك ²هو

فاسوق ٢٠ ان مادى اقلّ عساكر وكل ³من ملك منهم داريࢨاوش ⁴الهدى وحده سنة واحدة وقام من

فارس خمسة ملوك وملكوا خمسة وخمسين سنة ✣ وقولي ראיתי את האיל מנגח ונו

هو ان ⁵كانت له عساكر تعدّت الى ثلثة جهات وكان ذلك فى زمان كورش كما شرح

ישע מה. א ذلك فى فصل כה אמר יוי למשיחו ונו' من قوله אני לפניך وتمام القصّة ولذلك قال ודל

٦ חיות ונו' وهذا هو قوله דלתות נחושת אשבר ✣

٢١ والقهر الجدى ملك ياوان والقرن الكبيرة النى بين عࢨنيه هو

الملك الاوّل ✣

ينبغى ان نعود ايفا على ما تضمّنه الحزن ولم يفسّره جبريال ✣ قال בא מן

١٠ המערב ונו' قيل انه الاسكندر ⁶الذى ⁷وافى من اسكندريّة ✣ وقوله ואין נוגע בארץ

هو انه لم يحاربه احد ⁸منذ خرج من اسكندريّة الى ان ⁷وافى الى بابل ✣ وقد فسّر

קרן חזות بين عينيه انه الملك الاوّل وهو الاسكندر وزدنا شرح فى ما فعله الצפיר فقال

ויך ונו' וישבר את שתי קרניו وهو انه حارب العسكرين وهما خيل فارس ومادى ✣

وقوله וישליכהו ארצה هو ما فتح بلدا بلدا من بلدانهم ⁹وقتل من حاربه منهم ويمكن

١٥ انه قتل ارתحששתא الفرسى فعند ما اتّصل بالمدن ذلك لم يثبت احد منهم قدام

الاسكندر ✣ وقوله ולא היה מציל ונו' يعنى ¹⁰لم يحارب عنهم احد° ✣

٢٢ والمنكسرة ووقفن اربع تحتها اربع ممالك من الحرب يقفن

وليس بقوّته ✣

٢٣ ¹¹وفى اخر ملكهم عند ¹²انتهاء العاصين يقف ملك وقاح وفهم

٢٠ الروايات ✣

---

¹ حارون M.   ² Om. M.   ³ ש Heb.   ⁴ Om. M.   ⁵ كانت M; כאן Heb.

⁶ الى M.   ⁷ وافا M.   ⁸ מד Heb.   ⁹ وقتل M; وقيل Heb.   ¹⁰ لم يحارب

لם יהארב ענהם אחד Heb.   ¹¹ Arab. of ver. 23 om. in Heb.;   احد منهم M;

partly supplied inf. p. ٨٧, 6, by worse MSS.: ופי אכר מלכהם יקף מלך קוי אלונה ופהים

¹² انتهى M.   ¹² الאחכאיאת:

Line 4. ثلث.   شرحا. ١٢.

قال فى الحزن وكعظمو נשברה הקרن הגדולה وتعمدنه وهو انه عند ما وصل الاسكندر   فصل ٨
الى ¹ما اراده° ليس الاقتدار فعند ذلك انكسر وهو موته ⬩ وفسّر חזות ²ארבע מלכיות فاسوق ٢٣
وهم ³اربعة تلاميذ كانوا بعده اخذ كل واحد منهم جهة من جهات ⁴الدنيا من غير
حرب جرى بينهم فى اوّل امرهم ⬩ فقال מגני יעמדנה ليورى ان هاولاء الاربعة هم
يونانية ⬩ وقوله ולא בכחו يعنى وليس يكون لواحد منهم ولا لكلّهم قوّة המלך الاوّل ٥ ⬩
وقال فى الحزن ومن האחת וגו' وفسّره ובאחרית וגו' ليس يتمّ تفسيره الا فى الفصل
الكبير الاخير لكن قوله ومن האחת مهم يخا هذه האחת هى מלך הנגב لان ملك
العرب قام بينهم كما شرح ذلك فى المنام משתכל היות בקרניא ولنا الى هذا القول
عودة نشرح هولاء الاربعة ⬩ وقال فى الحزن מצעירה فدلّ ذلك على ان ملك הנגב كان
فى الوقت اصغر الاربعة تلاميذ الذى تقدّم ذكرهم ⬩ وقال ותגדל יתר אל הנגב هو ان ١٠
لم يبلغ واحد من ⁵الاربعة فى جهات العالم كما بلغت هذه القرن ⬩ وقال אל הנגב
قيل انه يشير به الى الامصار وقيل بلد الروم وقيل بلد للحجاز ⬩ والمזרח هو عمل الشرق
وخراسان كله ⬩ وאל הצבי ⬩ وزاد فى التفسير עז פנים ومبن חידות هو ما ⁶انفخ على
الله وكذب عليه ⬩ وقوله ומבן חידות هو انه سرق من كتب اليهود ⁷وخالف اشياء
ذكروها° واتّعى النبوّة وان جبرائيل خاطبه بها ⬩   ١٥

٢٤ ונעצם قوّته وليس بقوّته والعجائب يفسد وينجح ويفعل
ويفسد الاقوياء وشعب قديسين ⬩

٢٥ ومع اقباله ينجح المكر بيده وفى قلبه نعظم نفسه وبالسلو والهدو
يهلك الكثيرين وعلى رئيس الرؤساء يقف وبغير يد ⁹يعطب ⬩

قال فى الحزن وتفل ארצה وגו' وفسّره והשחית وגו' ⬩ فاما עצומים فهم اصحاب الدولة ٢٠
وهم روم وغيرهم الذى حاربهم واخذ بلدانهم ⬩ وעם קדושים هم يسرائيل ⬩ ولم نقل
כל עצומים وكل עם קדושים اذ لم يملك العالم باسره ⬩ وقال فى الحزن ותשלך אמת
ארצה وفسّره ונפלאות يشحيت وهذه النפلאות هو انه طعن على تورة الله جلّ ذكره وعلى

---

¹ Heb. מראדה   ² ארבע bis codd.   ³ اربع M. الاعلام ⁴ Heb.
⁵ الاربع M.   ⁶ Perh. انفخ (Heb. omit this sentence).   ⁷ אכבר ואשיא דכרוהא
Heb.   ⁸ Arab. of ver. 25 om. Heb.   ⁹ يعطب M in text; يعطل in marg.

فصل ٨   اقاويل انبيائه فاخذ ما اراده منها ووللفه له ١قلان كتابا وبطّل الباقى ٠ وقال فى

فاسوق ٣٥   الحزون وممنو هورم התמיד ولم ٢يفسّره فى هذا الفصل لانه على ظاهره ٣وسنذكره فى

الفصل الكبير الاخير ٠ وقال فى الحزون وعد שר הצבא הגדיל وفسّره وعל שר שדים وهذا

שר שדים يتّجه ان يكون يشير به الى ملك الروم لانه قد اخذ منهم ثلثة كراسى كما

٥ تقدّم ذكره فى المنام وقيل انه يشير به الى خلفائهم ٤الذين فى بابل ويكون هذا فعل

٥הקשיר الذى يقوم عليهم كما قال بعد هذا וזרועים ממנו יעמדו ونحن نترك الشرح

الى الفصل الرابع ونبيّنه ثمّ ٠ وقال فى الحزون ועשתה והצליחה وفسّره وעל שכלו וגו

وهذا المعنى قد ذكره ايضا فى الفصل الكبير وسنشرحه فى ועשה כרצונו המלך والشرح

التامّ ثم ونبيّن فيه ما هو התמיד وممكن מקדשו ومن هذا הפשע وسائر ما نحتاجه

١٠ فى هذا المعنى ٠ وزاد فى التفسير ובאפס יד ישבר والمراد فيه انه تتناقص احواله شى

شى فيعطب ويمزّ ٠ وبعد ان ذكرنا هذا الفصل باختصار نعود فيه ونذكر ما ليس لنا

اليه رجعة ٠ فنقول انه ذكر ارבع מלכיות فى الفصلين اعنى منام نبوخذناصر ومنام

دانيال وذكر دولة المسيح ايضا ولم يذكر ملك כשדים ولا ملك المسيح فى هذا ٦الفصل

لكنه ذكر ٧الثلث دول وهى ٧الثلث حيوانات فزادنا شرح فى ملك فارس ثلثة اشياء

١٥ احدها انه ملك منقسم فارس ومادى والثانى וכל חיות לא יעמדו كما تقدّم به الشرح

والثالث ان الاڤير يقتله وسائر ما تضمّنه هذا المعنى ٠ فهذه الثلثة تنضاف الى ثلثة

اشياء ذكرها فى ٨المنام ٠ احدها ולשטר חד הקימת والثانى ותלת עלעין בפומה

والثالث وכن אמרן לה קומי אכלי בשר שגיא كاثّه ذكر ثم حصول الثلثة جهات بيده وما

قد قيل لها קומי אכלי בשר שגיא: فاذا جمعنا بين الفصلين استوفينا جميع ما كان

٢٠ من ملك الفارس ٠ ونذكر ايضا ما ذكره من ملك اليونانيّة ونقول انه ذكر ثم سَفَره كما

قال ולה נפין ארבע די עוף על גבה وقال וארבעה ראשין לחיותא هو المقول ههنا وتعالينه

وغو٠ وزاد ههنا فى هذا الحزون شرح فى קרן חזות لان ٩ثم لم٠ يقسم الملك فيجعل بعضه

الملك الاول وبعضه ١٠الاربعة تلاميذ ٠ فقال כהתם הפשעים فدلّ ذلك على انهم يعصون

فاما ان يكون ذلك فى باب الدين واما ان يكون فى معنى الملك ويقرب ان يكون فى

---

١ قالون M.   ٢ نفסرה M; نפסרה Heb.   ٣ وسدكره M; וסנדכרה Heb.

٤ الذين or الذى M.   ٥ See Index.   ٦ الحازون M.   ٧ الثلثة M (bis).

٨ [الم]عنى M.   ٩ Only one of these words in M.   ١٠ الاربع M.

Line 1. وألّفه.   14. شرحا.   22. شرحا.

معنى الدين ❖ ثم زادنا ههنا فى قرن زغيرة فى ان سمّاه ملك قال ملك عز פנים וגו' ❖ فصل ٨

وقال ثم ולקדישי עליונין יבלה وزاد ههنا ונפלאות ישחית وسائر ما ذكره ❖ ولما لم يبق פסוק ٢٥

لما ذكره فى المنام من ذكر يوم الدين وملك المسيح شرح ¹امسك عنه ❖

٢٦ ومنظر المساء والصباح الذى قيل حقّ هو ❖ وانت ستّ المنظر

لانه الى ايّام كثيرة ❖   5

قوله הערב يريد به الذى رايت פלמוני يقول עד ערב בקר וגו' هو على ظاهره يعنى

هو ערב وבקر ليس له تاويل ²כמا לדאיל ³والצפיر تاويل وليس هو איל فى الحقيقة

وهذا هو فى الحقيقة لئلا تظنّ ان הערב تاويله دولة تنصرف وتاويل הבקר دولة

تظهر ❖ وقوله אלפים ושלש מאות هى الفين وثلث مايه ما جمعت בקר وערב جميعا

فتكون الف ⁴يوم ومايه وخمسين يوما الا ترى انه لم يقل אלפים וש' מ' ערב וא' וש' ١٠

מ' בקر كما قال اربعين يوم واربعين ليلة ❖ وقوله סתום החזון يعنى ⁵لا شكّ فيه°

وقيل انه اراد به اختم هذا الفصل على ما ذكرناه لك ❖ وقوله כי לימים רבים يعنى ان

هذا شى يكون بعد سنين كثيرة طويلة ❖

٢٧ وانا دانيال انتحبت وتوجعت ايام وقمت وعملت عمل الملك

واستوحشت على المنظر وليس مفهم لى ❖   15

لما سمع فى هذا الحزن وتشلك امت ארצה وما جانسه من القول اغتمّ وانتحب ❖

وقوله ימים ⁶هو سنة الى ان قتل בלשاصر ❖ وقوله ואקום ואעשה את מלאכת המלך

يشير الى ما تقدّم له فى زمان دارياوش ولم يكن ذلك من مراده لكن الملك الزمه

ذلك ❖ وقوله ואשתומם عرّف انه كان متفرّد عن الناس مثل قول سيد יחزקال עמ

ואשב וגו' משמים בתוכם ❖ ثم قال ואין מבין يريد ان فى هذه السنين لم يظهر ⁷אללה תע' ج. ١٥

له شى مما فى نفسه الى سنة احدى لدارياوش كانه [بيّن انه] كان بين المنام والحزن ٢١

سنتين لان المنام كان فى سنة احدى לבלשاصر والحزن فى سنة ثلث ومضى له سنة

ثلث לבלשاصر وكان هذا المذكور فى ⁸[فصل] سنة احدى لدارياوش فى اخر ⁹السنة ❖

---

¹ Heb. אערף ען דברה.   ² Obl. in M.   ³ פדאך לה תאויל add. K P X.

⁴ Om. M.   ⁵ Heb. לא תסאל פיה.   ⁶ Om. M.   ⁷ Om. M. يظهر is partly obl.

⁸ Om. B.   ⁹ M and most Heb.; אלסנה B. سنة احدى

Line 19. متفردا.

فصل ٩
فاسوق ١

٩ ١ فى سنة احدى لدارياوش بن احشويروش من نسل مادى الذى ملك على ملك كسديم ٠

هذا يمكن انه كان بعد ان طرح فى جبّ السباع ٠ وذكر اسم ابوة لانه كان مذكور لكنه غير احشويروش صاحب مردخاى واستير لان ذلك فارسىّ وهذا هو من مادى ٠
5 وقال אשר המלך וגו' لئلا نظنّ انه غير داريوش الذى فيل فيه דריוש מדאה קבל מלכותא ٠

٢ فى سنة احدى لملكه انا דانيبال تفطّنت فى الكتب عدد السنين الذى كان خطاب الله الى يرميا النبى لكمال لخرابات يروشالايم سبعين سنة ٠

10 لموضع ما طال الكلام اعاد بسنة احدة وزادنا لملكه ليعرّف ان قوله בשנת אחת לדריוש يريد به لملكه ٠ وقوله בינותי בספרים بشير الى كتب يرمياهو عمّ وذكر ذلك يرمياهو عمّ فى مواضع كثيرة فمرّة كتب ذلك فى السفر الذى بعث به الى بابل وهو قوله כי לפי מלאת לבבל שבעים שנה אפקוד אתכם وقال فى غيره ועבדו הגוים האלה את מלך בבל שבעים שנה ٠ وقوله למלאת לחרבות וגו' ليس يريد به ان مفى لחربات
15 ירושלים سبعين سنة لانه انما خربت من سنة תשע עשרה שנה لملك נבוכדנצר فكان لها فى هذا الوقت اثنين وخمسين سنة وانما اراد به سبعين سنة لملك بابل وقوله למלאת וגו' عند ما انقضت لبابل سبعين سنة ٠

٣ وجعلت وجهى الى الربّ الله لطلب صلاة وتضرّعات وصوم ومسح ورماد ٠

20 عند ما عرّف ذانيبال ان ملك بابل قد انقضى وقد ملك داريوش ولم يتمّ ما قال כי לפי מלאת וגו' احتاج الى ان يصلّى ويسأل الله تعֹ فى ذلك ٠ وقوله לבקש וגו'

כמֹ' יֹ'
כה' יֹ"א

---

1 Obl. in M.   2 דכר Heb.   3 وقوله للملوث لحربوث دروسالا .... فوله سعيم
M. وكان   5 تسع عسر سنة لֹ ...4 M. شانا ليس درد به ان مفا
6 ככוֹ Heb.   7 Perh. add. يريد به.   8 Om. M.   9 Om. or obl. in M.

Line 3. مذكورا، ابيه.

يريد بﻪ תפלה ותח׳ فقسم كلامه فقال תפלה ותח׳ ❖ فعرّف انﻪ ¹صلّى وهو صائم وعلى   فصل ٩

بدنﻪ مسح ويتمرّغ بالرماد ويسجد عليﻪ ❖   فاسوق ٣

---

⁴ وصليت للرب الاهى وقرّرت وقلت بطلبﺔ يا ربّ العالمين ²القادر

العظيم الهيوب حافظ العهد والفضل لمحبّيﻪ ولحافظى ³فرائضﻪ ❖

اعلم انﻪ ذكر فى الفاسوق الاوّل لفظﺔ תפלה ותחנונים وذكر فى هذا الفاسوق لفظ 5

תפלה ודוי ❖ اعلم ان هذه الصلاﺓ تنقسم على اربعﺔ ⁴معانى احدها تسبيح الله وهو

قولﻪ אנא יוי وتمام الفاسوق والثانى تعديد الذنوب والخطايا وذاك من ⁵فاسوق חטאנו

ועוינו الى ותחך וגו׳ والثالث تعديد ما جرى على يسرائيل من اجل ذنوبهم وذاك من

ותחך וגו׳ الى ועתה יוי אלהינו والرابع مسلﺔ الله تﻊ فى رجوعﻪ عن سخطﻪ فى معنى

البلد وفى معنى الامّﺔ وفى غفران الذنوب ❖ ولفظﺔ תפלה قد تجمع ⁶[فيها] الاربعﺔ 10

معانى وهو قولﻪ ועוד אני מדבר בתפלה وقد تجمع ثلثﺔ فقط لكنها تختلف فان قولﻪ

לבקש תפלה يقصد بﻪ الثلثﺔ المتقدّمﺔ الى ועתה יוי אלהינו وقولﻪ ואתפללה يخرج منﻪ

فصل الاقرار بالذنوب ويبقى تحت الثلثﺔ اعنى ⁷فاسوق ואתפללה ومن ותחך עלינו האלה

והשבועה الى اخر الصلاﺓ ❖ وجعل مقدّمﺔ الصلاﺓ ذكر افعال الله عز وجل وكذلك رسم

كل من يسل الله فى معنى يريده يجعل لمسلتﻪ مقدّمﺔ مثل قول سيّدنا موسى عَمّ יוי 15

אלהים אתה החלות וגו׳ ثم قال بعد ذلك אעברה נא ואראה فلذلك قال سيّد دانيال عَمّ האל   דבר׳ ג׳ כד

הגדול وتمامﻪ ❖ فذكر فى مقدّمﺔ صلاتﻪ ثلاثﺔ اشياء احدها הגדול ومعنى هذه اللفظﺔ

فى الخالق ⁸انﻪ فاعل الافعال° المبهرﺔ التى لا يقدر عليها غيره והנורא ومعناها

انﻪ يُهاب اذا انتقم من اعدائﻪ فيرتعدوا عند ذلك والثالث שומר הברית والחסد والمراد

فيﻪ هو وفا بما ⁹ضمنﻪ לאבותנו ברית אברהם ויצחק ויעקב ¹⁰وهى هذا الברית والחסד هو ما 20

ضمنﻪ فى הר סיני וברית ערבות מואב فسمّاها חסד من حيث انﻪ امر زائد ❖ فيكون قولﻪ

הגדול והנורא يشير بﻪ الى ما فعلﻪ معهم من المعجزات ¹¹فى מצרים والمدبر وفى الارض

ايضا ووفا بجميع ما ضمنﻪ ¹²للاباء ❖

---

¹ M. صلا   ² Heb. אלטאיק   ³ M وصاياء corr. فرائضﻪ; Heb. שראיעה.

⁴ Heb. אקסאם   ⁵ M. افسوق   ⁶ Om. M; some Heb. תנתמע פיהא   ⁷ M. افسوق

⁸ Obl. in M.   ⁹ M. ضمن لונא X; צמנﻪ לאבאינא   ¹⁰ وهى M.   ¹¹ من M.

¹² للاب M (ut videtur).

٥ اخطينا وانذبنا فسقنا وعصينا فسقنا وزوال ¹زلنا من وصاياك
فاسوق واحكامك ۰

قوله חטאנו يشير الى قوله לא השמידו את העמים וגו' وما جانسها فى معنى שבעה
גוים ۰ وقوله ועוינו ذلك فى معنى התועבות من ركوب الفروج المحرّمة وما جانسها ۰
٥ وقوله הרשענו هو فى معنى الظلم من הגזל והעשק والגנבה והונאה ונשך وתרבית وما
جانس ذلك ۰ وقوله ומרדנו هو فى معنى قتل الانبياء وضربهم وحبسهم ۰ ثم قال
וסור ممצותיך هو سائر الفرائض من السبوت والاقداس وما جانسها ۰ وقوله וממשפטיך
يشير به الى ظلم فى الاحكام ۰

٦ وما قبلنا قول عبيدك الانبياء التى خاطبوا باسمك الى ملوكنا
١٠ روسائنا وابائنا والى كل شعب الناس ۰

يعنى ما قبلنا قولهم لنا שובו שובו מדרכיכם הרעים ۰ وقوله ואל כל עם הארץ
بعد قوله ואבותינו يحتمل قولين احدهما ان قوله ואבותינו يشير به الى الشيوخ وكل
من له امر ²نافذ وقوله ואל כל עם הארץ يشير به الى الرعيّة والثانى يشير به الى
الגוים ۰ فذكر فى الفاسوق الاوّل انهم تركوا وصايا الله على فنونها وذكر فى هذا الفاسوق
١٥ انهم لم يقبلوا نصحا ولا توبيخا لهم ۰

٧ لك يا ربّ العدالة ولنا خزى الوجوه مثل هذا اليوم لآل يهونا
ولسكّان يروشالايم ولكل يسرائيل القريبيين والبعيدين فى كل
الاراضى ³التى ادحيتهم ثم بنكثهم الذى نكثوا بك ۰

قوله לך יוי הצדקה يعنى لك الحجّة ظاهرة علينا اذ لم تجود علينا ولنا للخزى لانا
تركنا عبادتك وعبدنا ما لا يستحقّ ذلك وكما قال כבשת גנב וגו' وذلك انهم خزوا عند
امم العالم عند ما شاهدوا قبيح افعالهم كما قال הובישו כי תועבה עשו ۰ ثم قال لאיש
يهودה وليوشبى يروشلم فجمع فى هذا القول الامّة باسرها وذكر اوّلا ملك يهودا ⁴وهو
الاجلّ ثم ذكر ملك يسرائيل ⁵كعادته فى ⁶كثير من (المواضع فى) الكتاب⁰ يقدّم يهودا

---

¹ Om. Heb.   ² Heb. يامر.   ³ M. الذى.   ⁴ M. وهم.   ⁵ M. كعادته.
⁶ M X؛ كثير من B etc. X M؛ الخطاب

على يسرائيل ويمكن ايضا انه قدّم يهوذا على بسرائيل فى هذا الموضع لان خزى يهوذا **فصل ٩**
اعظم من خزى يسرائيل كما قال وشمرون كحצי חטאתיך ⋄ وقوله הקרובים והرחוقים **فاسوق ٧**
يريد به القريبين من الارض والبعيدين منها كما قال הקרוبيم אليك او הרחוقيم ممك ⋄
יחזק' סז' נא
وقيل انه اراد به الذى اجلوا عن قرب والذى اجلوا [1] من زمان بعيد° وهم العشرة דבר' יג' ו
اسباط ⋄ وقال بمعلم اشر מעלו بך يعنى نكثوا بعهدك لانهم حلفوا لله تعّ وعاهدوه 5
فنكثوا به كما قال كي בגוד בגדו بي בيت يسرائيل وبيت يهوذا وقال הפרו בيت يسرائيل وبيت ירמ' ה. יא
שם יא. י
يهوذا את بريتى ⋄

٨ يا رب لنا خزى الوجوه لملوكنا وروسائنا ولابائنا الذى
اخطينا لك ⋄

اعاد لنا בשت הפנים ويتّجه فى ذلك ان الاوّل مقول فى جمهور الامّة وهذا مقول فى 10
خواصّ الامّة لقوله למלכينو ولשرينو ويكون قوله ولابوتينو يشير به الى الحكّام [2] والمشائخ
مثل قوله שבעים איש מזקני וגו' ويتّجه ايضا انه اعاده ليذكر فعلهم وفعل الله تعالى יחז' ח. יא
معهم كما قال

٩ للرب الهنا الرحمات والصفحات لانا عصينا به ⋄

قال ان الخزى علينا من وجهين احدهما لعظم ذنوبنا وغدرنا بالعهد والثانى هو 15
انه مع قبح افعالنا قد ابقى علينا ورحمنا وتجاوز عنّا كما قال וزכرת את درכך وגו' יחז' יו. סא. סג
وقال למען تزכري وبשت وגו' ⋄ وقال הرחميم והסליחות ومعناه انه كان يبقى عليهم
فى اوقات السخط كما قال ويحن יוי אותם وגو' وقال והסليحות [3]وذلك فى وقت انكسارهم מלכ' ב. יג. כג
مثل قوله ואתה אלוه סليحות وגו' وهذه كانت حالهم معه وهم فى الارض فامّا طول נחמ' ט. יז
للجالوت ورحماته دائمة عليهم كما قال ويتن אתم لرحميم وقال حسدى יוי وגו' ⋄ وقال كي תהل' קו. מו
مردنو بו يعنى وان كتّا عصيناه وقبحنا افعالنا وتغايينا فى المعاصى فرحماته علينا ⋄ איכה ג. כב
21

١٠ وما قبلنا قول الله الهنا لمسير بشرائعه الذى جعل قدّامنا
على يد عبيده الانبياء ⋄

قد قال فى ما تقدّم ولا שמענו وגו' فاعاده ليتمّم القول وذلك انه لما قال יוי لنا

---

[2] M. والشيوخ
[1] الذى اجلوا to עד בעד Heb.; but M is obl. from the first انجلوا
[3] Heb. יעני אנה יתנאו ענהם פי

فصل ٩ بشת הפ׳ וקال بعده ليiו الهينו الرحمים ונ׳ [فاضاف اليه ולא שמענו] فقال כי مردنו בו

فاسوق ١٠ ومعناه كما قلنا انهم فسخوا العهد فاضاف اليه ولא שמענו يعني [1]يجينا انبياوك

تامرنا بالرجوع الى شريعتك فلم نقبل فصار الذنب مضعف لانا غدرنا بعهدك ثم

خالفنا انبياك فلذلك اعاد ולא שמענו ✿ وقوله ביד عבديו הנביאים يشير الى كل

5 نبي بعثه الله تعالى الينا ممّن قد ذكر نبوته مدوّنة [2]وغيرهم [3][وهكذى تفسير ولא

שמענו بقول ייי الهينו ביד עבديו הנביאים] فعرّف ان الانبياء عمّ حثّونا على المسير في

شرائع الله تع ✿ وقال בתورתיו بلسان التكثير لان هي شرائع كثيرة [4]الجنسية كقوله

في القرابين زوאת תورה לעולה למנחة وقال في المأكول זوאت תورת הבהמה והעوף وכל

נפש חיה وقال في النجاسات | זואת תورת היולدת זوאת התورה לכל נגע הצرעת זوאת

10 תورת הזב: M def.

١١ وكل يسرائيل جازوا على شريعتك وزوال عن قبول قولك

فانصبّت علينا الحرامة والقسامة المكتوبة في شريعة موسى عبد

الله لانا اخطينا له ✿

قوله וכל ישראל ‹ليس› يشير به الى ‹كل› [الل]اشخاص الامّة اذ فيها انبياء

15 وصالحين كثيرين لكن القصد به الى اسباط يسرائيل اذ لم يخلُ سبط منهم بلا

خطا اعني عبادة الاوثان وغير ذلك من الذنوب فاما [في] قصّة العجل فقد عرفنا ان

שמ׳ לב. כו سبط لاو باسره لم يعبد العجل كقوله מי לייו אליه[5] يريد به من جملة الاسباط [6]يعني

لم يعبد العجل بل الله فقط فانضمّوا اليه כל بני לוו ولذلك استحقّوا المنزلة الجليلة

١٩ كقوله ولתת עليכم היום ברכה فلم يكن احد من الاسباط من لم يعبد الاوثان ويرتكب

الكبائر بل كان في خواصّهم كقوله כהניה חמסו תورתי ויחללו קدשي وقال הכהנים לא יחזק׳ כב. כו

امرو איה ייי وقوله המה מלכیהם שريהם כהنيهم ונביאיהם فلذلك قال וכל ישראל עברو ירמ׳ ב.ח.וכד

את תورתך يعني جازوا على ما فيها والقوها خلف ظهرهم كقوله וישליכو את תورתך נחמ׳ ס. כו

احري גום يعني جازوا على قولك على يد انبيائك ✿ واعاد هذه ليعرّف ان من اجل

انهم اطرحوا الתورה ولم يقبلوا قولك على يد انبيائك حلّت عليهم هذه القללות

---

[1] נאתנא Heb. M; (sic) وحسا [2] Om. Heb. [3] The bracketed words om.

Heb. [4] Om. Heb.; perh. الاجناس. [5] فقوله מי לייו אלيו add. B. [6] لله

ins. P.

Line 3. مضعفا.

المذكورة فى كتابك ❖ وهذه الالة هى التى قال فيها ارור האיש אשר יעשה פסל   **פסל**
ومsekة תועבת יוי وتمام الاثنى عشر فاسوق واليها اشار بقوله לעבדך בברית יוי אלהיך   **فصل ٩**
وبالاتו ❖ وقول והשבועה يشير الى بر#كة הר סיני وברית ערבות מואב الذى قطع مع   **فاسوق ١١**
الاباء فكانّ قول האלה يشير به الى فصل ארור האיש ונו' وقوله והשבועה هو فصل   **דבר' כ:ז טזו**
הברית فعرّف ان كلها חלّت بيسرائيل ❖

١٢ وثبت خطابه الذى خاطب علينا وعلى حكّامنا النى حكمونا
لاجابة علينا ببلّية عظيمة التى ما فعلت نحתت كل السماء كما فعلت
فى ירושלאيم ❖

قوله ויקם את דברו يشير به الى ما تواعدنا به الانبياء من הרעות المذكورة
❖ وقوله ועל שפטינו אשר שפטונו يشير به الى الملوك والحكّام الذى كانوا ظالمين واتلفوا   ١٠
الامة فلذلك חلّت البلايا بالكل ❖ وقوله אשר לא נעשתה תחת כל השמים يشير الى
ما اكلوا لحوم ابائهم واولادهم وما جانس ذلك ❖ ثم قال

١٣ كما هو مكتوب فى شريعة موسى كل هذه البلّيّة جاءت علينا
ولم نبتهل قبلة الله الهنا للرجوع من ذنوبنا وللارشاد بامانتك ❖

عرّف ان الذى قالته الانبياء كلّ مكتوب فى شريعة موسى عمّ وان الله عزّ وجلّ   ١٥
قد كان واقف الاباء على ذلك فلم يظلمهم بل ابقى عليهم وان ذنوبهم كانت توجب
اكثر من ذلك كقول עזרا كقول כי אתה אלהינו חשכת למטה מעונינו ❖ ثم عرّف ان مع   **עזרא ט: ג**
نزول البلاء بهم لكثرة الخطايا لم يرجعوا الى الله تعّ ويسألوا التجاوز عن سخطه كقوله
ואבקש מהם איש גודר גדר وتمام الاية ❖ وقوله ולהשכיל באמתך يعنى لم نتفرس فى   **יחזק' כב: ל**
ما واقفتنا عليه فكتّا نرتدع عن المعاصى لما علينا من العهود والمواثيق ❖   ٢٠

١٤ ورابط الله على البلّية [1]وجابها علينا ان عادل الله الهنا على
كل افعاله الذى فعل ولم نقبل قوله ❖

قال וישקד יוי על הרעה يعنى لما لم يتوبوا لم يصفح ولم يتجاوز عنهم ❖ وقوله כי
צדיק יוי אלהינו על כל מעשיו هو ان الله تعّ عادل فى جميع ما انزل بهم وان كان

فصل ۹ لم يفعل ذلك فى امّة من امم الدنيا كما فعل فى يروشالايم ۞ وقوله بعقب ذلك ولا

فاسوق ۱۴ شמענו בקול يشير به الى المنجلييں وقال مع كل بلاء نزل بنا وحصلنا فى الجالوث

تحت كلّ بلائهم لم يقبلوا من اللہ تعٰ ولم يرجعوا من معاصيهم ۞

۱۵ والآن يا رب يا الاهنا الذى اخرجت شعبك من ارض مصر

۵ بقدرة قوية وعملت لك اسما مثل هذا اليوم اخطينا فسقنا ۞

الى هذا الموضع انتهى فى تعديد الذنوب وذكر ما حلّ بالامّة من المصائب والبلايا ۞

ثم قال بعقب ذلك والآن يا رب العالمين انت الذى اخرجت شعبك من مصر بעשר

מכות واظهرت عزّهم وشرفهم على امم العالم فليس لك امة سواها ونحن كافينا

بالقبيح كقوله חטאנו רשענו ۞

۱۶ يا رب كجميع عدالتك يرجع الآن غضبك وحميتك من مدينتك

۱۰ يروشالايم جبل قدسك فانّ بخطايانا وبذنوب ابائنا يروشالايم

وشعبك لمعيرة لكل حوالينا ۞

قوله יוי ככל צדקותיך يعنى אجرنا على عاداتك القديمة التى كنت ترجع عن سخطك

۱۵ وترحمنا فقد تمت السبعون سنة وقد استوفت الارض حق عطلتها من השממות

والخرابلام ۞ وقوله ישב נא אפך وحمتمך يعنى ردّ يسرائيل اليها حتى تعمر ۞ وقال אפך

وحمتمך فقال אפך هو خراب المدينة اعنى مدينة القدس وقوله חמתך هو حرق ۞ وقوله

כי בחטאינו ובעונות אבותינו يعنى كي بخطايانا وبعونوتينا היתה يروشلم לחרפה لحرفه وبعونوتينا هيه عمك

لحرفه فصارت يروشلم חרפه لحريقها ووحشتها وصاروا يسرائيل חרפه بما نزل بهم

من البلاء والجالوث وخروجهم من بلدهم ۞ وذكر البلد والامّة لانه يريد من اللہ تعٰ

۲۰ عمارة البلد ورجوع يسرائيل من الجالوث اليه ۞

۱۷ والآن اسمع يا ربّ يا الاهنا الى صلاة عبدك والى تضرعاته

وانر وجهك على مقدسك المستوحش لاجل اسمك يا ربّ العالمين ۞

قوله אל תפלות עבדך يشير به الى الثلاثة اقسام الذى ذكرتها فى לבקש תפלה وقوله

فصل ٩   واك תחנוני يشير الى قوله יוי ككل צדקותיך وتمام هذا الفصل كما تقدّم بﻪ القول ⋄

فاسوق ١٧   وقوله והאר פניך المراد بﻪ سبب عمارتﻪ وبنيانﻪ ⋄ وقوله למען אדני يعني لاجل اسمك الذي عليه سمّيتﻪ بيتي ⋄ كانﻪ ذكر فى الفاسوق المتقدّم المدينة وذكر فى هذا الفاسوق القدس وجمع المدينة والامّة وذكر القدس مفرد لانّ المدينة يسكنونها يسرائيل والقدس هو موضع اخصّ من المدينة ⋄

٥

١٨ ميّل يا الاهى سمعك واسمع افتح عينك وانظر مستوحشاننا والمدينة التى سمّى اسمك عليها ان ليس على عدلنا نحن طارحين تضرّعاتنا قدّامك بل على رحمانك الكثيرين ⋄

رجع الى ذكر البلد فذكر ערי הקדש التى حوالى القدس فقال يا ربّ اسمع دعائى وانظر ما لحق مدن قدسك التى صارت שוממות محروقة بالنار فعمّرها باهلها ⋄ ثم ١٠ قال כי לא על צדקותינו هذا القول يدلّ على ان قوم اخر يصلّون كما يصلّى دانيال [1]كقوله ليس بصالحنا وافعالنا للجميلة [2]نتضرّع اليك لانا قد عصينا واكثرنا الذنوب لكن [3]تُكْلَاَنَﺎ على رحمتك الكثيرة فارحمنا وارحم بلداننا ⋄

١٩ يا رب اسمع يا رب اصفح يا رب اصغ واعمل ولا توخّر لاجلك يا الاهى لان اسمك قد سمّى على مدينتك وعلى امّتك ⋄ ١٥

ختم صلاتﻪ بقوله יוי שמעה ⋄ فقال שמעה ثم قال סלחה ثم قال הקשיבה ⋄ فقوله שמעה يعنى اسمع شكوى حالنا وما نزل بنا واصفح لذنوبنا ⋄ [4]وقوله הקשיבה يعنى اصغى الى تضرّعنا ثم قال ועשה وهو فى معنى امّتك ومدينتك وقدسك ⋄ وقوله למענך אלהי يعنى لان اسمك مدعى على مدينتك كما قلت כי הנה בעיר אשר נקרא שמי עליה ירמ' כה. כט אנכי וגו' وكذلك اسمك يقال אלהי ישראל فاعمل لاجل اسمك ولا تعظم ذنوبنا ٢٠ وخطايانا° ⋄

٢٠ وبعد انا متكلّم ومصلّى ومقرّ بخطيتى وخطية شعبى يسرائيل وطارح نضرّعى قدّام الربّ الاهى بسبب جبل قدس الاهى ⋄

---

[1] Perh. كانﻪ قال.   [2] codd. נצרע.   [3] BKX; text P. תכלאנא.   [4] B: הקשיבה

יעני אצג אלי תצרעאתי . . וקו' למענך אראד למען שמך כמ"ק כי הנה וגו' וכדלך אסמך עלי אֻמّתך יקאל עם יוי פאעמל מענא לאגّל אסמך:

Line 4. مفردا.   ١١. قوما.

[II. 3.]   N

فصل ۹   قوله מדבר يشير الى فاسوق אנא יוי האל הגדול ❖ وقوله ומתפלל يشير الى شكوى

فاسوق ۲۰ الاحوال [1]وتعديد المصائب ❖ وقوله ומתודה חטאתי يشير الى كل قول ذكره فى معنى

الذنوب سبعة عشر مرّة اوّلها חטאנו ועוינו واخرها ובעונות אבותינו ❖ وقوله חטאתי

וחטאת עמי ישראל كان الى هذا الموضع [2]يشرك نفسه مع الامّة [3]ولههنا قال חטאתי

5 וחטאת עמי فذكر خطيتة مفردة° ❖ قيل ان دانيال [4]الى ان كبر كان° تربى على ما

ربّاه والديه [5]ولما عقل لنفسه تغيّر عنه° فلذلك قال חטאתי ❖ وقيل انه قال חטאתי

من حيث [6]ان كل بنى ادم لا يخلصوا° من الخطا فمنهم (من) يقصد فمنهم من

يخطى وفى ذلك قال כי אדם אין צדיק בארץ ❖ وقيل انه قال חטאתי لانه ما كان   קהל׳ ז. כ

يمكنه ان [8]ينكر على الخطائين لعلوّ يد الاشرار° ❖ وقوله על הר קדש אלהי يعنى بسبب

10 جبل قدس الاهى ❖

۲۱ وبعد انا متكلم فى الصلاة والملاك جبريال الذى نظرت فى

المنظر فى الابتداء [9]مطير بلغب دانى الىّ عند وقت هديّة [10]المساء ❖

قوله מדבר בתפלה يجمع الصلاة كما هى من ואתפללה الى اخر الصلاة ❖ وقوله

אשר ראיתי בחזון בתחלة يشير الى فصل الحزون الذى رآه فى سنة ثلث لملك بلشاصر

15 كقوله ויקרא ויאמר גבריאל فعرّف انه بعثه اليه وكان دانيال قد انس به وهذا גבריאל

هو من جملة الملائكة والخواص الذى يقفوا قدام الכבוד الذى لهم [11]ستة اجنحة يطيرون

بها [12]كما قال ובשתים יעופף ❖ وقوله ביעף يعنى [13]بسرعة° ❖ [14]وقوله נוגע אלי כעת   ישע׳ ו. ב

מנחת ערב عرّف انه جاءه وقت المساء قال انه قبل صلاة الفرض وقال قوم بعدها

وهو الاقرب ان يكون صلّى صلاة الفرض ثم اعقب ذلك ואתפללה ❖ ومנחת ערב هى

20 עולת ערב لان لنا מנחה تفسيرها قربان كقوله ואל הבל ואל מנחתו والذى تقدّم ذكره   ברא׳ ד. ה

מבכורות צאנו ומחלביהן وكذلك قوله משאת كפי מנחת ערב يشير به الى עולת ערב ❖   תהל׳ קמא. ב

---

1 Om. K X.   2 ינעל K P X; text B.   3 והאהנא אפרד נפסה B.   4 Om. B K.

5 ולמא (codd.)—ענהא B בסהו 6 אד ליס יכלץ אנסאן B.   7 בקצד B (and).

8 ינכר עלי אלעצאה only B.   9 מתטאיר B.   10 אלגרוב B.   11 Om. B X.

12 كما—بسرعة om. X.   13 בסרה B.   14 בקו׳ X.

Line 6. والدوه.

فصل ٩   ٢٢ وفهمني وقال لى يا دانيال الآن خرجت لارشادك الفهم •

فاسوق ٢٢   قوله ויבן וידבר עמי يشير الى ما ذكره من שבעים שבעים وتمام القول • وقوله

עתה יצאתי يريد به خرجت من قدام الكبود وارسلت اليك لاعرّفك ما تحتاج الى

معرفته وتعرّفه ليسرائيل •

٢٣ فى ابتداء تضرّعائك خرج القول وانا جئت لاخبر به لانك رجل مشتهاات وتميّز القول وتفهّم فى المنظر •

قوله בתחלת يريد به منذ ابتديت تقول יוי ככל צדקותיך خرج للجواب وقد جئت لاخبرك بما أمرت ان اخبرك • اعلم انه لم يقل בתחלת תפלתך كانه مهما كان يذكر الذنوب وما حلّ بيسرائيل كان هوذا يسمع قوله فلما ابتدأ بقول יוי ככל צדקותיך جاء للجواب وجاء٤ جبريال وهذا رسم الصالحين مع بارئهم תع كقوله והיה טרם יקראו ואני אענה والقوم الذى كانوا عند الله تع نقص ¹آخّر للجواب عنهم عشرة ישׁ׳ סב׳ כד ايام كما علمنا من خبر يوحنن بن קרח واصحابه فلم يوّخره الله من اجل سيد يرميا هو يִרֶמיָהو יִרֶמ׳ מב عمّ وانما اخّره من جهة القوم • وقوله כי חמדות אתה يعنى انك تريد الوقوف على احوال القدس واحوال الامّة • وقوله ובין בדבר והבין يشير الى ما تقدّم من الكلام الذى سمعه من الملائكة فى المنام وفى الחזון جميعا فشرح له بعضها فى هذا الفصل ١٥ كما سنشرحه فى ما بعد فان فسّرنا בין והבין امرا او مصدرا فان ذلك مستمرّ لان المعنى لا يختلف •

٢٤ اسابيع هى سبعين انقطع على قومك وعلى مدينة قدسك لحبس الجرم (وقيل لاتمام او فراغ الجرم) ²واكمال ³الخطا ولاستغفار الذنب • ولاجابة عدل الدهور ولختم المنظر والنبى ولمسح قدس ٢٠ الاقداس •

عرّف ما يكون فى اربع מلכيות وذلك ان هذه السبعين اسبوع مرّ منها فى ملك كسديم ⁴سبع واربعين سنة وملك الفارس سبع وخمسين سنة وماية وثمانيين سنة

---

¹ אכד B; תאכר K P X.   ² ופנא B.   ³ אלחטא (sic) P X.   ⁴ Different
numbers in B: Chaldees 51, Persians 67, Greeks 180, Romans 192.

Line 11. نقصا; cp. WRIGHT, *Ar. Gr.* ii. § 136 a.

فصل ۹ للیوتانیّة ومایتین وستّة سنین لملك الروم فهذا هو تفصیل שבועים שבעים فقد دخل

فاسوق ۲۴ فی هذه السبعین اسبوع ملك الاربع حیوانات الا انه لم یتّسع فی ذكر ما جری منها

الا ما جری فی [1] زمان الروم من اخبار البیت الثانی وهذه السبعین اسبوع هی

اسابیع سنین שמטין یكون جملة ذلك اربع مایة وتسعین سنة وقد فصّلها فی ما

5 بعد ❖ وقوله נחתך על עמך یرید انه قطع من الله مثل ما قطع اربع مایة سنة

لابراهام אבינו ولبابل سبعین سنة فكذلك قطع هذه السبعین اسبوع ❖ وقوله על

עמך ועל קדשך من حیث ان الامّة قد لحقها فی هذه المدّة ضروب مختلفة فمنها محمودة

ومنها مذمومة فذكر فی هذا الفاسوق ستّة اشیاء ثلاثة منها محمودة وهی לכלא פשע

ולחתם חטאת ולכפר עון وثلاثة مذكورة على وجه اخر وهی ולהביא צדק עולמים

10 ולחתם חזון ונביא ולמשח קדש קדשים فمن هذه الستّة ما هو من اوّل الامر ومنها

ما هو بعد مدّة ثلث مایة سنة فقوله ולהביא צדק עולמים ולמשח קדש קדשים هذا

من اوّل حال بناء البیت واما ולחתם חזון ונביא فهو فی ملك یاوان واما ולחתם הפשע

ולחתם חטאת ולכפר עון فذاك فی توسّط السبعین [2] التی לבבל ❖ فقوله ולחלא הפשע

یرید به عبادت אלהים אחרים وما جانسها من התועבות ❖ واما ולחתם חטאת فهو ما

15 كان اخّر الایّام المقدّسة وسائر الاقداس ❖ ویدخل فی ولכפר עון سائر الذنوب التی

تجری من الناس بعضهم مع البعض فی الارواح وسائر الاموال والاملاك ❖ وقیل بفضّ

ذلك وقوله ولכפר עון هو فی معنی القرابین ❖ واراد بذلك ان فی كونهم فی بابل الی

انقضاء ملك بابل استوفی الله منهم ما استوجبوه من جهة ذبوبهم مضاف الی عد

د"ה ב. לו. כא רצתה הארץ את שבתותיה ❖ وقوله ולהביא צדק עולמים قال قوم انه یشیر به الی

20 כהנים גדולים وان قوله ולמשח קדש קדשים (یشیر به) [3] الی الاقداس والائمّة [4] ❖ وقیل

ان צדק עולמים هی القرابین وان למשח קדש קדשים هو כהן גדול واحتجّوا بقوله

د"ה א. לג. יד ויבדל אהרן להקדישו קדש קדשים وعلی القولین لیس بدّ من ذلك عند بناء البیت ❖

وبقی ولחתם חזון وهو قطع החזון والانبیاء من بین ישראיל فالחزان فهو فی معنی ما

یتنبا به لعتید كنبوة חגי وزכریا وملاכי من העתידות [5] והנביא هو ما یذكره

25 لوقته° ❖ فاما רוח הקדש فعند بعض العلماء انها انقطعت من زمان שלמה وبقیوا

---

¹ زمان supplied from B.   ² التی supplied from B.   ³ الی—קרשים supplied from
B; om. cett.   ⁴ ואלאמה codd.   ⁵ ואמא אלנביא פהו אלדי יתנבא לוקתה

Line 18. مضافا.   25. وبقیوا.

المسوررים ¹يقولون مزامير° التهلات كقوله عن زمان يحزقياهو ملك يهوذا ויאמר וגו' ۰ فصل ٩ ويتّجه ايضا ²فى قوله ولحتم حزون ونبيا اراد به ان كتب الانبياء ختمت وجمعت اربعة فاسوق ٣ وعشرين سفرا وضبطت ³دموسرות وسائر ما يحتاج اليه فى هذا الباب ۰ ⁴وادخل ר"ה ב. כ"ג. ولحتم حزون ونبيا ⁴بين להביא צ' ע' ⁵وبين ولمسح ק' ק' لأنّ النبوّة كانت بين ما قرّبت القرابين وبين مسحة קדש קדשים ۰

ᵗⁿ وتعرف وترتنش من خروج القول لإرداد ولبناء يروشالايم الى مسيح خليفة سبعة اسابيع واسابيع هى اثنين وستّين ترجع وتعمر رحبة وقطع ⁵وعجين الاوقات° ۰

ᵗⁿ وبعد اثنى وستّين اسبوع ⁶ينقطع المسيح وليس له والمدينة والقدس يفسد شعب الخليفة التجاى وحقّه (او نهايته) بالجرف ⁷والى انقضاء° الحرب منقطعة [على] ⁸المستوحشات ۰

قوله من موصا דבר قيل انه يشير به الى قول يرمياهو כי לפני מלאת וגו' وقيل כ"ם. ٠ انه يريد خروجه من عند الله ۰ وقوله لهشيب يريد به ارداد للجالوث مع כלי בית יוי ۰ وقوله عد مشيح نجيد يشير به الى כהן גדול فهو ⁹ممسوح בשמן המשחה وهو נגיד בית יוי ۰ وقيل ان المسيح כהن גדול والنجيد زרובבל בن שאלתיאל ۰ فعرّف انه ١٥ منذ ¹⁰خرب القدس ¹⁰وانجلت الاّمة الى ان يعمر בيت שני سبعة اسابيع وهى تسعة واربعين سنة وذلك ان لم يزل القوم فى البلد الى سنة ثلث وعشرين سنة من ملك نبوخذناصر وهم المسمّاين يوשבי الحربوت ¹¹فاجلاهم نבוזראדן רב טבחים وفيهم قال יחזק' לג. ד بשנת שלש وتمام القصّة فاذا القينا ثلثة وعشرين سنة من جملة سبعين ¹²سنة ירמ' נב. ל لבابل بقى سبعة واربعين سنة وسنة لدارياوש وسنة لكورש صارت ذلك تسع ٢٠

_____

¹ יעידון מא תקדם B.   ² אנה פי טי B.   ³ Sic.   ⁴ Supplied from B.   ⁵ ופי
צ'יק אלאוקאת B.   ⁶ תקטע K P X.   ⁷ ואלאנקצא K P X.   ⁸ וחשאת B.   ⁹ משיחו X,
משוח K.   ¹⁰ יכרב—תנגלי B; כרב—אנגלת K P X.   ¹¹ The passage which
follows is corrupt in codd.: פאנגלאהם בכתנאצר ופיהם קאל בשנת—פאמא X; K P
nearly the same (P); القصة—וفيهم and سنة وعشرين ثلثة om. B.   פאדא אלקינא
¹² Om. K X.

Line 18. المستمّون.

‏۰ شرح سفر دانيال ۰

فصل ۹ واربعين سنة وفى ذلك قال שבעים שבעה ۰ ثم قال ושבעים ששים וגו׳ وهى مدّة عمارة
فاسوق ۲٦ البيت الثانى الى ان جاء טיטוס הרשע ملك الروم اربع ماية سنة واربع وثلاثين
سنة ۰ فعرّف ان ترجع يروشلايم الى عمارتها في هذه المدّة۰ وقوله رحוב וחרוץ
وهى رحبات للحكّام وقوله חרוץ يريد به انفاذ الاحكام من القتل وغيره ۰ وقوله וبצוק
ויקרא ו. יד العתים قيل انه يشير به الى منحت كهن גדול التى قال فيها זה קרבן אהרן ובניו וגו׳ ۰

٦ وقال عתים من حيث ان نصفها بالغداة ونصفها بالعشى كقوله מחציתה וגו׳ ۰ وذكر
منحت كهن مفردة من حيث ان مهما تقرب فالمذبح عمال دائما ۰ وقوله ואחרי השבעים
וגו׳ عرّف ان عند انقضاء هذه الاثنين وستّين اسبوع ينقطع هذا المسيح المقدّم ذكره
بقوله עד משיח נגיד وهو زوال الكهن من المذبح ۰ وقوله ואין لا يعنى ليس له ولد
۱۰ ولا خليفة يكون بدله او يكون به وليس لهم طول الجالوت رياسة ۰ وقوله והעיר והקדש
תלים קלו. ז يشير الى يروشلايم ومקדש ייי ۰ وقوله ישחית يريد به يخرب ويحرق كقوله האמרים
ערו עד היסוד بה ۰ وقوله ועם נגיד הבא ³يشير الى عسكر الروم مع טיטוס ۰ وقوله۰
וקצו בשטף يريد به ومن ٤بقى من يسرائيل بعد القتل يجرفه يعنى يجليه ۰ وهذا
وصف ما حلّ بالقدس ويروشلايم والامّة ۰ ثم قال ועד קץ מלחמה يريد به الى اخر
۱٥ للحروب ٥وهى ٦حروب נוג تبقى ירושלם וערי יהודה שוממות على ما هو مشاهد
الى الان ۰

۲۷ ويقوى العهد للكثيرين اسبوع ¹واحد وفى نصف الاسبوع
يعطل الذبيحة والهدية ۷وعلى جناح الارجاس ⁸مستوحش والى
زمان الفناء (و)المنقطعة تنصبّ حمية الله على هذا المستوحش ۰

۲٥ بقى اسبوع واحد من السبعين اسبوع فيه فعرّف ان العدوّ قطع معهم
العهد على ⁹سبع سنين۰ الا يجليهم ولا يؤذيهم ۱۰وكان فى نصف۰ الاسبوع غدر
بهم وفسخ العهد وزعم بعض الناس ان الذى احوجه الى ذلك هو انه رآهم ۱۱هوذا
ينتقلون قوم بعد قوم ۱۲من البلد اذ راوا انه لا بدّ من جلوة ووقوعهم قدام العدوّ

---

¹ הרן KPX; om. B.   ² B only; om. cett.   ³ وقوله يشير الى .. om. KX.
٤ יבקא KPX.   ⁵ והו codd.   ⁶ חרב B.   ⁷ ואלי KX.   ⁸ יסתוחש
KPX.   ⁹ עלי אסבוע ואחד B.   ¹⁰ פלמא מצי B.   ¹¹ Om. KX.
¹² ען C

فقالوا نمرّ من انفسنا ¹خير لنا۰ ۰ وقال قوم ان يسرائيل قتلوا עرﻟﻴם كانوا فى فصل ۹
البلد وهم اجلّاء الروم فلمّا فعلوا ذلك غدر بهم وفتح البلد واحرق القدس وبطل فاسوق ٢٧
القرابين ²منﻪ كقولﻪ ושבﻴﺚ זבﺢ ומנחה وعلى ما فى الاخبار انﻪ اقام فى بيت اللﻪ تعّ ──────
وﺛﻦ وقرّب الحزﻳﺮ على مذبح اللﻪ تعّ ۰ وقولﻪ וכנﻒ שקﻮﺻﻴם هو عسكر الروم المسمّاون
שקﻮﺻﻴم فهم الذين خربوا القدس كقولﻪ ﻣﺸﻤﻢ ۰ ثم قال ועד כﻟﻪ يريد بﻪ الى ان ٥
يعمل اللﻪ تعّ כ וﻻ فى زوال الامم وخاصّة باذوم כﻟﻪ فى البلد ونﺤﺮﺻﻪ فى الملك ۰
وقولﻪ תתﻚ על שﻮﻣﻢ يريد (بﻪ) תתﻚ חﻣﺚ ﻳﻴﻲ على هذا البلد الذى سيصير שﻮﻣﻢ حتى
يجون يسرائيل ويعمرونﻪ ۰ وعرّف اللﻪ هذا لدانيال من اجل انﻪ كان يريد ان يقف
على ما يكون من الامّة والقدس فى زمان الثلث ممالك لانﻪ قد علم ان ليس بدّ
من عمارة القدس ورجوع للجالية فقد كان يجوز ان ³يبقون على حالهم كما ⁴كان ١٠
فى زمان ملك الفارس واليونانيّة فعرّفﻪ ان ليس بدّ من خراب البلد وجالوث الامّة
حتى يعرف ذلك ويعرفوﻪ يسرائيل فعند ذلك الم قلبﻪ وتوجّع بذلك ۰

١١۰ فى سنة ثلث لكورش ملك فارس خطاب انكشف لدانيال
النى سمّى اسمﻪ بلطشاصر وحقّ الخطاب وجيش كبير وفهم
الخطاب وفهم لﻪ فى المنظر۰ ١٥

عرّف ان فى سنة ثلث لكورش ⁵ظهر لﻪ ﻣﻼك۰ وخاطبﻪ بجميع ما اراد اللﻪ تعّ
كشفﻪ لﻪ ۰ وهذا الفصل الرابع ۰ وذلك ⁶ان فى ملك بلشاصر دفعتين ودفعة فى ملك
دارياوش ۰ وهذا الرابع ۰ كأنّﻪ الى سنة احدى لكورش كان فى عمالة السلطان كما
شرحنا ذلك فى قولﻪ ויהﻲ דניﻻﻝ וﻧﻮ ثم خرج عن عمل السلطان لانﻪ اعتفى وخاصّة עزרא ﻧ. ﻧ
عند ما وقع النداء كقولﻪ מﻲ בﻛﻢ מﻛﻞ עﻣﻮ وايضا كان شاخ ⁷وتعلّق قلبﻪ بما اخبر عنﻪ
عما يكون من خراب البلد ورجوع الامّة الى للجالوث كما تقدّم بﻪ الشرح ۰ ثم انﻪ ٢١
اخذ فى التشقّى والصوم ليسل اللﻪ عما فى نفسﻪ وذلك انﻪ كان يستعين على ما

---

¹ אצﻟﻪ (l. אצﻟﻪ) B. يبقون (ﻳَﺒﻘَﻮّﺍ for) B ;ﻳﺒﻜﻲ   ² منﻪ ins. C; om. cett.   ³ يبقون B
cett.   ⁴ كانوا C.   ⁵ נﻄﺮ מ׳ cett. Perh. كان.   ⁶ ﻧﻨﻪ C; ﻧﻨﻪ C D   ⁷ ותשﺘﻧﻞ B;
ﻗﻠﺒﻪ איﻨﺎ وﺗﻌﻠﻚ وﺷﺎﻙ ﻗﻠﺒﻪ א׳) D כﻟﺒﻪ א׳)   איﻨﺎ om. C) C D K P X. B is very different
in this paragraph; e.g. the third and fourth citations are in inverted order.

Line 4. ﻭﺛﻨﺎ,ﺍﻟﻤﺴﻤﻮﻥ.

فصل ١٠ يطلبه بالتشقّى كما تقدّم به (الذكر) فى الفصل المتقدّم ❖ وقوله دבר נגלה يعنى
فاسوق ا كلام كان معلق ومغلق شرحه له فظهر بعد ما كان مستورا ❖ ثم قال ואמת הדבר
يريد كلام على ظاهره ليس هو من جنس المنام ولا من جنس الحزن كما شرحنا
ذلك فى تفسير ומראה הערב והבקר وذلك انه اربع دفعات ذكر هذه اللفظة التى
5 معناها ❖ ❖ ❖ واحد فهذا الثانية وبعدها אבל אגיד לך את הרשום בכתב אמת والرابعة
ועתה אמת אגיד לך ❖ وقال אשר נקרא שמו ولم يقول אשר שמו בלטשאצר ❖ قال
قوم ان بقى هذا الاسم عليه ولم يخلع عنه وقيل لما قال אשר נקרא ولم يقول שמו ב'
دلّ ذلك على انه كان يسمى بدله الى وقت زوال ملك كسديم ثم زال بزوال الملك
وهو قريب ❖ ثم قال וצבא גדול يعنى شرح خبر צבא גדול اما ان يكون אדום واما
10 ان يكون ישמעאל كما سنشرحه فى ועשה כרצונו המלך ❖ وقوله ובין את הדבר ובינה لا
يريد شرح الكلام الذى يتقدّم وشرح المراءة الذى נظרה وهو الحزن ونحن نبيّن ذلك
فى ما بعد ❖

٢ فى تلك الايّام انا دانيال كنت متحزّن ثلثة اسابيع ايّام ❖

٣ خبز المشتهات [1]لم اكل ولحما وخمرا [1]لم يدخل الى فمى
15 [2]ودهن [1]لم اندهّن الى كمال ثلاثة اسابيع [3]ايّام ❖

قوله בימים ההם يريد به فى سنة ثلث لكورش وهى الثلاثة اسابيع ايّام التى تشقّى
فيها وقوله שלשה שבעים ימים اورى الفرق بين هذه الاسابيع وبين שבעים שבעים لان
تلك (ال)اسابيع سنين وهذه ايّام فلذلك قال ימים ❖ ثم قال היתי מתאבל ذكر اشياء
استعملها فى هذه الاسابيع وهى الطعام والشراب والعطر فذكر من الطعام الخبز واللحم
20 ومن الشراب الخمر وقال فى الخبز חמדות اذ كان ليس بدّ له من اكل الخبز فبيّن
انه لا ياكل الخبز الدرمك الخاصة ❖ وقال فى البشر والداين لא בא אל פי اذ لم ياكله ولم
يشربه اصلا ❖ فكانّه ياكل خبز الشعير او [4]المخشكار وادمه بقول وحبوب ولعله كان
ياكل شيا من الفاكهة ❖ ثم ذكر الدهن والعطر كقوله וסוך לא סכתי وقد علمنا انه
لا بدّ من ان يغيّر ملبوسه فيلبس الخشن وانه ايضا [5]لم يحضر الافراح ❖ وهذه كلها

---

[1] B: om. دهن [2]   מא אכלת (K לם אכלת) .. מא דכל .. מא דכל .. העטיר לם תעטרת
DKX.   [3] הי איאם B.   [4] אלכשאכאר וקיל אלכשכאר D.   [5] לא CKX.
Line 5. وهذه.   6. يقل.   14. لحم etc.

من ¹مبسوطات האבלוﬨ وقد بقى القول فى الصوم فقال قوم انه ²صامها لقول   فصل ١٠

الملاك כי מן היום הראשון אשר וﬁ' فقال ان الصوم احد اقسام التشقّى وليس هو   فاسوق ٣

بعيد فالزم نفسه ان يدوم على هذا التحزّن الى ان يكشف الله له ما يكشف من

احوال الامّة مثل ما الزم داود نفسه عمّ من التشقّى الى ان كشف ³له الله ما ارادﮦ

كقوله אם אבוא באהﬥ ביﬨי ✦ ⁴وتفعل اولياء الله هذا لعلمها ان الله يجيبهم الى   ﬨﬣﬥים קﬥב. ﬔ

سوالهم فاما اهل لڄالية⁵ فليس لهمۥ ان يتجاسروا على ذلك بل ⁷يقومون ويسالون ٦

الله فى ما يجوز ان يسالون ⁸مثلﮦ ✦ ويجب ⁹لنا ان نبيّن هذا اﬥבﬡ֗ר الذى منع

نفسه عن اكله اتى لحم هو من اللحوم فنقول انه يشير به الى ما جاز له اكله لانه

انما امتنع فى هذه الايّام عن هذه الاربعة التى كان يفعلها فى ما تقدّم له من الايّام

الماضية ورجع الى مثل ذلك بعد ان انكشف له ما كشف الله له فاما ما كان محرّم ١٠

عليه ابدا فليس له مدخل فى هذا القول فليس يجوز ان يكون قوله وבﬡ֗ר يقصد به

الى لحم البهائم والطيور والاسماك المحرّمة ولا ايضا الى لحم البقر والغنم الذى ¹⁰انما

ينطلق عند اتمام الشروط التى تضمّنها الشريعة كما شرحنا ذلك فى تفسير التورا

وﬗﬤﬨ מﬗײַﬨ التى الفناء ✦ فان قال قائل ممن لا يعرف اللغة فما هو هذا اللحم قلنا

لحم طائر وبهائم برّيّة واسماك فان قال ¹¹من اين لنا ان السمك בﬡ֗ר في لغتنا قيل ١٥

له ان ¹²الطائر والاسماك يسمّى בﬡ֗ר° وليس فرق بين السمك وغيره لكن نوجدك

ذلك بنصّ وهو قول الرسول عمّ ואﬨﬣ אמרﬨ בﬡ֗ר אﬨײַ ﬥﬣﬨ ثم قال بعدﮦ הﬠﬠﬢ ﬡ ו﬋ײַ֗ר וﬁ'   במ﬐﬙﬒ יﬡ. ﬔﬡ

فذكر غنم وبقر ثم ذكر السمك فدلّ ذلك على ان السمك בﬡ֗ר مثل البقر والغنم ثم

سمّى الطائر בﬡ֗ר الا ترى انه سمّى السلوى בﬡ֗ר كقوله הﬠﬡ֗ר עוﬔײַ בײַ ﬡײַ﬩ﬣײַ וﬗﬤﬥﬡ   במﬔ' יﬡ. ﬥﬔ

¹³جمع الطائر مع الوحش كقوله כﬠ ײַ﬩שׁ כﬠ בﬡ֗ר ﬔﬔﬠ בײַבּבּﬠ ﬣﬠﬡ وقصّة نوح عمّ تدلّ   וﬠשּׁﬢ יﬠ. ﬠﬔ

على ذلك فقد بان لك ان كل حيوان ¹⁴اسمﮦ בﬡ֗ر لا محالة الان ليس يجوز ان   ﬔﬠ

يحتجّ علينا من يطلق اللحم فى لڄالية بقول دانيال ובﬡ֗ר ויײַ ﬥﬡ בﬡ ﬡﬥ פﬁ مع

كون مذبح الله عمّال والقرابين دائمة عليه لانه قد بنى المذبح منذ سنة ✦

---

¹ ﬔבשּׁوשּׁמﬡﬨ B.   ² ﬩﬐מﬣﬡ C; perh. ﬩﬐﬐מﬣ.   ³ Om. K X.   ⁴ ﬨ﬐עﬥ
D K P X.   ⁵ المدنيين المقتدرين ins. after لڄالية B K.   ⁶ فما سبيلهم B K.
⁷ يﬢﬠﬔײַ B K.   ⁸ Perh. مثلهم.   ⁹ Ins. C only.   ¹⁰ Om. C X.
¹¹ Ins. D only.   ¹² כﬠ ﬡﬥﬗﬡ﬚ײַ י﬩מﬡ בﬡ֗ר B.   ¹³ جميع K P X.
¹⁴ Om. P X.

فصل ١٠
فاسوق ٤

٤ وفى اليوم الرابع وعشرين من الشهر الاول وانا كنت على شطّ
النهر الكبير هو الدجلة ٠

يدلّ هذا النصّ (على) انه كان بعد تقضّى الثلثة اسابيع فعلمنا انه ابتدى بالتشقّى
من اليوم الثالث من الشهر وعرّف انه كان سائر على شطّ الدجلة فظهر له هذا الملاك
5 واعلم انه فى الחזון لم يكن فى الحقيقة على نهر اولى وانما راى فى الחزון كانه على
النهر وهذا كان يقظة (وهو) فى الحقيقة قائم على النهر ٠ ولم ¹يعلم اين كان منه
هل فى الموصل ام فى بابل او ²فى غيرها ³لان الدجلة اول خروجها من فوق الموصل
وينصبّ على البطائح⁰ ٠

٥ ⁴فشلت عينى ونظرت وانا شخص واحد ملبس مقدارِيّة
١٠ وحقواه مشدودان بمنطقة من ⁵ابريز ٠

ירמ׳ י׳. ט　　اوفز اسم مكان كقوله وذهب מאופז ٠

٦ وجثّته مثل لون الجوهر الازرق ووجهه مثل منظر البرق
وعينيه مثل مشاعل النار وانرعيه وساقيه مثل لون النحاس الغلى
وصوت كلامه مثل صوت جمهور العسكر ٠

M
16
يجب ان تعلم ان ليس هذا الملك جبريال كما ظنّ قوم لان جبريال كان قد انس
به ولم يكن منظره هذا المنظر الهائل العظيم بل قد رآه بعقب الصلاة ولم يلحقه شى
من هذا الذى لحقه كما سنذكر ذلك كما يصف احد من الملائكة التى نظرها كما
وصف هذا الملاك لهوله ولخوفه منه ⁶وسنذكر ما نحتاج اليه فى هذا الباب عند قوله
והנה מיכאל וגו׳٠ ٠ ثم وصف ⁷لون جسمه فعرّف ⁸انه من عنقه الى ركبه يشبه لون
20 لجوهر الازرق وان وجهه مثل البرق الخاطف ولونه احمر على رسم البرق وعرّف ان
عيناه ⁹مثل مشاعل النار التى لها صفير الى بعيد ¹⁰وعرّف ان ذراعيه وساقيه مثل

لون النحاس المغلي وهو اصفر وان صوته يسمع عن بعد كما يسمع صوت العسكر كما فصل ١٠
قال בקול המון وكل هذا تهوّل ناظرها ولباسه ثياب مقداريّة متشمّرة على ١عمل فاسوق ٢
المحارب الذى تكون ثيابه ٢مشدود(ة) الوسط وذلك لانه ٣جاءه من الحرب كما سنذكر —
ذلك فى ما بعد ٠

٧ ونظرت انا دانيل وحدى المنظر والقوم الذين كانوا معى لم ٥
ينظروا المنظر غير ان قلقة عظيمة وقعت عليهم وهربوا فى ٤الاختباء ٠

اعلم انه لم ير الملاك على الشط وانما ٥رآه فى الهواء فوق ٦النهر متعالى عن الماء
كما قال فى اخر الفصل אשר ממעל למימי היאר فعرّف انه رآه بهذه الصورة الهائلة
الفزعة ٠ ثم قال והאנשים ונו׳ فدلّ ذلك على انه كان معه قوم فنظر هو ولم ينظر غيره
وقد قال לבדי وقد علمنا انه وحده نظر فما المعنى بقوله והאנשים ונו׳ الجواب فى ذلك ١٠
انه اورا انهم وان كانوا لم ينظروا فقد احسّوا شى ولحقهم من ذلك חרדה وبحتمل ان
لحقهم ذلك من اجل هول صوته فسمعوا الصوت ولم ينظروا الصورة لانه قال לא ראו את
המראה ولم يقل לא שמעו ٧ولكنهم لما سمعوا صوته وقعت عليهم رعدة فهربوا على
وجوههم ٠ ويمكن ان هولاء قوم خرجوا معه لضرب لم يذكره الكتاب ٠ وكذلك
الآباء سمعوا صوت صوت الله فوقعت عليهم رعدة وخوف فهربوا الى بعد كما قال וירא שמות כ. יח
העם וינועו ٠
١٦

٨ وانا تبقيت وحدى ونظرت هذا المنظر ٨العظيم ولم يبق فىّ قوّة
وبهاء وجهى انقلب علىّ الى مغسس وما حبست قوّة ٠

٩قد قال فى الفاسوق المتقدم וראיתי אני דניאל ונו׳ ثم قال بقيت انا وحدى وليس
معى من يونسنى ٠ ١٠وقوله ולא נשאר בי כח يريد به قوّة للوقوف٥ وقوله ثانية ולא עצרתי ٢٥
כח يريد به ولم يبق فىّ قوّة للحركة وقوله והודי נהפך ונו׳ كانه ١١اصفر وجهه كما يلحق
الناس فى وقت موتهم ٠

---

¹ Obl. in M. ² CKX. משמרה משדור ³ لفاه M (وافاه؟). ⁴ الاحتى M;
Heb. אלכבי ⁵ رآه om. M. ⁶ الماء CMX. ⁷ ولكنهم K; لكن M;
cett. לכנהם ⁸ Om. M. ⁹ قد M (in the previous line, where the scribe had
commenced by mistake, وقد); Heb. וקד ¹⁰ وقوله—للوقوف M only. ¹¹ اصفار M.

فصل ۱۰ ۹ وسمعت صوت خطبه وعند سماعى صوت خطابه وانا كنت سابت
فاسوق ۹ على وجهى ووجهى على الارض ⋄

قوله נרדם על פני كانه غشى عليه ساعة ⋄

۱۰ وانا يد دنت بى ۱وضربتنى على ركبى ۲واكفّ رجليّ ⋄

5 ۳هذا يد ملك راى ان يره الملك محرك٤ حتى قام من على وجهه وصار على
اربعة مثل البهائم ولم يكن فيه قوّة يجلس على نفسه ولم يقوم ايضا ⋄

۱۱ وقال لى يا دانيال يا رجل المتمناات افهم فى الخطاب الذى
انا مخاطبك وقف على وقوفك فان الساعة بعثت اليك وعند
مخاطبته ٥معى بهذا الخطاب وقفت مرتعد ⋄

۱۵ امره بشيين احدهما اجعال بالك مما هوذا بخاطبه به وعرّفه ان الله بعث به اليه
والثانى ليقف على رجليه حتى يسمع كلامه فعرّف انه وقف لكنه وقوف على غير
ثبات بل مرتعد ⋄

۱۲ وقال لى لا تفزع يا دانيال فان من اليوم ٥الاوّل الذى
جعلت فى قلبك للتفهّم والتشقّى قدام الاهك سُمعوا خطبك وانا
۱۵ جئتُ بسبب خطبك ⋄

قوله אל תירא يعنى لا تخاف ان تكون قد نقصت حالتك عند الله ان فى صلاتك
جاءك للخطاب وانت تصلّى وقد مفى لك فى هذه الدفعة ثلثة اسابيع ولم يجئك
للجواب فان من اوّل يوم ابتدات بالتشقّى ٦قد سمعوا خطبك لكن كان لى شغل قطعنى
عن المجىّ اليك ⋄ وقوله נשמעו דבריך يدلّ على انه كان ايضا يسل الله فى ان يفهمه
۲۰ ما كان يريد ان يفهمه وعرّفه ان مجيّه فى هذا الوقت ٧هو ليعرّفه ما كان يرى الله
ان يعرّفه اياه ⋄

---

۱ وطريتنى all.   ۲ وكفوف يدّ B.   ۳ هذا and هذا C M (يدّ[s] lost);
هذا—محرك C M   X. هذا اليه الملك K؛ هذا اليه يد ملك
ins. B.   ٦ وقد M.   ٧ Om. M.   ٤ Om. C M.   ٥ Om. M C D K X؛

١٣ ورئيس ملك فارس واقف حنائى واحد وعشرين يوما وهوذا فصل ١٠
ميخائيل احد الملائكة الاوّلين جاء لينصرنى وانا تبقّيت ثمّ ١لصف فاسوق ١٣
ملوك فارس ✧

١٤ وجئتُ لتفهيمك الذى يصادف شعبك فى اخر الايّام فان ايضا
الوحى للايّام ✧ ٥

١٥ وعند ٢مخاطبته معى مثل هذه الخطب جعلت وجهى على
الارض وانخرست

عرّفه ان الذى منعه ان يجى من اوّل يوم هو محاربته לשׂר פרס والغرض فى ذلك
هو انه كان يحاربه الى ٣ان مات كورش فلما مات كورش تركه وجاء الى دانيال ٤وسنوفى
ما نحتاج اليه فى هذا المعنى فى فاسوق واני בשׁנת אחת וג' فقال له كما تفرّغت א.א.ט.
من محاربة שׂר פרס جئتُ لافهمك ما يلحق امّتك فى اخر الزمان وهو وقت انقضاء ١١
الاربع ممالك ✧ وقوله כי עוד וג' يعنى ان هذا החזון الذى نظرت فى ما تقدّم هو
الى اخر الزمان وهو קץ اربع מלכיות ✧ وعند ما انتهى كلام الملك الى هذا القول
زادت رعدته عليه ولم يكن فيه ٥قوّة للوقوف ووقع على وجهه ✧ ثم قال ונאלמתי
وهو انه لم يبق له قوّة ٦يخاطبه على ما تقدّم من قوله بل انخرس ولم يتكلّم اصلا ✧ ١٥

١٦ وانا كشبه بنى ادم دانى على شفتىّ ٧وفتحت فاى وتكلّمت
وقلت للواقف ٨حنائى يا سيّدى فى المنظر انقلبوا امغاصى علىّ
وما حبست قوّة ✧

١٧ وكيف يقدر عبد سيّدى هذا للكلام مع سيّدى هذا وانا من
الوقت لم يثبت ٩فىّ قوّة ونسمة لم تبق فىّ ✧ ٢٠

راى كان ملك يشبه انسان يانس اليه ويمكن ان يد الملك دنت بفيه مثل قوله
فى يشاعيا عَمّ ויעף وتمامه ومثله قول يرميا عَمّ וישלח וג' فعند دنوّ الملاك به انفتح ١.י.
פ.ו.א.

¹ ענד C M X.   ² מכאאטבתה M; مخاطبة P.   ³ Om. M.   Heb. וסנסתוף
⁵ Om. M.   ⁶ على مخاطبته C K P X; מכאטכה B; لخاطبه M; מכאאטבתה M.   ⁷ فتحت M.
⁸ חדאى M.   ⁹ פיא bis P.

✤ شرح سفر دانيال ✤

فصل ١٠ فمه وتكلّم كقوله ואפתח וגו׳ ✤ وقوله אל העמד נגדי يشير الى الملاك الكبير الذى

فاسوق ١٧ كان يخاطبه ✤ وقال هذا القول على سبيل الاعتذار اليه يعنى لولا ما دخلنى من

الفزع وضعفت قوّتى لقمت قائماً كما امرتنى وعمد על עמדך ✤ وقال נהפכו צירי مثل

שמואלא.ב.ד.יט قوله فى كثة عيلى ותכרע ותלד כי נהפכו עליה ציריה ✤ ¹وقوله והיך יוכל يعنى ليس

5 فى قدرتى ان اثبت لمخاطبة مثل سيدى ولا بلغت [منزلتى] هذه المنزلة ✤ وقوله ואני

מעתה يعنى منذ وافيتك لم تبق لى قوّة ولا حركة كما قال ונשמה לא נשארה בי ويجوز

איוב כו.ד انه ²אراد به ولم يبق لى عقل ممّا قد ذهلت لان لنا نשמה يريد به العقل مثل قوله

לב. ח ³ונשמת מי° ومثل ונשמת שדי תבינם ✤

١٨ وعاودنى ودنانى كمنظر ادميّ وقوّانى ✤

10 عند ما دنت يده به تكلّم ولم يكن فيه قوّة للوقوف وعاود ذلك الملك الذى

تقدّم ذكره ودنا به فعند ذلك قوّى للوقوف ✤ كان الملاك الكبير هو ממעל למ
صمي

היאך ⁴وانه راى يده ولم يَرَ غير يده واخر رآه وانس به ومرّة دنا بشفتيه ومرّة دنا به

ولعلّه اخذ يده ونشله ⁵كقوله ויחזקני° ✤

١٩ وقال لا تخشا يا رجل المتمنّاات سلامة لك اشتد وشدن

15 وعند تخاطبه معى ⁶اشتدّيت وقلت يتتكلم سيدى ان قد ⁷شدّيتنى ✤

القائل له אל תירא هو الملك الكبير ومعناه لا تفزع على نفسك من الوقت قُم

واشتدّ وقوى قلبك واسمع ما اقوله لك فلما سمع كلامه قوى قلبه ولا بدّ من ان

يكون قد قام على رجليه ✤

٢ وقال البس علمت لما جئت البك والساعه ارجع للمحاربة مع

20 رئيس فارس وانا خارج وانا رئيس ياوان جائ ✤

قوله הידעת يشير الى ما تقدّم له من القول وهو قوله ואני באתי כדבריך وتمام

القول فقال له قد عرّفتك لاى معنى جئت والساعة فليس بدّ من ⁸ان ارجع لأحارب

---

¹ واخر راى يده ولا يد غير يده M. ² بقوله M. ³ Ins. B only. ⁴ قوله M.
(ولا for ولאם) M B; text D K P X. ⁵ Om. M. ⁶ אשתדית B K X; اشتدت
M C P. ⁷ For شَدّدتنى (apparently) M. ⁸ Om. M.

مع رئيس فارس فى معنى الاربعت ملوك الذى ¹تقوم لفارس وقد شرح ذلك فى ما فصل ١٠
بعد ۞ وقوله ואני יוצא يعنى اخرج من محاربة رئيس فارس وبعده ²يجى؞ שר יון ولا فاسوق ٢
يذكر له ما يكون بعد ياوان ۞

<hr>

٢١ لكن حقًّا اخبرك بالمرسوم فى الكتاب حقّ وليس احد متنقوّى
معى على بطلان هولاء الا ميخائيل رئيسكم ۞ 5

قوله את הרשום בכתב אמת يشير الى ما سمعه فى المنام الذى كتبه כמו قال באדין
חלמא כתב فقال ذلك المرسوم فى الكتاب وله باطن ³انا اذكره لك على ظاهره ليس له
تاويل ۞ وقوله ואין אחד מתחזק يريد وليس واحد ⁴يعيننى على بطلان هذه الممالك
غير ميخائيل فقط ۞ وقوله שרדם عرّف ان ميخائيل שר ישראל فعرّف ان هذا الملك
الذى كان يكلّمه هو يعزل الممالك مع ميخائيل ۞ وقوله על אלה يحتمل انه قصد ١٠
به الى מלכי פרס فقط لانه تقدّم ذكرهم ويحتمل انه اراد به اربع מלכיות فعرّف ان
هذين الملكين ⁵يتعاضدان على عزل هذه الممالك كلهم ولم يذكر هذا الملك الكبير انه
رئيس احد دولة من هذه الدول فيقرب فيه ان ميخائيل كان يحارب اعداء يسرائيل
فقط وهذا الملاك يحارب صاحب كل دولة اذا تمّ وقت دولتهم ويعزله ۞

١١١ وانا فى سنة احدى لدارياوش المادى وقوفى لمقوى له ١٥
ولمحصص له ۞

عرّفه انه كما انه اعان ميخائيل على | قتل كورش كذاك اعانه على قتل دارياوش   M def.
המדי او موته ۞ ويجب ان نلبث ههنا قليلا ونذكر طرفا ممّا ⁶نحتاج الى ذكره بقول
مختصر فى معنى الملائكة ۞ فنقول فى ذلك انه لا سبيل الى دفع ظاهر النصّ من
قول اللّه تعّ ومن قول انبيائه الا بعد ان يعتاص ويمتنع بحيث يكون العقل ٢٠
يدفعه او نصّ محكم يدفعه فيُعلم عند ذلك ان لهذا النصّ تخريج يوفق بينه وبين
العقل وبين النصّ المحكم ويكون قد استعمل ⁷ذلك على طريق من الطرق على سبيل
المجاز والاتساع كما ذكرنا ذلك فى عدّة مواضع فى التورا وسائر كتب الانبياء عمّ ۞
فاما ما يردّه العقل ⁸من قوله انحدر اللّه وصعد اللّه فلمّا كان العقل يمنع ذلك بحيث

<hr>

¹ ‏בקו‎ Heb.   ² مجى M.   ³ وانا M B.   ⁴ نعينى M.   ⁵ يعاضدا M.
⁶ ‏יחתאן‎ codd. من انحدار B C;   ⁷ من ذلك D K X; النى ذلك B C P Q.   ⁸ كف B C;
‏אללה וצער‎ P X; text K.

انه ان حملناه على ظاهره يجب عنده ان يكون للخالق تعّ جوهرة يحلّ الامكنة فصل ۱۱

فيكون فى مكان دون مكان وانه يتحرك ويسكن وكان ذلك من صفات المخلوقين فاسوق ۱

المحدودين فيوصف بصفاتهم فيجب ان يكون لتلك النصوص تخريج ١فاما ان يتاوّل

للاسم المذكور واما (ان) ٢يتاوّل للفعل ◆ فاما ما ٣يتاوّل للاسم فهو וירד ייי ויעל

5 ויל׳ فانما نثبت الفعل ٣للشخص الموصوف بالنزول والصعود ٤لكن القصد فى ذلك

الى ملاك اللہ او وقار اللہ او رسول اللہ باختصار لفظة ◆ واما ما يتاوّل ٥للفعل فهو

كقول القائل فرح اللہ وشقّ على اللہ وغار اللہ وما جرى هذا المجرى فهذه اعراض منفية

عن البارّى عز وجل وانما فيه معنى (يجب) ان يذكر حسب ما احتمل القول ◆ فبحيث

ان نظر العقل يدلّ على ذلك استعملت اللغة الاتساع والمجاز فى ذلك ◆ وما كان

10 النصّ يدفعه ايضا فيجب ان ٦يتاول النص المحتمل الوجهين وما ٧زاد على ذلك ◆

الان نصوص نواطق الكتاب ليس تدفع ان يكون خلق اللہ تعّ ملائكة كما لا يدفع

العقل فلا سبيل الى دفعها لا على قول من يقول انها حوادث ولا على قول من يقول

انہ يحدثها ويعدمها ◆ وذلك انا وجدنا فى كتاب اللہ تعّ مواضع يذكر فيها الملائكة

وهى على قسمين فقد تظهر حسّا فيشاهدها الانسان يقظة كما يشاهد سائر الاشياء

15 المرائّة وقد يشاهدها فى المنام كما يشاهد اشياء غير الملائكة ايضا ◆ فاما ما يشاهد

يقظة فذاك مثل ما ظهر لهاغار وليعقوب وموسى وبلعام ويهوشوع وجذعون ومانوح

وداود ونبوخذناصر ودانيال ◆ وفى المنام ابيملين على رأى قوم ويعقوب وبلعام ◆

وقد يسمع السامع كلامهم من غيره ان يراهم كما سمعت هاغار وسمع ابراهام وكذلك

شمويل وكذلك دانيال واذا كان هذا فى اخبارنا فلا وجہ لدفع هذه النصوص ◆ ٨وفى

20 المعلوم انہ لا يدرك بحاسّة البصر غير للجسم وان العرض لا يقوم بنفسہ فيجب ان يكون

الملك جسم وللجسم لا يحدث | نفسہ فقد وجب ان يكون لہ محدث احدثہ وهو مما M

يمكن عليہ البقاء فاذا كان الملك مخلوقا فيجوز عليہ البقاء فما الذى يوجب إعدامہ ◆

فان ظنّ ظانّ ان الملاك انما هو ٩مخلوقا لوقتہ لمعنى ١٠للخطاب او غير ذلك ١١فاذا تمّ ذلك°

فلا وجہ لبقائہ قيل لہ وما الذى يدلّ على انہ خلق فى الحال وانہ انما خلق للخطاب

25 او لمعنى ١٢ما يريده° للحال ١٣لا لغيرها ◆ فان قال وايش للملاك من الافعال غير

---

¹ Om. X. ² נתאול codd. ³ ללשבץ BK; ואלשבץ CDPQX. ⁴ לכנה
codd. ⁵ אלפ׳ codd. (C) אלפאעל C). ⁶ Om. CDPQX; יתנאול B. ⁷ יזאד BDK.
⁸ Perh. ومن. ⁹ מכלוקה X. ¹⁰ حطاب M. ¹¹ Om. M. ¹² يوجبہ M;
¹³ او لغبرها M. Heb. אן ירידה

فصل ۱۱ الرسالة وما جانسها مما هو لوقته قلنا [1]له التسبيح والتمجيد لخالقه الا ترى ان النبى

فاسوق ۱ مصطفى للرسالة ومع ذلك فليس للخطاب خلق فقط ۰ ثم وجدنا فى اخبارنا [2]بقاء

الملاك من ذلك بقاء الكبود بين بنى يسرائيل تسع ماية سنة وقول دانيال عن جبريال

והאיש וגו' وبين الوقتين سنه ولا يجوز ان يظنّ [3]انه شخص مثل شخص فان ذلك لا

يستحقّ ان يكون ذلك شخص خلق منذ سنة ثم انه انعدم وخلق مثله او يكون هو ه

بعينه وايضا فان قول هذا الملاك المخاطب لدانيال هوذا يقول ان لى مدّة فى حرب

وانى محارب لمن بقى منهم كما قال ואין אחד וגו' وقوله ايضا ובעת ההיא יעמד וגו'

M def. فهذه النصوص تدلّ على بقائهم فعند | هذا البيان يبطل قول القائل انها | تخلق
M inc.

لوقتها وتنعدم ۰ فاما مراتبها فلا شكّ انها تفضل بعضها على بعض كما [4]ذكرنا ذلك

תהל' קג' א فى صدر تفسير يحزقيال وفى تفسير لدود ברכי נפשי את יוי بكلام واسع الا ترى

۱۱ ان فى هذا الفصل يقول فى الواحد כמראה אדם فعرّف انه قرب منه ولم يفزع منه

وكان يفزع ويذهل من الملاك الكبير وهذا متّسع فى اخبارنا وقدرها محدودة حسب ما

جعل لخالق لها الا ترى ان يعقوب ابونا عمّ لمّا صارع الملاك عجز الملاك فى لحال عن

برא' לב' כה تخليته كما قال וירא וגו' وان كان صورها هائلة فان الله قد يمكن بنى ادم من

۱۵ مشاهدتها غير الكبود الكبير [5]العظيم [6]الذى التمس الرسول عمّ من الله تعّ ان يوريه

שמו' לג' כ اياه فقال לא תוכל وגו' وقال له וראית וגו' فدلّ ذلك على انه يرى ظهره ولا يرى وجهه ۰

فهذا قول باختصار فى هذا الباب ونحن معولين على شرح ما تقدّم لنا فى غير هذا

الموضع لكن [7]لم يحسن نحمل هذا القول فى هذا المكان ۰ فقوله עמדי למחזיק וגו'

عرّف ان العمل لميخائيل وان هذا الملاك يعاونه فى ذلك ۰

۲۰ [8]والساعة يقينا اخبرك (اى قول على ظاهره) هونا بقى ايضا ۲

---

[1] Om. M.   [2] مقام M.   [3] אנה שכן מתל שכן כלק מנד סנה C; using this

ولا يجوز ان يظنّ انه شخص مثل شخص خلق we may rewrite the whole passage thus:

M شرحنا   [4] منذ سنة ثم انعدم وخلق مثله فان ذلك لا يستحقّ ان يكون هو بعينه ۰

[5] العظم M.   [6] الى M.   [7] لم يحسن يعبّر على هذا الفصل من عـ ن ـدك... ..

ذلك .. ى M; لم يحسن نحمل هذا القول فى هذا الملكان .Heb نחמל Q; ימהל B K;

for نحמל P X; هذا نחמל C).   [8] M corruptly: والساعة هوذا اخبرك بقول على ظاهره ۰

والان .Heb have والساعة

Line 13. ابانا.

فصل ۱۱ ثلثة ملوك ۱تقوم لفارس والرابع يبسر يسار كبير اكثر من الكل وعند
فاسوق ۲ قوّته يثير الكل لملك ياوان ❖

عرّف ان بعد كورش اربعة ملوك وهم احشويروش صاحب مردخای وبعده ارتحششت
الصغير وبعده داریاوش الفارسی وهم الثلثة الذی قيل ۳فيهم הנה עוד שלשה וגו׳ ❖
5 ۳وقوله והרביעי וגו׳ يشير الى۵ ارتحششت صاحب עזרא ונחמיא عمّ وفی قول יעשיר וגו׳
اعلم انه قد عرّف ان كورش حصلت له خزائن الملوك فايسر يسارا كبيرا كما قال
ישע׳ מה. ג ונתתי וגו׳ وقد بيّن يسار احشويروش فی ספר המגלה كما قال בהראותו את עשר כבוד וגו׳
אסת׳ א. ד
قعرّف فی هذه الاية ان ارتحششت اكثر يسارا من ۴كل ملوك فارس فمع ما انه اكثر
يسارا من الكل فانه غُيِّر فی ملكه ۵اكثر من الكل لانه ملك ثلثة وثلاثين سنة ❖
10 ثم عرّف انه اذا بلغ فی يساره ينقضی ملكه ويحصل للجميع لملك ياوان كقوله יעיר
הכל وهذا لم يشرحه فی الחלום ولا فی الחזון وشرحه ههنا ❖

۳ و يقف ملك جبّار ويتسلّط تسلّط كبير ويعمل كرضائه ❖

قوله עמד يعنی يثبت على الملك ❖ وقوله מלך גבור هو المقول فی החזון קרן חזות
בין עיניו وهو الاسكندر ۶وذلك لانه فتح المدن الكبار واخباره مذكورة مشهورة ❖ وقوله
15 ומשל וגו׳ ذلك من حيث ان ۷ملوك فارس ملكوا ثلث جهات على ما ذكرنا۸فی تفسير
۹ועלעין فی قوله ותלת עלעין בפמה בין שנוהי وقوله ראיתי את האיל מנגח ימה וצפונה
ונגבה والاسكندر ملك اربع جهات العالم كما قال فيه די תשלם בכל ארעא وقال ועשה
כרצונו يعنی يقتل من يريد ويملك من يريد ولا يردّ احد امره من جنس قوله فی
M des. נבוכדנצר די הוא צבא הוא מחי وتمام القول ❖ |

20 ۴ وعند وقوفه تنكسر ملكه وتنقسم لاربع جهات السماء وليس
لعقبه ولا كسلطانه الذی تسلّط لان تنقلع ملكه وللاخرين غير
هولاء ❖

قوله תשבר מלכותו هو عند موت الاسكندر اضطرب الملك ❖ وقوله ותחץ هو ان

۱ Om. M.   ۲ Ins. C only.   ۳ وهاربيعی—مكول [وقوله .. يشير الى
M.   ۴ Om. (apparently) M.   ۵ اكبر C K P Q X.   ۶ وقال نבור Heb. وهو
۷ Ins. C only.   ۸ Om. M.   ۹ C only; العلما cett.

وقع بين روسائه مشاجرة فاصطلح اهل المملكة على ان ياخذ كل واحد جهة من جهات   **فصل ١١**
العالم وذاك من حيث انه لم يخلف ولد يملك فى مكانه لقوله ולא לאחריתו   وقوله   **فاسوق ٢**
ولא כמשלו يعنى مع كون هولاء الاربعة فى اربع جهات العالم لم يكن ¹فيهم ضبط ——◦——
الملك والقوّة مثل ما كان فى الاسكندر ❖ وقوله כי תנתש מלכותו يعنى ينقلع ملك
اليونانيّة الذى له اربع جهات الدنيا وقام قوم بعد قوم ملكوا بعد هولاء الاربعة   5
الى ان تمّت لهم ماية ²وثمانين سنة على ما تضمّنته الاخبار ❖ وقوله ولאחרים מלבד
אלה يريد انه قام بعد ذلك قوم ملكوا على ³سنن المتقدّمين وقد تقدّم ذكر هولاء
كقوله כהתם הפשע وهم פשעים فى معنى السنن والملك ❖

❖ ويتقوّى ملك الندب ومن رؤسائه ويتقوّى عليه ويتسلّط سلطان
كبير سلطانه ❖   10

اعلم ان الملك انقسم لاربعة فكل واحد اخذ على رسم المتقدّم ذكرهم ويعلم
ذلك من قوله מלך הנגב מלך הצפון وسنشرح ذلك فى موضع اخر بشرح بيّن لكن لم
يذكر من الاربعة ملوك غير ملك الندب وملك الصفون ⁴ومن هذا يشبه ان⁵ ملك الغرب
وملك الشرق جلس كل واحد فى جهته ولم يطلب غيرها فلم يجر بينهم حرب ولذلك
لم يذكرهم الكتاب وذكر ملك الندب وملك الصفون من حيث انهم جرى لهم اخبار حروب   15
فمن اجل ذلك ذكرهم دون ملك الغرب والشرق ويتّجه ايضا ان ملك الغرب وملك
الشرق انضاف كل واحد منهما الى واحد من الملكين ❖ وقوله ומן שריו قيل فيه
انه واحد من روساء الملك الذى تقدّمه كأنّه كان מלך הנגב الذى سبقه يونانيّ وهذا
كان رئيس من روسائه وقيل انه يريد به ومن روساء מלך הצפון ⁵عصى وتقوّى على
מלך הצפון وهو قول قريب لان الفاسوق الذى بعده يشدّ هذا التفسير ❖ وقوله ויחזק   20
עליו يريد به ان מלך הנגב تقوّى على מלך הצפון ❖ وقوله ממשל רב هو ان عمله
اكبر واوسع من عمل غيره وهو عمل الروم لان هذا מלך הנגב هو ملك الروم وهو اوّل
ملك قام لهم ❖

◦ ولانقضاء سنين يتصاحبوا وبنت ملك الندب تجى الى מלך הצפון

———————————

فصل ١١ ليعمل صلح ولا تحسس قوّة النراع ولا تثبت نراعه بل تسلّم هى
فاسوق ٦ ومحيبها والمنشيها ومقوّيها فى الاوقات ✦

قال ولقض شنים ولم يذكر كم سنين هى لعلها سنين كان بينهم موافقة فغدر
ملك الحفون بملك النحب فمن اجل ذلك ارسل ملك النحب عساكر الى ملك الحفون وهذا
5 نظير ما جرى لسذوم مع كذرلاعمر انهم اطاعوه اثنى عشر سنة ثم عصوا عليه فغزاهم ✦
برא' יד. ג وقوله يتحبرو يريد به اجتماعهم للحرب مثل قوله كل אלה חברו ✦ وقوله وبت ملك
النحب يريد به جمع عساكر مثل בت מצרים בת צור وكثير مثل ذلك فى كتابنا ✦ وقوله
לעשות מישרים يريد به تطلب منه ان يرجع يصالحه ويدوم على ما كان عليه من
جنس ما طلب سنحريب ملك اشور من حزقياهو ويمكن انه اراد منه ان يقول
10 بمذهبه وكان ملك الحفون يعبد الاوثان فلم يستجيب ملك الحفون الى ما اراده منه ملك
1 النحب فخرج يحارب عسكر ملك النحب فلم يكن لعسكر ملك النحب ثبات قدام ملك الحفون
كقوله ولא تעצר כח הזרוע واعلم ان הזרוע هى عساكر ملك النحب كانها تنهزم قدام
ملك الحفون فعند ذلك تستأمن اليه كقوله ותנתן היא ומביאיה והילדה ✦ فقوله תנתן
היא يقصد الى الجند ✦ وقوله ומביאיה يشير الى نقباء العسكر ✦ وقوله והילדה يشير
15 الى مدبّر العسكر الذى انصبه ملك النحب يدبّر العسكر وسار معه لان الملك نفسه لم
يجى مع العسكر وذلك لاحد حالين اما لانه حقر ملك الحفون 2وبان عنده ان عسكره
يهلك ملك الحفون او يكون ايضا فزع اذا خرج عن بلده تضطرب عليه احواله فلم يبرح
من مكانه ✦ وقوله ומחזיקה בעתים يشير الى قوم كانوا فى جملة هذا العسكر على
سبيل المعونة لهم ولم يكونوا فى الاصل من عسكره 3لكن كان يستعين بهم بمال
20 يدفعه اليهم فكان اذا احتاج اليهم يخرجون فى عسكره ثم يرجعون الى مكانهم
فلذلك قال ومחזיקה בעתים ✦

٧ ويقف من عرق سنوخها على كرسيّه ويجى الجيش ويدخل
فى محصن ملك الحفون ويعمل فيهم ويقوى ✦

٨ وايضا معبودانهم مع الات تمتّيهم 4فضّة ونهب° بالسبى يدخل
25 مصرا وهو سنين يثبت من ملك الحفون ✦

---

1 הצפון D K X.   2 וכאן codd.   3 לבן D P; לאן cett.   4 Om. P X.

عرّف انه لم يكن لملك הננב قوّة بقاوم ملك הצפון بل مات على انكساره ¹وذلك فصل ١١
فبعد ان انصرف قام [بدلك] ²ملك في مكانه كقوله כנו ٭ وفي قوله מנצר שרשיה فاسوق ٨
يدلّ (على) انه لم يكن ولده لكن كان من ذرّيّة الملك من بني عمّه وكان رجل
جبّار فقاد العساكر وجاء معه خوفا من ان يلحق عسكره كما لحق العسكر الاوّل ٭
وقوله ויבא אל החיל يعني يجي [العسكر] الى العسكر الذي استأمن الى ملك הצפון ٥
فكما يرونه قد وافى يرجعون اليه وعند ذلك يتقوّى ويجيء الى المدن للحصينة الذي
لملك הצפון وخاصّة مدينة الملك ٭ وقوله ועשה בהם يريد يعمل فيهم ملحمة ويتقوّى
عليهم فيقتل قوم منهم اعني من اصحاب للحرب ٭ ثم عرّف انه ياخذ معبوداتهم حنقا
عليهم من جنس فعل ملك اشور بعدلي ישראל كقوله גם אתו לאשור יובל ٭ وقوله הוש
نسيحيهم هم رؤساء الملك وامراوه ٭ ولم يقع الملك بيده اما ان يكون هرب على رأي ١٠
قوم واما ان يكون راسله واستجاب الى ان يطيعه فيعطيه ما اراده الملك المتقدّم كما
شرحنا في قوله לעשות מישרים وهو القريب في نفسي لكن لم يرض ملك הננב ³من
ملك הצפון بذلك الا بعد ان اخذ معبوداتهم مع سائر ذخائرهم حتى لا يبقى لهم حال
بل يبقى ملك הצפون ضعيفا جدّا فعند ذلك يضطرّ الى ⁴اوّل الطاعة لملك הננב
كقوله بعده ١٥

٩ ويدخل تحت ملك ملك הננב وحينئنٍ يرجع الى ارضه ٭

يعني يدخل ملك הצפון تحت طاعة ملك הננב وبعد ذلك يرجع ملك הננב الى ادمته ٭
وقوله והוא שנים יעמד يريد يبقى هو بعد موت ملك הצפון مثل قوله אך אם יום או שמו כא. כא
יומים يريد به يبقى حتى فكانّه ملك הננב الاوّل يموت وملك הצפון حتّى ثم يموت
ذلك ملك הצפון في حياة ملك הננב الثاني فيموت ذليل مؤدّي طاعة لملك הננב ٭ ٢٠

١٠ وبنيه يتحرّشون ويحشرون جمهور عساكر كبار ويجيء مجى
ويجرف ويجوز ويرجع ويتحرّش الى محصنه ٭

١١ ويتنرّر ملك הננב ويخرج ويتحارب معه مع ملك הצפון
ويوقف جمهور عسكر كبير ويسلّم الجمهور بيده ٭

فصل ۱۱ ‏ ۱۲ ويحمل العسكر ويرتفع قلبه ويلقى (او يطرح) الربوات ولا

فاسوق ۱۲ ‏ يتحصّن احد ٠

قد بان ان ملك الجنوب الاوّل كان اوّل امره قوىّ ثم اندقّ وانّ ملك الצפון كان اوّل

امره ضعيف ثم تقوّى على ملك الجنوب ثم يرجع يذلّ بيد ملك الجنوب ويموت على

5 مثل ذلك فاوّله ضعيف واخره ضعيف ٠ ثم عرّف ان بعد موته يقوم اولاده بعده على

الملك ولم يذكر عددها لكنهم كانوا امراء وتحت يد كل واحد منهم عساكر وكان الواحد

منهم اكبر حال والباقون تحت يده فقالوا نعمل كما عمل ملك الجنوب الثانى وناخذ

ثار ابينا منه فاجتمع رأيهم كلهم على ذلك ٠ وقال יתגרו ولم يقل بماذا يتحرّرشون

فالذى يلوح فيه هو انهم راسلوه بترك ما كان اخذه من ابيهم من البلدان او يخرج

10 شى مما رسمه عليه فلم يجيبهم الى ذلك فعندها جمعوا عساكر واخذوا يدخلون

بلد بلد من ملك الجنوب وملك الجنوب لم يبرح من مكانه خوفا منهم ٠ وقال اوّلا ובניו

יתגרו ليعرّف ان كلهم راسلوا מלך הנגב ثم قال ובא ובא ושטף يشير الى واحد الاجلّ

فيهم ٠ وقوله וישב ויתגרו يدلّ على انه اوّلا اخذ بلدان من מלך הנגב وحصلت له

ولم يستجرى ان يجى الى مدينة מלך הנגב فلما راى ان מלך הנגב لم يتحرّك من موضعه

15 استجرى وغزاه الى مدينة ملكه فلذلك قال וישב ויתגרה עד מעזה ٠ فعند ذلك اضطّر

ملك الجنوب الى الخروج اليه ٠ وقوله ונלחם עמו ثم قال עם מלך הצפון يقرب فيه انه

قصد اوّلا العساكر ثم قصد الملك نفسه فلما راى انه قصده اوقف فى وجهه عسكر خشن

حتى يصدّون عنه ولعلهم ان يظفرون بملك الجنوب فعند ذلك يتسلّم מלך הנגב ذلك

العسكر الخشن الذى اوقف מלך הצפון ويكبر قلب מלך הנגب وينهزم מלך הצפון بنفسه

20 ويعود الى بلده ٠ وقوله והפיל רבאות كانه اخذ من عسكر מלך הצפון ما اراده وقتل

عالم من الناس من العساكر وغيرها ٠ وقوله ולא יעוז يعنى لا يكون لاحد ثبات قدامه

بل الكل ينخذلون بين يديه ثم تمرّ له مدّة طويلة على مثل ذلك ويقرب عندى ان

هذا ملك الجنوب هو الذى احرق القدس واجلى امّتنا ومن ذلك الوقت تقوّوا الروم وغلبت

دولتهم وصارت حيوانة كبيرة عظيمة كقوله عنها דחיلא وينبغى ان تعلم ان هذه

25 الحروب المذكورة جرت فى سنين كثيرة نحو [1]مايتى سنه فليس ذلك مقول فى اشخاص

وانما هو مقول فى الملك ٠

---

[1] X. מאתי

Line 3. قوّيّا.   4. ضعيفا.   10. يجّبهم.   11. بلدا etc.   17. عسكرا etc.

18. يصدّوا.   21. عالما.   25. مقولا.

١٣ ثم يرجع ملك الڅقون ويوقف جمهور عساكر اكثر من العساكر فصل ١١
الاولى ولانقضاء الاوقات سنين يجى مجى بجيش كبير وبسرح فاسوق ١٣
عظيم ٠

تقرب ان هذا ملك الڅقون غير المنهزم وعرّف انه يحشر عساكر اكثر من
العساكر المتقدّمة التي تسلّمها ملك الننب ٠ وقوله ولقض العتمم سنمم ولم يقل ولقض ٥
سنين يشير به الى قول شبوعيم شبعيم نحتك على عمك وعل عير كدشك او يكون اراد به
بعد انقضاء سنين جرت بينهم موافقة بعد الهزيمة وكانوا ١يدون طاعة الى ملك
الننب لقوّته وبعد انقضاء هذه المدّة يحشر ملك الڅقون هذه العساكر ويقصد ملك الننب كما
سنذكر ذلك فى ما بعد ٠

١٤ وفى ²تلك الاوقات كثيرين يقفون على ملك الننب وبنى مثغرى ١٠
قومك يرتفعون لتثبيت الوحى وينعثرون ٠

قال فى الفاسوق المتقدّم ولقض العتمم سنمم فرجع يعرّف ان فى تلك الاوقات تكبر
حال ملك الننب فتلتقّ اليه عساكر كبار ويذلّ ملك الڅقون ٠ وقوله وبنى فريصى عمك
قيل انه يشير الى اصحاب يشوَ الذى تقول النصارى انه المسيح وهم الذى عملوا
الانجيل واسماؤهم معروفة الواحد متاى الشرطىّ الثانى مرقس صيّاد السمك والثالث ١٥
لوقا الطبيب تلميذ ³فولس ابا شاؤول الرابع يوحنا قرابة يشوع وهو الذى تولّى ⁴من
يشوَ ما تولّى فاليهم يشير بقوله وبنى فريصى عمك لانهم اثغروا الدين ولا شكّ فى ان
عالم من يسرائيل تنصّروا معهم ٠ وقوله ينشاو هو انه صار لهم محلّ كبير عظيم
وذكر كبير ٠ وقوله لهعميد ونو' عرّف ان كان قصدهم ليثبتوا ليشوع الحزن ⁵كما هو
مشهور من ⁶دعواهم فى اناجيلهم واخبارهم ٠ وقوله ونكشلا ان كان اشار به الى ٢٠
اصحاب يشوع المراد به خروجهم عن دين يسرائيل وان كان اشار به الى الامّة لقوله
عمك فاراد سقوط يسرائيل بعد ذلك لانهم صاروا مطالبين بقتل الله فكم قتل من
يسرائيل ⁷من ذلك الوقت والى ان يفرج الله تقع عن امّته فلذلك قال ونكشلا قال فعرّف
ان هلك يسرائيل منهم وبهم ٠ فاوّلا اهلكونا ملوكنا وانبياوَنا الكذّابين فهم كانوا

فصل ۱۱ سبب زوال دولتنا وجاليتنا وهؤلاء سبب هلاكنا طول لجالوث ونزول البلاء بنا ‏¹ولذلك فاسوق ۱۴ تاوّل قوم منا فى اوّل ملك كرن זעירא فاملكونا ✦

۱۵ ويجىى ملك הצפון ويصبّ الحسك ويشتّص مدينة الملك وانزعة [ال]ملك הנגב لا يثبتون وقوم مختاريه وليس قوّة ٥ للثبات ٥

بعد ان ادخل فى الوسط خبر يشوע واصحابه وما يجرى علينا منهم رجع يتمّم ما كان من ملك הצפון عند ما حشر تلك العساكر فيجب ان نلحق قوله ויבא ملك הצפון بقوله فى الفاسوق المتقدّم יבוא בוא בחיל גדול ✦ فعرف ان ملك הצפון يجى الى بلد الروم وبحاصر مدينة الملك وياخذها لقوله ولכד عیر مبצرות قيل انها مدينة قסطנطنيا ٥ ۱۰ وقوله זרועות הנגב ונו' [و]هم المقول فيهم רבים יעמדו על מ' הנ' وهم عساكر كبار التقت لمלך הנגב وعضدته ✦ ثم قال ועם מבחריו وهم عساكر كانت له خاصّة ثقاته فلا يقفوا هؤلاء ايضا قدام ملك הצפון فيقتل عالم من عساكر ملك הנגב ويستأمن عالم الى ملك הצפון من عسكر ملك הנגב ويعضدوه كقوله بعده

۱۶ ويعمل الجاى البه كرضائه وليس من يثبت قدامه ويثبت فى ۱۵ ارض السرّاء ويفنى ببيه ٥

قوله ויעש ونו' يشير الى من يجيه من عند ملك הנגב وهم قوم جبابرة اجلّاء فعرّف انهم يعملون ما يريده ملك הצפון ويفتحون له ابواب ‏²ويعملها فى عمل الروم فعند ذلك لا يثبت احد قدامه من بلدان ملك הנגב ويكون فى ذلك الوقت قد انبسطت الروم فى بلد يسرائيل وملكوها وخاصّة بلد بيت المقدس ويكون لهم فيها عساكر كبار ۲۰ فيقصدهم ملك הצפون ومعه عساكره ويقيم فى ارض يسرائيل مدّة طويلة كقوله ויעמד בארץ הצבי ويقتل عالم من الروم كقوله וכלה בידו ٥

۱۷ ويجعل للدخول بصلابة كل ملكه والمستقبمبين معه ويعمل وبنت النساء يعطيه لافسادها ولا تثبت ولا له تكون ٥

عرّف ان ملك הצפون يقصد بلدان ملك הנגב القوّية بالرجال الحصينة ٥ قوله ויشרים

فصل ١١ عما قيل ان قوم من يسرائيل يكونون معه كتّاب وغير ذلك فيعرّفوه ما هو مكتوب
١٧ فاسوق من اقباله فيثق بقولهم ويعمل عليه كقوله ועשה ۞ وقوله ובת נשים וג' قيل انه يشير
به الى بيت المقدّس فعرّف انه يخرب مواضع للروم بيع لعبادتهم وموضع كرسيّ
يكون لهم ولعل الله تعّ يمكنه من ملك الندب ويعمل به هذه الاعمال من اجل
٥ ما عمل ملك الندب فى البيت الثانى وما عمله بيسرائيل فكان ذلك بعض العزّاء
لامّته ۞ ثم عرّف انه لا يقيم بالشام فتبقى له على اسمه بل ينصرف عنها الى
موضع اخر فيثبتوا فيها الروم على ما كانوا كقوله ולא יעמד וג' ۞

١٨ ويجعل وجهه الى جزائر ويشنص كثيرين ويعطل هذا الامير
معيرته غير ان معيرته يرق الىه ۞

١٠ عرّف انه يقصد للجزائر التى كانت لملك الندب ۞ لعله يشير الى ١بلد الثغار ٢وهم
طرسوس وقبروس وغيرها فيفتحها ويقتل ويغنم وليس قصده المقام فى عمل الندب
وانما قصده ان يستوفى حقّ ما عمله به ملك الندب وكان ملك الندب يعيّر ملك
الصفون بما عمل به عند ما غزاه الى عير مصوّاو فاذا عمل ملك الصفون هذه الاعمال
بملك الندب فعند ذلك تزول معيرة ملك الندب عن ملك الصفون كقوله והשבית קצין
١٥ حرفته هذا القصّ هو ملك الصفون ۞ ثم قال بلتى حرفته يعنى ومع ما انه عطل
المعيرة عنه رجع يعيّر ملك الندب وذلك ان ملك الندب الذى احرق بيت المقدّس لم يغزُ
ملك الصفون وانما عند ما غزاه ملك الصفون عمل ما عمل بعسكر ملك الصفون فاما هذا
فانه غزاه الى مدينته وقتل فى عسكره وفتح بلدان كثيرة وقتل فيهنّ فعمل ملك الصفون
بملك الندب اعظم من فعل ملك الندب به فلذلك قال بلتى حرفته ישיב לו ۞ ٣فهذا
٢٠ ٤شرح ما جرى بين ملك الصفون وملك الندب وهى ثلث دفعات الوقعة الاولى غزت عساكر
ملك الندب الى ملك الصفون [وظفرت به] ٥والثانية غزا ملك ٥الندب الى ملك ٥الصفون
۞ ۞ ۞ ۞ ۞ ۞ ۞ فكانت عليه ۞ فحصلت الوقعة الاولى والثانية لملك
الندب على ملك الصفون والثالثة لملك الصفون على ملك الندب فقد حصل لملك الندب
دفعتين وواحدة لملك الصفون وهذه الثلث وقعات كانت فى مدّة طويلة نيّف على
٢٥ شّ سنة كما شرحنا فى ما تقدّم وكان كرسيّ ملك الصفون فى عمل بغداذ وهذا اخر
حرب جرى بين هذين الملكين ۞

---

١ Perh. بلاد. ٢ وهم om. X; קברס, טרסוס codd. ٣ פהדה codd. ٤ שרח P only;
שרוח cett. ٥ الندب الصفون and transposed in D X.

فصل ۱۱
فاسوق ۱۹
۱۹ ويرّد وجهه الى حصون ارضه ويعثر ويسقط ولا يوجد ۰

عرف انه بعد ان يعمل هذه الاعمال يعود الى بغداذ التى هى كرسىّ ملكه وعند ذلك ينعثر فى موضع كرسيّه فيمكن ان يكون [ان] بعض حاشيته يقتله وبخفى امره ولم يعلم به كقوله ונכשל ונפל וג' ۰

۲۰ ويقف على مركزه مجيز المقتضى المقتضى بهجة الملك ونحو ايّام احاد يعطب ولا بملاقاة ولا بحرب ۰

اذا قال على كنه المراد به انه يجلس الثانى فى مكان المتقدّم واذا لم يقل على كنه يكون فى موضع اخر فعرّف انه يجلس فى مكانه اخر ليس له جبروة ولا فتوح ولا حرب ووصف من احوال شيّين احدهما מעביר נוגש والثانى הדר מלכות فاما מעביר נוגש فقال فيه بعض العلماء انه دفع للخراج عن الناس فلم يكون على الناس منه كلفة مشقّة ولا مونة وزعم بعض العلماء ان من اخباره انه كان يلزم الناس غلق ابوابهم من نصف النهار وينصرف الناس الى الاكل والشرب ومن كان ضعيف فله جراية من مائدة السلطان فينقضى الزمان فى اكل وفى شرب وفرح وسرور ولباس جيّد بهتّ فلذلك قال הדר מלכות ۰ وعرّف ان ليس تطول مدّته كقوله ובימים אחדים عرّف انه يعطب بغير ملاقاة ولا حرب وحكا من يعرف هذه الامور ان العرب كبست الموضع وكان الناس فى اكل وشرب فكبسوا الملك وقتلوه وهو اخر ملك للماجوس ببغداذ ومنهم تسلّمت ملوك العرب الى يومنا هذا ۰

۲۱ ويقف على مركزه حقير ولا يجعلوا عليه بهاء ملك ويجى بعلو ويبسّط الملك بالملاسات ۰

۲۲ وعساكر الجرف ينجرفوا من قدّامه وينكسروا وايضا خليفة العهد ۰

قال نذزه هو ان كل ملك قام من هؤلاء الممالك كان له قومة ودمائة الا هذا فان لم يكن له مقدار واخباره واخباره معروفة فليس نحتاج نبسطها ۰ وقوله ובא בשלוה يعنى يدخل بلد بلد بغير حرب وبغير حمار كما فعل غيره ممن تقدّم ۰ وقوله והחזיק מלכות בחלקלקות هو ما ادّعى من الحزن وسائر ما ذكره فى الحلام من قوله ופם ממלل רברבן ומלין לצד ¹وقوله فى تفسير الحزن ומבין חידות ۰ وقوله וזרעות השטף

---

¹ כקי' codd.

هي عساكر كبار الذي למלך הצפון وعساكر الروم ايضا فعرّف انهم ينهزمون من قدامه   فصل ١١ וינכסרו ✦ وقوله وعم נגיד ברית قيل انه صاحب الروم كقوله והעיר והקדש פاسوق ٢٢ ישחית עם נגיד הבא وقيل فيه נגיד ברית من حيث انه كان عاهد יسرائيل كقوله והגביר ברית לרבים שבוע אחד وقيل انه قصد به الى ملوك בני ישראל الذي ذلّوا بني דוד تحت يدهم ✦

5

٢٣ ومن التصاحب البه يعمل مكر ويعلو ويعظم بقليل من الناس ✦

قيل ان القصد بقوله ומן התחברות אליו يشير الى صاحب الرجل איש הרוח وهو עמر واحد من العشرة فعرّف انه يعشه مرمة مع يسرائيل وغيرهم [1]واخباره مشروحة مشهورة فعرّف انه يعلو ويعظم بيسير من الناس معه ✦

٢٤ بسلو وبسمان المدينة يدخل ويعمل ما لم يعملوا اباوه ولا اباء ١٠ ابائه النهب والسلب والسرح لهم يبنر وعلى الحصون يدبّر تدبيرات والى وقت ✦

قال في ما تقدّم ובא בשלוה وذلك مقول في איש הרוח وهذا مقول في هذا المذكور ✦ وقوله ובמשמני מדינה [و]هى المدن الكبار التى فيها ارباب النعم ✦ وقوله ועשה אשר לא עשו ונ׳ يشير الى الفتح والقتل وعرّف انه لم يكن لقدمائه شى مما وصل اليه ✦ ١٥ ثم قال בזה ושלל ורכוש להם יבזור وهو انه كان يقنع بالغذاء اليسير والثوب الحقير والمركوب الدنيّ ✦ واذا فتح البلدان ونهبها حصّلها كلها للجهاد ولا يأخذ لنفسه منها شىء لذلك قال בזה ושלל ורכוש להם יבזור ✦ قوله בזה (اما ان) يشير به الى الناس فانه كان يسبى منهم واما انه يشير به الى الجواهر والآلات الرفيعة ✦ وقوله [2]ושלל הثياب ورכوש بهائم مركوبة وابقار وغنم ✦ وقوله ועל מבצרים ونّ قصد به الى ٢٠ حصون في عمل العراق كانت لملك الצفون [3]فتحها بحيّل وتدبير كقوله יחשב מחש׳ وقوله ועד עת يريد به وقت نهاية امره في اقباله فاذا جاء وقت ادباره انعكست احواله ✦

٢٥ ويثور قوّته وقلبه على ملك الننب بجيش كبير وملك الننب

---

[1] ואכבארהם codd.   [2] ושלל ישיר בה אלי אלת׳ P.   [3] פפתחוהא codd.

فصل ١١
فاسوق ٢٥
‏يتحرش للحرب بجيش كبير وعظيم جدّا ولا يثبت ان يدبّرون
علیه تدبيران ٭

‏وآكلى طعامه يكسروه وجيشه يجرف ويقعون قتلَى كثيرين ٭

قوله ויער כחו ולבבו هو انه لم يعدّ ملك الننب شى وهو مع ذلك النفر اليسير الذى
كان معه فى مبادئ امره الذى قيل فيهم במעט ונו' فكان كل وقت يسلّمون قوم بعد
قوم فكثر عسكره ٭ فهذه الوقعة كانت بين عمر ابن خطاب والروم الذين كانوا
فى الشام فذكر بعض العلماء انه دخل عمر الى بيت المقدّس فاستعدّ ملك الروم
لمحاربته وانفضوا للحرب فى مرج عمواس بقرب بيت المقدّس فذكر لعمر عسكر كبير
كقوله בחיל גדול ولذلك لقيه מלך הננב הם بعسكر عظيم لكن عسكر الروم كان اكثر
من عسكر الاسلام لانه زاد عليه ²لقوله ועצום עד מאד ٭ وقال ולא יעמד يشير الى
عسكر מלך הננב كانه انهزم عند ما التقى للحرب ٭ وقوله כי יחשב يشير الى عسكره
عند ما راى اقبال صاحب الاسلام غدروا بملك الننب حتى ان غلمانه للخاصة التى
³جرايته عليهم° من مائدته هم اعطوه اذ لم ينصحوه بالحرب ٭ فعند ذلك تمكّن
الاسلام من الروم وقتل منهم خلق عظيم كقوله ונפלו חללים فعند ذلك تسلّم ארץ
ישראל صاحب الاسلام من الروم الى يومنا هذا ٭

‏وكلى الملكين قلبهم الى الاسابة وعلى اخوان واحد يتنكلّمون
بالكنب ولا ينبح ان قد بقى انقضاء الى الوقت ٭

قال فى ما تقدّم ולא נתנו עליו ונו' فمهما لم ياخذ بيت المقدّس من الروم لم
يسمّيه لهم ملك وعند ما تسلّموا بيت المقدّس سمّاه ملك ٭ فقوله ושניהם המלכים
الواحد للعرب والاخر للروم ٭ وقوله לבבם למרע يعنى [يكون] ⁴يسون الى يسرائيل كل
واحد منهم على ضرب على ما هو ظاهر من الاسلام ومن النصارى ٭ وقوله ועל שלחן
אחד قيل انه يشير به الى يسرائيل وسمّاهم שלחן אחד בحيث ان אדום ريشمعال كل
واحد منهم ياكل طعام الاخر ٭ وقال دانيال فى تفسير منام نبوخذناصر מתערבين
בזרע אנשא كما شرحنا معناها فعرّف ثم اختلاطهم فى الزبجة وكذلك هم مختلطين

---

¹ B. ינרד.   ² Perh. بقوله.   ³ Perh. جرايتهم عليه.   ⁴ P; יאסון X; יסן
יכון (only) B K.

Line 16. وكلا.

فى باب الماكل كقوله فى الجميع המתקרשים והמטהרים אל הגנות فالمتكرسيم هم   **فصل ١١**
הערלים لانهم يدّعون القدوسيّة اذ يقولون فلان القديس ووقت التقديس قد جاء   **فاسوق ٢٧**
ولهم قرابين ويدّعون ان لهم كهنة قديسين وماء المعموديّة ولذلك لا يستحمّون من   ——
الجنابة ✤ فاما الاسلام فليس يرون ذلك بل يستحمّون من الجنابة ولذلك سمّاهم   يشׁעׁ سـ. יׁ
مطهرين ✤ فالערלים يستعملون لفظة קדושה وهؤلاء يستعملون لفظة טהרה وقوله אל   5
הגנות يشير به الى دعوا كل واحد منهم [كتاب وصاحب و]انّ لهم للجتّة كما هو
مذكور فى كتابهم ويقولون ✤ وقوله אחר אחד בתוך يريد به ان كلهم اتّفقوا على
ان التورا قد نسخت وان شرع اخر ورد بعده وانه دين ليس ينسخ بغيره ✤ فلما
قام الاسلام قالوا فى التورا مثل ما قال النصارى وقالوا ان كتاب صاحبهم قد نسخ
دين النصارى بغيره ✤ ثم عرّف ان המתקרשים هم اكلين لحم الخنزير وعرّف ان   10
المطهرين هم אוכלי שקץ ועכבר ومع ان الاسلام تحرّم لحم الخنزير فليس يجتنبون
اكل طعام الערלים فهم ياكلون على مائدة واحدة ويسرائيل مائدة واحدة اذ لا ياكلون
لحم خنزير ولا שקץ ولا עכבر فقوله ועל שלחן אחד هم يسرائيل من هذا الوجه ✤ وان
قلنا ان שלחן אחد يفيد شيئين (ف)احدهما انهم يجلسون على שלחן אחد والثانى
انهم [1]يكذبون على الله تعّ وعلى امّته ✤ وقوله ولא תצלח يشير الى يسرائيل يعنى   15
ولا تنجح لهم حال جل يكونون [2]مدابير مخاذيل فلذلك قال ולא תצלח ✤ وقوله כי
עוד קץ למועד يعنى مهما قد بقى الى كى קץ מלכיות الى ان تنقضى فحينئذ [3]يخذل يدبر
ادوم ويشمعال وينجحون يسرائيل ✤ واعلم ان هذا الفاسوق يخدم هذه المدّة
الطويلة منذ ظهر الاسلام الى اخر للجالوث ✤

٢٨ ويرجع الى ارضه بسرح عظيم وقلبه على عهد القدس ويعمل   20
ويرجع الى ارضه ✤

رجع يتمّم ما تقدّم ذكره فى الفاسوق المتقدّم وهو انه ذكر فى الفاسوق المتقدّم ما
ينزل بملך הגנב من العطب والقتل فعرّف ان صاحب الاسلام يرجع الى الموضع
الذى كان مقامه فيه قيل انه كان مقامه بدمشق فرجع الى ثم بسرح عظيم غُنم
من عسكر ملك הגנב ✤ وقوله ولבבו يعنى قلبه على اذاء يسرائيل كقوله فى الفاسوق   25
المتقدّم لבدم למرע وكذى يحكى ان كان هذا الرجل شديد العداوة ليسرائيل اعنى

---

[1] יכדל only B D K X; يخرجون=יכרנון ; יכדבון P.   [2] מדברין P.   [3] ידבר
only P.

فصل ۱۱ عمر بن لخطاب ۞ وقوله ועשה يعني يعمل مراده فى يسرائيل برسوم رسمها عليهم
فاسوق ۲۸ وهم اليهود المقيمين ببيت المقدس وبعد ذلك يعود الى بلده ۞ وهذه وقعة جرت
على ملك الجنب عند بيت المقدّس ۞ ثم قال

۲۹ للوقت يرجع ويدخل فى الجنب ولا يكون مثل ۱الاولى ولا
۵ مثل الاخيرة ۞

الى هذا الفاسوق انتهى ذكر ما جرى فى مبادئ ملك يشمعال ومن هذا الفاسوق
يذكر ما يكون فى اخر امرهم ۞ وذلك انه قال فى الفاسوق المتقدّم كי עוד קץ למועד
فعرّف ان اذا جاء המועד وبلغ الى اخر امره ישוב يعنى يرجع يدخل فى الجنب وهو
انه يدخل فى عمل الروم وهذا قد ابتدى من سنين فى ناحية الغرب وهو (ان)
۱۰ ملك مערب الذى هو الان ملك مصر بعث عساكر الى عمل الروم ۞ وقوله ولא תהיה
כראשונה ונו׳ يشير به الى ما كان فى اول ظهور ملكه فاوّلا هو ما كسر ثلث كراسى
كما تقدّم الشرح فى ותلת עליون وايضا فى ما قاله فى ما تقدّم ויער כחו ונו׳ فالى
هذا يشير بقوله ولא תהיה כראשונה ۞ ۲وقوله וכאחרנה يشير الى ما سنذكره فى
تفسير ובעת קץ יתגנח עמו فالاولى كانت كلها لصاحب يشمعال يشير على ملך הנגב
۱۵ والاخيرة تكون كلها لملך הנגב على يشمعال وهذه الوقعة المتوسّطة ليس تكون لا
مثل المتقدّمة ولا مثل الاخيرة بل تكون على حالة متوسّطة تجرى بينهم فلذلك
قال ولא תהיה כראשונה וכאחרונה ۞

۳۰ ويدخلون فيه مغازبيين وقبرسيين وينكسر ويرجع ويزغم على
عهد القدس ويعمل ويرجع ويفظن على تاركى عهد القدس ۞

۲۰ يمكن ان يكون قوله يבאו בו ציים هو دخولهم فى دينه وبتجد ان يكون اراد به
دخول تحت الطاعة لا دخول فى الدين ۞ وقوله ונכאה ليس عاطف عليه وانما هو
عاطف على الناس وعلى البلدان يعنى ينكسر كل واحد منهم بين يديه ۞ وقوله
חעם על [עזבי] ברית קדש فيه معنى فهو ان هذا الملك المذكور كان اوّل امره قصد
يسرائيل بالاذاء ثم تركهم واخر الامر يعود عليهم وهذا باب لم ينتظر بعد ۞

---

۱ אלאולה codd. (as frequently; cp. FLEISCHER, *Kl. Schr.* i. 337). ۲ Om. P X.

Line 21. عاطفا.

وقوله ٱשב ويبن ونו' يشير الى قوم من يسرائيل تركوا دين يسرائيل ودخلوا فى دينه **فصل ١١**
فيحسن اليهم فدلّ قوله هذا على انه يطالب بترك الدين فقوم يثبتوا على دين **فاسوق ٣٠**
يسرائيل فيزغم عليهم وقوم يتركوا ويدخلوا فى دينه فيحسن اليهم فسنبيّن ذلك ____
فى اخر الفصل [على ما يبين ذلك فى موضعه] ۰

٣١ وانزعة منه يقفون ويبدلوا المقدس الحصين ويزيلون الدائم ٥
ويجعلون الرجس مستوحش ۰

عرّف انه يحارب اوّلا ملك هنند كقوله لمועד يשوב ثم عرّف حال يسرائيل معه
ثم رجع يعرّف ما يعمله بامّته كقوله וזרעים ممنو هى عساكر تنفذ الى بيت عبادتهم
وتعمل هذه الاشياء احدها وחללו المقدس المنع وهو الذى تقدم ذكره فى الحزن
كقوله והשליך مكن مקدשו ثم قال והשליך وقال ههنا وחללו المقدس فقوله והשליך يريد ١٠
به انه يخربه ويلقيه الى الارض وחללו يريد به انه يطرح فيه القتلى ويصير مثل
المزابل ومواضع القذر ۰ وقوله והסירו התמיד يريد به انهم يبطلون الحجّ وان لا يحجّ
الناس بعد ذلك ولا يصلّوا على رسمهم ولا يضحوا على رسومهم وقوله התמיד لانه كان فى
الستّة كان دائما لا يفترون عن الحجّ وهو مثل قوله فى الفصل المتقدم وممنو هورم
התמיד وزاد ههنا ونتنو השקוץ משמם ويقرب فيه انه يريد الצלמים التى فى البيت ١٥
דבר' כ'ט ٠ ١٦ م"א ٠ ١٤ ٠ ח
مثل وتراوا את שקוציהם ومثل ولכמוש שקוץ מואב وهذه الצלמים كانت قديمة لم
يمكنه يزيلها فى قديم الزمان فازالها فى هذا الوقت والى هذا المعنى يشير بقوله יוי
תהל' ٠ ٠ ٢٠
בעיר צלמם תבזה واعلم ان فى الحزن ذكر اشياء مجملة فجاء ههنا فصّلها شى شى
فقوله الان ونتنو השקוץ משמם ان كان على نفس الצלה فيكون الغرض فيه هو انه
يبقى ملقى بعد ما كان عزيز ١مصون وان ردّدناه الى موضعه فيكون الغرض فيه كون ٢٠
الموضع مستوحش خراب لا يقربه احد وقد ذكر سيد يشعياهو عمّ فى صلاته بقوله
ارمان ٢זרים מעיר לעולם לא יבנה فهذا הארמון هو البيت وقوله זרים اذ فيه צלמים **כה ٠ ב**
وقوله לעולם לא יבנה من حيث انه قد خرب ولا يبنى ابدا والدهر وان ردّدناه الى
القائلين به فيكون الغرض فيه انهم يحزنون ممّا قد نزل بقدسهم كما قد حزن
يسرائيل عند ما نزل بهم البلاء وخرب قدسهم ۰
٢٥

---

۳۲ ومظلمین العهد یدلس بالملاسات وشعب عارفی الالاه یشتدوا
ویعملوا ❖

رجع الی قوله ושב ויבן על עזבי ונו' فهذا زیادة فی شرحه فعرّف انه ¹یدلسهم
بکلام سلس لیّن وهو ²انه یخرج قوم من امّتنا لضرب من ضروب امور الدنیا ویجی
۵ الی فواسیق فی המקרא مقولة علی المسیح یوجهونها الی صاحب الوقت ویفسّرونها
علیه ³ویتاوّل السبت والعید فیهلکوا ویخرجوا من الدین فقال فیهم ومرشیعی ברית
من حیث انهم یظلمون ویخرجون من עול התורה وعهود یسرائیل ❖ وقوله ⁴ועם
יודעי אלהיו יחזיקו ועשו یشیر الی قوم من یسرائیل یقفون علی مذهب صاحب الوقت
وانه لم سرّ لا یقفوا علیه کثیر من یسرائیل فهلکوا وقوم هم علماء یفتّشوا علی
۱۰ دینه ویروا انه فاسد ویشتدّوا بالתورה ویعملوا بها ولا یخرجوا عن دین یسرائیل کما
خرج غیرهم وهذا قد بدا فی جهة الغرب مذ سنین کثیرة وخرج کثیر من یسرائیل
عن الدین وقالوا بقوله وهذا مشهور وقال علی الذی لم یخرجوا عن الدین ועם
יודעי אלהיו יחזיקו ועשו ❖

۳۳ ومرشدی الشعب یفهموا للکثیرین وینعثرون بالسیف وبسبی
۱۵ وباللهیب ونهب ایّام ❖

هؤلاء המשכילים هم יודעי אלהיו ❖ وقوله ויבינו לרבים یفهمون خلق کثیر من
یسرائیل مذهب ویقوّوا ایدیهم بدین الله فلا یخرجون من الدین فاذا رآهم لا یدخلون
فی دینه اشتدّ غضبه علیهم کما فعل بُختناصر ﺑﺤﻨﻨﻴﺎ میسائیل وعزریا وطرحهم فی اتون
النار وکذلك یعمل هذا بیسرائیل فقوم یقتلهم بالسیف وبعضهم بالنار کقوله בחרב
۲۰ ובלהבה وبعضهم بسبی ونهب رجالهم واثامهم ❖ ثم قال ימים وبیقرب انه مدّة سنة
واعلم انه قال ועם قال على עזבי ב' ק' قبل حروعیم ممنو یعمدو وقال بعده ומرשיעי ברית
لیعرّف انه تجری علی یسرائیل ضرّه قبل خراب البیت ⁵کقوله فی الاوّل ועם علی
עוزבי ברית قدس وقال ועשה ثم شرح ذلك فی هذا الفاسوق بחרב ובלהבה ❖ وقوله
ונכשלו یشیر به الی القوم الذی تبعوا המשכילים لان המשכילים ذکرهم فی الفاسوق
۲۵ الذی بعده ❖

---

¹ ידוסהם B K.   ² אנהם P X.   ³ Perh. ویتاوّلون.   ⁴ Om. till end of paragraph P X.   ⁵ וקו' codd.

٣٣ وعند انعثارهم ينصروا نصرة يسيرة وينعطفوا معهم كثيرين فصل ١١
بالملاسات ✧   فاسوق ٣٣

بعد ان قال ونكشلو بحرب وبلهبة قال بعد ذلك وبهكشلم يعزرو ولم يبيّن بما
ذا ينصروا فزعم بعض العلماء ان اللّه تعالى يقيم لهم מושיע مثل אסתר המלכה
وقيل انهم ينصروا بمعنى ان اللّه يبيد المتولّي اذاءهم ✧ وقوله ונלוו עליהם רבים 5
يمكن انه يشير به الى الذى [٠]משעו لان هذه اللفظة تقع على الدخول فى الدين
كقوله فى من دخل فى الدين وبنى נכר הנלוים על יי فعرّف ان مع ما ان اللّه ينصر ישע' נו. ו
هؤلاء المنعثرين بحرب وبلهبة هوذا ¹يدخلون كثيرين فى دين هذا الرجل وذلك بما
يستعمل معهم من الחלקלקות ✧ وهذا الחלקלקות هو نظير ما قاله فى ما تقدّم
ومحزيق מלכות בחלקלקות فكذلك هذا الثانى له חלקלקות يجذب بها الناس ١٠
الى دينه ✧

٣٥ ومن المرشدين ينعثروا لسبك بهم ولتنقية ولتتبيض الى وقت
انقضاء (او دهابة) ✧

ذكر اوّلا ما يعمل بتباع المعلمين من قوله ونكשלו ונו' ان اللّه يعضدهم ويلطف
فى بابهم ثم عرّف ما عرّف بالמשכילים فعرّف انهم ينعثروا ايضا ✧ وقوله ١٥
بالמשכילים לצרף ולברר ונו' ولم يقل ²مثله فى تباعهم من حيث ان التباع يلحقوا
المقدّمين فاذا راوا ان الמשכילים قد انعثروا استركّت ايديهم فان كان انعثار
الמשכילים بالسيف والحريق فيقولون اذا كان اللّه قد تعّ قد مكّن من المعلّمين فاى
شى نترجّى فتضعف يدهم اذ يقولون لو كان ديننا حق لم يمكّن اللّه تعّ من
معلّمينا كما لم يمكّن من حننيا מيסائيل وعزريا وان كان قال יכשלو بخروجهم ٢٠
عن الدين نظير قوله قوله ³תלמידה يשوע להעמיד חזון ونكשלו فانه اشدّ من القتل
اذ يقولون لو كان دين يשﻉ حق لم يخرجوا منه معلّمينا ولقد كانوا يثبتوا عليه
كما ثبت حننيا מيסائيل وعزريا ✧ فعند ذلك يكون السبك اذ يثبت من يثبت
ولا يغيّر ما يجرى على المعلّمين ومن لم تكن عقيدته جيّدة يخرج عن الدين
فلذلك قال לצרוף بهم ولברר وسنشرح معانى هذه الثلث الفاظ فى يثبררו ونو' ✧ ثم ٢٥

---

¹ ירסלון X.   ² מתלהם D X.   ³ תלמאדה D K.

فصل ۱۱ عرّف انه يجرى هذا عليهم وعلى المعلمين وقد بقى الى وقت نهاية الكم كما
فاسوق ۳۵ سنذكر ذلك فى ما بعد ♦

۳٦ ويعمل كرضائه هذا الملك ويرتفع ويتكبّر وينتكبّر وعلى كل ۱قادر وعلى
الاه الاشراف ينتكلّم بالعجائب وينجح الى وقت فراغ الزغم فان
۵ المنقطعة قد انفعلت ♦

۳۷ والى الاه ابائه لا يميّز وعلى شهوة الناس وعلى كل اله لا
يميّز بل على كل معبود ينتعظّم ♦

۳۸ ولالاه الاقوياء على مركزه يكرم ولالاه لم يعرفه ابائوه يكرم
بنهب وفضة وبجوهر عزيز وبالمتمنّاات ♦

۱۰ ۳۹ ويعمل لحصون الاقوياء مع الاه غريب الذى يثبت يكثر الوقار
ويسلّطهم بالكثيرين والادمة يقسم بالثمن ♦

قوله ועשה כרצונו يتّجه ان يكون قصد [به] الى ۲الملك باسره منذ قوّى حال
يشمعال الى اخر امره ۳في ذكر هذه العشرة اشياء التى [ذكرها] (اوّلها) (ועשה כרצונו
המלך) واخرها وادمه يحلق بمحبّ ويتّجه ان يكون يشير به الى صاحب هولاء
۱۵ הזרועים الذى بخرب المقدس ويبطل للحجّ فانّ القولين مستمرّدين ♦ الان قد تقدّم
ذكر ما يفعله فى اذوم وفى يسرائيل وفى המקדש ورجع الان يذكر جمل افعاله فقال
اوّل ועשה כרצונו وهذا يشبه ما قلناه فى الكبش والعتود اعنى ملك الفارس وملك
اليونانيّة وهو ان امره نافذ يعمل ما يريده وليس احد يقاومه فيما يريده ولا ۴يكبر
عليه وذلك لعظم حاله وانه يصل الى ما يريده ♦ ثم قال ויתרומם ויתגדל על כל אל
۲۰ اعلم انه ذكر فى هذا الفصل ستّة الاهات ۵الاول ויתרומם ויתגדל על כל אל والثانى
وعل אל אלים ידבר נפלאות والثالث ועל אלהי אבתיו לא יבן والرابع ועל כל אלוה
لا يبن والخامس ולאלוה מעוזים والسادس ולאלוה אשר לא ידעוהו אבתיו وليس
דבר.۳۰ من هذه الستّة الاه هو للخالق غير قوله ועל אל אלים ידבר נפלאות وذلك مثل قوله

---

۱ מעבוד X. כקו' אוולא ۲ מלך X. ۳ פדבר codd. P X. יכסר ۵
ויתגדל X.

فصل ١١ الثلاثة[1] ◦ وقيل فى الهى الالهيم والباقى يشير به الى معبودات هى غير ال الهيم
فاسوق ٣٩ منها انه لا يلتفت اليها ويتعاظم عليها واثنين منها يكرمهما وهو قوله ولالهاه
مَعُوزّيم عَل كَنو يَكبِّد ثم قال ولالوه اشر لا يَدعوهو اَبوتاو ولم يقل فى الخالق انه
يعبده او لا يعبده وانما قال يتكلم بالعجائب من جنس قوله فى ما تقدّم ومَلاح لَصَد
وَنو[ ] وقوله فى اَلوه مَعُوزّيم يَكبِّد ولم يقل يعبد وقال فى غير الخالق وغير هؤلاء ٥
المعبودين لا يبن فالذى يقرب فيه انه يظهر عبادة للخالق جل وعلا لكنه يتكلّم
فيه بما لا يجوز فان كان على الملك منذ ابتدى فهو مشروح من قولهم وما يعتقده
للجمهور منهم وان كان على هذا الاخير فاخبر عن مذهبه ايضا انه كذا يقول وقال فى
المعبودات الاخر كِى عَل كَل يِتنَدَّل وليس يريد به انه يتعظّم على المعبودات نفسها وانما
يريد به على عبادها والقائلين بها لانه يطعن على المذاهب (وقيل على اهلها)[2] ١٠
وقوله وعَل الهى اَبوتاو لا يَبِن يقصد به الى° مذاهب اَبائه الذين كانوا يعبدون
الاوثان ان كان ذلك على پَسول وان كان على الاخير فهو انه يبطل المذاهب التى
بيدهم ولذلك يخرب البيت ◦ وقوله وعَل حَمدَت نَشيم يريد به بيت المقدس التى
تعظّمها[3] الناس والامم° انه ابطل ان تكون القبلة بل يستدبرها ويستقبل الموضع الذى
يَحِجّون اليه وان كان على الملك الاخير فيكون المراد به البيت الذى يَحِجّون اليه ١٥
لانه يخرّبه. ويقرب ايضا فى تفسير وعَل حَمدَت نَشيم [يشير][4] انه معبود[5] صورة° ذكَ
لانه شهوة النساء الرجال للمتعة فتكون هذه الصورة فى قبلتهم ولذلك قال وعَل حَمدَت
نَ بعد وعَل الهى اَبوتاو وقبل وعَل كَل اَلوه ليدلّ على انه [فى] معبود خاصّ ◦
والمراد فى قوله يَبِن انه يلتفت اليه فذلك انه ذكر هذه اللفظة فى هذا الموضع ثلث
دفعات والمراد فيه معنى واحد فاوّلها يَشَب ويَبِن عَل عَزبِى ب ق ك والثانى (والثالث) ٢٠
فى هذا الفاسوق ◦ وقوله ولالهاه مَعُوزّيم اما ان يكون اسم معبود كما قال قوم انه
الات والعُزّى[6] فهذا مشهور معروف واما ان يكون° اسم غيرها ويتّجه ايضا ان يكون
قوله مَعُوزّيم يشير الى قوم اسمهم مَعُوزّيم وفيهم قال لمَبَصَرى مَعُوزّيم كانّه لهم معبود
ومذهب يرى ان يكرمه ولا يسقطه وقال فى اَلوه مَعُوزّيم يَكبِّد فقط وقال فى الاَلاء
الاخر يَكبِّد بَزَهَب ובכَسِّف ◦ وقوله وبَحَمودوت يشير الى الات نفيسة نظير חَמودות ٢٥
بَزَهَب ◦

عزرا ח. כז وقوله وَعَشَه لمَبَصَرى מَעُזّيم עِם אَلوه نَכَر يَحتمل قولين اما ان يكون

---

[1] تلתה X.   [2] على—l. ١١ om. P X.   [3] P only; cett. الامم; perh. النساء.
[4] Om. K.   [5] Perh. صورة معبود.   [6] اسم om. X.

R 2.

فصل ۱۱ يحاربهم لانهم لم يطيعوه فمن استءام اليه بقوله اكرمه ووهب له ورفع

فاسوق ۳۹ منزلته كقوله אשר יכיר ירבה כבוד והמשילם ברבים واما ان يكون قال وعשה למבצري

מעזים ثم بيّن ايش يعمل معهم فقال אשר יכיר ירבה כבוד فكانه لهؤلاء المعازيم

مذهبان او معبودان فالواحد يقول به كما تقدّم القول به ולאלוה מעזים ولهم

5 معبود اخر او مذهب اخر لا يقول به كقوله עם אלוה נכר فهم الان يختلفوا فى

عبادتهم فهذا الملك يريد المعبود الواحد ولا يرى الاخر ٠ وذكر ثلثة اشياء [ما]

يعملها مع من يقول بقوله אחש ها ירבה כבוד وهو ما يوصله اليه من الاموال والخلع

والثانى يامّره على البلدان كقوله והמשילם والثالث يعطيه اقطاع كقوله

وאדמה יחלק במחיר يريد به اراضى لها اثمان كبار ويجوز ايضا ان اراد به جعل هذا

10 مقام الثمن لانهم تركوا مذهبهم ودخلوا فى مذهبه وهذا الذى يهلك עזבי ברית

קדש وذلك انهم يرون ان كل من دخل فى مذهبه يبلغ الى هذه المراتب ومن لم

يقل بقوله قتل واحرق فيخرجوا عن الدين فلذلك תلف عالم من اמّتنا ¹فى اوّل

هذا الملك والى الان قد خرج عالم من الامّة فى جهة الغرب ايضا فاما يسرائيل عندما

اظهر الله اياته بمصر وفى سينى كان الناس معتقدين مذهب بני ישראל بخوف

15 سيف ولا لرجاء مراتب وهم עرב רב والذى الزمنا الله فى شريعتنا هو انه من دخل فى

دنر' כה. יט ديننا نواسيه من غلّاتنا كما نواسى الايتام والارامل كقوله لنر ولايتوم ولالمنة فاما

ان ندفع اليه مراتب جليلة فلا ٠ ومن قوله فى هذا الفصل והצלחה דלّ (على) انه

يقبل فى سائر اموره الى ان يفنى سخط الله تقع على اמّته وليس بعد سلطان هذا

الملك ملك اخر وهو آخِرُ الممالك التى تذلّ يسرائيل ٠

20 ۴۰. وفى وقت النهاية ²يتناطح معه ملك الجنوب ويتعصّف عليه

ملك الצפון بركب وفرسان وبالمراكب الكبار ويدخل فى الاراضى

ويجرف ويجوز ٠

۴۱ ويدخل فى ارض السرّاء وكثيرات ينعثروا وهنه الاراضى

تنفلت من يده الشراة وמואב وطرف بني עמון ٠

---

٤٢ ويرسل يده فى الاراضى وارض مصر لا تكون لفليتة ❖

٤٣ ويتسلّط بكنوز الذهب والفضة وبكل متمنات مصر والنوبة والحبش فى خطاه ❖

٤٤ واخبار ينهشوه من الشرق والعراق ويخرج بحمية كبيرة لاستيصال ولاصطلام كثيربن ❖

٤٥ ويغرس مضارب فازتة وبين البحرين لجبل القدس ويجىّ الى حتّه (او نهايته) وليس له ناصر ❖

قوله وכעת קץ هذا الקץ يجمع شيين احدهما انقضاء اقبال هذا الملك والثانى انقضاء الزغم على يسرائيل ❖ عرّف ان فى الاخرة ١ينعكس عليه وذلك انه اوّل ظهور كرن זעירה حارب ملك الذنب واخذ منه ثلاث كراسى على ما شرحنا ذلك فى قوله ותלתה מלכין واخذ منهم الشام والامصار ثم تسلّم من מלך הצפון العراق وبلد خراسان والى حدّ ٢باب الابواب يفتح بلد بلد وياخذه كقوله بشلاوة ובمשמני مدينة وتمام القول ❖ فاذا انتهى اقباله رجع هذين الملكين اعنى מלך הנגב ומלך הצפון عليه كقوله فى מלך הנגב ויתננה عمو وقال فى מלך הצפון ويشتعر عليه وقد ظهر طرفا من فعل מלך הנגב فى زماننا وهى وقعات جرت فاخذ من ثغور المسلمين انطاكية وطرسوس وعين زربة وتلك الناحية وقد بقى لهم دفعات اخر تكون بعد هذا ❖ واما מלך הצפון فلم يكن منه بعد شى ❖ فقال فى מלך הנגב יתננה عمو لانه قريب منه ٣ ❖ ❖ قرب الشام ❖ وقال فى מלך הצפון ويشتعر عليه لانه يجى من قرب باب الابواب ❖ وقد كتّا وعدنا ان نبيّن فى هذا الفاسوق قوله מלך הצפון ומלך הנגב الى من يشير وذلك ان بعض علمائنا يذهب الى ان מלך הצפון يشير به الى ملك العرب لانه تسلّم من מלך הצפון بغداذ ٤التى كان كرسى الماجوس فيها فنحن نبيّن ازالة هذه الشبهة ❖ يجب ان تعلم ان هذه الاربع ممالك التى ذكرها فى منام نبوخذناصر وفى منام دانيال تنقسم فالملك الاوّل ملك العالم ومن ملك العالم باسره لا يُنسب الى جهة دون جهة بل قد يُنسب الى المدينة التى كرسيّه فيها كقوله ملك

---

١ תנעכם codd.   ٢ Gloss in X שער השערים דרבנד.   ٣ Perh. add يجى من.

٤ אלדי codd.

فصل ۱۱ بَابَل فاما ان يكون يقال ملك مَعرَب او مِزرح او צָפוֹן او נֶגֶב فلا ولذلك لا تَجد شيا

פסוק ۴۵ من ذلك فى ملك כַּשְׂדִים ولا فى ملك مدى وفرس والاسكندر الذى هو الملك الاوّل

لليونانيّة وانما قال ملك הצפון وملك הַנֶּגֶב بعد موت الاسكندر وانقسم ملكه لاربعة

تلاميذه وتحن لاربع روחוֹת فصار يقول ملك הנגב ملك הצפון فلو كان ملك

5 الاسلام فى احد للجهات اما נֶגֶב واما צָפוֹן كان يَحسن يقول فيه ملك הצפון وملك

הנגב واذ قد اخذ من נֶגֶב ومن צָפוֹן ومزرح ومَعرَب لم يَجُز ان يَنسب الى جهة من

للجهات فهذا اصل صحيح ٭ الان ليس يَجوز ان يكون ملك الاسلام ملك הצפון ولا נֶגֶב

ولذلك قال יִתְגָּרֶה عِمّو يشير الى المتقدّم ذكره كقوله ועשה כרצונו המלך فعَرَّف ان ملك

הנגב يناطحه فليس هو ملك הנגב وكذلك قال וישתער עליו ملك הצפון اليه يشير

10 بان ملك הצפון يَتحرّك اليه ويجيه مثل الريح العاصف فقد صحّ ان ليس ملك הצפון

ملك الاسلام ٭ ثم قال בְרֶכֶב وبفرسيم ובאניות רבות لم يبيّن ايما منهما يجيه

برכב وبفرسيم والاقرب فيه ان ملك הצפון يوافيه برכב وبفرسيم ويجيه ملك הנגב فى

במד' כד' כד' הַיָּם באניות وفى ذلك قال וצים מיד כתים ٭ وقال ובא ولم يقل وبאו فكان ذلك

على الملكين جميعا اعنى ملك הצפון وملك הנגב فكذا نقول ان الملكين يتعاضدا

15 عليه ولم نعلم ايّهما من قول دانيال عَمّ لكِنّا نعلم ذلك من قول نبى اخر شرحه

وهو قول יُوֹאָל بن פֶּתוֹאֵל عَمّ وذلك انه ذكر ثلثة فصول الواحد תִּקְעוּ שׁוֹפָר בְּצִיּוֹן الاوّل

والثانى (תקעו שופר בציון الثانى) والثالث קָרְאוּ זֹאת בַּגּוֹיִם קַדְּשׁוּ מִלְחָמָה فالاول

مقول على בختنصر والثانى على هذا ملك الصفون المذكور فى هذا الفصل وهو قوله וְאֵת

הַצְּפוֹנִי אַרְחִיק מֵעֲלֵיכֶם وهذا نشرح لك كيف يكون ذلك والثالث مقول على נוֹג ٭

ג' כ'

20 اعلم ان صاحب الاسلام المقيم ببغداد غير ولد عبّاس هو من الצفون وقد كانوا كُقّار

فى الاصل فهذا يمشى لهم مع ولد عبّاس الخليفة[1] فليس بدّ لصاحب هؤلاء الزراעים

من اخذ ذلك البلد اعنى بغداد ويندفع قدامه ولعله يقتل فيهم فعند ذلك يتعصّبون

من قبل القوم الذى اندفعوا من قدامه ويجون الى بابل قاصدا كما تنبت الانبياء

עَمّ وهو فصل فى يشعياهو عَمّ משא בבל ונו' وكذلك نبوّة يرمياهو عَمّ وقال فيهم אשר כסף

ג' א'

25 וזהב לا يَحسبو لانهم يطلبون اخذ الثار ممّا جرى عليهم ممّن تسلّم البلد منهم فيجتمعون

ويجون اليه قاصدين فاليها يشير بقوله هَهُנا וישתער עליו מَהצפון ٭ وقوله ובא

בשטף ועבר اراد به يدخل فى عمل الملك الذى اخذه من عمل العبّاس ويفتح ارض

بابل بالسيف وبخرج خلق من يسرائيل عند قدومه وقصدهم אֶרֶץ יִשְׂרָאֵל عمّا شرح فصل ١١
ذلك سيّد يرمياهو عمّ بقوله צִיּוֹן יִשְׂאֽלוּ דֶרֶךְ ثم يقصد מֶלֶךְ הַצָּפוֹן عمل هذا الملك فاسوق ٤٥
فيخرج من بابل الى الشام فكل بلد ¹يلقاه يفتحه بالسيف اذ ليس قصده اولا ان
يثبت له كرسيّ الملك وانما قصده تلف البلدان التى تحت يد الذى هو صاحب
‫ ‬ن. ה.
الاسلام وعرّف انه يقتل من لقى كقوله וְיִשְׁלַח יָדוֹ בַּאֲרָצוֹת وعرّف انه يجئ الى אֶרֶץ ٥
יִשְׂרָאֵל كقوله וּבָא בְּאֶרֶץ הַצְּבִי ❖ وقوله יִכְשֵׁלוּ يشير الى أكثر [من] المدن والضياع
التى فى אֶרֶץ יִשְׂרָאֵל وايضا كل ²ساحل البحر ❖ ثم قال וְאֵלֶּה יִמָּלְטוּ מִיָּדוֹ فذكر אֱדוֹם
وهو جبل الشرى وמוֹאָב وطرف בְּנֵי עַמּוֹן ولم يذكر ايش السبب فى ذلك فلو كان
تخلّف عنها لضعف يده لم تكن هذه البلدان باعظم من بابل ومصر لكنّه لا
يشتغل بها اذ ليس لها حال ولا ملك ولا يسار ولا يحتفل بها ويمرّ كثير من ١٠
يسرائيل اليها كقوله עַל אֶרֶץ מוֹאָב יָגוּרוּ בָךְ נִדָּחֵי מוֹאָב הֱוִי סֵתֶר לָמוֹ מִפְּנֵי שׁוֹדֵד יש' י"ו. ד
فزعم قوم انهم يمرّوا اليها من قبل هذا الملك وقول الكتاب תִּקְעוּ שׁוֹפָר בַּצִּיּוֹן يورى ان
يسرائيل يكونون فى صيون ❖ وعرّف انه يمرّ الى ارض مصر لانه عمل الملك ايضا ولم
يذكر انه نهب بلد مصر غير ذلك لموضع ما فيها من الذخائر والاموال كقوله וּמָשַׁל
וגו' ❖ وقوله וְלוּבִים וגו' عرّف ان فى ذلك الوقت ³יִתְבָּעֵהוּ قوم من כּוּשִׁים וְלוּבִים كقوله ١٥
בְּמִצְעָדָיו او يكون اراد به فى سفره الى مصر يهلك כּוּשִׁים וְלוּבִים وهم فى عمل مصر
ايضا ❖ وقوله וּשְׁמֻעוֹת יְבַהֲלֻהוּ عرّف انه بعد حصوله فى نهاية عمل مصر الى حدّ
الغرب يتّصل به اخبار מִמִּזְרָח וּמִצָּפוֹן ⁴وهى دخول يسرائيل من הַבְּרִיָּה الى אֶרֶץ יִשְׂרָאֵל
كما سنستوفى الكلام فى هذا المعنى فى ما بعد فاذا دخل من הַבְּרִיָּה الى אֶרֶץ יִשְׂרָאֵל
يفتحوها بالسيف وينطرد من قدامهم اعداؤهم فاذا اتّصل ذلك بِمֶלֶךְ הַצָּפוֹן وهو فى ٢٠
اخر عمل مصر رجع الى الشام لاصطلامهم وابادتهم كقوله לְהַשְׁמִיד וּלְהַחֲרִים רַבִּים يشير
الى يسرائيل لانهم دخلوا خلق كثير فاذا اتّصل خبر رجوعه بيسرائيل انحشدوا الى
صيون ويفعلوا ما قال بوאל بن פתואל عمّ تقעו שׁוֹפָר בְּצִיּוֹן وتمام القصّة ❖ هذا
يفعلونه عند ما ויטע אהלו אפדנו قيل انه يضرب مضاربه عند עַמּוֹאָס وبين هذا
الموضع وبين القدس اربع فراسخ وقيل انه יְחַטַּ فى بّريّة תקוע وهذا ايضا موضع واسع ٢٥
فاذا مدّ ثم مضاربه على انه يباكرهم الى القدس يبعث اللـه تعـ ملاكه מִיכָאֵל
فيهلك عسكره باسره فيموتون كلهم ويبقى ملقى نتن على وجه الصحراء حتى يجيف

فصل ۱۱ وينتن كقولﻩ ואת הצפוני ארחיק מעליכם והדחתיו אל ארץ ציה فمن ثم يُعلم ان

فاسوق ٥۰ هذا الفصل مقول فى מלך הצפון وذكر ما يكون من حال يسرائيل عند قدومﻩ

عليهم ❖

١ ۱۲ وفى ذلك الوقت يثبت ميخائيل الرئيس الكبير الواقف

٥ على بنى قومك وتكون وقت شدّة التى لم تكن مثلها من كون

حرب الى ذلك الوقت وفى ذلك الوقت ينفلت كل المكتوب فى

الديوان ❖

قولﻩ ובעת ההיא يشير الى قولﻩ ובעת קץ יתגנח עמו وهو اوقات עדן ועדנין ופלג

עדן وفى قولﻩ ¹יעמד ולא יקول° יבוא وغير ذلك من الالفاظ ²** * هو انها

۱۰ مدّة ³ثلث سنين ونصف ❖ ووقوفﻩ لشيين احدهما لبطلان الممالك على ما تقدّم

القول بﻩ وאين אחד מתחזק וגו' والثانى لخلاص يسرائيل من شدائد تجرى عليهم ❖

وقد قال שרכם وزادنا ههنا انﻩ השר הגדול ذلك ذلك فدلّ على انﻩ عظيم فى الملائكة ❖

وفى قولﻩ ונהיתה עת צרה ثم قال אשר לא נהיתה دليل على انﻩ شى لم يكن ⁴مثلﻩ

من דור הפלגה وليس يريد بﻩ انﻩ لم يكن من جنسﻩ فى العالم لانﻩ ليس يخلو

۱٥ جوع او سيف او وبا او مرض او فقر وسائر ما هو موجود فى العالم وكذلك مطالبة

الدين فقد وجدنا بختناصر طالب ميسائيل وعزريا بالسجود للصنم الذى عملﻩ

وانما القصد فيﻩ الى ما قد شرحﻩ עוذﻩ הנביא آسا ملك יהודא وكذلك ذكرﻩ زכריا

ﻩ"ﻩ.ב. כ.ﻩ النبى عﻩ فقال עוذﻩ ובעתים ההם אין שלום ליוצא ולבא וגו' وقولﻩ וכתתו גוי בגוי

ﻩ. ١ וגו' وقال זכריا כי לפני הימים וגו' ❖ واصل هذه الצرות هو ان הזרועים يطلبون ان

۲۰ ياخذون ملك العباسة من بابل على ما قال العلماء ثم انهم يمنعون الحونين من

الصلاة فى מכות التى جرت لهم بها العادة ويبطلون ذكر איש הרוח فيقع بينهم

السيف ويستظهرون عليهم הזרועים ويقتلون فيهم مقتلة عظيمة ويهرب منهم قوم

כא. يג الى יער בערב جياع عطاشى كقول يشعياهو عﻩ משא בערב וגו' وقال כי מפני חרבות

נדדו وتمام القول فدلّ ذلك على مرورهم من السيف والقتل وسبب مرورهم الى تلك

۲٥ الناحية لعلمهم انﻩ ليس يمكنهم الرجوع الى بلدانهم اذ הקושר قد تمكن

---

¹ Perh. ولم يقل.   ² Perh. add معنى.   ³ Om. B K Kit.   ⁴ Kit. מן נַנַסֵה

فصل ۱۲ ¹فيدبّرون ان يهربون الى بنى عمّهم القائلين بقولهم فيقيمون عندهم يلقونهم
فاسوق ۱ بالطعام والماء لتعيش ارواحهم فى ذلك الوقت يبتدى السيف فى يشمعال بعضهم
مع بعض ولم يتمّ للقشرים ملك لان صاحبهم يطالب الناس بترك دينهم الذى لـ
نحو اربع مائة سنة لا سيّما بغير معجز الا بالسيف فيقع بينهم السيف فتبطل عند
ذلك دواوين السلاطين ولا يكون كرسّى ملك ولا مصالح على الطرق ولا طوف وحارس 5
فى المدن ولا دكّان يفتح ولا تجار يسافرون ولا قطر ينزل من السماء ولا زرّاع ولا كرّام
ولا انسان يتّجه لـ معاش فعند ذلك يكون للجوع ²الكبير والوبا الكبير مع السيف
فعند ذلك يتمّ كلة ونحرَצה ولا يبقى من الناس الا اليسير وتخرب البلدان وتستوحش
الطرق وتشتغل الامم بعضها مع بعض فعند ذلك يتمّ ليسرائيل للخروج ³من بينهم
الى مدبر العمים والى الاحوال يشير بقوله وهيתה עت צרה אשר לא נהיתה מהיות 10
גוי ובקى ملك الצفن الى بابل ويخرجون من بابل الى ارض يسرائيل قبل التشويش
الكبير وفى ذلك الوقت يكون ⁴خبط فى [ارض يسرائيل] (بابل) قبل خروجهم لقوله
יرم' נא. נה צاו מתוכה עמי وقال ומן ירך لببكم وقال ובעת ההיא ימלט עמך כل הנמצא כתוב
בספר ۞ قال ימלט עמך من حيث ان البلاء يحلّ بالגויم كما تقدّم بـ القول ولما
قال כל הנמצא כתوب בספر علمنا ان ليس كل يهودّى يتخلّص وانما يتخلّص المكتوب 15
ד"ה. ב. ב. יו دون غيره اعنى اشرار يسرائيل الذى لم يتوبوا فى ذلك الوقت لانه قال וישב בצר לו
دبר' ד. ל ال ייי الهى يسرائيل وقال בצر لك ומצاוך فان من تاب بقى ومن لم يتب هلك
עמوس מ. ל بالسيف بيد العدوّ وبافات اللـ تعّ كقوله بחרب ימותו כל חטאי עמی فلذلك قال כל
ישע' סה. י הנמצا كتوب בספر واعلم انه قال فى افعال הרשעים הנה כתוبة لفنى مثل قوله فى
מלא' ג. יו افعال הصالحين ויכתב ספר זכרون لفنى ייי وليس يجوز ان يكون قوله ههنا כל 20
הנמצا كتوب בספר على الجّيّد والردّى وانما هو على ما تقدّم بـ القول وقد شرح
ذلك سيّد يشعياهو عمّ بقوله وנكتوב כل הכתוב لحياة بيروشلم فعرّف ان ينفلت منهم
المكتوب للبقاء وقال بعد ذلك אم רחצ ייי את צوات בנوت ציון فدلّ ذلك على ان
المكتوب للبقاء هو الذى قد تنظّف من الاوساخ والدمى ۞ فمن كان بين الامم
تلف بالسيف ومن لم يتلف بيد الامم وخرج مع الناس الى مدبر العمים اهلكه 25
يחזק' כ. לח اللـ تعّ كقوله وברוتى مكم המوردים והفوשעים وليس يتمّ ان نذكر ما يكون فى

<hr/>

¹ פיתדברון P X.   ² Perh. الكثير.   ³ P only; om. cett.
⁴ סכט B X.

[II. 3.]   S

فصل ۱۲ ذلك الوقت على الاستقصاء لانه يحتاج الى ¹كتاب براسه ولانا قد ذكرنا فى كل سفر

فاسوق ۱ من تقاسيم المقرا الذى فسّرناه ما احتمل الموضع ✧

— ❊ —

۲ وكثيربن من ادمة التراب يقومون هولاء لبقاء الدهر وهولاء لمعيرات لنكال الدهر ✧

5   عرّف ان فى ذلك الزمان يقوم كثير من الموتى قال فيهم مثل قوله وربים מעמי

אהה׳ ח. יב   האדץ מתיהדים اذ ليس يقومون كل الموتى وانما يقوم ²بعضها وقد شرحنا ذلك فى

לו   היתה עלי יד ייי فى سفر بحزقال عمّ بشرح واسع وتكلمنا ايضا طرفا من ذلك فى

יד. יב   تفسير ايوب فى قوله ואיש שכב ולא יקום هاهنا منه طرف ✧ فنقول اوّلا اند

بتّر بخلاص الامّة بقوله ובעת ההיא ימלט עמך ثم ²بتّر باقامة الموتى ليعرّف ان

10   الاحياء والموتى جميعا ينظرون الفرج وكما انه قسم الاحياء قسمين بعض يبقى

وبعض يتلف كذلك قسم من يقوم من الموتى على قسمين منهم לחיי עולם ومنهم

לחרפות ✧ وقد شرح بحزقال عمّ ان الذين يقومون جالوثيّين لقوله هنه امرام

יבשו עצמותינו ואבדה תקותנו وليس هذا حال موتى الدولة ولذلك قال سيد يشعياهو

כ. יט   عمّ יחיו מתיך ثم قال הקיצו ורננו مثل قوله هاهنا מישני אדמת עפר لكن ثم اختصر

15   على ذكر صلحاء الامّة وهاهنا ذكر الفربين جميعا لقوله אלה לחיי עולם ואלה לחרפות

ולדראון وقد شرح ذلك سيد يشعياهو عمّ فى اخر سفره ³كقوله וראו בפגרי האנשים

הפשעים בייי وهذا ⁴وصف ⁵מן° ما صار من° مَن مات فى لجالوث وجاهر الله تعّ بكبائر

الذنوب ✧ وقوله לחרפות לדראון עולם فاما الحرفوت فذلك لانهم كانوا يعيرون اخيار

الامّة المتحسّرين المهمومين المغمومين على ما نزل بالامّة من البلاء وعلى بيت الله

20   ⁵كما قال عن° الصالح فى فصل הושיעני אלהים כי באו מים עד נפש כי עליך נשאתי

ההל׳ סט׳. ה   חרפה כי קנאת ביתך אכלתני ואבכה ואתנה לבושי שק חרפה שברה לבי ונו׳ فكانوا ياكلون

הוש׳ כ׳. א   ويشربون ويتقّى زمانهم بالطرب والفرج وقد نهانا الله تعّ عن ذلك بقوله אל תשמח

ישראל אל גיל כעמים وما كفاهم انهم لا يعملون ما قال الله تعّ حتى يبغضون

من اطاعه ويعيرونه باستعماله الدين والتحزن والتنسّك فلذلك دعا عليهم فى اخر

25   الفصل كقوله יהי שלחנם לפניהם לפח תחשכנה עיניהם מראות שפך עליהם זעמך ימחו

---

¹ כתאב K P; אלכתאב cett.   ² בעצّהם P X.   ³ لقוّ codd.   ⁴ מא צאר פי

only B; און מן מאת פי only K P X.   ⁵ כמא קאל ען כף׳ P X; B K; כَן פי

מספר חיים فاذا انشقّ هر הזיתים وصار بين الشقّين وهدة عظيمة صارت تلك فصل ۱۲
الوهدة موضع عقاب هؤلاء الרשעים واذا كان يوم السبت وراس الشهر خرجوا יسראיל فاسوق۲
يوم الاحد ومن غد راس الشهر الى هؤلاء المعاقبين ونظروا ما حلّ بهم فيعيّرونهم
به كقوله והנחם שמכם לשבועה לבחירי فكان הرשעים يعيرون الصالحين ظلما وهم ישע׳ סה׳ סו
بعيرون הرשעים بحقّ فلذلك قال لחرفوت ۰ وقال לدران ذلك لما يشاهدونهم في ٥
ضجيج عظيم من الم النار ولدغ للحياة كقوله כي תולעתם לא תמות ومن قوله لدران
עولם ان عقاب هؤلاء הرשעים دائم ليس له نهاية وكل موضع يقول فيه עולם وليس
ثم دليل يدلّ على نهاية اما عقل واما سمع ۱ فيجب ان يكون ذلك مويّد بل العقل
يوجب ان يكون عقاب הرשעים مويّد لا انقضاء له ۰ ثم نقول في ما يرد به النقّ من
۲اللفظ المفهوم وله ظاهرة فليس سبيل الى التاويل فيه بان نخرجه عن ظاهره فيجب عند ۱۰
هذا ان قول מישני אدمת עפر انه على ظاهره وليس المراد به لجالوثيين الممثّلين في
لجالوث بالموتى وخاصّة ليس في هذا الفصل قول ليس هو على ظاهره بل على كله على
ظاهره ومن المعلوم انه لما كان החזון الذى نظره دانيal فسّره له גבريال لانه كان له
تاويل فلما جاء ۳الى قول אלפים ושלש מאות וני׳ قال له ומראה וני׳ אمت هو على ما
شرحناه وكذلك قال في صدر هذا الفصل הנה אמت ونعته אמת אני لך فكل هذا الفصل على ظاهره ۱۵
فيجب ان يكون قول ورבים وني׳ على ظاهره وليس ذلك مما ينكره العقل والسمع
على ما بيّنا وهذا في اخبارنا ان الله תع احيا ولد השونמית وكذلك الميّت الذى دنا
בעצموت אليشע فاذا هذا قد جرى وليس ذلك محال كان ايضا ما ضمنه الله
عز وجل من اقامة موتى יسראيل يتمّ ولما قال فيهم اله لحرفوت لدران עولم كان
ذلك خليد في المثابين ۴والمعاقبين على امر واحد والله تع يقيم موتى لجالوث وقت ۲۰
الفرقان واما موتى الدولة فيقومون مع من يقوم من كل من مات ليثاب او يعاقب
وذلك عند براءة שמים חدشים وارض חدشة فان ليس بد من تغيّر يحدث في هذا
السماء والارض لقوله שאו מרם עיניכם وتمامه والى ذلك يشير ايوب بقوله עד בלתי يשע׳ מ׳ כו
שמים לא יקיצו فهذا كان معروف عند كل الناس ان اقامة الموتى يكون عند ما איוב יד׳ יב
يحدث ذلك في السماء والارض ولذلك قال עד בלتي שמים לא יקيצו فاما اقامة موتى יד׳ יב
يسראيل فيكون قبل ذلك فهذا طرف ذكرناه في ذلك الموضع اذ لم يجوز ان نجوز عليه ۲٦
ولا نذكر فيه قول ۰

۱ פינב P; פונב BK X; אלי قول ۳ אלאלפאט BK. אלפان X; אלפفان P; אللفان ۲ אলאלفان P.
۴ والمعوكبين X. cett. אلقول

فصل ۱۲ ٣ والمرشدين يبصّون مثل بصيص السماء ومعدّلين الكثيرين مثل
فاسوق ٣ الكواكب للابد والدهر ۰

كانَ قسم الاحياء على قسمين والموتى على قسمين كما شرحنا ذلك فى ما
تقدّم وقال بعد ذلك והמשכילים فافرد المصيكلايم عن العوامّ ليعرف منزلتهم انها
5 زائدة على غيرهم من الامّة وهذا قيل فى من يقوم من القبر ۰ عرّف ان ٰديباجة
وجوههم تكون مثل لون الرقيع وهو ان لَه بصيص عظيم مثل ذلك مثل وجه سيّد موسى
عليه السلام وهذا نور يكسيهم اللـه تعَ ليبين شرفهم وليس يدفع ذلك انهم
يلتذّون بـه ۰ وقولـه ומצדיקי הרבים هم الذى ردوا الناس من الفساد الى الدين وقولـه
מלא׳ ג.۱ הרבים לيدلّ انهم ٢ردوا الكثيرين نظير قولـه فى הכהנים ורבים השיב מעון فعرّف
10 انهم يرشدون الناس الى الدين بما يعلّمونهم מצות ייַ ومع ذلك يردّونهم عن المعاصى
وذلك انهم قد اشتغلوا בתורת ייַ وقصدوا اللـه تعَ فى ان ٣يرشدهم الى معرفة شرائعـه
وهم חמישי דרך وصلاتهم مدوّنة واقوالهم مشروحة اثنين وعشرين بيت كل بيت
ثمانية فواسيق وهم القائلون لمن طلب التعليم הוי כל צמא وقال فى فصل הנה ישכיל
עבדי בדעתו יצדיק צדיק עבדי فذكر فى هذا الفصل شقاء המשכיל وامراضه وكثرة علمـه
15 ودينـه فاليهم يشير بقولـه והמשכילים יזהירו כזהר הרקיע وقولـه ככוכבים على معنيين
احدهما فى انوارها والثانى البقاء والدوام لا ينقطع لעולمه وهذا يفعلـه اللـه تعَ
معهم بعد ان يوريهم ישועת ישראל وعمارة القدس ويقيمون مدّة حتى يرون ٤من
نظرة٥ وحينئذ ينقلهم الى دار الثواب ويقرب انهم يكونون مع الملائكة فى العلو
זכר׳ ג.۱ كقولـه فى יהושע בן יהוצדק ונתתי לך מהלכים כל درك بدل ما علّموا يسرائيل التورا
20 وردّوهم عن ذنوبهم ٥وتشقّوا فى الجالوث والزموا انفسهم للحزن وغيرهم اشغلوا يسرائيل
بتعليم للخرافات واخذوا اموالهم وربّوا ابدانهم بالاكل والشرب وانصرفوا مسرورين ولم
يعملوا الواجب واكسبوا الناس الذنوب وعلّموهم ما يسخط اللـه عليهم فلذلك لا محالة
عقوبتهم اشدّ عقوبة من تبّاعهم ۰

٤ وانت يا دانيال [ال]ستّ الكلم واختم السفر الى وقت الانقضاء
25 والنهاية يطوفون كثيرين وتكثر المعرفة ۰

---

¹ דבאגّה codd.   ² רדו codd.   ³ ירשדוהם PX.   ⁴ Perh. منتظرـه or منظرـه.
⁵ ותשקי X.

الى ههنا عرّف الملك ما يكون من وقته ذلك الى اخر الامور كقوله له فى اول **فصل ١٢**
كلامه انى جئت لاخبرك بما يكون [1]الى اخر الزمان قال وانت يا دانيال سدّ هذه الكلم **فاسوق ٤**
بمعنى خليها على جملتها ولا تطالب بكشف اكثر مما قيل لك • وقوله **وחתום**
הספר يعنى اختم كتابك هذا بما قد قيل لك ولا تنتظر شى اخرو ذلك انه ما كان
يجوز ان ينكشف اليه [2]فى القول اخر° فقال (חתום) فعرّفه انه لم يبق قول يقال **٥**
له • ثم قال **עד עת קץ** ليورى انه [3]لا ينكشف لاحد الى اخر للجالوث وكل من يدّعى
انه [4]يقف على **קץ** نلوت مبطل • وقوله **ישוטטו רבים** يشير به الى **המשכילים**
[5]وطالبى العلم وهذا الطوف يكون على وجهين **احدهما** يطوفون البلدان لطلب
العلم [فى كتاب الله تعّ] لانه يظهر فى كل صقع علماء [6]فيطوفون طالبى العلم **ח. יב**
ليتعلموا من العلماء وقد شرح ذلك سيّد عاموس عمّ بقوله **ונעו מים ערים ומצפון ح. יב**
وهذا يكون فى اول امرهم وبعد ذلك يكشف الله تعّ لهم عند حرقتهم للطلب **١١**
والثانى ישוטטו فى كتاب الله تعّ كمن يطلب الكنوز فعند ذلك تكثر المعرفة
وهذه المعرفة فى شيين **احدهما** معرفة **מצות** والثانى معرفة **הקץ** وليس
يكشف الله تعّ **הקץ** الا بعد ان يعرفوا **מצות** وهم **יראי יוי** كقوله **סוד יוי ליראיו תהל' כה. יד**
وليس ذلك الا بالبحث والنظر والتفتيش عن قول الله تعّ كقوله **הורני יוי דרך חקיך ١٥
נל עיני** فهذه الاقاويل ونظراؤها [7]تدلّ على بطلان قول اصحاب التقليد مثل قول
الفيومى وغيره الذين اهلكوا يسرائيل بما دوّنوا وقالوا ليس يجوز ان تعرف فرائض
الله تعّ من البحث لانه يوّدّى الى خلف ويجب التقليد لخلفاء الانبياء وهم اصحاب
המשנה والתלמוד وان كل اقاويلهم من الله تعّ فاطغى الناس بكتبه المزخرفة ويشهد
لمن كذّب على كتاب الله تعّ بالصدق فهو اذن اشدّ مطالبة منهم والله تعّ ياخذ **٢٠**
حقّ امّته منه ومن امثاله •

• ونظرت انا دادنيال وانا [8]بملاكين اخرين واقفين الواحد ههنا
على شطّ النهر وواحد ههنا على شطّ [9]النهر من° الجانب الاخر •

بعد ان سمع دانيال جميع ما قيل له الى **ישוטטו** ولم يكن مع الملك الذى كان

¹ Perh. فى. ² في الקץ اكثر K P; perh. في الקץ اكثر° . ³ لם codd. ⁴ Om. D P X;
במלאכאן B; text K. ⁵ וטאלב D X. ⁶ פיטוף X. ⁷ ידל codd. ⁸ במלאכאן
etc. P X. ⁹ Ins. K; om. cett.

فصل ١٢ يخاطبه ملك اخر فلما فرغ كلامه راى ملاكين اخرين الواحد معه فى الناحية التى
فاسوق ٥ هو واقف فيها والاخر من لجانب الاخر وفى قوله אחרים احد ثلثة اقاويل اما ان
يكون ¹عرّف ان ليس هما الملاكين الذين نظرهما فى الحزن الاوّل فى ואשמעה فكان
الواحد سائل لصاحبه عما فى نفس دانيال واجابه الاخر وكذلك هؤلاء سال الملك
٥ الاخر ועד מתי קץ נפלאות فقد كتّا نظنّ ان هؤلاء الملاكين هم اولئك الملكين فقال
אחרים فعرّف ان هؤلاء غير هؤلاء واما ان يكون قال אחרים لئلا نظنّ انه يشير الى
الملاكين الذين تقدم ذكرهما فى هذا الفصل احدهما והנה יד נגעה בי والثانى והנה
כדמות בני אדם فعرّف ان هؤلاء غير هؤلاء فيجب عند ذلك انه راى فى هذه
الدفعة خمسة ملائكة اثنين فى ما تقدم وثلاثة فى هذا الوقت واما ان يكون قال
١٠ אחרים لئلا نظنّ ان احدهما الملاك الكبير واخر معه فلذلك قال אחרים فصاروا
ثلثة ملائكة ۰

٦ فقال للملك ملبس الثياب المقداريّة المشمّرة الذى فوق النهر
الى متى انقضاء هذه العجائب ۰

٧ وسمعت الملك ملبس الثياب المقداريّة الذى فوق ماء النهر
١٥ ورفع يمينه وشماله الى السماء وحلف بحىّ الدهر ان الى وقت
ووقتين ونصف وعند فراغ تفتتت يد شعب القدس ²تفنين كل
هنه ۰

قوله ויאמר לאיש هو قول واحد من الملاكين ولم يقل ויאמרו فكتّا نقول ان
الاثنين سالة ولم نعلم ايّهما ولم يذكر ³له المعنى فى نظره الواحد الذى لم يسال ولا
٢٠ يجيب فالاشبه فيه ان السائل هو الذى من تلك الناحية والذى كان واقف معه
هو ليونسه او ⁴ليجيب دانيال على سماع المسلة وجواب المجيب والى الان لم نعلم
ان كان الملاك الكبير واقف وبيّن ههنا انه كان واقف فى الهواء فوق الماء وانه لم
يكن واقف على الارض لانه لم يكن ⁵من الملائكة التى تهبط من السماء الى الارض

---

¹ עארף codd. ² תפנין B K P; תפנן D X. ³ Perh. لنا. ⁴ Perh.
ليوجب على دانيال. ⁵ מע codd.

فصل ۱۲   وانما بعثه الله تَعَ لمعنى دانيال لا لغيره ٭ فساله עד מתי קץ הפלאות وهذه הפלאות
فاسوق ۷   يقصد بها الى هذه הצרות التى تجرى فى اخر الاوقات ٭ وقوله עד מתי يعنى كم

يكون مدّتها فاجابها كاجابة فلمونى للسائل الاول الذى قال له עד מתי החזון

۱ وكذلك اجاب ۲ هذا الملاك للسائل عن مسلته ولم يكن قصد السائل ليقف هو على

ذلك لان الملائكة تقف على السرّ ۳ الذى يقول لدانيال ואתה דניאל סתום החזון وانما

۵ سال هو ليسمع منه دانيال للجواب فان سأل سائل لاىّ معنى لم يرد هذا القول عن

غير مسلة اجبنا بانه يمكن ان يكون السبب فى ذلك هو ليورى ان لولا مسلة

الملك له لم يرد للجواب لانه من الاسرار الكبار ٭ ثم ان لم يرد للجواب من غير يمين

فعرّف ان الملك الكبير حلف يمينا ليعرّف انه ليس له استثناء لانها مدّة لا تطول

وهذه اليمين ليس ۴ هى من اجل دانيال عَمَ وانما هى من اجل يسرائيل الذين ۱۰

يكنون فى عت ترّه واورى عظم اليمين وذلك فى شيين احدهما رفع اليدين

بـرا׳ יד. כב   واليمين برفع اليدين تعظم اليمين الا ترى انه يقول سيد ابراهام عَمَ הרימותי

ידי אל יוי وقال للخالق عز وجل נשאתי ידי فى عدّة مواضع والثانى انها يمين باسم

ירמ׳ כד. כי   يوى وهى اليمين العظيمة ليس اعظم منها يقول הנני נשבעתי בשמי הגדול ٭

وتفسير وحى עולם ان البارى تبارك اسمه חי حَتَّى لا يزول وفى اللغة חי اسم للحىّ كقوله ۱۵

بـرا׳ ו. יש   ومكل החי وكقوله חי יוי وقد يعمل اسم للحيوة نظير חי פרעה ولم يجز ان نفسّرها
بـرا׳ מב. יו

مثل חי פרעה فيجب ان نفسّرها حَتَّى لا חَيَاة ٭ ثم عرّف انه حلف كي למועד

מועדים וحاصي وهذا يشبه قوله עד עדן ועדנין وפلג עדن ليس بينهما فرق اصلا ونرى ان

نجمع المواضع المذكور فيها الاوقات المتعلقة بالقץ وهى ثمانية احدها قول سيّد

י. יד   يشعياهو عَمَ ועתה דבר יוי בשלש שנים כשני שכיר والثانى בעוד שנה כשני שכיר
כא. יו

۲۱   والثالث ויתיהבון בידה עד עדן والرابع עד ערב בקר אלפים ושלש מאות ונצדק קדש

والخامس ونكשלו בחرب ובלהבה בשבי ובבזה ימים كي למועד מועדים

والسابع ومعت הוסר התמיד والثامن אשרי המחכה ٭ فاما قوله בשלש שנים

فقد عرّفنا اوّلها واخرها فاوّلها منذ ובא אل مقدسى להתפلل ولا يوكل وهم החוננים

الذى يطلبون ان يصلّوا على رسمهم فيمنعوهم הזרעים كما تقدّم به القول آنفا ۲۵

واخرها ونקלה כבוד מואב والقصد فيه هو انه يسخف وقار מואב ويصير قليل العدد

---

۱ ולדלך codd.   ۲ Ins. P; om. cett.   ۳ Perh. الا ترى انه يقول.   ۴ Ins. D;
om. cett.

فصل ۱۲ كقوله מעט מזער ويصير حينئذ لا مقدار له كقوله ומזער ۲ולا ۳يكون فيهم ۴رئيس
فاسوق ۷ مقدّم كقوله لا ۵כביר ۰ والثانى اوّله هروب المصلّيين الى יער בערב كما تقدّم
القول واخرة وكلّه كل כבוד קדר فلا يبقى لقدر כבוד ويقلّ فيها جبابرتة وهذه السنة
هى من جملة الثلاث سنين لكن اذ مرّ منها سنة כלה כבוד קדר وفى اخرها

5 ונקלה وهو اَلّ يبقى له כבוד اصلا ۰ فاما عدن ועדנין وפלג עדן فهو على ما تقدّم به
القول اما ان يكون اراد به ان مدّة ما يقيم عليها فى ما يفعله بيشمعال ويسرائيل
עדן ועדנין وפלג עדן واما ان يكون اراد به يُجعلوا يسرائيل بيد هذا הקושר الى ان
يبقى من زمان הקץ עדן ועדנין وפלג עדן ومن الاقرب فى النفس ان هذا الذى وصف
فعله انه يبطل للحجّ وبخرب البيت ويلقى دين ۶يسرائيل يدوم على ما هو عليه الى

10 ان يبتدى עדן ועדנין وפלג עדן وعند ذلك يزول ويتلف كقوله فيه ובאפס יד ישבר
وليس يدلّ ذلك على مدّة كونه على تلك للحال وعند زوال ملكه تبتدى העדנין فاذا
ابتدت העדנין ابتدت الצרות المذكورة كما تقدّم به الشرح وعند نهايتها تنتهى
الצרות وبُعلم ذلك من قوله ههنا كי למועד מועדים וחצי וככלות נפץ יד עם קדש
תכלינה כל אלה ۰ الان قد بيّن ان عند ابتداء העדנין تبتدى الצרות وتنتهى عند

15 فراغ העדנין فاما אלפים ושלש מאות قد تقدّم القول انها الف يوم وخمس ماية يوم
وعرّف ان نهايتها ונצדק קדש ولم يذكر اوّلها والاقرب فى ذلك هو ان تدوم الצרות
على يسرائيل من هذا الملك الذى بخرب מכות الذى يبقى دين ۶يسرائيل الى الارض
אלפים ושלש מאות منها سنة واحدة ونכשלו בחרב ובלהבה בשבי ובבזה ولكن منتهى
هذه الאלפים ושלש מאות ونצדק קדש وقوله ונצדק קדש هو ضدّ ותשלך אמת ארצה

20 فاما ان يكون اراد به ظهور سيد الياهو عَمّ واما ان يكون دخول يسرائيل الى الارض
من مدبر העמים ويقرب فيه ان هذا האלפים ושלש מאות بعضها فى زمان هولاء
الזרועים وبعضها من עדן ועדנין وפלג עדן لان فيها يخرجون يسرائيل الى مدبر
העמים كما تقدّم به القول فقد تبيّن الان ان ونכשלו בחרב قبل העדנין وان אלפים
ושלש מאות بعضها يكون فى زمان הزרועים وبعضها فى جملة עדן ועדנין وפלג עדן

25 وقد تقدّم القول منّا ان עדן وقت واحد وان עדנין يدلّ على اكثر من واحد ولا يدلّ
على اثنين دون ثلثة والذى يقرب هو (انه) وقت قوله ומעת הוסר התמיד كما
سنبيّن ذلك فى تفسيرة ونذكر بعد ذلك אשרי המחכה ۰ وقوله וככלות נפץ יד עם

۱ קולה X. ۲ولا P; ולם cett. ۳يכن codd. ۴ רווס מקדמין P.
۵ סכיר BDK. ۶ Perh. يشمعال.

קדש هو ما لحق يسرائيل فى هذه السنين من הצרות. واعلم ان ثم وقت تكون **فصل ١٢**
צרה على يسرائيل دون غيرهم ووقت تكون צרה على العالم باسره وقد شرح ذلك **فاسوق ٧**
سيّد يرمياهو عمّ بقوله קול חרדה שמענו פחד ואין שלום שאלו נא וראו وقال بعده
הוי כי גדול היום ההוא מאין כמהו وعت צרה وقوله קול חרדה שמענו يشير بـه الى
اخبار التى تتّصل بيسرائيل وهو قول سيّد يشعياهو מכנף הארץ זמירות שמענו צבי **כד. י**
לצדיק وقال פחד ואין שלום وهو قوله פחד ופחת ופח وهذا צרה تشتمل على العالم **6**
باسره وذكر ذلك فى الفاسوق الذى بعده كقوله מדוע ראיתי כל גבר ידיו על חלציו
כילדה ثم قال وعت צרה היא ليعقب وفى ذلك احد قولين اما ان يكون يشير الى ما
تقدّم مما يجرى على يسرائيل فى زمان הזרועים ونכשלו فهى צרה גדולה واما ان
يكون يشير بـه الى ما يلحقهم بعد دخولهم من مدبר העמים الى الارض وذلك فى **10**
ثلث اوقات اولها ما يجرى عليهم من الצفوני كما تقدّم القول بـه فى ויצא בחמה
גדולה وبعده المذكورة فى مزمور אלהים אל דמי לך وهو قول (فى) אהלי אדום **תהל' פג**
וישמעאלים وبعده נוד وهو اخر ما يجرى عليهم من הצרות فكأنّه يجرى عليهم اولا
צרה فى زمان הזרועים وبعده من מלך הצفוני وبعده אהלי אדום وبعده נוד وفى
جملة هذه السنين يكون السبك وفى ذلك وנ، والبعده قال והבאתי את השלשית באש ❖ **זכר' י. ט**

16   ۸ وانا سمعت ولم افهم فقلت يا سيّدى ايش اخر هنه ❖

قال دانيال سمعت قول الملك כי למועד מועדים וחצי ولم افهم ❖ اعلم انـه لم
يعلم ثلاث اشياء احدها هو انه لم يعلم المועד كم من الزمان كما شرحنا فى עדן
ועדנין ופלג עדן وذلك ان מועד ועדן وעת معنى هذه الثلاثة الفاظ واحد فقد يكون عت
طرفة عين وساعة وما فوق ذلك (مثل) سنين فعند ما قال למועד لم يدلّ ذلك **20**
على وقت محدود والثانى انه لم يقف على اوّل هذه המועדים من اين تبتدى
والثالث ان מועדים لفظ لا يدلّ على اثنين دون ثلاثة فلذلك قال ولא אבין ❖ وقوله
واومرה אדני كانه قال لم افهم قال فان كان ما قلت فان كان يجوز ان تعرّفنى ايش اخر هذه
الامور فاجابه عن الشيين احدهما اجابة عن سواله מה אחרית אלה و(الاخر) اجابة
عن قول ולא אבין وان كان الملك لم يسمع ولא אבין كقوله **25**

۹ فقال مرّ يا دانيال فان مسدودة ومختومة الكلم الى وقت
النهاية (او الانقضاء) ❖

فصل ۱۲ ۱۰. يتنقّوا ويتبيّضوا وينسبكوا كثيرين ويعصون كثيرين ولا يفهموا
فاسوق ۱۰ كل الاشرار والمرشدين يفهموا ٭

قال כי סתומים من جنس ما تقدّم له مثله فى قوله ואתה דניאל סתום החזון
لكن الذى تقدّم هو قول لدانيال وليس فى ذلك دليل على ان غيره لا يقف
5 عليه فقال له כי סתומים וחתומים ليعرّف انها סתומים וחתומים عن كل بنى ادم ٭
وقال עד עת קץ فعرّف ان الى ذلك الوقت هى סתומים ومن (بعد) هذا الوقت
ينكشف ٭ ثم عرّفه ان (فى) ذلك الوقت الذى هو עת קץ יתבררו ٭ يجب ان
تعلم انه عرّف ان الקץ ليس يجى الا بعد تصفية الامّة من العصاة ٭ ويجب ان
نلبث ههنا قليلا واقول ان للفرج المنتظر نصوص تتضمّن علامات تحدث تدلّ
10 عليها وهى على قسمين أحدهما فعل الامّة والثانى فعل الله تعّ فاما افعالنا
فهى رجوعنا الى الله تعّ واما افعال الله تعّ فهى اشياء كثيرة ونحن نذكرها ٭ اما

דבר' ד' ל رجوعنا الى الله تعّ فقول الرسول عمّ بצר לך ומצאוך וفصل והיה כי יבאו אליך וג'
שם ל

وقال הושע יד' ב שובה ישראל עד יוי קחו עמכם דברים שובו בنים שובבים لكنهم ليس يرجعون
الى الله تعّ الا بعد شدائد كبار كما تقدّم القول به قبل (فى) هذا الفصل وقال
ישע' נמ' כ ובעת ההיא ימלט עמך وقال ובא לציון גואל ٭ وقد اشتبه على قوم من اليهود قوله
נמ' י' فى يشعياهو וירא כי אין איש וג' فظنّ ان قد لا يتوبون يسرائيل ويجيهم الفرقان

17 ۱عن غير توبة° وهذا خطا اذ لو كان يجى الفرقان عن غير توبة لما اخّر الله الفرج
هذه المدة الطويلة وانما نقول انه قسمة اهل الجالية فى اخر هذه الدولة الاخرة على
قسمين الواحد قوم اخيار يطلبون العلم ويجتهدون فيه ويكثّرون من الصوم والتشقّى
20 ويلبسون المسوح ويتمرّغون بالرماد متواضعين يسلون الله تعّ فرج امّته والثانى قوم
منهمكين فى المعاصى غارقين فى فعل الذنوب الكبائر ومع ذلك يبغضون الفريق
الصالح ويطعنون عليه ويرونه بصورة المنافقة ويحرّمونه ويبعدونه اذ ليس يقول بقولهم
ישע' נח' ב ولا يرى مذهبهم فاما الفريق الاوّل فهو الذى وصف افعاله فى قوله ואותי יום יום
ידרשון ودעת דרכי יחפצון فانكر عليهم ان يجرى بينهم ²فى عوامّهم ظلم فى معاملات
25 واحكام ولا يغيرونها ³وقلّة افتقاد ضعفاهم على ما تصمّنه الفصل والفريق الكبير
נמ' א الذى هو جمهور الامّة قال له הן לא קצרה יד יוי מהושיע כי אם עונותיכם היו מבדילים

---

¹ Om. PX.   ² פי P; מן cett.   ³ וקולה codd.

فصل ١٢   כי כפיכם נגואלו בדם الى ان قال وتهي האמת נעדרת فالى هذا الفاسوق اشار بقوله וירא

فاسوق ١٠   كي אין איש ומשתומם כי אין מפגיע وفى قوله ותושע לו زروع [1] تنبيت تحريك הצרות

على هؤلاء הרשעים حتى يتوب من يتوب ويهلك من يهلك فاما ان يكون וירא كي

يשע' سי. ה   אין איש باسرها فذلك فى غاية البعد وقال للفريق الاوّل שמעו דבר יוי החרדים

אל דברו فعرّف ان اخوتهم يبغضوهم ويشتموهم ومع ذلك يقولون ان رضى الله تع 5

فينا ومن اجلنا يكون الفرقان وهم فى ذلك مبطلين فهذا ذكر طرفا مما ذكر لنا

فى رجوعهم الى الله تع وبعده يكون الفرقان وقد نقدم لنا فى ישוטטו רבים ותרבה

הדעת طرف ايضا ونرى ان نبيّن كيف سياقة رجوع يسرائيل الى الله تع وما الذى

يفعلوه لخاصّ منهم وما الذى يفعلوه العوامّ فنقول ان لخاصّ منهم يقبل على

التورا مع [2] حصوله باسوأ حال من الفقر والضيق الشديد وبعدّة اعدائه من الامة 10

ومن الفرق الكبير وهم تميمي דרך وتباعهم والفريق الكبير يتناقص القائلين بقول

مقدّميه ويقترون قوم بعد قوم الى ان تبتدى אלפים ושלש מאות وفى وقت بطلان

كراسى الدول واشتغال الناس فى הצרות تبطل مواد رؤساء اليهود ويبطل امرهم النافذ

ويطلبهم العدو صاحب الوقت فعند ذلك يظهر للجماعة القائلين برياستهم ان

لحقّ فى جهة الفريق وعلى يده يكون الفرقان فيرجعون الى التورا ويتركون تقليد 15

المتمسكين بكتب قدمائهم وليس يوخّر عند ذلك الفرقان وقد شرحنا ذلك

شرحا شافيا على سياقة موافاة فى تفسير שיר השירים مما يطول شرحه ههنا فهذا ما

ذكره الكتاب من افعالنا فاما ما ذكر من فعل الله تع فهو ينقسم ايضا على

قسمين احدهما ما يكون من حالنا قبل الفرقان عند توبتنا وقد ذكره فى שירת

האזינו השמים وهو قوله كي ידין יוי עמו وعرّف ان الله تع ياخذ حقّ امته من 20

اعدائهم ويتراجع اليهم بالصفح عند ما يبلغون الى الفقر ولا يبقى فيهم من له حال

كقوله كي يراה كي אזלת יד ومعنى אזלת יד اوّلا ضعف الفقر ثم لا يكون فيهم خادم

سلطان كما كانوا اذ كان فيهم عمّال جهابذة وغير ذلك وكان احوالهم متماسكة بهم

فيفتقروا بعد ما كانوا مياسير من جهة السلطان ومياسير التجار [3] يتركوا المكاسب

زכر' ח. י   كما تقدّم به القول فى قوله كي לפני הימים ההם שכר האדם לא נהיה فلذلك قال אזלת

יד وقال ואפס עצור ועזוב يعنى لا يكون لواحد منهم جاء ان يحبس ويطلق كما كان 26

والثانى وصف حال הגוים وهو قوله كي נקם ושלם فعرّف ان مهما امور הגוים

---

[1] תוכבית codd.   [2] Perh. حصولهم.   [3] So P; ותרכו cett.

فصل ١٢ منتظمة فى ملكهم نحن مقيمين على ادبارنا وطول جاليتنا واذا بدوا ينكسوا يتصل

فاسوق ١٠ ادبارهم ويهلكوا عن قرب كقولﮫ كي קرוב יום אידם فهذه ثلثة علامات الישׁועה فاذا

ظهرت تيقّنوا المשׂכילים بالفرقان فلذلك قال كי סתומים וחתומים הדברים עד עת קץ

فعند قرب الקץ يبين ذلك وراء الله تعٰ اللطيف باتمﮥ ان يخفى ذلك عنها لانﮫ لو

5 وقفوا على طول لجالية لتلف عالم من العوامّ لكنﮫ تركﮫ على الرجاء ينتظرون الفرج

وينصلحون قوم بعد قوم ويزول سخط الله تعٰ واذا قرب الوقت ظهرت لهم العلامات

فيعلمون ان الوقت قد جاء ويتمسّكون بالدين ولا يخرجون عنﮫ الا اليسير كما

تقدّم القول بﮫ ❖ ثم قال יתבררו فقسم الناس على ثلثة اقسام بخرج ¹ارבعة على ما

هوذا اشرح اعلم انﮫ قد كان قال لצרוף בהם ولבחر ولלבن فرجع اعادة ليورى ان ذلك

10 يكون وقت الקץ فاما قولﮫ יתבררו فالظاهر منﮫ التنفية والنقد كما ينقد الحبّ من

يرמ׳ ו. יח الفضول والتراب والحجر مثل قولﮫ מثل לא لצرות ولא لظاهر وكما ينقد الصيرفيّ الدرهم لجيّد

من الزيف فيعزل لجيد من الردى الذى كان مختلط معﮫ والمراد فى ذلك هو ان كان

فى الامّة صالحين وتائبين فهم للحنطة وفيهم اشرار الامّة اكلهم لحرام مبدلين

²السבות والاعياد مرتكبين الفواحش لا يتوبون فيميّز الله تعٰ بينهم بما يهلك

15 الاشرار فمنهم من يفنى بالسيف وقوم بالوبا كما تقدّم القول بﮫ انفا فى וברותי מכם

יחזק׳ כ. לח המורדים והפושעים בי وقال בחרב ימותו כל חטאי עמי فلذلك قال יתבררו قد حصل

עמוס ט. י قسمان قوم צדיקים على الكمال وقوم هم רשעים גמורים ثم قال יתלבנו وهم قوم

متوسّطين فى الدين يفعلون المצות لا على سبيل الكمال فهم مثل ثوب قد حصلت

19 فيﮫ اثر وسخة فيحتاج الى قلع تلك الطبوع منﮫ ثم يغسل كقولﮫ فى هذا المعنى

ישׂ׳ סד. ה وכבגד עדים כל צדקותינו فاذا قربت الצרות تركوا ما بايديهم من تلك الذنوب وكما

יرמ׳ ב. כב قال للقدماء כי אם תכבסי בנתר فهولاء دون طبقة ³من قيل فيهم יתבררו اذ كان

اولئك צדיקים גמורים وهولاء متوسّطين وهذه اوصاف القوم لخارجين عن الفريق

الكبير ثم قال ויצרפו وهو وصف الفريق الكبير فمثّلهم بفضّة وذهب فيﮫ الغشّ مختلط

وهى المذاهب التى ورثوها من ابائهم ويقولون بما يقولون لهم روساؤهم ويقترّون

25 بها فيدخلوا تحت الצרות فيسبكهم حتى يتركونها ويرجعون الى תורת יוֹי وهذا وصف

حالهم قرب ظهور سيّد الياهو عمّ كما شرحنا ذلك فى غير هذا السفر اعنى فى سفر

תהלים ❖ ثم قال והרשיעו רשעים يشير بﮫ الى מרשיעי ברית وهم القسم الذى ذكرتﮥ

---

¹ Perh. ארבعا.   ² אלסבת X.   ³ من P; ممن B K X

فى يتبرّرو يعنى انهم يزيدوا عصيان وقال ولا يبينו يعنى لا يجعلون بالهم الى ما فصل ١٢ هو مكتوب فى ديوان الله تعّ فكانوا يرجعون الى الله تعّ ولا يخرجون عن دينه وهم فاسوق ١٠ المتاوّلين للنصوص على ما تقدّم به القول انفا • ثم قال והמשכילים יבינו وذلك انهم يرجعون الى الكتاب [الله تعالى] فيميّزوا ما فيه فيعلمون ان الذى ذكره الله تعّ فى كتابه قد جاء فيقفون على ذلك فيوقفون اسرائيل عليها فعند ذلك يتمسّكون ٥ بالدين ويتركون ما بايديهم من المعاصى كما قال יחזיקו ועשו كما شرحناه •

١١ ومن وقت ازالة الدائم واجعال الرجس خاوى مستوحش ايّام عدّها الف يوما ومايتين وتسعين يوما •

رجع شرح له ما لم يقف عليه من قوله כי למועד מועדים וחצי كما تقدّم قولنا فيه فبيّن له ان مועד מועדים هى الف ومايتين وتسعين يوما فعلم ان قوله מועד ١٠ محصور على سنة واعلم ان מועדים هو سنتين لا اكثر وعرّف ان וחצי هو اقلّ من سنة وبيّن له ان ابتداء عدد هذه الاربعة سنين الا كسر من وقت הוסר התמיד • اعلم ان قد ذكر התמיד ثلث دفعات قال اوّلا וממנו הוסר התמיד והשלך מכון מקדשו ولم يذكر ثم من فاعله فجاء فى القول عرّف انه فعل قوم من أصحاب الدولة كقوله חרועים ממנו יעמדו وزادنا شرح فى قوله וחללו ונתנו השקוץ משומם على ما شرحناه ١٥ واعاده ههنا ليعرّف دانيال (و)ليعرفنا ايضا ان ابتداء המועדים من وقت הוסר התמיד وعند نهاية هذه الايّام التى هى الف ومايتى وتسعين [سنة] [و]תنقضى الצرות كقوله תכלינה כל אלה فقد شرح له ما لم يعلمه فعلمه وينبغى ان نذكر المعنى فى قوله מועד מועדים וחצי ولم يقل לשלשה מועדים فافرد מועד وجمع מועדים فنقول فى ذلك ما يتّجه وهو انه لمّا كانت هذه המועדים سنين على ما قلنا واوّلها מעת הוסר ٢٠ התמיד وان قول سيد يشعياهو عمّ בשלש שנים כשני שכיר هى מועד מועדים [וחצי] كما قلنا فى ما تقدّم من كلامنا وقلنا انه عرّفنا ان سنة من هذه الثلاث سنين يكون فيها زوال כבוד קדר وقلّة جبابرته كقوله وبعود שنة כשני שכיר فهو המועד الاوّل فيكون قوله כי למועד يشير به الى السنة الاولى من هذه الثلث سنين التى تكون فيها יכלה כל כבוד קדר فاما السنتين فتكون على ضرب واحد وهو ان يكون ٢٥ فيها ונקלה כבוד מואב الى اخر امره ولم يذكر سيّد يشعياهو النصف سنة بعد שלש שنين لانه زمان بعد تلف يشمعال ويقرب فيه ان هذا النصف على التقريب لانه اكثر من نصف سنة هو منذ يكبس מלך הצפון بابل الى ان يدخلون يسرائيل من مدبر

فصل ١٢ העמים فيتلف מלך הצפון عند ذلك ثم بيّن ان قوله כשני שכיר انها سنين قمريّة

فاسوق ١١ فتكون الثلث سنين ستة وثلاثين شهرا [1]عدد ايامها الف ومايتى وتسعين

يوما بقى من الف يوما ومايتى وتسعين يوما مايَة يوما وستة وعشرين يوما فهو

פלג עדן على ما قلناه فان חצי فى لغتنا قد يكون نصف شطرين وقد يكون اقلّ

5 واكثر كما تقدم من قوله חצי שרף باش فيكون قوله פלג עדן هو الاكثر لا الاقلّ

ويكون פלג עדן يجرى فى العالم خبط من ملك הצפון منذ يتلف يشمعال ولا يبقى

له رئيس ويخرج من بابل الى ان يتلف فى ארץ ישראל كما شرحنا فى ושמועות

יבהלוהו ٠

١٢ طوبى الراقب ويبلغ الى ايّام هى الف وثلثة ماية خمسة

١٥ وثلاثين يوما ٠

هذه الايام ليس هى من الايّام المذكورة ولم يذكر اوّلها من اى وقت تبتدى

والى اىّ وقت تنتهى اذ ليس هى من ايّام الممالك اصلا ٠ وقال אשרי המחכה وهذا

المحكة هو الذى قد حصل فى עת מועדים وهوذا يعدّها وقد علم انها مدّة يسيرة

تتقّى ويتخلّص من الצרות وهو يبلغ الى هذه الالف وثلثماية خمسة وثلاثين يوما

תהל' צ' א وهم الاخيار תמימי דרך وتبّاعهم وقد ذكر ذلك سيد موسى عمّ فى فصل יושב בסתר

16 עליון كما شرحناه فى موضعه وقال فى اخر الفصل ארך ימים אשביעהו وقد يموت قوم

فى ايّام המועדים ولا يبلغون الى هذه الايّام فلذلك قال אשרי המחכה ויגיע اذ ليس

كل מחכה יגיע فيه فيقرب فيه ان اوّلها منذ יהלך מלך הצפון فيظهر عند ذلك اقبال

ירמ' ל"א ס يسرائيل ويزاد ويزاد توافرهم وفيها يكون קבץ ישראל الثانى الذى فيه הנני מביא אותם

20 מארץ צפון בבכי יבואו وفى هذه الايّام يظهر المسيح عمّ ويكونون يسرائيل مطمئنّين

واخر هذه الايّام يجى נוד ويظهر الله فيه تقع نقמות وهو اخر يوم من هذه الالف

وثلث ماية وخمسة وثلثين يوما ثم بعد נוד تكون دولة المسيح على اهل العالم

باسره فجعل هذه الالف وثلثماية خمسة وثلاثين مفردة على هذه من حيث ان

فيها كدرا الا انها بعد تقّى الدول وفيها اكثر ما ننتظره ٠

---

[1] Numbers the same in all (B D P X Kit.); to be corrected from Comm. on Isaiah i. 174 b; عدد ايّامها الف يوم وخمسة ... يبقى مايتان وخمسة وعشرين يوما وستون يوما.

١٣ وانت مرّ الى الحتّ (او الانتهاء) وتقرّ وتقف الى قرعتك فصل ١٢
فاسوق ١٣
لانقضاء الايام (او اليمين) ❖

قد كان قال له לך דניאל ولم يقل الى اين فبيّن له ذلك فقال مرّ اى انصرف
على غمومك ¹انت وبسرائيل الى القبر كما انصرف (الاباء) الى وقت الקץ ❖ وقوله يشע' نז. ד
ותנוח يريد به في قبرك مثل ינוחו על משכבותם ولم نعلم اين قبرة ويقرب انه في بابل
لانه لم يطلع في בית שני على ما يلوح لنا لانه בשנת שלש لכורש كان في بابل وقد ٦
كان القوم صعدوا في سنة احدى لكورش ملك فارس ❖ وقال ותעמוד يعني تقوم من
القبر ❖ وقوله לגורלך اما ان يكون الى دار الثواب الذى يستحقّه واما ان يكون الى
ارض ישראל الذى له فيها גורל ويعيش زمان طويل في زمان الفرقان ويفرح بقدس
رب العالمين وجمع شمل الامّة وبعد ذلك ينقله اللﮥ تعّ حتّى الى دار الثواب بين ١٠
الملائكة وهو الاقرب في نفسي ❖ ثم عرّف متى يقوم للثواب فقال لקץ הימין ويقرب فيه
انه عند نهاية الالف وثلث ماية وخمس وثلاثين يوما يقيمه اللﮥ تعّ ²وبحييه الى
גורלו وفي ذلك الوقت ايضا يكون ما وعد اللﮥ تعّ به من اقامة موتاهم كقولﮥ
هنه اني فوتح את קברותיכם وبوربهم مواعيده كقولﮥ זכרני ייי ברצון עמך נסל اللﮥ יחזק' לז. יב
תהל' קו. ד
تعّ ان يقرب ذلك في اتّامنا واتّامكم ولا يحترمنا ويحترّمكم وفور لخطّ من علم كتابه
وكشف سرائرﮥ والتمسّك بدينﮥ وبقدس قدسﮥ وبوربنا عمارته لمعن שמו הגדול ولمعن ١٦
رحميﮥ الربيم امن ❖

*   *   *   *   *   *   *   *   *   *

وقد تكلّمنا في هذا الفصل حسب ما لاح لنا انه قريب من جميع ما سمعنا
من معلمين للجالية وما قرأناه في كتبهم واللﮥ تعّ يغفر ويصفح عن الزلل والغلط
بجودة وكرمه ونرى ان نتبع ذلك ما قاله غيرنا في هذه الמועדים والקץ ليقف عليها ٢٠
من اراد ان يقف ❖ وذلك ان العلماء الذى سبقوا قبل يوسف بن بختوى رحمﮥ
الرحمن فسّروا الفים ושלש מאות ויمים الف ماتين وتسعين والف ושלש מאות سنين
لا اتّام فاما الرّبابيين فانهم ذكروا الקץ وزعموا ان من سنة ثلث لكورش الى الקץ
الف وثلث ماية وخمسة وثلثين سنة وقد عبر هذا منذ سنين فقد سقط قولهم
وكل من قال بقولهم وكذلك الفيومّي هّم فسّرها سنين وقد بطل ايضا ولﮥ في تفسير ٢٥

---

¹ انت ins. P; om. cett.—انصرف ال   ² Perh. ويحييﮥ.

مועד מועדים וחצי بدع عجيبة وقد ردّ عليه سلمون بن يروحام رحمه الله تعّ وقد ١٢

اسوق غنينا عن الردّ عليه من حيث انه ايضا قد عبر الوقت ولم يجرِ الקץ وكذلك قوم ١٣

من القرّائين فسّروا אלפים שלש מאות سنين منذ יخرجوا الآباء من مصر والى الקץ

وقد عبر ايضا منذ سنين ولم يصحّ قولهم فاما سلمون بن يروحام رحمه الله تعّ فانه

في تفسير ولا אתנו יודע עד מה اسقط ان يعرف الקץ وتفسير תפלת עני כי יעטוף הל׳ עד׳ ם

פ קב׳ יד

في כי בא מועד اثبت الקץ وقد عبر وبطل ووافق غيره في تفسير אלפים وفي تفسير ٦

ימים אלף وزعم ايضا انها ايّام وخالفهم في ומעת הוסר התמיד فزعم ان قوله ומעת ה׳

הת׳ يريد به خراب בית שני فوافق بنيامين النهوندي رحمه الله تعّ في ان הוסר

התמיד (هو خراب) בית שני وخالفه في ان هذه الאיّام (ايّام) لا سنين وبنيامين

رحمه الله تعّ مشى على اصله في انها سنين فرد سلمون بن يروحام رحمه الله تعّ ١٠

هذه الايّام اعني אלף ומאתים وتسعيم الى الثلث ونصف الذي فيها قال وחצי השבוע

ישבית זבח ומנחה وكل واحد قد اخذ طريق وغلط الكل في جعلهم ימים سنين فاما

بنيامين النهوندي فجعل אלפים ושלש מאות سنين من خراب שילה ומעת הוסר התמיד من خراب

בית שני وقد بقى على حسابه نحو اربع ماية سنة وهذا قول باطل ويفسد جميع ما ذهبوا

اليه شيان احدهما هو انهم ادّعوا انهم يقفون على الקץ والكتاب قال כי סתומים וחתומים ١٥

الدبرים فكل من يدّعي انه يقف عليه قبل عت קץ فقد ادّعى ما ليس يصحّ والثاني

انهم جعلوا الימים سنين ومن المعلوم انه لما قال שבועים اراد ان يفرق بين ימים وبين سنين

في هذا اللفظ فليس شى من هذه الثلثة المذكورين سنين اعني אלפים ושלש מאות אלף

ومאتים وتسعيم وאלף שלש מאות שלשים וחמשה بل الكل ايّام فاما الذي فسّرها

ايّام لا سنين فقد قال ان هذه الثلثة هى واحد بعد الاخر اعني جعل אלפים ושלש ٢٠

מאות العدد الواحد وجعل אלף מאתים وتسعيم العدن الثاني وجعل אלף ושלש מאות

العدن الثالث وزعم ان نصف العدن لم يذكر في كم يوم هو فيجوز ان يكون نصف

العدن الاول وهذا اقرب لعمري من قول غيره ۰ وقد ذكرنا نحن ما قرب منّا وما

لاح لنا ومن الله نسل التجاوز عن الخطا والزلل لان الذي جرى لنا ليس هو قول حتم

بل على سبيل التقريب فقد قال جل ذكره כי סתומים וחתומים הדברים עד עת קץ ٢٥

ومن אללה ١   כרנו B ; כרונ X. ٢   הדא codd. ٣   אנגד B. ٤   Om. B. ٥
B. اسال الصفح واليه اتضرع ان ינجאה عن الزلل والجلل

فصل ١٢ [1]وفى هذا الزمان ينكشف على يد المשכילים كما قال והמשכילים יבינו يقرب الله
فاسوق ١٣ تعالى ظهورهم برحمته ورآفته

• אמן •

---

[1] אמן—وفى X adds מאיה. om. X. ויקרב ענדי אן יכון אלפרקאן ענדה פי ארבע מאיה

למלכות זעירה חש במ אמן ברוך נתן ליעף כח ולאין עונים עצמה ירבה ושלום:

וענדה אן אלפרקאן יכון ענד תקצי מאיה למלכות ישמעאל פתם אנה מצّי פכאן B adds

שארחה אלחכם ר יפת אבו עלי ז″ל לה מן קבל דלך אלתאריך כנחו אלמאיה סנה

פצאר לה נחו אלסבע מאיה סנة וכסר אלחכם מתופי ז″ל יבוא שלום ינוח על משכבו

אמן ושלום:
